Journey of Transformation

Second Edition

Seton Hall University

macmillan learning
curriculum solutions

bedford/st.martin's ▪ hayden-mcneil ▪ w.h. freeman ▪ worth publishers

Printed in the United States of America

10 9 8 7 6 5 4 3 2 1

ISBN 978-0-7380-8852-5

Macmillan Learning Curriculum Solutions
14903 Pilot Drive
Plymouth, MI 48170
www.macmillanlearning.com

Sciglitano 8852-5 F16

TABLE OF CONTENTS

EPIGRAPH

The purpose of education is to show a person how to define himself authentically and spontaneously in relation to his world—not to impose a prefabricated definition of the world, still less an arbitrary definition of the individual himself. The world is made up of the people who are fully alive in it: that is, of the people who can be themselves in it and can enter into a living and fruitful relationship with each other in it. The world is, therefore, more real in proportion as the people in it are able to be more fully and more humanly alive: that is to say, better able to make a lucid and conscious use of their freedom. Basically, this freedom must consist first of all in the capacity to choose their own lives, to find themselves on the deepest possible level. A superficial freedom to wander aimlessly here and there, to taste this or that, to make a choice of distractions (in Pascal's sense) is simply a sham. It claims to be freedom of "choice" when it has evaded the basic task discovering who it is that chooses. It is not free because it is unwilling to face the risk of self-discovery.

The function of a university is, then, first of all to help the student discover himself: to recognize himself, and to identify who it is that chooses.

This description will be recognized at once as unconventional and, in fact, monastic. To put it in even more outrageous terms, the function of the university is to help men and women save their souls and, in so doing, to save their society: from what? From the hell of meaninglessness, of obsession, of complex artifice, of systematic lying, of criminal evasions and neglects, of self-destructive futilities.

Thomas Merton, "Learning to Live" 358–59

TO THE READER

What is the best way to live? No question is more important. The readings assembled in this volume each attempt to address it. When reading them you may find that they sometimes offer remarkably similar answers, but in other ways they diverge significantly. In the latter case, you, the reader, are confronted with a challenge—which *is* the best way to live? How are you to decide? Not to decide is not an option, since this is not just any question, but the question about how we are to live. Whatever your goals, plans, dreams—however you go about the day to day business of living, you are already operating with some ideas about how this question is to be answered. Most likely these ideas have their origins in the influences that have shaped you up to this point in your life—family, friends, peers, religious tradition, and the values embodied in American society. Perhaps you have been influenced by things you have read, listened to, or watched. Whatever the sources of ideas, values, and goals that guide your approach to life, the aim of this course is to get you to think about how you live and why. One of the best ways to begin thinking about these questions is to consider what others who have thought deeply about them have said.

Most of the texts found in this reader are considered "classics." But you are not being asked to read them simply because others have judged them to be classics. Rather, the reason why they have been designated classics is because, regardless of their age, these works have shown a remarkable ability to speak to people across the centuries. We read them for their abiding relevance, not because they are old. Bear this in mind as you read. Perhaps this is your first encounter with these texts. If so, you may find at least some of them to be unfamiliar, challenging, or even frustrating to read. In the case of a book such as the Bible, you may have the opposite experience. If you come from a religious tradition that takes the Bible to be the word of God, you may think that you already know what it means.

In any case, regardless of the level of familiarity or unfamiliarity you bring to these texts, it is important to adopt certain intellectual attitudes when reading. The first would be openness. Many of the authors you will be reading come from perspectives other than your own. In order to understand them you will need to make an effort to enter into their perspective.

A second and related attitude you will need is intellectual humility. When confronted with readings that are difficult or unfamiliar you may be tempted to dismiss the ideas encountered as stupid or irrelevant. Resist this temptation. Be open to the possibility that the author you are reading is smarter than you are, has thought more deeply about these things than you have, and is offering a perspective on how to live that needs to be taken seriously. If you are confused, annoyed, or frustrated by a particular reading, it is not a sign that the author is a dope; your reaction might very well indicate that you need to delve more deeply into the text in order to grasp the author's meaning. As a general rule, it is wise to bear in mind that you need to understand an author before you are capable of forming a judgment about what you have read.

A third quality you will need in approaching these readings is an attitude of attentiveness. The selections found in this volume are not meant to be perused superficially. They are meant to be read with care and reflection. They have been carefully selected and edited so that you can get a basic sense of the authors without being overwhelmed with an enormous amount of reading. One of the primary reasons for doing this is so that you will have time to read attentively. Please give the readings the attention they deserve.

Finally, it might be useful to consider why we designate certain courses as "core." At the risk of stating the obvious, it is because "core" means essential, fundamental, basic; and, as noted above, there is no question more important than the question concerning how we are to live. Notice also that the focus here is on fundamental *questions*. The aim of a course such as "Journey of Transformation" is to get you, the reader, to consider certain questions about what makes for a worthwhile life. We trust that, over time, you will work out answers for yourself. This book is written with the conviction that the authors included here can be of some help in that process.

OVERVIEW

One of the most appealing features for both students who take CORE 1101: "The Journey of Transformation" and CORE 2101: "Christianity and Culture in Dialogue," and for the professors who teach them, is that these two Signature Courses are often taught through the lens of the particular scholarly discipline of the professor who teaches them. "The Journey of Transformation," the course that you are about to embark upon, is a journey; and hopefully you will be transformed by having taken it, as well as enriched by the disciplinary perspective of your professor for the course. While it may seem both a cliché and trite, this course has the potential to truly transform the way you understand the Catholic tradition intellectually and spiritually, the world in which you live, and, most importantly, your own personal life. This is true both metaphorically and literally.

Over the past 20 years, neuroscience research has demonstrated that what we think and the ideas to which we expose ourselves have a direct impact upon our physical, emotional, and spiritual wellbeing. Our brains, it seems, are much more malleable than we believed. Therefore, in many ways, we are what we think. Based on the theory of neuroplasticity, which is the technical term for the malleability of the brain, the ideas that you will explore in "The Journey of Transformation" have the potential not only to transform you intellectually and spiritually but also to have positive effects upon the structure of your brain and upon your sense of wellbeing.

The course begins with a reading from *Nostra Aetate*, a document written during the Second Vatican Council. *Nostra Aetate* addresses the relationship between Christianity and Catholic Christianity in particular, and non-Christian religious traditions. We might think of the selection from *Nostra Aetate* as setting the tone for the rest of the course. The aim of this first reading is to highlight what is universally good and true in the non-Christian traditions, most especially in relation to the other two Abrahamic religious traditions, Judaism and Islam, as well as all that is true and good in Hinduism and Buddhism. *Nostra Aetate* also outlines what it is about the Christian Revelation that is unique in relation to these non-Christian traditions.

From there we move on to Plato's *Republic* and particularly to the famous "allegory of the cave." This selection actually has a lot in common with the selection from the *Bhagavad Gita* that you will read a bit later in the semester. Both the "allegory of the cave" in Plato's *Republic* and the selection from the *Gita* stress that there is a stark contrast between how we humans perceive truth from actual Truth. Hopefully, reading both of these texts will inspire you to embark on your own search for a firsthand experience of Truth with a capital "T" and to awaken you from your deluded sense of reality to that which is "really" Real. After reading the *Republic*, you will read Plato's *Apology*, or, more correctly, *The Apology of Socrates*, which tells the story of the trial of Socrates and his death sentence by poisoning. In many ways the *Apology* is about what happens when one questions the cherished beliefs of one's society, such as Socrates did. Perhaps here we can think of the transformative effects of living philosophy as a way of life. To do so can often transform one's worldview with such depth and poignancy that it no longer is possible to remain quiet, even though to speak out, as Socrates did, cost him his life. Social change agents are not always appreciated by the societies and cultures that are the targets of such agents.

Christianity shares a common heritage with Judaism and with the ancient Greeks. The Hebrew Scriptures, which Christians commonly refer to as the Old Testament or the First Testament, and the writings of Plato and other Greek philosophers of the time, were foundational to the thinking of the early Fathers of the Church. Therefore, it's fitting after Plato that our next selections are drawn from the Hebrew Bible, specifically from the Books of Genesis, Exodus, and Ruth. Each of these three readings stresses the themes of journey and transformation, respectively. In Genesis we read the story of Abraham being called by God to go forth from his homeland to a new place. In Exodus, the Hebrew people are led by God from enslavement in Egypt to wander in the desert for 40 years, mysteriously led by God in the form of a "pillar of smoke" to the Promised Land where God has promised them they will thrive and flourish. In Ruth, we read about the relationship between Ruth and her mother-in-law Naomi. Despite Naomi's attempts to convince Ruth not to follow her back to Bethlehem, Ruth nevertheless pledges her fidelity to go with Naomi wherever she may go.

From the readings in the Hebrew Scriptures we move on to the selections from the foundational text of Christianity, the New Testament. Specifically, we read Luke's Gospel in which the ultimate transcendent mystery of God's personal love is revealed and embodied in the person and life of Jesus of Nazareth. Having grounded ourselves in the Gospel narrative of Jesus' earthly life as written by Luke, we move on to read selections of Augustine's *Confessions*, thought by some scholars to be one of the first autobiographies and the prototype for that genre up to the present time.

While Augustine does not have a major role in the Eastern or Greek Church, his impact is significant in the Latin or Roman Church where his theology has played, and still plays, an important role in how the Church understands the redemptive role of Jesus' life, death, and resurrection in the economy of salvation. In this sense, reading Augustine's *Confessions* is the model par excellence of and for a journey of transformation. Following Augustine, we are offered selections from Dante's *Divine Comedy*, a poetic masterpiece if ever there was one. Dante takes his readers on a visionary journey through Hell, Purgatory, and Paradise, the invisible worlds of the Christian cosmos. A product of the medieval world with its privileging of allegorical and symbolic approaches to reading texts, the many different levels of meaning that such an approach to reading Dante provides have been a source of spiritual transformation for those who have read him from the time in which he wrote to the present. Perhaps reading Dante's *Divine Comedy* will have a similar transformative effect on you.

While during the course of the semester you will also read selections from other more modern sources to be chosen by your professor, we end "The Journey of Transformation" with a selection from Pope Benedict's *Deus Caritas Est* (God Is Love), a contemporary reflection on one of the most important of Christian doctrines, "God is Love." In this encyclical, the transformative effects of God's Love are elucidated by insights Pope Benedict offers his readers about the different forms of human love in relation to God's Love—the transformative effects of God's Love in personal human relationships, including erotic love; the relationship between Christian Charity and political justice; the relationship between the Church and the state; and, the symbiotic relationship of all of the foregoing by which the world can be transfigured and transformed by the power of Love.

Hopefully, through reading and thinking deeply about each of these important selections, as well as by discussing them in class with your professor and with your fellow students, you will gain important insights into what it means to be human, what really matters and is of lasting value in terms of your own life journey, and the riches the Catholic intellectual tradition has to offer to potentially help you grow as a human being and to inspire you to make a valuable contribution to the world in which we live in these first few decades of the 21st century.

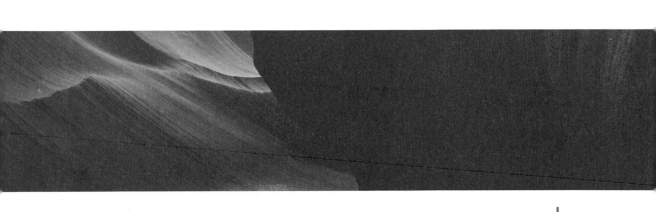

I

Nostra Aetate

Editors' Introduction

It is not an overstatement to say that the Second Vatican Council has had (and continues to have) a greater impact on the Catholic Church than any event since the Protestant Reformation. Vatican Two was an ecumenical council, that is, a meeting of representatives of the entire Church, consisting mainly of the world's Catholic bishops. The Council was called by Pope John XXIII in January of 1959. One of the main purposes behind Pope John's calling of an ecumenical council was to provide the Church with an opportunity for updating (*aggiornamento* in Italian), especially with regard to the Church's attitude toward the modern world. It would not be accurate, though, to say that Pope John set out to "modernize" the Church. His intention was to draw upon tradition in order to address contemporary questions. In his opening address to the Council, John warned those assembled not to heed the "prophets of gloom" in their midst, who saw only the negative aspects of modern society. The pope was not advocating an uncritical acceptance of everything modern, but he was nudging the Church in the direction of a more open yet critical stance toward modernity. He also made a point of reminding his listeners that while the substance of the Catholic faith was permanent and abiding, the way that faith was expressed could vary in accordance with the needs of the time and place. The Council met from October 9, 1962 to December 8, 1965 in four two to three month sessions. It produced sixteen documents: four major Constitutions, nine Decrees, and three Declarations (including *Nostra Aetate*). The legacy and proper understanding of the Council is still debated, and these debates show little sign of abating any time soon.

One result of the Council's work on which there is near unanimous agreement is that *Nostra Aetate* represented a significant change in the attitude of the Catholic Church toward other religions. It was promulgated on October 28, 1965. The brevity of the declaration belies its importance as a breakthrough in inter-religious dialogue. Nowhere is this change more evident than in the document's treatment of Judaism and the Jewish people. Centuries of negative attitudes toward Judaism were repudiated in the space of one paragraph. The Jewish roots of Christianity are emphasized, the collective charge against the Jewish people for the death of Jesus is rejected, and anti-Semitism is decried. If today's readers of the text take for granted the attitude toward other religions displayed in the document, this may be due in part (at least among Catholics) to the fact that the teaching of *Nostra Aetate* has been taken to heart over the last five decades. Beginning as it does with the recognition that the quest for meaning is common to all people, *Nostra Aetate* is a fitting text with which to begin a volume that takes this quest to be its central focus.

DECLARATION ON THE RELATION OF THE CHURCH TO NON-CHRISTIAN RELIGIONS

1. In our time, when day by day mankind is being drawn closer together, and the ties between different peoples are becoming stronger, the Church examines more closely her relationship to non-Christian religions. In her task of promoting unity and love among men, indeed among nations, she considers above all in this declaration what men have in common and what draws them to fellowship.

One is the community of all peoples, one their origin, for God made the whole human race to live over the face of the earth.(1) One also is their final goal, God. His providence, His manifestations of goodness, His saving design extend to all men,(2) until that time when the elect will be united in the Holy City, the city ablaze with the glory of God, where the nations will walk in His light.(3)

Men expect from the various religions answers to the unsolved riddles of the human condition, which today, even as in former times, deeply stir the hearts of men: What is man? What is the meaning, the aim of our life? What is moral good, what is sin? Whence suffering and what purpose does it serve? Which is the road to true happiness? What are death, judgment and retribution after death? What, finally, is that ultimate inexpressible mystery which encompasses our existence: whence do we come, and where are we going?

2. From ancient times down to the present, there is found among various peoples a certain perception of that hidden power which hovers over the course of things and over the events of human history; at times some indeed have come to the recognition of a Supreme Being, or even of a Father. This perception and recognition penetrates their lives with a profound religious sense.

Religions, however, that are bound up with an advanced culture have struggled to answer the same questions by means of more refined concepts and a more developed language. Thus in Hinduism, men contemplate the divine mystery and express it through an inexhaustible abundance of myths and through searching philosophical inquiry. They seek freedom from the anguish of our human condition either through ascetical practices or profound meditation or a flight to God with love and trust. Again, Buddhism, in its various forms, realizes the radical insufficiency of this changeable world; it teaches a way by which men, in a devout and confident spirit, may be able either to acquire the state of perfect liberation, or attain, by their own efforts or through higher help, supreme illumination. Likewise, other religions found everywhere try to counter the restlessness of the human heart, each in its own manner, by proposing "ways," comprising teachings, rules of life, and sacred rites. The Catholic Church rejects nothing that is true and holy in these religions. She regards with sincere reverence those ways of conduct and of life, those precepts and teachings which, though differing in many aspects from the ones she holds and sets forth, nonetheless often reflect a ray of that Truth which enlightens all men. Indeed, she proclaims, and ever must proclaim Christ "the way, the truth, and the life" (John 14:6), in whom men may find the fullness of religious life, in whom God has reconciled all things to Himself.(4)

The Church, therefore, exhorts her sons, that through dialogue and collaboration with the followers of other religions, carried out with prudence and love and in witness to the Christian faith and life, they recognize, preserve and promote the good things, spiritual and moral, as well as the socio-cultural values found among these men.

3.   The Church regards with esteem also the Moslems. They adore the one God, living and subsisting in Himself; merciful and all-powerful, the Creator of heaven and earth,(5) who has spoken to men; they take pains to submit wholeheartedly to even His inscrutable decrees, just as Abraham, with whom the faith of Islam takes pleasure in linking itself, submitted to God. Though they do not acknowledge Jesus as God, they revere Him as a prophet. They also honor Mary, His virgin Mother; at times they even call on her with devotion. In addition, they await the day of judgment when God will render their deserts to all those who have been raised up from the dead. Finally, they value the moral life and worship God especially through prayer, almsgiving and fasting.

Since in the course of centuries not a few quarrels and hostilities have arisen between Christians and Moslems, this sacred synod urges all to forget the past and to work sincerely for mutual understanding and to preserve as well as to promote together for the benefit of all mankind social justice and moral welfare, as well as peace and freedom.

4.   As the sacred synod searches into the mystery of the Church, it remembers the bond that spiritually ties the people of the New Covenant to Abraham's stock.

Thus the Church of Christ acknowledges that, according to God's saving design, the beginnings of her faith and her election are found already among the Patriarchs, Moses and the prophets. She professes that all who believe in Christ—Abraham's sons according to faith (6)—are included in the same Patriarch's call, and likewise that the salvation of the Church is mysteriously foreshadowed by the chosen people's exodus from the land of bondage. The Church, therefore, cannot forget that she received the revelation of the Old Testament through the people with whom God in His inexpressible mercy concluded the Ancient Covenant. Nor can she forget that she draws sustenance from the root of that well-cultivated olive tree onto which have been grafted the wild shoots, the Gentiles.(7) Indeed, the Church believes that by His cross Christ, Our Peace, reconciled Jews and Gentiles, making both one in Himself.(8)

The Church keeps ever in mind the words of the Apostle about his kinsmen: "theirs is the sonship and the glory and the covenants and the law and the worship and the promises; theirs are the fathers and from them is the Christ according to the flesh" (Rom. 9:4–5), the Son of the Virgin Mary. She also recalls that the Apostles, the Church's main-stay and pillars, as well as most of the early disciples who proclaimed Christ's Gospel to the world, sprang from the Jewish people.

As Holy Scripture testifies, Jerusalem did not recognize the time of her visitation,(9) nor did the Jews in large number, accept the Gospel; indeed not a few opposed its spreading.(10) Nevertheless, God holds the Jews most dear for the sake of their Fathers; He does not repent of the gifts He makes or of the calls He issues-such is the witness of the Apostle.(11) In company with the Prophets and the same Apostle, the Church awaits that day, known to God alone, on which all peoples will address the Lord in a single voice and "serve him shoulder to shoulder" (Soph. 3:9).(12)

Since the spiritual patrimony common to Christians and Jews is thus so great, this sacred synod wants to foster and recommend that mutual understanding and respect which is the fruit, above all, of biblical and theological studies as well as of fraternal dialogues.

True, the Jewish authorities and those who followed their lead pressed for the death of Christ;(13) still, what happened in His passion cannot be charged against all the Jews, without distinction, then alive, nor against the Jews of today. Although the Church is the new people of God, the Jews should not be presented as rejected or accursed by God, as if this followed from the Holy Scriptures. All should see to it, then, that in catechetical work or in the preaching of the word of God they do not teach anything that does not conform to the truth of the Gospel and the spirit of Christ.

Furthermore, in her rejection of every persecution against any man, the Church, mindful of the patrimony she shares with the Jews and moved not by political reasons but by the Gospel's spiritual love, decries hatred, persecutions, displays of anti-Semitism, directed against Jews at any time and by anyone.

Besides, as the Church has always held and holds now, Christ underwent His passion and death freely, because of the sins of men and out of infinite love, in order that all may reach salvation. It is, therefore, the burden of the Church's preaching to proclaim the cross of Christ as the sign of God's all-embracing love and as the fountain from which every grace flows.

5. We cannot truly call on God, the Father of all, if we refuse to treat in a brotherly way any man, created as he is in the image of God. Man's relation to God the Father and his relation to men his brothers are so linked together that Scripture says: "He who does not love does not know God" (1 John 4:8).

No foundation therefore remains for any theory or practice that leads to discrimination between man and man or people and people, so far as their human dignity and the rights flowing from it are concerned.

The Church reproves, as foreign to the mind of Christ, any discrimination against men or harassment of them because of their race, color, condition of life, or religion. On the contrary, following in the footsteps of the holy Apostles Peter and Paul, this sacred synod ardently implores the Christian faithful to "maintain good fellowship among the nations" (1 Peter 2:12), and, if possible, to live for their part in peace with all men,(14) so that they may truly be sons of the Father who is in heaven.(15)

Notes

1. Cf. *Acts* 17:26

2. Cf. *Wis.* 8:1; *Acts* 14:17; *Rom.* 2:6–7; 1 *Tim.* 2:4

3. Cf. *Apoc.* 21:23f.

4. Cf 2 *Cor.* 5:18–19

5. Cf St. Gregory VII, *letter XXI to Anzir (Nacir), King of Mauritania* (Pl. 148, col. 450f.)

6. Cf. *Gal.* 3:7

7. Cf. *Rom.* 11:17–24

8. Cf. *Eph.* 2:14–16

9. Cf. *Lk.* 19:44

10. Cf. *Rom.* 11:28

11. Cf. *Rom.* 11:28–29; cf. dogmatic Constitution, *Lumen Gentium* (Light of nations) AAS, 57 (1965) pag. 20

12. Cf. *Is.* 66:23; *Ps.* 65:4; *Rom.* 11:11–32

13. Cf. *John.* 19:6

14. Cf. *Rom.* 12:18

15. Cf. *Matt.* 5:45

Nostra Aetate. Declaration on the Relation of the Church to Non-Christian Religions. Pope Paul VI, October 28, 1965. Copyright © Libreria Editrice Vaticana. Reprinted with permission of Libreria Editrice Vaticana.

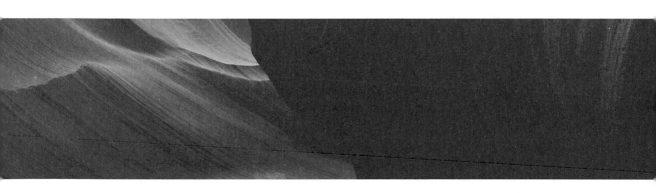

II

Plato

Editors' Introduction

Nowhere is philosophy as a way of life presented more eloquently and beautifully than in the dialogues of Plato. Central to these dialogues is the figure of Socrates, who was Plato's teacher and mentor. Socrates left no writing of his own, so it is mainly through Plato that we know about the Socratic way of philosophizing. There seems to be general agreement among scholars that of Plato's nearly thirty works, the earlier dialogues probably capture the essence of the historical Socrates more closely than the later dialogues, where Plato begins to use Socrates as a mouthpiece for his own philosophical views.

Plato (427–347 B.C.) was born into an aristocratic family in Athens. To be an adult male citizen of a Greek city-state *(polis)* such as Athens normally meant taking an active part in its civic life. It is clear from many of Plato's dialogues that he took an enormous interest in the relationship between the philosophical life and the world of politics. However, having seen Socrates condemned to death by the citizen-jurors of Athens, Plato withdrew from active engagement in politics. Instead, he founded a school known as the Academy, whose most famous student was the philosopher Aristotle. Apparently the lure of politics continued to exert a pull on Plato, and in the later part of his life he attempted to put his political philosophy into practice in the Greek city-state of Syracuse (in present day Sicily). These efforts were unsuccessful, and Plato returned to Athens. Following his teacher Socrates, Plato's approach to philosophy emphasizes the idea of conducting one's life by following one's questions. At least in the early dialogues, Socrates rarely if ever comes to a definite conclusion about the questions he raises. Philosophy, so understood, is literally "love of wisdom," without any implication that wisdom is already possessed by the philosopher. To turn Plato's philosophy into a series of doctrines or answers to philosophical questions is to seriously distort its meaning and purpose. Plato deliberately chose to write in dialogical form, so as to engage his readers in a process of questioning. And from his esteemed teacher he learned that the best place to begin is by questioning oneself.

APOLOGY OF SOCRATES

When reading the *Apology*, it will quickly become clear that Socrates does not seem to be apologizing for anything (if by "apology" we mean saying we are sorry for having done something wrong). Instead, "apology" as used here is more accurately understood as Socrates' defense of himself at his trial. The dialogue is an account, written by Plato, of one of the most famous trials in history. How much of the dialogue records "what actually happened" and how much is based upon Plato's recollection or imagination is still debated. The main reason to read the *Apology* is that it is such a wonderful example of what it means to practice philosophy as a way of life. Today it is more common to think of philosophy as an academic discipline, forced on students as part of their university education. But for Socrates, philosophy was fundamentally about how to live. Approach the dialogue with this in mind.

The trial of Socrates (469–399 B.C.) took place in Athens in 399 B.C. The court that tried him was composed of 501 citizen jurors, selected by lot. The decision of the court was based upon a majority vote. It is worth noting that Athens was at the time undergoing a period of political unrest, with the result that the city was agitated and full of tensions. Some of Socrates' friends and allies were in the thick of this crisis, and he may very well have been a victim of the passions unleashed by the conflicts besetting the city. But the dialogue also makes it clear that Socrates had made enemies for himself by his relentless questioning of the beliefs of Athenian society.

The work is divided into three parts. The first part consists of Socrates' actual defense, including his response to the specific charges leveled against him. This section constitutes most of the dialogue. The second part is a short speech given by Socrates after his conviction in which he proposes what he deems to be the most appropriate penalty. The dialogue ends with Socrates' warning to Athens in which he prophesies that his death will not bring about the end of the city's woes. As the dialogue concludes, readers are left wondering whether Socrates' speech to his accusers is much of a defense at all, and what that could mean.

How you, O Athenians, have been affected by my accusers, I cannot tell; but I know that they almost made me forget who I was—so persuasively did they speak; and yet they have hardly uttered a word of truth. But of the many falsehoods told by them, there was one which quite amazed me;—I mean when they said that you should be upon your guard and not allow yourselves to be deceived by the force of my eloquence. To say this, when they were certain to be detected as soon as I opened my lips and proved myself to be anything but a great speaker, did indeed appear to me most shameless—unless by the force of eloquence they mean the force of truth; for if such is their meaning, I admit that I am eloquent. But in how different a way from theirs! Well, as I was saying, they have scarcely spoken the truth at all; but from me you shall hear the whole truth: not, however, delivered after their manner in a set oration duly ornamented with words and phrases. No, by heaven! but I shall use the words and arguments which occur to me at the moment; for I am confident in the justice of my cause (Or, I am certain that I am right in taking this course.): at my time of life I ought not to be appearing before you, O men of Athens, in the character of a juvenile orator—let no one expect it of me. And I must beg of you to grant me a favour:—If I defend myself in my accustomed manner, and you hear me using the words which I have been in the habit of using in the agora, at the tables of the money-changers, or anywhere else, I would ask you not to be surprised, and not to interrupt me on this account. For I am more than seventy years of age, and appearing now for the first time in a court of law, I am quite a stranger to the language of the place; and therefore I would have you regard me as if I were really a stranger, whom you would excuse if he spoke in his native tongue, and after the fashion of his country:—Am I making an unfair request of you? Never mind the manner, which may or may not be good; but think only of the truth of my words, and give heed to that: let the speaker speak truly and the judge decide justly.

And first, I have to reply to the older charges and to my first accusers, and then I will go on to the later ones. For of old I have had many accusers, who have accused me falsely to you during many years; and I am more afraid of them than of Anytus and his associates, who are dangerous, too, in their own way. But far more dangerous are the others, who began when you were children, and took possession of your minds with their falsehoods, telling of one Socrates, a wise man, who speculated about the heaven above, and searched into the earth beneath, and made the worse appear the better cause. The disseminators of this tale are the accusers whom I dread; for their hearers are apt to fancy that such enquirers do not believe in the existence of the gods. And they are many, and their charges against me are of ancient date, and they were made by them in the days when you were more impressible than you are now—in childhood, or it may have been in youth—and the cause when heard went by default, for there was none to answer. And hardest of all, I do not know and cannot tell the names of my accusers; unless in the chance case of a Comic poet. All who from envy and malice have persuaded you—some of them having first convinced themselves—all this class of men are most difficult to deal with; for I cannot have them up here, and cross-examine them, and therefore I must simply fight with shadows in my own defence, and argue when there is no one who answers. I will ask you then to assume with me, as I was saying, that my opponents are of two kinds; one recent, the other ancient: and I hope that you will see the propriety of my answering the latter first, for these accusations you heard long before the others, and much oftener.

Well, then, I must make my defence, and endeavour to clear away in a short time, a slander which has lasted a long time. May I succeed, if to succeed be for my good and yours, or likely to avail me in my cause! The task is not an easy one; I quite understand the nature of it. And so leaving the event with God, in obedience to the law I will now make my defence.

I will begin at the beginning, and ask what is the accusation which has given rise to the slander of me, and in fact has encouraged Meletus to prove this charge against me. Well, what do the slanderers say? They shall be my prosecutors, and I will sum up their words in an affidavit: 'Socrates is an evil-doer, and a curious person, who searches into things under the earth and in heaven, and he makes the worse appear the better cause; and he teaches the aforesaid doctrines to others.' Such is the nature of the accusation: it is just what you have yourselves seen in the comedy of Aristophanes (Aristoph., Clouds.), who has introduced a man whom he calls Socrates, going about and saying that he walks in air, and talking a deal of nonsense concerning matters of which I do not pretend to know either much or little—not that I mean to speak disparagingly of any one who is a student of natural philosophy. I should be very sorry if Meletus could bring so grave a charge against me. But the simple truth is, O Athenians, that I have nothing to do with physical speculations. Very many of those here present are witnesses to the truth of this, and to them I appeal. Speak then, you who have heard me, and tell your neighbours whether any of you have ever known me to hold forth in few words or in many upon such matters...You hear their answer. And from what they say of this part of the charge you will be able to judge of the truth of the rest.

As little foundation is there for the report that I am a teacher, and take money; this accusation has no more truth in it than the other. Although, if a man were really able to instruct mankind, to receive money for giving instruction would, in my opinion, be an honour to him. There is Gorgias of Leontium, and Prodicus of Ceos, and Hippias of Elis, who go the round of the cities, and are able to persuade the young men to leave their own citizens by whom they might be taught for nothing, and come to them whom they not only pay, but are thankful if they may be allowed to pay them. There is at this time a Parian philosopher residing in Athens, of whom I have heard; and I came to hear of him in this way:—I came across a man who has spent a world of money on the Sophists, Callias, the son of Hipponicus, and knowing that he had sons, I asked him: 'Callias,' I said, 'if your two sons were foals or calves, there would be no difficulty in finding some one to put over them; we should hire a trainer of horses, or a farmer probably, who would improve and perfect them in their own proper virtue and excellence; but as they are human beings, whom are you thinking of placing over them? Is there any one who understands human and political virtue? You must have thought about the matter, for you have sons; is there any one?' There is,' he said. 'Who is he?' said I; 'and of what country? and what does he charge?' 'Evenus the Parian,' he replied; 'he is the man, and his charge is five minae.' Happy is Evenus, I said to myself, if he really has this wisdom, and teaches at such a moderate charge. Had I the same, I should have been very proud and conceited; but the truth is that I have no knowledge of the kind.

I dare say, Athenians, that some one among you will reply, 'Yes, Socrates, but what is the origin of these accusations which are brought against you; there must have been something strange which you have been doing? All these rumours and this talk about you would never have arisen if you had been like other men: tell us, then, what is the cause of them, for we should be sorry to judge hastily of you.' Now I regard this as a fair challenge, and I will endeavour to explain to you the reason why I am called wise and have such an evil fame. Please to attend then. And although some of you may think that I am joking, I declare that I will tell you the entire truth. Men of Athens, this reputation of mine has come of a certain sort of wisdom which I possess. If you ask me what kind of wisdom, I reply, wisdom such as may perhaps be attained by man, for to that extent I am inclined to believe that I am wise; whereas the persons of whom I was speaking have a superhuman wisdom which I may fail to describe, because I have it not myself; and he who says that I have, speaks falsely, and is taking away my character. And here, O men of Athens, I must beg you not to interrupt me, even if I seem to say something extravagant. For the word which I will speak is not mine. I will refer you to a witness who is worthy of credit; that witness shall be the God of Delphi—he will tell you about my wisdom, if I have any, and of what sort it is. You must have known Chaerephon; he was early a friend of mine, and also a friend of yours, for he shared in the recent exile of the people, and returned with you. Well, Chaerephon, as you know, was very impetuous in all his doings, and he went to Delphi and boldly asked the oracle to tell him whether—as I was saying, I must beg you not to interrupt—he asked the oracle to tell him whether anyone was wiser than I was, and the Pythian prophetess answered, that there was no man wiser. Chaerephon is dead himself; but his brother, who is in court, will confirm the truth of what I am saying.

Why do I mention this? Because I am going to explain to you why I have such an evil name. When I heard the answer, I said to myself, What can the god mean? and what is the interpretation of his riddle? for I know that I have no wisdom, small or great. What then can he mean when he says that I am the wisest of men? And yet he is a god, and cannot lie; that would be against his nature. After long consideration, I thought of a method of trying the question. I reflected that if I could only find a man wiser than myself, then I might go to the god with a refutation in my hand. I should say to him, 'Here is a man who is wiser than I am; but you said that I was the wisest.' Accordingly I went to one who had the reputation of wisdom, and observed him—his name I need not mention; he was a politician whom I selected for examination—and the result was as follows: When I began to talk with him, I could not help thinking that he was not really wise, although he was thought wise by many, and still wiser by himself; and thereupon I tried to explain to him that he thought himself wise, but was not really wise; and the consequence was that he hated me, and his enmity was shared by several who were present and heard me. So I left him, saying to myself, as I went away: Well, although I do not suppose that either of us knows anything really beautiful and good, I am better off than he is,— for he knows nothing, and thinks that he knows; I neither know nor think that I know. In this latter particular, then, I seem to have slightly the advantage of him. Then I went to another who had still higher pretensions to wisdom, and my conclusion was exactly the same. Whereupon I made another enemy of him, and of many others besides him.

Then I went to one man after another, being not unconscious of the enmity which I provoked, and I lamented and feared this: but necessity was laid upon me,—the word of God, I thought, ought to be considered first. And I said to myself, Go I must to all who appear to know, and find out the meaning of the oracle. And I swear to you, Athenians, by the dog I swear!—for I must tell you the truth—the result of my mission was just this: I found that the men most in repute were all but the most foolish; and that others less esteemed were really wiser and better. I will tell you the tale of my wanderings and of the 'Herculean' labours, as I may call them, which I endured only to find at last the oracle irrefutable. After the politicians, I went to the poets; tragic, dithyrambic, and all sorts. And there, I said to myself, you will be instantly detected; now you will find out that you are more ignorant than they are. Accordingly, I took them some of the most elaborate passages in their own writings, and asked what was the meaning of them—thinking that they would teach me something. Will you believe me? I am almost ashamed to confess the truth, but I must say that there is hardly a person present who would not have talked better about their poetry than they did themselves. Then I knew that not by wisdom do poets write poetry, but by a sort of genius and inspiration; they are like diviners or soothsayers who also say many fine things, but do not understand the meaning of them. The poets appeared to me to be much in the same case; and I further observed that upon the strength of their poetry they believed themselves to be the wisest of men in other things in which they were not wise. So I departed, conceiving myself to be superior to them for the same reason that I was superior to the politicians.

At last I went to the artisans. I was conscious that I knew nothing at all, as I may say, and I was sure that they knew many fine things; and here I was not mistaken, for they did know many things of which I was ignorant, and in this they certainly were wiser than I was. But I observed that even the good artisans fell into the same error as the poets;—because they were good workmen they thought that they also knew all sorts of high matters, and this defect in them overshadowed their wisdom; and therefore I asked myself on behalf of the oracle, whether I would like to be as I was, neither having their knowledge nor their ignorance, or like them in both; and I made answer to myself and to the oracle that I was better off as I was.

This inquisition has led to my having many enemies of the worst and most dangerous kind, and has given occasion also to many calumnies. And I am called wise, for my hearers always imagine that I myself possess the wisdom which I find wanting in others: but the truth is, O men of Athens, that God only is wise; and by his answer he intends to show that the wisdom of men is worth little or nothing; he is not speaking of Socrates, he is only using my name by way of illustration, as if he said, He, O men, is the wisest, who, like Socrates, knows that his wisdom is in truth worth nothing. And so I go about the world, obedient to the god, and search and make enquiry into the wisdom of any one, whether citizen or stranger, who appears to be wise; and if he is not wise, then in vindication of the oracle I show him that he is not wise; and my occupation quite absorbs me, and I have no time to give either to any public matter of interest or to any concern of my own, but I am in utter poverty by reason of my devotion to the god.

There is another thing:—young men of the richer classes, who have not much to do, come about me of their own accord; they like to hear the pretenders examined, and they often imitate me, and proceed to examine others; there are plenty of persons, as they quickly discover, who think that they know something, but really know little or nothing; and then those who are examined by them instead of being angry with themselves are angry with me: This confounded Socrates, they say; this villainous misleader of youth!—and then if somebody asks them, Why, what evil does he practise or teach? they do not know, and cannot tell; but in order that they may not appear to be at a loss, they repeat the ready-made charges which are used against all philosophers about teaching things up in the clouds and under the earth, and having no gods, and making the worse appear the better cause; for they do not like to confess that their pretence of knowledge has been detected—which is the truth; and as they are numerous and ambitious and energetic, and are drawn up in battle array and have persuasive tongues, they have filled your ears with their loud and inveterate calumnies. And this is the reason why my three accusers, Meletus and Anytus and Lycon, have set upon me; Meletus, who has a quarrel with me on behalf of the poets; Anytus, on behalf of the craftsmen and politicians; Lycon, on behalf of the rhetoricians: and as I said at the beginning, I cannot expect to get rid of such a mass of calumny all in a moment. And this, O men of Athens, is the truth and the whole truth; I have concealed nothing, I have dissembled nothing. And yet, I know that my plainness of speech makes them hate me, and what is their hatred but a proof that I am speaking the truth?—Hence has arisen the prejudice against me; and this is the reason of it, as you will find out either in this or in any future enquiry.

I have said enough in my defence against the first class of my accusers; I turn to the second class. They are headed by Meletus, that good man and true lover of his country, as he calls himself. Against these, too, I must try to make a defence:—Let their affidavit be read: it contains something of this kind: It says that Socrates is a doer of evil, who corrupts the youth; and who does not believe in the gods of the state, but has other new divinities of his own. Such is the charge; and now let us examine the particular counts. He says that I am a doer of evil, and corrupt the youth; but I say, O men of Athens, that Meletus is a doer of evil, in that he pretends to be in earnest when he is only in jest, and is so eager to bring men to trial from a pretended zeal and interest about matters in which he really never had the smallest interest. And the truth of this I will endeavour to prove to you.

Come hither, Meletus, and let me ask a question of you. You think a great deal about the improvement of youth?

Yes, I do.

Tell the judges, then, who is their improver; for you must know, as you have taken the pains to discover their corrupter, and are citing and accusing me before them. Speak, then, and tell the judges who their improver is.—Observe, Meletus, that you are silent, and have nothing to say. But is not this rather disgraceful, and a very considerable proof of what I was saying, that you have no interest in the matter? Speak up, friend, and tell us who their improver is.

The laws.

But that, my good sir, is not my meaning. I want to know who the person is, who, in the first place, knows the laws.

The judges, Socrates, who are present in court.

What, do you mean to say, Meletus, that they are able to instruct and improve youth?

Certainly they are.

What, all of them, or some only and not others?

All of them.

By the goddess Here, that is good news! There are plenty of improvers, then. And what do you say of the audience,—do they improve them?

Yes, they do.

And the senators?

Yes, the senators improve them.

But perhaps the members of the assembly corrupt them?—or do they too improve them?

They improve them.

Then every Athenian improves and elevates them; all with the exception of myself; and I alone am their corrupter? Is that what you affirm?

That is what I stoutly affirm.

I am very unfortunate if you are right. But suppose I ask you a question: How about horses? Does one man do them harm and all the world good? Is not the exact opposite the truth? One man is able to do them good, or at least not many;—the trainer of horses, that is to say, does them good, and others who have to do with them rather injure them? Is not that true, Meletus, of horses, or of any other animals? Most assuredly it is; whether you and Anytus say yes or no. Happy indeed would be the condition of youth if they had one corrupter only, and all the rest of the world were their improvers. But you, Meletus, have sufficiently shown that you never had a thought about the young: your carelessness is seen in your not caring about the very things which you bring against me.

And now, Meletus, I will ask you another question—by Zeus I will: Which is better, to live among bad citizens, or among good ones? Answer, friend, I say; the question is one which may be easily answered. Do not the good do their neighbours good, and the bad do them evil?

Certainly.

And is there anyone who would rather be injured than benefited by those who live with him? Answer, my good friend, the law requires you to answer—does any one like to be injured?

Certainly not.

And when you accuse me of corrupting and deteriorating the youth, do you allege that I corrupt them intentionally or unintentionally?

Intentionally, I say.

But you have just admitted that the good do their neighbours good, and the evil do them evil. Now, is that a truth which your superior wisdom has recognized thus early in life, and am I, at my age, in such darkness and ignorance as not to know that if a man with whom I have to live is corrupted by me, I am very likely to be harmed by him; and yet I corrupt him, and intentionally, too—so you say, although neither I nor any other human being is ever likely to be convinced by you. But either I do not corrupt them, or I corrupt them unintentionally; and on either view of the case you lie. If my offence is unintentional, the law has no cognizance of unintentional offences: you ought to have taken me privately, and warned and admonished me; for if I had been better advised, I should have left off doing what I only did unintentionally—no doubt I should; but you would have nothing to say to me and refused to teach me. And now you bring me up in this court, which is a place not of instruction, but of punishment.

It will be very clear to you, Athenians, as I was saying, that Meletus has no care at all, great or small, about the matter. But still I should like to know, Meletus, in what I am affirmed to corrupt the young. I suppose you mean, as I infer from your indictment, that I teach them not to acknowledge the gods which the state acknowledges, but some other new divinities or spiritual agencies in their stead. These are the lessons by which I corrupt the youth, as you say.

Yes, that I say emphatically.

Then, by the gods, Meletus, of whom we are speaking, tell me and the court, in somewhat plainer terms, what you mean! for I do not as yet understand whether you affirm that I teach other men to acknowledge some gods, and therefore that I do believe in gods, and am not an entire atheist—this you do not lay to my charge,—but only you say that they are not the same gods which the city recognizes—the charge is that they are different gods. Or, do you mean that I am an atheist simply, and a teacher of atheism?

I mean the latter—that you are a complete atheist.

What an extraordinary statement! Why do you think so, Meletus? Do you mean that I do not believe in the godhead of the sun or moon, like other men?

I assure you, judges, that he does not: for he says that the sun is stone, and the moon earth.

Friend Meletus, you think that you are accusing Anaxagoras: and you have but a bad opinion of the judges, if you fancy them illiterate to such a degree as not to know that these doctrines are found in the books of Anaxagoras the Clazomenian, which are full of them. And so, forsooth, the youth are said to be taught them by Socrates, when there are not unfrequently exhibitions of them at the theatre (Probably in allusion to Aristophanes who caricatured, and to Euripides who borrowed the notions of Anaxagoras, as well as to other dramatic poets.); and they might pay their money, and laugh at Socrates if he pretends to father these extraordinary views. And so, Meletus, you really think that I do not believe in any god?

I swear by Zeus that you believe absolutely in none at all.

Nobody will believe you, Meletus, and I am pretty sure that you do not believe yourself. I cannot help thinking, men of Athens, that Meletus is reckless and impudent, and that he has written this indictment in a spirit of mere wantonness and youthful bravado. Has he not compounded a riddle, thinking to try me? He said to himself:—I shall see whether the wise Socrates will discover my facetious contradiction, or whether I shall be able to deceive him and the rest of them. For he certainly does appear to me to contradict himself in the indictment as much as if he said that Socrates is guilty of not believing in the gods, and yet of believing in them—but this is not like a person who is in earnest.

I should like you, O men of Athens, to join me in examining what I conceive to be his inconsistency; and do you, Meletus, answer. And I must remind the audience of my request that they would not make a disturbance if I speak in my accustomed manner:

Did ever man, Meletus, believe in the existence of human things, and not of human beings?...I wish, men of Athens, that he would answer, and not be always trying to get up an interruption. Did ever any man believe in horsemanship, and not in horses? or in flute-playing, and not in flute-players? No, my friend; I will answer to you and to the court, as you refuse to answer for yourself. There is no man who ever did. But now please to answer the next question: Can a man believe in spiritual and divine agencies, and not in spirits or demigods?

He cannot.

How lucky I am to have extracted that answer, by the assistance of the court! But then you swear in the indictment that I teach and believe in divine or spiritual agencies (new or old, no matter for that); at any rate, I believe in spiritual agencies,—so you say and swear in the affidavit; and yet if I believe in divine beings, how can I help believing in spirits or demigods;—must I not? To be sure I must; and therefore I may assume that your silence gives consent. Now what are spirits or demigods? Are they not either gods or the sons of gods?

Certainly they are.

But this is what I call the facetious riddle invented by you: the demigods or spirits are gods, and you say first that I do not believe in gods, and then again that I do believe in gods; that is, if I believe in demigods. For if the demigods are the illegitimate sons of gods, whether by the nymphs or by any other mothers, of whom they are said to be the sons—what human being will ever believe that there are no gods if they are the sons of gods? You might as well affirm the existence of mules, and deny that of horses and asses. Such nonsense, Meletus, could only have been intended by you to make trial of me. You have put this into the indictment because you had nothing real of which to accuse me. But no one who has a particle of understanding will ever be convinced by you that the same men can believe in divine and superhuman things, and yet not believe that there are gods and demigods and heroes.

I have said enough in answer to the charge of Meletus: any elaborate defence is unnecessary, but I know only too well how many are the enmities which I have incurred, and this is what will be my destruction if I am destroyed;—not Meletus, nor yet Anytus, but the envy and detraction of the world, which has been the death of many good men, and will probably be the death of many more; there is no danger of my being the last of them.

Some one will say: And are you not ashamed, Socrates, of a course of life which is likely to bring you to an untimely end? To him I may fairly answer: There you are mistaken: a man who is good for anything ought not to calculate the chance of living or dying; he ought only to consider whether in doing anything he is doing right or wrong—acting the part of a good man or of a bad. Whereas, upon your view, the heroes who fell at Troy were not good for much, and the son of Thetis above all, who altogether despised danger in comparison with disgrace; and when he was so eager to slay Hector, his goddess mother said to him, that if he avenged his companion Patroclus, and slew Hector, he would die himself—'Fate,' she said, in these or the like words, 'waits for you next after Hector;' he, receiving this warning, utterly despised danger and death, and instead of fearing them, feared rather to live in dishonour, and not to avenge his friend. 'Let me die forthwith,' he replies, 'and be avenged of my enemy, rather than abide here by the beaked ships, a laughing-stock and a burden of the earth.' Had Achilles any thought of death and danger? For wherever a man's place is, whether the place which he has chosen or that in which he has been placed by a commander, there he ought to remain in the hour of danger; he should not think of death or of anything but of disgrace. And this, O men of Athens, is a true saying.

Strange, indeed, would be my conduct, O men of Athens, if I who, when I was ordered by the generals whom you chose to command me at Potidaea and Amphipolis and Delium, remained where they placed me, like any other man, facing death—if now, when, as I conceive and imagine, God orders me to fulfil the philosopher's mission of searching into myself and other men, I were to desert my post through fear of death, or any other fear; that would indeed be strange, and I might justly be arraigned in court for denying the existence of the gods, if I disobeyed the oracle because I was afraid of death, fancying that I was wise when I was not wise. For the fear of death is indeed the pretence of wisdom, and not real wisdom, being a pretence of knowing the unknown; and no one knows whether death, which men in their fear apprehend to be the greatest evil, may not be the greatest good. Is not this ignorance of a disgraceful sort, the ignorance which is the conceit that a man knows what he does not know? And in this respect only I believe myself to differ from men in general, and may perhaps claim to be wiser than they are:—that whereas I know but little of the world below, I do not suppose that I know: but I do know that injustice and disobedience to a better, whether God or man, is evil and dishonourable, and I will never fear or avoid a possible good rather than a certain evil. And therefore if you let me go now, and are not convinced by Anytus, who said that since I had been prosecuted I must be put to death; (or if not that I ought never to have been prosecuted at all); and that if I escape now, your sons will all be utterly ruined by listening to my words—if you say to me, Socrates, this time we will not mind Anytus, and you shall be let off, but upon one condition, that you are not to enquire and speculate in this way any more, and that if you are caught doing so again you shall die;—if this was the condition on which you let me go, I should reply: Men of Athens, I honour and love you; but I shall obey God rather than you, and while I have life and strength I shall never cease from the practice and teaching of philosophy, exhorting any one whom I meet and saying to him after my manner: You, my friend,— a citizen of the great and mighty and wise city of Athens,—are you not ashamed of heaping up the greatest amount of money and honour and reputation, and caring so little about wisdom and truth and the greatest improvement of the soul, which you never regard or heed at all? And if the person with whom I am arguing, says: Yes, but I do care; then I do not leave him or let him go at once; but I proceed to interrogate and examine and cross-examine him, and if I think that he has no virtue in him, but only says that he has, I reproach him with undervaluing the greater, and overvaluing the less. And I shall repeat the same words to every one whom I meet, young and old, citizen and alien, but especially to the citizens, inasmuch as they are my brethren. For know that this is the command of God; and I believe that no greater good has ever happened in the state than my service to the God. For I do nothing but go about persuading you all, old and young alike, not to take thought for your persons or your properties, but first and chiefly to care about the greatest improvement of the soul. I tell you that virtue is not given by money, but that from virtue comes money and every other good of man, public as well as private. This is my teaching, and if this is the doctrine which corrupts the youth, I am a mischievous person. But if any one says that this is not my teaching, he is speaking an untruth. Wherefore, O men of Athens, I say to you, do as Anytus bids or not as Anytus bids, and either acquit me or not; but whichever you do, understand that I shall never alter my ways, not even if I have to die many times.

Men of Athens, do not interrupt, but hear me; there was an understanding between us that you should hear me to the end: I have something more to say, at which you may be inclined to cry out; but I believe that to hear me will be good for you, and therefore I beg that you will not cry out. I would have you know, that if you kill such an one as I am, you will injure yourselves more than you will injure me. Nothing will injure me, not Meletus nor yet Anytus—they cannot, for a bad man is not permitted to injure a better than himself. I do not deny that Anytus may, perhaps, kill him, or drive him into exile, or deprive him of civil rights; and he may imagine, and others may imagine, that he is inflicting a great injury upon him: but there I do not agree. For the evil of doing as he is doing—the evil of unjustly taking away the life of another—is greater far.

And now, Athenians, I am not going to argue for my own sake, as you may think, but for yours, that you may not sin against the God by condemning me, who am his gift to you. For if you kill me you will not easily find a successor to me, who, if I may use such a ludicrous figure of speech, am a sort of gadfly, given to the state by God; and the state is a great and noble steed who is tardy in his motions owing to his very size, and requires to be stirred into life. I am that gadfly which God has attached to the state, and all day long and in all places am always fastening upon you, arousing and persuading and reproaching you. You will not easily find another like me, and therefore I would advise you to spare me. I dare say that you may feel out of temper (like a person who is suddenly awakened from sleep), and you think that you might easily strike me dead as Anytus advises, and then you would sleep on for the remainder of your lives, unless God in his care of you sent you another gadfly. When I say that I am given to you by God, the proof of my mission is this:—if I had been like other men, I should not have neglected all my own concerns or patiently seen the neglect of them during all these years, and have been doing yours, coming to you individually like a father or elder brother, exhorting you to regard virtue; such conduct, I say, would be unlike human nature. If I had gained anything, or if my exhortations had been paid, there would have been some sense in my doing so; but now, as you will perceive, not even the impudence of my accusers dares to say that I have ever exacted or sought pay of any one; of that they have no witness. And I have a sufficient witness to the truth of what I say—my poverty.

Some one may wonder why I go about in private giving advice and busying myself with the concerns of others, but do not venture to come forward in public and advise the state. I will tell you why. You have heard me speak at sundry times and in divers places of an oracle or sign which comes to me, and is the divinity which Meletus ridicules in the indictment. This sign, which is a kind of voice, first began to come to me when I was a child; it always forbids but never commands me to do anything which I am going to do. This is what deters me from being a politician. And rightly, as I think. For I am certain, O men of Athens, that if I had engaged in politics, I should have perished long ago, and done no good either to you or to myself. And do not be offended at my telling you the truth: for the truth is, that no man who goes to war with you or any other multitude, honestly striving against the many lawless and unrighteous deeds which are done in a state, will save his life; he who will fight for the right, if he would live even for a brief space, must have a private station and not a public one.

I can give you convincing evidence of what I say, not words only, but what you value far more—actions. Let me relate to you a passage of my own life which will prove to you that I should never have yielded to injustice from any fear of death, and that 'as I should have refused to yield' I must have died at once. I will tell you a tale of the courts, not very interesting perhaps, but nevertheless true. The only office of state which I ever held, O men of Athens, was that of senator: the tribe Antiochis, which is my tribe, had the presidency at the trial of the generals who had not taken up the bodies of the slain after the battle of Arginusae; and you proposed to try them in a body, contrary to law, as you all thought afterwards; but at the time I was the only one of the Prytanes who was opposed to the illegality, and I gave my vote against you; and when the orators threatened to impeach and arrest me, and you called and shouted, I made up my mind that I would run the risk, having law and justice with me, rather than take part in your injustice because I feared imprisonment and death. This happened in the days of the democracy. But when the oligarchy of the Thirty was in power, they sent for me and four others into the rotunda, and bade us bring Leon the Salaminian from Salamis, as they wanted to put him to death. This was a specimen of the sort of commands which they were always giving with the view of implicating as many as possible in their crimes; and then I showed, not in word only but in deed, that, if I may be allowed to use such an expression, I cared not a straw for death, and that my great and only care was lest I should do an unrighteous or unholy thing. For the strong arm of that oppressive power did not frighten me into doing wrong; and when we came out of the rotunda the other four went to Salamis and fetched Leon, but I went quietly home. For which I might have lost my life, had not the power of the Thirty shortly afterwards come to an end. And many will witness to my words.

Now do you really imagine that I could have survived all these years, if I had led a public life, supposing that like a good man I had always maintained the right and had made justice, as I ought, the first thing? No indeed, men of Athens, neither I nor any other man. But I have been always the same in all my actions, public as well as private, and never have I yielded any base compliance to those who are slanderously termed my disciples, or to any other. Not that I have any regular disciples. But if any one likes to come and hear me while I am pursuing my mission, whether he be young or old, he is not excluded. Nor do I converse only with those who pay; but any one, whether he be rich or poor, may ask and answer me and listen to my words; and whether he turns out to be a bad man or a good one, neither result can be justly imputed to me; for I never taught or professed to teach him anything. And if any one says that he has ever learned or heard anything from me in private which all the world has not heard, let me tell you that he is lying.

But I shall be asked, Why do people delight in continually conversing with you? I have told you already, Athenians, the whole truth about this matter: they like to hear the cross-examination of the pretenders to wisdom; there is amusement in it. Now this duty of cross-examining other men has been imposed upon me by God; and has been signified to me by oracles, visions, and in every way in which the will of divine power was ever intimated to any one. This is true, O Athenians, or, if not true, would be soon refuted. If I am or have been corrupting the youth, those of them who are now grown up and have become sensible that I gave them bad advice in the days of their youth should come forward as accusers, and take their revenge; or if they do not like to come themselves, some of their relatives, fathers, brothers, or other kinsmen, should say what evil their families have suffered at my hands. Now is their time. Many of them I see in the court. There is Crito, who is of the same age and of the same deme with myself, and there is Critobulus his son, whom I also see. Then again there is Lysanias of Sphettus, who is the father of Aeschines—he is present; and also there is Antiphon of Cephisus, who is the father of Epigenes; and there are the brothers of several who have associated with me. There is Nicostratus the son of Theosdotides, and the brother of Theodotus (now Theodotus himself is dead, and therefore he, at any rate, will not seek to stop him); and there is Paralus the son of Demodocus, who had a brother Theages; and Adeimantus the son of Ariston, whose brother Plato is present; and Aeantodorus, who is the brother of Apollodorus, whom I also see. I might mention a great many others, some of whom Meletus should have produced as witnesses in the course of his speech; and let him still produce them, if he has forgotten—I will make way for him. And let him say, if he has any testimony of the sort which he can produce. Nay, Athenians, the very opposite is the truth. For all these are ready to witness on behalf of the corrupter, of the injurer of their kindred, as Meletus and Anytus call me; not the corrupted youth only—there might have been a motive for that—but their uncorrupted elder relatives. Why should they too support me with their testimony? Why, indeed, except for the sake of truth and justice, and because they know that I am speaking the truth, and that Meletus is a liar.

Well, Athenians, this and the like of this is all the defence which I have to offer. Yet a word more. Perhaps there may be some one who is offended at me, when he calls to mind how he himself on a similar, or even a less serious occasion, prayed and entreated the judges with many tears, and how he produced his children in court, which was a moving spectacle, together with a host of relations and friends; whereas I, who am probably in danger of my life, will do none of these things. The contrast may occur to his mind, and he may be set against me, and vote in anger because he is displeased at me on this account. Now if there be such a person among you,—mind, I do not say that there is,—to him I may fairly reply: My friend, I am a man, and like other men, a creature of flesh and blood, and not 'of wood or stone,' as Homer says; and I have a family, yes, and sons, O Athenians, three in number, one almost a man, and two others who are still young; and yet I will not bring any of them hither in order to petition you for an acquittal. And why not? Not from any self-assertion or want of respect for you. Whether I am or am not afraid of death is another question, of which I will not now speak. But, having regard to public opinion, I feel that such conduct would be discreditable to myself, and to you, and to the whole state. One who has reached my years, and who has a name for wisdom, ought not to demean himself. Whether this opinion of me be deserved or not, at any rate the world has decided that Socrates is in some way superior to other men. And if those among you who are said to be superior in wisdom and courage, and any other virtue, demean themselves in this way, how shameful is their conduct! I have seen men of reputation, when they have been condemned, behaving in the strangest manner: they seemed to fancy that they were going to suffer something dreadful if they died, and that they could be immortal if you only allowed them to live; and I think that such are a dishonour to the state, and that any stranger coming in would have said of them that the most eminent men of Athens, to whom the Athenians themselves give honour and command, are no better than women. And I say that these things ought not to be done by those of us who have a reputation; and if they are done, you ought not to permit them; you ought rather to show that you are far more disposed to condemn the man who gets up a doleful scene and makes the city ridiculous, than him who holds his peace.

But, setting aside the question of public opinion, there seems to be something wrong in asking a favour of a judge, and thus procuring an acquittal, instead of informing and convincing him. For his duty is, not to make a present of justice, but to give judgment; and he has sworn that he will judge according to the laws, and not according to his own good pleasure; and we ought not to encourage you, nor should you allow your-selves to be encouraged, in this habit of perjury—there can be no piety in that. Do not then require me to do what I consider dishonourable and impious and wrong, especially now, when I am being tried for impiety on the indictment of Meletus. For if, O men of Athens, by force of persuasion and entreaty I could overpower your oaths, then I should be teaching you to believe that there are no gods, and in defending should simply con-vict myself of the charge of not believing in them. But that is not so—far otherwise. For I do believe that there are gods, and in a sense higher than that in which any of my accusers believe in them. And to you and to God I commit my cause, to be determined by you as is best for you and me.

•   •   •

(The jurors vote 281 to 220 to find Socrates guilty.) There are many reasons why I am not grieved, O men of Athens, at the vote of condemnation. I expected it, and am only surprised that the votes are so nearly equal; for I had thought that the majority against me would have been far larger; but now, had thirty votes gone over to the other side, I should have been acquitted. And I may say, I think, that I have escaped Meletus. I may say more; for without the assistance of Anytus and Lycon, any one may see that he would not have had a fifth part of the votes, as the law requires, in which case he would have incurred a fine of a thousand drachmae.

And so he proposes death as the penalty. And what shall I propose on my part, O men of Athens? Clearly that which is my due. And what is my due? What return shall be made to the man who has never had the wit to be idle during his whole life; but has been careless of what the many care for—wealth, and family interests, and military offices, and speaking in the assembly, and magistracies, and plots, and parties. Reflecting that I was really too honest a man to be a politician and live, I did not go where I could do no good to you or to myself; but where I could do the greatest good privately to every one of you, thither I went, and sought to persuade every man among you that he must look to himself, and seek virtue and wisdom before he looks to his private interests, and look to the state before he looks to the interests of the state; and that this should be the order which he observes in all his actions. What shall be done to such an one? Doubtless some good thing, O men of Athens, if he has his reward; and the good should be of a kind suitable to him. What would be a reward suitable to a poor man who is your benefactor, and who desires leisure that he may instruct you? There can be no reward so fitting as maintenance in the Prytaneum, O men of Athens, a reward which he deserves far more than the citizen who has won the prize at Olympia in the horse or chariot race, whether the chariots were drawn by two horses or by many. For I am in want, and he has enough; and he only gives you the appearance of happiness, and I give you the reality. And if I am to estimate the penalty fairly, I should say that maintenance in the Prytaneum is the just return.

Perhaps you think that I am braving you in what I am saying now, as in what I said before about the tears and prayers. But this is not so. I speak rather because I am convinced that I never intentionally wronged any one, although I cannot convince you—the time has been too short; if there were a law at Athens, as there is in other cities, that a capital cause should not be decided in one day, then I believe that I should have convinced you. But I cannot in a moment refute great slanders; and, as I am convinced that I never wronged another, I will assuredly not wrong myself. I will not say of myself that I deserve any evil, or propose any penalty. Why should I? because I am afraid of the penalty of death which Meletus proposes? When I do not know whether death is a good or an evil, why should I propose a penalty which would certainly be an evil? Shall I say imprisonment? And why should I live in prison, and be the slave of the magistrates of the year—of the Eleven? Or shall the penalty be a fine, and imprisonment until the fine is paid? There is the same objection. I should have to lie in prison, for money I have none, and cannot pay. And if I say exile (and this may possibly be the penalty which you will affix), I must indeed be blinded by the love of life, if I am so irrational as to expect that when you, who are my own citizens, cannot endure my discourses and words, and have found them so grievous and odious that you will have no more of them, others are likely to endure me. No indeed, men of Athens, that is not very likely. And what a life should I lead, at my age, wandering from city to city, ever changing my place of exile, and always being driven out! For I am quite sure that wherever I go, there, as here, the young men will flock to me; and if I drive them away, their elders will drive me out at their request; and if I let them come, their fathers and friends will drive me out for their sakes.

Some one will say: Yes, Socrates, but cannot you hold your tongue, and then you may go into a foreign city, and no one will interfere with you? Now I have great difficulty in making you understand my answer to this. For if I tell you that to do as you say would be a disobedience to the God, and therefore that I cannot hold my tongue, you will not believe that I am serious; and if I say again that daily to discourse about virtue, and of those other things about which you hear me examining myself and others, is the greatest good of man, and that the unexamined life is not worth living, you are still less likely to believe me. Yet I say what is true, although a thing of which it is hard for me to persuade you. Also, I have never been accustomed to think that I deserve to suffer any harm. Had I money I might have estimated the offence at what I was able to pay, and not have been much the worse. But I have none, and therefore I must ask you to proportion the fine to my means. Well, perhaps I could afford a mina, and therefore I propose that penalty: Plato, Crito, Critobulus, and Apollodorus, my friends here, bid me say thirty minae, and they will be the sureties. Let thirty minae be the penalty; for which sum they will be ample security to you.

(The jurors vote to condemn Socrates to death.) Not much time will be gained, O Athenians, in return for the evil name which you will get from the detractors of the city, who will say that you killed Socrates, a wise man; for they will call me wise, even although I am not wise, when they want to reproach you. If you had waited a little while, your desire would have been fulfilled in the course of nature. For I am far advanced in years, as you may perceive, and not far from death. I am speaking now not to all of you, but only to those who have condemned me to death. And I have another thing to say to them: you think that I was convicted because I had no words of the sort which would have procured my acquittal—I mean, if I had thought fit to leave nothing undone or unsaid. Not so; the deficiency which led to my conviction was not of words—certainly not. But I had not the boldness or impudence or inclination to address you as you would have liked me to do, weeping and wailing and lamenting, and saying and doing many things which you have been accustomed to hear from others, and which, as I maintain, are unworthy of me. I thought at the time that I ought not to do anything common or mean when in danger: nor do I now repent of the style of my defence; I would rather die having spoken after my manner, than speak in your manner and live. For neither in war nor yet at law ought I or any man to use every way of escaping death. Often in battle there can be no doubt that if a man will throw away his arms, and fall on his knees before his pursuers, he may escape death; and in other dangers there are other ways of escaping death, if a man is willing to say and do anything. The difficulty, my friends, is not to avoid death, but to avoid unrighteousness; for that runs faster than death. I am old and move slowly, and the slower runner has overtaken me, and my accusers are keen and quick, and the faster runner, who is unrighteousness, has overtaken them. And now I depart hence condemned by you to suffer the penalty of death,— they too go their ways condemned by the truth to suffer the penalty of villainy and wrong; and I must abide by my award—let them abide by theirs. I suppose that these things may be regarded as fated,—and I think that they are well.

And now, O men who have condemned me, I would fain prophesy to you; for I am about to die, and in the hour of death men are gifted with prophetic power. And I prophesy to you who are my murderers, that immediately after my departure punishment far heavier than you have inflicted on me will surely await you. Me you have killed because you wanted to escape the accuser, and not to give an account of your lives. But that will not be as you suppose: far otherwise. For I say that there will be more accusers of you than there are now; accusers whom hitherto I have restrained: and as they are younger they will be more inconsiderate with you, and you will be more offended at them. If you think that by killing men you can prevent some one from censuring your evil lives, you are mistaken; that is not a way of escape which is either possible or honourable; the easiest and the noblest way is not to be disabling others, but to be improving yourselves. This is the prophecy which I utter before my departure to the judges who have condemned me.

Friends, who would have acquitted me, I would like also to talk with you about the thing which has come to pass, while the magistrates are busy, and before I go to the place at which I must die. Stay then a little, for we may as well talk with one another while there is time. You are my friends, and I should like to show you the meaning of this event which has happened to me. O my judges—for you I may truly call judges— I should like to tell you of a wonderful circumstance. Hitherto the divine faculty of which the internal oracle is the source has constantly been in the habit of opposing me even about trifles, if I was going to make a slip or error in any matter; and now as you see there has come upon me that which may be thought, and is generally believed to be, the last and worst evil. But the oracle made no sign of opposition, either when I was leaving my house in the morning, or when I was on my way to the court, or while I was speaking, at anything which I was going to say; and yet I have often been stopped in the middle of a speech, but now in nothing I either said or did touching the matter in hand has the oracle opposed me. What do I take to be the explanation of this silence? I will tell you. It is an intimation that what has happened to me is a good, and that those of us who think that death is an evil are in error. For the customary sign would surely have opposed me had I been going to evil and not to good.

Let us reflect in another way, and we shall see that there is great reason to hope that death is a good; for one of two things—either death is a state of nothingness and utter unconsciousness, or, as men say, there is a change and migration of the soul from this world to another. Now if you suppose that there is no consciousness, but a sleep like the sleep of him who is undisturbed even by dreams, death will be an unspeakable gain. For if a person were to select the night in which his sleep was undisturbed even by dreams, and were to compare with this the other days and nights of his life, and then were to tell us how many days and nights he had passed in the course of his life better and more pleasantly than this one, I think that any man, I will not say a private man, but even the great king will not find many such days or nights, when compared with the others. Now if death be of such a nature, I say that to die is gain; for eternity is then only a single night. But if death is the journey to another place, and there, as men say, all the dead abide, what good, O my friends and judges, can be greater than this? If indeed when the pilgrim arrives in the world below, he is delivered from the professors of justice in this world, and finds the true judges who are said to give judgment there, Minos and Rhadamanthus and Aeacus and Triptolemus, and other sons of God who were righteous in their own life, that pilgrimage will be worth making. What would not a man give if he might converse with Orpheus and Musaeus and Hesiod and Homer? Nay, if this be true, let me die again and again. I myself, too, shall have a wonderful interest in there meeting and conversing with Palamedes, and Ajax the son of Telamon, and any other ancient hero who has suffered death through an unjust judgment; and there will be no small pleasure, as I think, in comparing my own sufferings with theirs. Above all, I shall then be able to continue my search into true and false knowledge; as in this world, so also in the next; and I shall find out who is wise, and who pretends to be wise, and is not. What would not a man give, O judges, to be able to examine the leader of the great Trojan expedition; or Odysseus or Sisyphus, or numberless others, men and women too! What infinite delight would there be in conversing with them and asking them questions! In another world they do not put a man to death for asking questions: assuredly not. For besides being happier than we are, they will be immortal, if what is said is true.

Wherefore, O judges, be of good cheer about death, and know of a certainty, that no evil can happen to a good man, either in life or after death. He and his are not neglected by the gods; nor has my own approaching end happened by mere chance. But I see clearly that the time had arrived when it was better for me to die and be released from trouble; wherefore the oracle gave no sign. For which reason, also, I am not angry with my condemners, or with my accusers; they have done me no harm, although they did not mean to do me any good; and for this I may gently blame them.

Still I have a favour to ask of them. When my sons are grown up, I would ask you, O my friends, to punish them; and I would have you trouble them, as I have troubled you, if they seem to care about riches, or anything, more than about virtue; or if they pretend to be something when they are really nothing,—then reprove them, as I have reproved you, for not caring about that for which they ought to care, and thinking that they are something when they are really nothing. And if you do this, both I and my sons will have received justice at your hands.

The hour of departure has arrived, and we go our ways—I to die, and you to live. Which is better God only knows.

THE REPUBLIC

Plato's *Republic* (written around 380 B.C.) is generally considered one of the greatest (if not the greatest) of his dialogues. While *The Apology* is an early dialogue, *The Republic* comes from Plato's middle period. What this means (among other things) is that although the figure of Socrates as Plato actually recalled him is still very much in evidence, Plato is also beginning to expound his own philosophy by placing it in the mouth of his teacher.

The overarching theme of *The Republic* is the nature of justice. In the course of considering this question, a good part of the work is taken up discussing the relationship between justice as manifest in the soul and justice as embodied in the city-state (*polis*). Socrates poses the issue in a provocative way by asking his friends (and us) why someone should be just in a world where justice does not always pay, and where the unjust seem to prosper. In the view of Socrates (and Plato), a city or state will be just when the souls of those who comprise it are properly ordered, and when the proper ordering of the soul is reflected in the proper ordering of the state. At the same time, Socrates also underlines the fact that it is difficult if not impossible for a person to possess a just (that is, properly balanced) soul in a city-state that is itself disordered. On this point it is crucial to bear in mind that, for the Greeks, human beings are social and political by nature. There is no such thing for them as an "individual" apart from the community. So if the community is unjust it will have a terrible effect on the souls of its members. We need to be very careful here about what it is that Plato is doing in the dialogue. There is a common misperception that he was designing an "ideal state" or utopia. This mistaken notion needs to be strongly qualified if not thrown out completely. Why? Because for Plato, the "city founded in speech" by Socrates has a greater degree of reality than the corrupt *polis* in which he lived. For Plato, what we tend to refer to as "the real world" is actually a world of appearances in which opinion (rather than true knowledge) reigns. In his view most people live most of their lives without knowledge of the true nature of reality. Plato depicts this situation in the allegory of the cave. Those few persons fortunate enough to escape from the cave and to gain knowledge of what is truly real are the philosophers, the "lovers of wisdom." If these philosophers were to rule, the city-state could be healthy and just.

But what are the chances of this happening? *The Republic* ends on an ambivalent note (as do so many of Plato's dialogues). On one hand, Socrates confesses to his young friend Adeimantos that it is unlikely that the city he has described will ever come to pass in this world. But that is not cause for despair. As Socrates reminds Adeimantos, "It matters nothing whether it exists anywhere or shall exist; for he (the philosopher) would practice the principles of this city only, no other." In other words, whether the city exists or not on earth, those who are wise and just will lead their lives in accordance with its principles, regardless of the cost. In this way we are brought back to the question with which *The Republic* began: whether it is worthwhile to be just in a world that is so often unjust. The dialogue ends with Socrates reminding his audience that even if justice is not to be realized in this world, it will count for a great deal in the afterlife. In the myth of Er he describes the eternal consequences that follow from the pursuit of justice and injustice. Socrates concludes by exhorting his hearers that the myth "would save us, if we would be guided by it."

Allegory of the Cave

Socrates. Glaucon.

Socrates. And now, I said, let me show in a figure how far our nature is enlightened or unenlightened: Behold human beings living in an underground den, which has a mouth open towards the light and reaching all along the den; here they have been from their childhood, and have their legs and necks chained so that they cannot move, and can only see before them, being prevented by the chains from turning round their heads. Above and behind them a fire is blazing at a distance, and between the fire and the prisoners there is a raised way; and you will see, if you look, a low wall built along the way, like the screen which marionette players have in front of them, over which they show the puppets.

I see.

And do you see, I said, men passing along the wall, carrying all sorts of vessels, and statues[1] and figures of animals made of wood and stone and various materials, which appear over the wall? Some of them are talking, others silent.

You have shown me a strange image, and they are strange prisoners.

Like ourselves, I replied; and they see only their own shadows, or the shadows of one another, which the fire throws on the opposite wall of the cave?

True, he said; how could they see anything but the shadows if they were never allowed to move their heads?

And of the objects which are being carried in like manner they would only see the shadows?

Yes, he said.

And if they were able to converse with one another, would they not suppose that they were naming what was actually before them?

Very true.

---

1   Thus the prisoners see only shadows cast by images of real things,—not even shadows cast by real things themselves.

And suppose further that the prison had an echo which came from the other side, would they not be sure to fancy when one of the passers-by spoke that the voice which they heard came from the passing shadow?

No question, he replied.

To them, I said, the truth would be literally nothing but the shadows of the images.

That is certain.

And now look again, and see what will naturally follow if the prisoners are released and disabused of their error. At first, when any one of them is liberated and compelled suddenly to stand up and turn his neck round and walk and look towards the light, he will suffer sharp pains; the glare will distress him, and he will be unable to see the realities of which in his former state he had seen the shadows; and then conceive some one saying to him that what he saw before was an illusion, but that now, when he is approaching nearer to being and his eye is turned towards more real existence, he has a clearer vision,—what will be his reply? And you may further imagine that his instructor is pointing to the objects as they pass and requiring him to name them,—will he not be perplexed? Will he not fancy that the shadows which he formerly saw are truer than the objects which are now shown to him?

Far truer.

And if he is compelled to look straight at the light, will he not have a pain in his eyes which will make him turn away to take refuge in the objects of vision which he can see, and which he will conceive to be in reality clearer than the things which are now being shown to him?

True, he said.

And suppose once more, that he is reluctantly dragged up a steep and rugged ascent, and held fast until he is forced into the presence of the sun himself, is he not likely to be pained and irritated? When he approaches the light his eyes will be dazzled, and he will not be able to see anything at all of what are now called realities.

Not all in a moment, he said.

He will require to grow accustomed to the sight of the upper world. And first he will see the shadows best, next the reflections of men and other objects in the water, and then the objects themselves; then he will gaze upon the light of the moon and the stars and the spangled heaven; and he will see the sky and the stars by night better than the sun or the light of the sun by day?

Certainly.

Last of all he will be able to see the sun, and not mere reflections of him in the water, but he will see him in his own proper place, and not in another; and he will contemplate him as he is.

Certainly.

He will then proceed to argue that this is he who gives the season and the years, and is the guardian of all that is in the visible world, and in a certain way the cause of all things which he and his fellows have been accustomed to behold?

Clearly, he said, he would first see the sun and then reason about him.

And when he remembered his old habitation, and the wisdom of the den and his fellow-prisoners, do you not suppose that he would felicitate himself on the change, and pity them?

Certainly, he would.

And if they were in the habit of conferring honors among themselves on those who were quickest to observe the passing shadows and to remark which of them went before, and which followed after, and which were together; and who were therefore best able to draw conclusions as to the future, do you think that he would care for such honors and glories, or envy the possessors of them? Would he not say with Homer, "Better to be the poor servant of a poor master," and to endure anything, rather than think as they do and live after their manner.

Yes, he said, I think that he would rather suffer anything than entertain these false notions and live in this miserable manner.

Imagine once more, I said, such an one coming suddenly out of the sun to be replaced in his old situation; would he not be certain to have his eyes full of darkness?

To be sure, he said.

And if there were a contest, and he had to compete in measuring the shadows with the prisoners who had never moved out of the den, while his sight was still weak, and before his eyes had become steady (and the time which would be needed to acquire this new habit of sight might be very considerable), would he not be ridiculous? Men would say of him that up he went and down he came without his eyes; and that it was better not even to think of ascending; and if any one tried to loose another and lead him up to the light, let them only catch the offender and they would put him to death.

No question, he said.

This entire allegory, I said, you may now append, dear Glaucon, to the previous argument; the prisonhouse is the world of sight, the light of the fire is the sun, and you will not misapprehend me if you interpret the journey upwards to be the ascent of the soul into the intellectual world according to my poor belief, which, at your desire, I have expressed—whether rightly or wrongly God knows. But, whether true or false, my opinion is that in the world of knowledge the idea of good appears last of all, and is seen only with an effort; and, when seen, is also inferred to be the universal author of all things beautiful and right— parent of light and of the lord of light in this visible world, and the immediate source of reason and truth in the intellectual; and that this is the power upon which he who would act rationally either in public or private life must have his eye fixed.

I agree, he said, as far as I am able to understand you.

Moreover, I said, you must not wonder that those who attain to this beatific vision are unwilling to descend to human affairs; for their souls are ever hastening into the upper world where they desire to dwell; which desire of theirs is very natural, if our allegory may be trusted.

Yes, very natural.

And is there anything surprising in one who passes from divine contemplations to the evil state of man, misbehaving himself in a ridiculous manner; if, while his eyes are blinking and before he has become accustomed to the surrounding darkness, he is compelled to fight in courts of law, or in other places, about the images or shadows of images of justice, and is endeavoring to meet the conceptions of those who have never yet seen absolute justice?

Anything but surprising, he replied.

Any one who has common sense will remember that the bewilderments of the eyes are of two kinds, and arise from two causes, either from coming out of the light or from going into the light, which is true of the mind's eye, quite as much as of the bodily eye; and he who remembers this when he sees any one whose vision is perplexed and weak, will not be too ready to laugh; he will first ask whether that soul of man has come out of the brighter life, and is unable to see because unaccustomed to the dark, or having turned from darkness to the day is dazzled by excess of light. And he will count the one happy in his condition and state of being, and he will pity the other; or, if he have a mind to laugh at the soul which comes from below into the light, there will be more reason in this than in the laugh which greets him who returns from above out of the light into the den.

That, he said, is a very just distinction.

But then, if I am right, certain professors of education must be wrong when they say that they can put a knowledge into the soul which was not there before, like sight into blind eyes.

They undoubtedly say this, he replied.

Whereas, our argument shows that the power and capacity of learning exists in the soul already; and that just as the eye was unable to turn from darkness to light without the whole body, so too the instrument of knowledge can only by the movement of the whole soul be turned from the world of becoming into that of being, and learn by degrees to endure the sight of being, and of the brightest and best of being, or in other words, of the good.

Very true.

And must there not be some art which will effect conversion in the easiest and quickest manner; not implanting the faculty of sight, for that exists already, but has been turned in the wrong direction, and is looking away from the truth?

Yes, he said, such an art may be presumed.

And whereas the other so-called virtues of the soul seem to be akin to bodily qualities, for even when they are not originally innate they can be implanted later by habit and exercise, the virtue of wisdom more than anything else contains a divine element which always remains, and by this conversion is rendered useful and profitable; or on the other hand, hurtful and useless. Did you never observe the narrow intelligence flashing from the keen eye of a clever rogue—how eager he is, how clearly his paltry soul sees the way to his end; he is the reverse of blind, but his keen eyesight is forced into the service of evil, and he is mischievous in proportion to his cleverness?

Very true, he said.

But what if there had been a circumcision of such natures in the days of their youth; and they had been severed from those sensual pleasures, such as eating and drinking, which, like leaden weights, were attached to them at their birth,[2] and which drag them down and turn the vision of their souls upon the things that are below—if, I say, they had been released from these impediments and turned in the opposite direction, the very same faculty in them would have seen the truth as keenly as they see what their eyes are turned to now.

Very likely.

Yes, I said; and there is another thing which is likely, or rather a necessary inference from what has preceded,—that neither the uneducated and uninformed of the truth,

---

2   Plato means: "If the son should be freed from the tendencies to the world of change (the world of 'becoming') which have become attached to the soul by the pleasures of eating and drinking, and hold it down like leaden weights," etc.

nor yet those who never make an end of their education, will be able ministers of State; not the former, because they have no single aim of duty which is the rule of all their actions, private as well as public; nor the latter, because they will not act at all except upon compulsion, fancying that they are already dwelling apart in the islands of the blest.

Very true, he replied.

Then, I said, the business of us who are the founders of the State will be to compel the best minds to attain that knowledge which we have already shown to be the greatest of all—they must continue to ascend until they arrive at the good; but when they have ascended and seen enough we must not allow them to do as they do now.

What do you mean?

I mean that they remain in the upper world; but this must not be allowed; they must be made to descend again among the prisoners in the den, and partake of their labors and honors, whether they are worth having or not.

But is not this unjust? he said; ought we to give them a worse life, when they might have a better?

You have again forgotten, my friend, I said, the intention of the legislator, who did not aim at making any one class in the State happy above the rest; the happiness was to be in the whole State, and he held the citizens together by persuasion and necessity, making them benefactors of the State, and therefore benefactors of one another; to this end he created them, not to please themselves, but to be his instruments in binding up the State.

The Myth of Er

Well, I said, I will tell you a tale; not one of the tales which Odysseus tells to the hero Alcinous, yet this too is a tale of a hero, Er the son of Armenius, a Pamphylian by birth. He was slain in battle, and ten days afterwards, when the bodies of the dead were taken up already in a state of corruption, his body was found unaffected by decay, and carried away home to be buried. And on the twelfth day, as he was lying on the funeral pile, he returned to life and told them what he had seen in the other world. He said that when his soul left the body he went on a journey with a great company, and that they came to a mysterious place at which there were two openings in the earth; they were near together, and over against them were two other openings in the heaven above. In the intermediate space there were judges seated, who commanded the just, after they had given judgment on them and had bound their sentences in front of them, to ascend by the heavenly way on the right hand; and in like manner the unjust were bidden by them to descend by the lower way on the left hand; these also bore the symbols of their deeds, but fastened on their backs. He drew near, and they told him that he was to be the messenger who would carry the report of the other world to men, and they bade him hear and see all that was to be heard and seen in that place. Then he beheld and saw on one side the souls departing at either opening of heaven and earth when sentence had been given on them; and at the two other openings other souls, some ascending out of the earth dusty and worn with travel, some descending out of heaven clean and bright. And arriving ever and anon they seemed to have come from a long journey, and they went forth with gladness into the meadow, where they encamped as at a festival; and those who knew one another embraced and conversed, the souls which came from earth curiously enquiring about the things above, and the souls which came from heaven about the things beneath. And they told one another of what had happened by the way, those from below weeping and sorrowing at the remembrance of the things which they had endured and seen in their journey beneath the earth (now the journey lasted a thousand years), while those from above were describing heavenly delights and visions of inconceivable beauty. The story, Glaucon, would take too long to tell; but the sum was this:—He said that for every wrong which they had done to any one they suffered tenfold; or once in a hundred years—such being reckoned to be the length of man's life, and the penalty being thus paid ten times in a thousand years. If, for example, there were any who had been the cause of many deaths, or had betrayed or enslaved cities or armies, or been guilty of any other evil behaviour, for each and all of their offences they received punishment ten times over, and the rewards of beneficence and justice and holiness were in the same proportion. I need hardly repeat what he said concerning young children dying almost as soon as they were born. Of piety and impiety to gods and parents, and of murderers, there were retributions other and greater far which he described. He mentioned that he was present when one of the spirits asked another, 'Where is Ardiaeus the Great?' (Now this Ardiaeus lived a thousand years before the time of Er: he had been the tyrant of some city of Pamphylia, and had murdered his aged father and his elder brother, and was said to have committed many other abominable crimes.) The answer of the other spirit was: 'He comes not hither and will never come. And this,' said he, 'was one of the dreadful sights which we ourselves witnessed. We were at the mouth of the cavern, and, having completed all our experiences, were about to reascend, when of a sudden Ardiaeus appeared and several others, most of whom were tyrants; and there were also besides the tyrants private individuals who had been great criminals: they were just, as they fancied, about to return into the upper world, but the mouth, instead of admitting them, gave a roar, whenever any of these incurable sinners or some one who had not been sufficiently punished tried to ascend; and then wild men of fiery aspect, who were standing by and heard the sound, seized and carried them off; and Ardiaeus and others they bound head and foot and hand, and threw them down and flayed them with scourges, and dragged them along the road at the side, carding them on thorns like wool, and declaring to the passers-by what were their crimes, and that they were being taken away to be cast into hell.' And of all the many terrors which they had endured, he said that there was none like the terror which each of them felt at that moment, lest they should hear the voice; and when there was silence, one by one they ascended with exceeding joy. These, said Er, were the penalties and retributions, and there were blessings as great.

Now when the spirits which were in the meadow had tarried seven days, on the eighth they were obliged to proceed on their journey, and, on the fourth day after, he said that they came to a place where they could see from above a line of light, straight as a column, extending right through the whole heaven and through the earth, in colour resembling the rainbow, only brighter and purer; another day's journey brought them to the place, and there, in the midst of the light, they saw the ends of the chains of heaven let down from above: for this light is the belt of heaven, and holds together the circle of the universe, like the under-girders of a trireme. From these ends is extended the spindle of Necessity, on which all the revolutions turn. The shaft and hook of this spindle are made of steel, and the whorl is made partly of steel and also partly of other materials. Now the whorl is in form like the whorl used on earth; and the description of it implied that there is one large hollow whorl which is quite scooped out, and into this is fitted another lesser one, and another, and another, and four others, making eight in all, like vessels which fit into one another; the whorls show their edges on the upper side, and on their lower side all together form one continuous whorl. This is pierced by the spindle, which is driven home through the centre of the eighth. The first and outermost whorl has the rim broadest, and the seven inner whorls are narrower, in the following proportions—the sixth is next to the first in size, the fourth next to the sixth; then comes the eighth; the seventh is fifth, the fifth is sixth, the third is seventh, last and eighth comes the second. The largest (or fixed stars) is spangled, and the seventh (or sun) is brightest; the eighth (or moon) coloured by the reflected light of the seventh; the second and fifth (Saturn and Mercury) are in colour like one another, and yellower than the preceding; the third (Venus) has the whitest light; the fourth (Mars) is reddish; the sixth (Jupiter) is in whiteness second. Now the whole spindle has the same motion; but, as the whole revolves in one direction, the seven inner circles move slowly in the other, and of these the swiftest is the eighth; next in swiftness are the seventh, sixth, and fifth, which move together; third in swiftness appeared to move according to the law of this reversed motion the fourth; the third appeared fourth and the second fifth. The spindle turns on the knees of Necessity; and on the upper surface of each circle is a siren, who goes round with them, hymning a single tone or note. The eight together form one harmony; and round about, at equal intervals, there is another band, three in number, each sitting upon her throne: these are the Fates, daughters of Necessity, who are clothed in white robes and have chaplets upon their heads, Lachesis and Clotho and Atropos, who accompany with their voices the harmony of the sirens—Lachesis singing of the past, Clotho of the present, Atropos of the future; Clotho from time to time assisting with a touch of her right hand the revolution of the outer circle of the whorl or spindle, and Atropos with her left hand touching and guiding the inner ones, and Lachesis laying hold of either in turn, first with one hand and then with the other.

When Er and the spirits arrived, their duty was to go at once to Lachesis; but first of all there came a prophet who arranged them in order; then he took from the knees of Lachesis lots and samples of lives, and having mounted a high pulpit, spoke as follows: 'Hear the word of Lachesis, the daughter of Necessity. Mortal souls, behold a new cycle of life and mortality. Your genius will not be allotted to you, but you will choose your genius; and let him who draws the first lot have the first choice, and the life which he chooses shall be his destiny. Virtue is free, and as a man honours or dishonours her he will have more or less of her; the responsibility is with the chooser—God is justified.' When the Interpreter had thus spoken he scattered lots indifferently among them all, and each of them took up the lot which fell near him, all but Er himself (he was not allowed), and each as he took his lot perceived the number which he had obtained. Then the Interpreter placed on the ground before them the samples of lives; and there were many more lives than the souls present, and they were of all sorts. There were lives of every animal and of man in every condition. And there were tyrannies among them, some lasting out the tyrant's life, others which broke off in the middle and came to an end in poverty and exile and beggary; and there were lives of famous men, some who were famous for their form and beauty as well as for their strength and success in games, or, again, for their birth and the qualities of their ancestors; and some who were the reverse of famous for the opposite qualities. And of women likewise; there was not, however, any definite character in them, because the soul, when choosing a new life, must of necessity become different. But there was every other quality, and they all mingled with one another, and also with elements of wealth and poverty, and disease and health; and there were mean states also. And here, my dear Glaucon, is the supreme peril of our human state; and therefore the utmost care should be taken. Let each one of us leave every other kind of knowledge and seek and follow one thing only, if peradventure he may be able to learn and may find some one who will make him able to learn and discern between good and evil, and so to choose always and everywhere the better life as he has opportunity. He should consider the bearing of all these things which have been mentioned severally and collectively upon virtue; he should know what the effect of beauty is when combined with poverty or wealth in a particular soul, and what are the good and evil consequences of noble and humble birth, of private and public station, of strength and weakness, of cleverness and dullness, and of all the natural and acquired gifts of the soul, and the operation of them when conjoined; he will then look at the nature of the soul, and from the consideration of all these qualities he will be able to determine which is the better and which is the worse; and so he will choose, giving the name of evil to the life which will make his soul more unjust, and good to the life which will make his soul more just; all else he will disregard. For we have seen and know that this is the best choice both in life and after death. A man must take with him into the world below an adamantine faith in truth and right, that there too he may be undazzled by the desire of wealth or the other allurements of evil, lest, coming upon tyrannies and similar villainies, he do irremediable wrongs to others and suffer yet worse himself; but let him know how to choose the mean and avoid the extremes on either side, as far as possible, not only in this life but in all that which is to come. For this is the way of happiness.

And according to the report of the messenger from the other world this was what the prophet said at the time: 'Even for the last comer, if he chooses wisely and will live diligently, there is appointed a happy and not undesirable existence. Let not him who chooses first be careless, and let not the last despair.' And when he had spoken, he who had the first choice came forward and in a moment chose the greatest tyranny, his mind having been darkened by folly and sensuality, he had not thought out the whole matter before he chose, and did not at first sight perceive that he was fated, among other evils, to devour his own children. But when he had time to reflect, and saw what was in the lot, he began to beat his breast and lament over his choice, forgetting the proclamation of the prophet; for, instead of throwing the blame of his misfortune on himself, he accused chance and the gods, and everything rather than himself. Now he was one of those who came from heaven, and in a former life had dwelt in a well-ordered State, but his virtue was a matter of habit only, and he had no philosophy. And it was true of others who were similarly overtaken, that the greater number of them came from heaven and therefore they had never been schooled by trial, whereas the pilgrims who came from earth having themselves suffered and seen others suffer, were not in a hurry to choose. And owing to this inexperience of theirs, and also because the lot was a chance, many of the souls exchanged a good destiny for an evil or an evil for a good. For if a man had always on his arrival in this world dedicated himself from the first to sound philosophy, and had been moderately fortunate in the number of the lot, he might, as the messenger reported, be happy here, and also his journey to another life and return to this, instead of being rough and underground, would be smooth and heavenly. Most curious, he said, was the spectacle—sad and laughable and strange; for the choice of the souls was in most cases based on their experience of a previous life. There he saw the soul which had once been Orpheus choosing the life of a swan out of enmity to the race of women, hating to be born of a woman because they had been his murderers; he beheld also the soul of Thamyras choosing the life of a nightingale; birds, on the other hand, like the swan and other musicians, wanting to be men. The soul which obtained the twentieth lot chose the life of a lion, and this was the soul of Ajax the son of Telamon, who would not be a man, remembering the injustice which was done him in the judgment about the arms. The next was Agamemnon, who took the life of an eagle, because, like Ajax, he hated human nature by reason of his sufferings. About the middle came the lot of Atalanta; she, seeing the great fame of an athlete, was unable to resist the temptation: and after her there followed the soul of Epeus the son of Panopeus passing into the nature of a woman cunning in the arts; and far away among the last who chose, the soul of the jester Thersites was putting on the form of a monkey. There came also the soul of Odysseus having yet to make a choice, and his lot happened to be the last of them all. Now the recollection of former toils had disenchanted him of ambition, and he went about for a considerable time in search of the life of a private man who had no cares; he had some difficulty in finding this, which was lying about and had been neglected by everybody else; and when he saw it, he said that he would have done the same had his lot been first instead of last, and that he was delighted to have it. And not only did men pass into animals, but I must also mention that there were animals tame and wild who changed into one another and into corresponding human natures—the good into the gentle and the evil into the savage, in all sorts of combinations.

All the souls had now chosen their lives, and they went in the order of their choice to Lachesis, who sent with them the genius whom they had severally chosen, to be the guardian of their lives and the fulfiller of the choice: this genius led the souls first to Clotho, and drew them within the revolution of the spindle impelled by her hand, thus ratifying the destiny of each; and then, when they were fastened to this, carried them to Atropos, who spun the threads and made them irreversible, whence without turning round they passed beneath the throne of Necessity; and when they had all passed, they marched on in a scorching heat to the plain of Forgetfulness, which was a barren waste destitute of trees and verdure; and then towards evening they encamped by the river of Unmindfulness, whose water no vessel can hold; of this they were all obliged to drink a certain quantity, and those who were not saved by wisdom drank more than was necessary; and each one as he drank forgot all things. Now after they had gone to rest, about the middle of the night there was a thunderstorm and earthquake, and then in an instant they were driven upwards in all manner of ways to their birth, like stars shooting. He himself was hindered from drinking the water. But in what manner or by what means he returned to the body he could not say; only, in the morning, awaking suddenly, he found himself lying on the pyre.

And thus, Glaucon, the tale has been saved and has not perished, and will save us if we are obedient to the word spoken; and we shall pass safely over the river of Forgetfulness and our soul will not be defiled. Wherefore my counsel is, that we hold fast ever to the heavenly way and follow after justice and virtue always, considering that the soul is immortal and able to endure every sort of good and every sort of evil. Thus shall we live dear to one another and to the gods, both while remaining here and when, like conquerors in the games who go round to gather gifts, we receive our reward. And it shall be well with us both in this life and in the pilgrimage of a thousand years which we have been describing.

SYMPOSIUM (SELECTIONS)

The *Symposium* (dated sometime between 385–378 B.C.) recounts a drinking party held at the home of the tragic poet Agathon. The Greek word *symposion* literally means "drinking together." At this particular party, the guests agree that because of their hangovers from the previous evening's festivities, they will go easy on the drinking. Rather than get drunk again they agree to take turns giving speeches in honor of love. The Greek language has several words for "love," but during this symposium the participants will focus on "eros" or desire.

The dialogue is narrated by Apollodorus, a friend of Socrates, who is reporting what he heard about the evening from another friend of Socrates, Aristodemus, who attended the party but did not give a speech. Those who gave speeches during the symposium were: Phaedrus (a friend of Plato); Pausanias (a legal expert); Erixymachus (a physician); Aristophanes (the great comic playwright); Agathon; Socrates; and Alcibiades (a young, popular, handsome, talented but unscrupulous Athenian politician).

In the excerpts that follow, the theme of the dialogue is introduced, followed by the speeches of Aristophanes and Socrates. As befits the character of a comic playwright, Aristophanes' speech seems to be both poking fun at Greek myths and making a serious point about the nature of love. In the case of Socrates, after questioning Agathon, Socrates recalls how he learned about love from a wise woman seer by the name of Diotima of Mantinea. Whether Diotima was a historical figure or a fictional character created by Plato is a matter of debate. Regardless of the verdict on this question, it is with the teaching of Diotima (as conveyed by Socrates) that the dialogue reaches its greatest degree of complexity and depth in its treatment of love.

This was the style of their conversation as they went along. Socrates dropped behind in a fit of abstraction, and desired Aristodemus, who was waiting, to go on before him. When he reached the house of Agathon he found the doors wide open, and a comical thing happened. A servant coming out met him, and led him at once into the banqueting-hall in which the guests were reclining, for the banquet was about to begin. Welcome, Aristodemus, said Agathon, as soon as he appeared—you are just in time to sup with us; if you come on any other matter put it off, and make one of us, as I was looking for you yesterday and meant to have asked you, if I could have found you. But what have you done with Socrates?

I turned round, but Socrates was nowhere to be seen; and I had to explain that he had been with me a moment before, and that I came by his invitation to the supper.

You were quite right in coming, said Agathon; but where is he himself?

He was behind me just now, as I entered, he said, and I cannot think what has become of him.

Go and look for him, boy, said Agathon, and bring him in; and do you, Aristodemus, meanwhile take the place by Eryximachus.

The servant then assisted him to wash, and he lay down, and presently another servant came in and reported that our friend Socrates had retired into the portico of the neighbouring house. 'There he is fixed,' said he, 'and when I call to him he will not stir.'

How strange, said Agathon; then you must call him again, and keep calling him.

Let him alone, said my informant; he has a way of stopping anywhere and losing himself without any reason. I believe that he will soon appear; do not therefore disturb him.

Well, if you think so, I will leave him, said Agathon. And then, turning to the servants, he added, 'Let us have supper without waiting for him. Serve up whatever you please, for there is no one to give you orders; hitherto I have never left you to yourselves. But on this occasion imagine that you are our hosts, and that I and the company are your guests; treat us well, and then we shall commend you.' After this, supper was served, but still no Socrates; and during the meal Agathon several times expressed a wish to send for him, but Aristodemus objected; and at last when the feast was about half over—for the fit, as usual, was not of long duration—Socrates entered. Agathon, who was reclining alone at the end of the table, begged that he would take the place next to him; that 'I may touch you,' he said, 'and have the benefit of that wise thought which came into your mind in the portico, and is now in your possession; for I am certain that you would not have come away until you had found what you sought.'

How I wish, said Socrates, taking his place as he was desired, that wisdom could be infused by touch, out of the fuller into the emptier man, as water runs through wool out of a fuller cup into an emptier one; if that were so, how greatly should I value the privilege of reclining at your side! For you would have filled me full with a stream of wisdom plenteous and fair; whereas my own is of a very mean and questionable sort, no better than a dream. But yours is bright and full of promise, and was manifested forth in all the splendour of youth the day before yesterday, in the presence of more than thirty thousand Hellenes.

You are mocking, Socrates, said Agathon, and ere long you and I will have to determine who bears off the palm of wisdom—of this Dionysus shall be the judge; but at present you are better occupied with supper.

Socrates took his place on the couch, and supped with the rest; and then libations were offered, and after a hymn had been sung to the god, and there had been the usual ceremonies, they were about to commence drinking, when Pausanias said, And now, my friends, how can we drink with least injury to ourselves? I can assure you that I feel severely the effect of yesterday's potations, and must have time to recover; and I suspect that most of you are in the same predicament, for you were of the party yesterday. Consider then: How can the drinking be made easiest?

I entirely agree, said Aristophanes, that we should, by all means, avoid hard drinking, for I was myself one of those who were yesterday drowned in drink.

I think that you are right, said Eryximachus, the son of Acumenus; but I should still like to hear one other person speak: Is Agathon able to drink hard?

I am not equal to it, said Agathon.

Then, said Eryximachus, the weak heads like myself, Aristodemus, Phaedrus, and others who never can drink, are fortunate in finding that the stronger ones are not in a drinking mood. (I do not include Socrates, who is able either to drink or to abstain, and will not mind, whichever we do.) Well, as of none of the company seem disposed to drink much, I may be forgiven for saying, as a physician, that drinking deep is a bad practice, which I never follow, if I can help, and certainly do not recommend to another, least of all to any one who still feels the effects of yesterday's carouse.

I always do what you advise, and especially what you prescribe as a physician, rejoined Phaedrus the Myrrhinusian, and the rest of the company, if they are wise, will do the same.

It was agreed that drinking was not to be the order of the day, but that they were all to drink only so much as they pleased.

Then, said Eryximachus, as you are all agreed that drinking is to be voluntary, and that there is to be no compulsion, I move, in the next place, that the flute-girl, who has just made her appearance, be told to go away and play to herself, or, if she likes, to the women who are within (compare Prot). To-day let us have conversation instead; and, if you will allow me, I will tell you what sort of conversation. This proposal having been accepted, Eryximachus proceeded as follows:—I will begin, he said, after the manner of Melanippe in Euripides, 'Not mine the word' which I am about to speak, but that of Phaedrus. For often he says to me in an indignant tone:—'What a strange thing it is, Eryximachus, that, whereas other gods have poems and hymns made in their honour, the great and glorious god, Love, has no encomiast among all the poets who are so many. There are the worthy sophists too—the excellent Prodicus for example, who have descanted in prose on the virtues of Heracles and other heroes; and, what is still more extraordinary, I have met with a philosophical work in which the utility of salt has been made the theme of an eloquent discourse; and many other like things have had a like honour bestowed upon them. And only to think that there should have been an eager interest created about them, and yet that to this day no one has ever dared worthily to hymn Love's praises! So entirely has this great deity been neglected.' Now in this Phaedrus seems to me to be quite right, and therefore I want to offer him a contribution; also I think that at the present moment we who are here assembled cannot do better than honour the god Love. If you agree with me, there will be no lack of conversation; for I mean to propose that each of us in turn, going from left to right, shall make a speech in honour of Love. Let him give us the best which he can; and Phaedrus, because he is sitting first on the left hand, and because he is the father of the thought, shall begin.

No one will vote against you, Eryximachus, said Socrates. How can I oppose your motion, who profess to understand nothing but matters of love; nor, I presume, will Agathon and Pausanias; and there can be no doubt of Aristophanes, whose whole concern is with Dionysus and Aphrodite; nor will any one disagree of those whom I see around me. The proposal, as I am aware, may seem rather hard upon us whose place is last; but we shall be contented if we hear some good speeches first. Let Phaedrus begin the praise of Love, and good luck to him. All the company expressed their assent, and desired him to do as Socrates bade him.

Aristodemus did not recollect all that was said, nor do I recollect all that he related to me; but I will tell you what I thought most worthy of remembrance, and what the chief speakers said.

The Speech of Aristophanes

Aristophanes professed to open another vein of discourse; he had a mind to praise Love in another way, unlike that either of Pausanias or Eryximachus. Mankind, he said, judging by their neglect of him, have never, as I think, at all understood the power of Love. For if they had understood him they would surely have built noble temples and altars, and offered solemn sacrifices in his honour; but this is not done, and most certainly ought to be done: since of all the gods he is the best friend of men, the helper and the healer of the ills which are the great impediment to the happiness of the race. I will try to describe his power to you, and you shall teach the rest of the world what I am teaching you. In the first place, let me treat of the nature of man and what has happened to it; for the original human nature was not like the present, but different. The sexes were not two as they are now, but originally three in number; there was man, woman, and the union of the two, having a name corresponding to this double nature, which had once a real existence, but is now lost, and the word 'Androgynous' is only preserved as a term of reproach. In the second place, the primeval man was round, his back and sides forming a circle; and he had four hands and four feet, one head with two faces, looking opposite ways, set on a round neck and precisely alike; also four ears, two privy members, and the remainder to correspond. He could walk upright as men now do, backwards or forwards as he pleased, and he could also roll over and over at a great pace, turning on his four hands and four feet, eight in all, like tumblers going over and over with their legs in the air; this was when he wanted to run fast. Now the sexes were three, and such as I have described them; because the sun, moon, and earth are three; and the man was originally the child of the sun, the woman of the earth, and the man-woman of the moon, which is made up of sun and earth, and they were all round and moved round and round like their parents. Terrible was their might and strength, and the thoughts of their hearts were great, and they made an attack upon the gods; of them is told the tale of Otys and Ephialtes who, as Homer says, dared to scale heaven, and would have laid hands upon the gods. Doubt reigned in the celestial councils. Should they kill them and annihilate the race with thunderbolts, as they had done the giants, then there would be an end of the sacrifices and worship which men offered to them; but, on the other hand, the gods could not suffer their insolence to be unrestrained. At last, after a good deal of reflection, Zeus discovered a way. He said: 'Methinks I have a plan which will humble their pride and improve their manners; men shall continue to exist, but I will cut them in two and then they will be diminished in strength and increased in numbers; this will have the advantage of making them more profitable to us. They shall walk upright on two legs, and if they continue insolent and will not be quiet, I will split them again and they shall hop about on a single leg.' He spoke and cut men in two, like a sorb-apple which is halved for pickling, or as you might divide an egg with a hair; and as he cut them one after another, he bade Apollo give the face and the half of the neck a turn in order that the man might contemplate the section of himself: he would thus learn a lesson of humility. Apollo was also bidden to heal their wounds and compose their forms. So he gave a turn to the face and pulled the skin from the sides all over that which in our language is called the belly, like the purses which draw in, and he made one mouth at the centre, which he fastened in a knot (the same which is called the navel); he also moulded the breast and took out most of the wrinkles, much as a shoemaker might smooth leather upon a last; he left a few, however, in the region of the belly and navel, as a memorial of the primeval state. After the division the two parts of man, each desiring his other half, came together, and throwing their arms about one another, entwined in mutual embraces, longing to grow into one, they were on the point of dying from hunger and self-neglect, because they did not like to do anything apart; and when one of the halves died and the other survived, the survivor sought another mate, man or woman as we call them,— being the sections of entire men or women,— and clung to that. They were being destroyed, when Zeus in pity of them invented a new plan: he turned the parts of generation round to the front, for this had not been always their position, and they sowed the seed no longer as hitherto like grasshoppers in the ground, but in one another; and after the transposition the male generated in the female in order that by the mutual embraces of man and woman they might breed, and the race might continue; or if man came to man they might be satisfied, and rest, and go their ways to the business of life: so ancient is the desire of one another which is implanted in us, reuniting our original nature, making one of two, and healing the state of man. Each of us when separated, having one side only, like a flat fish, is but the indenture of a man, and he is always looking for his other half. Men who are a section of that double nature which was once called Androgynous are lovers of women; adulterers are generally of this breed, and also adulterous women who lust after men: the women who are a section of the woman do not care for men, but have female attachments; the female companions are of this sort. But they who are a section of the male follow the male, and while they are young, being slices of the original man, they hang about men and embrace them, and they are themselves the best of boys and youths, because they have the most manly nature. Some indeed assert that they are shameless, but this is not true; for they do not act thus from any want of shame, but because they are valiant and manly, and have a manly countenance, and they embrace that which is like them. And these when they grow up become our statesmen, and these only, which is a great proof of the truth of what I am saying. When they reach manhood they are lovers of youth, and are not naturally inclined to marry or beget children,—if at all, they do so only in obedience to the law; but they are satisfied if they may be allowed to live with one another unwedded; and such a nature is prone to love and ready to return love, always embracing that which is akin to him. And when one of them meets with his other half, the actual half of himself, whether he be a lover of youth or a lover of another sort, the pair are lost in an amazement of love and friendship and intimacy, and one will not be out of the other's sight, as I may say, even for a moment: these are the people who pass their whole lives together; yet they could not explain what they desire of one another. For the intense yearning which each of them has towards the other does not appear to be the desire of lover's intercourse, but of something else which the soul of either evidently desires and cannot tell, and of which she has only a dark and doubtful presentiment. Suppose Hephaestus, with his instruments, to come to the pair who are lying side by side and to say to them, 'What do you people want of one another?' they would be unable to explain. And suppose further, that when he saw their perplexity he said: 'Do you desire to be wholly one; always day and night to be in one another's company? for if this is what you desire, I am ready to melt you into one and let you grow together, so that being two you shall become one, and while you live live a common life as if you were a single man, and after your death in the world below still be one departed soul instead of two—I ask whether this is what you lovingly desire, and whether you are satisfied to attain this?'— there is not a man of them who when he heard the proposal would deny or would not acknowledge that this meeting and melting into one another, this becoming one instead of two, was the very expression of his ancient need (compare Arist. Pol.). And the reason is that human nature was originally one and we were a whole, and the desire and pursuit of the whole is called love. There was a time, I say, when we were one, but now because of the wickedness of mankind God has dispersed us, as the Arcadians were dispersed into villages by the Lacedaemonians (compare Arist. Pol.). And if we are not obedient to the gods, there is a danger that we shall be split up again and go about in basso-relievo, like the profile figures having only half a nose which are sculptured on monuments, and that we shall be like tallies. Wherefore let us exhort all men to piety, that we may avoid evil, and obtain the good, of which Love is to us the lord and minister; and let no one oppose him—he is the enemy of the gods who opposes him. For if we are friends of the God and at peace with him we shall find our own true loves, which rarely happens in this world at present. I am serious, and therefore I must beg Eryximachus not to make fun or to find any allusion in what I am saying to Pausanias and Agathon, who, as I suspect, are both of the manly nature, and belong to the class which I have been describing. But my words have a wider application—they include men and women everywhere; and I believe that if our loves were perfectly accomplished, and each one returning to his primeval nature had his original true love, then our race would be happy. And if this would be best of all, the best in the next degree and under present circumstances must be the nearest approach to such an union; and that will be the attainment of a congenial love. Wherefore, if we would praise him who has given to us the benefit, we must praise the god Love, who is our greatest benefactor, both leading us in this life back to our own nature, and giving us high hopes for the future, for he promises that if we are pious, he will restore us to our original state, and heal us and make us happy and blessed.

The Speech of Socrates/Diotima

Socrates then proceeded as follows:—

In the magnificent oration which you have just uttered, I think that you were right, my dear Agathon, in proposing to speak of the nature of Love first and afterwards of his works—that is a way of beginning which I very much approve. And as you have spoken so eloquently of his nature, may I ask you further, Whether love is the love of something or of nothing? And here I must explain myself: I do not want you to say that love is the love of a father or the love of a mother—that would be ridiculous; but to answer as you would, if I asked is a father a father of something? to which you would find no difficulty in replying, of a son or daughter: and the answer would be right.

Very true, said Agathon.

And you would say the same of a mother?

He assented.

Yet let me ask you one more question in order to illustrate my meaning: Is not a brother to be regarded essentially as a brother of something?

Certainly, he replied.

That is, of a brother or sister?

Yes, he said.

And now, said Socrates, I will ask about Love:— Is Love of something or of nothing?

Of something, surely, he replied.

Keep in mind what this is, and tell me what I want to know—whether Love desires that of which love is.

Yes, surely.

And does he possess, or does he not possess, that which he loves and desires?

Probably not, I should say.

Nay, replied Socrates, I would have you consider whether 'necessarily' is not rather the word. The inference that he who desires something is in want of something, and that he who desires nothing is in want of nothing, is in my judgment, Agathon, absolutely and necessarily true. What do you think?

I agree with you, said Agathon.

Very good. Would he who is great, desire to be great, or he who is strong, desire to be strong?

That would be inconsistent with our previous admissions.

True. For he who is anything cannot want to be that which he is?

Very true.

And yet, added Socrates, if a man being strong desired to be strong, or being swift desired to be swift, or being healthy desired to be healthy, in that case he might be thought to desire something which he already has or is. I give the example in order that we may avoid misconception. For the possessors of these qualities, Agathon, must be supposed to have their respective advantages at the time, whether they choose or not; and who can desire that which he has? Therefore, when a person says, I am well and wish to be well, or I am rich and wish to be rich, and I desire simply to have what I have—to him we shall reply: 'You, my friend, having wealth and health and strength, want to have the continuance of them; for at this moment, whether you choose or no, you have them. And when you say, I desire that which I have and nothing else, is not your meaning that you want to have what you now have in the future?' He must agree with us—must he not?

He must, replied Agathon.

Then, said Socrates, he desires that what he has at present may be preserved to him in the future, which is equivalent to saying that he desires something which is non-existent to him, and which as yet he has not got:

Very true, he said.

Then he and every one who desires, desires that which he has not already, and which is future and not present, and which he has not, and is not, and of which he is in want;— these are the sort of things which love and desire seek?

Very true, he said.

Then now, said Socrates, let us recapitulate the argument. First, is not love of something, and of something too which is wanting to a man?

Yes, he replied.

Remember further what you said in your speech, or if you do not remember I will remind you: you said that the love of the beautiful set in order the empire of the gods, for that of deformed things there is no love—did you not say something of that kind?

Yes, said Agathon.

Yes, my friend, and the remark was a just one. And if this is true, Love is the love of beauty and not of deformity?

He assented.

And the admission has been already made that Love is of something which a man wants and has not?

True, he said.

Then Love wants and has not beauty?

Certainly, he replied.

And would you call that beautiful which wants and does not possess beauty?

Certainly not.

Then would you still say that love is beautiful?

Agathon replied: I fear that I did not understand what I was saying.

You made a very good speech, Agathon, replied Socrates; but there is yet one small question which I would fain ask:—Is not the good also the beautiful?

Yes.

Then in wanting the beautiful, love wants also the good?

I cannot refute you, Socrates, said Agathon:— Let us assume that what you say is true.

Say rather, beloved Agathon, that you cannot refute the truth; for Socrates is easily refuted.

And now, taking my leave of you, I would rehearse a tale of love which I heard from Diotima of Mantineia (compare 1 Alcibiades), a woman wise in this and in many other kinds of knowledge, who in the days of old, when the Athenians offered sacrifice before the coming of the plague, delayed the disease ten years. She was my instructress in the art of love, and I shall repeat to you what she said to me, beginning with the admissions made by Agathon, which are nearly if not quite the same which I made to the wise woman when she questioned me: I think that this will be the easiest way, and I shall take both parts myself as well as I can (compare Gorgias). As you, Agathon, suggested (supra), I must speak first of the being and nature of Love, and then of his works. First I said to her in nearly the same words which he used to me, that Love was a mighty god, and likewise fair; and she proved to me as I proved to him that, by my own showing, Love was neither fair nor good. 'What do you mean, Diotima,' I said, 'is love then evil and foul?' 'Hush,' she cried; 'must that be foul which is not fair?' 'Certainly,' I said. 'And is that which is not wise, ignorant? do you not see that there is a mean between wisdom and ignorance?' 'And what may that be?' I said. 'Right opinion,' she replied; 'which, as you know, being incapable of giving a reason, is not knowledge (for how can knowledge be devoid of reason? nor again, ignorance, for neither can ignorance attain the truth), but is clearly something which is a mean between ignorance and wisdom.' 'Quite true,' I replied. 'Do not then insist,' she said, 'that what is not fair is of necessity foul, or what is not good evil; or infer that because love is not fair and good he is therefore foul and evil; for he is in a mean between them.' 'Well,' I said, 'Love is surely admitted by all to be a great god.' 'By those who know or by those who do not know?' 'By all.' 'And how, Socrates,' she said with a smile, 'can Love be acknowledged to be a great god by those who say that he is not a god at all?' 'And who are they?' I said. 'You and I are two of them,' she replied. 'How can that be?' I said. 'It is quite intelligible,' she replied; 'for you yourself would acknowledge that the gods are happy and fair— of course you would— would you dare to say that any god was not?' 'Certainly not,' I replied. 'And you mean by the happy, those who are the possessors of things good or fair?' 'Yes.' 'And you admitted that Love, because he was in want, desires those good and fair things of which he is in want?' 'Yes, I did.' 'But how can he be a god who has no portion in what is either good or fair?' 'Impossible.' 'Then you see that you also deny the divinity of Love.'

'What then is Love?' I asked; 'Is he mortal?' 'No.' 'What then?' 'As in the former instance, he is neither mortal nor immortal, but in a mean between the two.' 'What is he, Diotima?' 'He is a great spirit (daimon), and like all spirits he is intermediate between the divine and the mortal.' 'And what,' I said, 'is his power?' 'He interprets,' she replied, 'between gods and men, conveying and taking across to the gods the prayers and sacrifices of men, and to men the commands and replies of the gods; he is the mediator who spans the chasm which divides them, and therefore in him all is bound together, and through him the arts of the prophet and the priest, their sacrifices and mysteries and charms, and all prophecy and incantation, find their way. For God mingles not with man; but through Love all the intercourse and converse of God with man, whether awake or asleep, is carried on. The wisdom which understands this is spiritual; all other wisdom, such as that of arts and handicrafts, is mean and vulgar. Now these spirits or intermediate powers are many and diverse, and one of them is Love.' 'And who,' I said, 'was his father, and who his mother?' 'The tale,' she said, 'will take time; nevertheless I will tell you. On the birthday of Aphrodite there was a feast of the gods, at which the god Poros or Plenty, who is the son of Metis or Discretion, was one of the guests. When the feast was over, Penia or Poverty, as the manner is on such occasions, came about the doors to beg. Now Plenty who was the worse for nectar (there was no wine in those days), went into the garden of Zeus and fell into a heavy sleep, and Poverty considering her own straitened circumstances, plotted to have a child by him, and accordingly she lay down at his side and conceived Love, who partly because he is naturally a lover of the beautiful, and because Aphrodite is herself beautiful, and also because he was born on her birthday, is her follower and attendant. And as his parentage is, so also are his fortunes. In the first place he is always poor, and anything but tender and fair, as the many imagine him; and he is rough and squalid, and has no shoes, nor a house to dwell in; on the bare earth exposed he lies under the open heaven, in the streets, or at the doors of houses, taking his rest; and like his mother he is always in distress. Like his father too, whom he also partly resembles, he is always plotting against the fair and good; he is bold, enterprising, strong, a mighty hunter, always weaving some intrigue or other, keen in the pursuit of wisdom, fertile in resources; a philosopher at all times, terrible as an enchanter, sorcerer, sophist. He is by nature neither mortal nor immortal, but alive and flourishing at one moment when he is in plenty, and dead at another moment, and again alive by reason of his father's nature. But that which is always flowing in is always flowing out, and so he is never in want and never in wealth; and, further, he is in a mean between ignorance and knowledge. The truth of the matter is this: No god is a philosopher or seeker after wisdom, for he is wise already; nor does any man who is wise seek after wisdom. Neither do the ignorant seek after wisdom. For herein is the evil of ignorance, that he who is neither good nor wise is nevertheless satisfied with himself: he has no desire for that of which he feels no want.' 'But who then, Diotima,' I said, 'are the lovers of wisdom, if they are neither the wise nor the foolish?' 'A child may answer that question,' she replied; 'they are those who are in a mean between the two; Love is one of them. For wisdom is a most beautiful thing, and Love is of the beautiful; and therefore Love is also a philosopher or lover of wisdom, and being a lover of wisdom is in a mean between the wise and the ignorant. And of this too his birth is the cause; for his father is wealthy and wise, and his mother poor and foolish. Such, my dear Socrates, is the nature of the spirit Love. The error in your conception of him was very natural, and as I imagine from what you say, has arisen out of a confusion of love and the beloved, which made you think that love was all beautiful. For the beloved is the truly beautiful, and delicate, and perfect, and blessed; but the principle of love is of another nature, and is such as I have described.'

I said, 'O thou stranger woman, thou sayest well; but, assuming Love to be such as you say, what is the use of him to men?' 'That, Socrates,' she replied, 'I will attempt to unfold: of his nature and birth I have already spoken; and you acknowledge that love is of the beautiful. But some one will say: Of the beautiful in what, Socrates and Diotima?—or rather let me put the question more clearly, and ask: When a man loves the beautiful, what does he desire?' I answered her 'That the beautiful may be his.' 'Still,' she said, 'the answer suggests a further question: What is given by the possession of beauty?' 'To what you have asked,' I replied, 'I have no answer ready.' 'Then,' she said, 'let me put the word "good" in the place of the beautiful, and repeat the question once more: If he who loves loves the good, what is it then that he loves?' 'The possession of the good,' I said. 'And what does he gain who possesses the good?' 'Happiness,' I replied; 'there is less difficulty in answering that question.' 'Yes,' she said, 'the happy are made happy by the acquisition of good things. Nor is there any need to ask why a man desires happiness; the answer is already final.' 'You are right.' I said. 'And is this wish and this desire common to all? and do all men always desire their own good, or only some men?—what say you?' 'All men,' I replied; 'the desire is common to all.' 'Why, then,' she rejoined, 'are not all men, Socrates, said to love, but only some of them? whereas you say that all men are always loving the same things.' 'I myself wonder,' I said, 'why this is.' 'There is nothing to wonder at,' she replied; 'the reason is that one part of love is separated off and receives the name of the whole, but the other parts have other names.' 'Give an illustration,' I said. She answered me as follows: 'There is poetry, which, as you know, is complex and manifold. All creation or passage of non-being into being is poetry or making, and the processes of all art are creative; and the masters of arts are all poets or makers.' 'Very true.' 'Still,' she said, 'you know that they are not called poets, but have other names; only that portion of the art which is separated off from the rest, and is concerned with music and metre, is termed poetry, and they who possess poetry in this sense of the word are called poets.' 'Very true,' I said. 'And the same holds of love. For you may say generally that all desire of good and happiness is only the great and subtle power of love; but they who are drawn towards him by any other path, whether the path of money-making or gymnastics or philosophy, are not called lovers—the name of the whole is appropriated to those whose affection takes one form only—they alone are said to love, or to be lovers.' 'I dare say,' I replied, 'that you are right.' 'Yes,' she added, 'and you hear people say that lovers are seeking for their other half; but I say that they are seeking neither for the half of themselves, nor for the whole, unless the half or the whole be also a good. And they will cut off their own hands and feet and cast them away, if they are evil; for they love not what is their own, unless perchance there be some one who calls what belongs to him the good, and what belongs to another the evil. For there is nothing which men love but the good. Is there anything?' 'Certainly, I should say, that there is nothing.' 'Then,' she said, 'the simple truth is, that men love the good.' 'Yes,' I said. 'To which must be added that they love the possession of the good?' 'Yes, that must be added.' 'And not only the possession, but the everlasting possession of the good?' 'That must be added too.' 'Then love,' she said, 'may be described generally as the love of the everlasting possession of the good?' 'That is most true.'

'Then if this be the nature of love, can you tell me further,' she said, 'what is the manner of the pursuit? what are they doing who show all this eagerness and heat which is called love? and what is the object which they have in view? Answer me.' 'Nay, Diotima,' I replied, 'if I had known, I should not have wondered at your wisdom, neither should I have come to learn from you about this very matter.' 'Well,' she said, 'I will teach you:— The object which they have in view is birth in beauty, whether of body or soul.' 'I do not understand you,' I said; 'the oracle requires an explanation.' 'I will make my meaning clearer,' she replied. 'I mean to say, that all men are bringing to the birth in their bodies and in their souls. There is a certain age at which human nature is desirous of procreation—procreation which must be in beauty and not in deformity; and this procreation is the union of man and woman, and is a divine thing; for conception and generation are an immortal principle in the mortal creature, and in the inharmonious they can never be. But the deformed is always inharmonious with the divine, and the beautiful harmonious. Beauty, then, is the destiny or goddess of parturition who presides at birth, and therefore, when approaching beauty, the conceiving power is propitious, and diffusive, and benign, and begets and bears fruit: at the sight of ugliness she frowns and contracts and has a sense of pain, and turns away, and shrivels up, and not without a pang refrains from conception. And this is the reason why, when the hour of conception arrives, and the teeming nature is full, there is such a flutter and ecstasy about beauty whose approach is the alleviation of the pain of travail. For love, Socrates, is not, as you imagine, the love of the beautiful only.' 'What then?' 'The love of generation and of birth in beauty.' 'Yes,' I said. 'Yes, indeed,' she replied. 'But why of generation?' 'Because to the mortal creature, generation is a sort of eternity and immortality,' she replied; 'and if, as has been already admitted, love is of the everlasting possession of the good, all men will necessarily desire immortality together with good: Wherefore love is of immortality.'

All this she taught me at various times when she spoke of love. And I remember her once saying to me, 'What is the cause, Socrates, of love, and the attendant desire? See you not how all animals, birds, as well as beasts, in their desire of procreation, are in agony when they take the infection of love, which begins with the desire of union; whereto is added the care of offspring, on whose behalf the weakest are ready to battle against the strongest even to the uttermost, and to die for them, and will let themselves be tormented with hunger or suffer anything in order to maintain their young. Man may be supposed to act thus from reason; but why should animals have these passionate feelings? Can you tell me why?' Again I replied that I did not know. She said to me: 'And do you expect ever to become a master in the art of love, if you do not know this?' 'But I have told you already, Diotima, that my ignorance is the reason why I come to you; for I am conscious that I want a teacher; tell me then the cause of this and of the other mysteries of love.' 'Marvel not,' she said, 'if you believe that love is of the immortal, as we have several times acknowledged; for here again, and on the same principle too, the mortal nature is seeking as far as is possible to be everlasting and immortal: and this is only to be attained by generation, because generation always leaves behind a new existence in the place of the old. Nay even in the life of the same individual there is succession and not absolute unity: a man is called the same, and yet in the short interval which elapses between youth and age, and in which every animal is said to have life and identity, he is undergoing a perpetual process of loss and reparation—hair, flesh, bones, blood, and the whole body are always changing. Which is true not only of the body, but also of the soul, whose habits, tempers, opinions, desires, pleasures, pains, fears, never remain the same in any one of us, but are always coming and going; and equally true of knowledge, and what is still more surprising to us mortals, not only do the sciences in general spring up and decay, so that in respect of them we are never the same; but each of them individually experiences a like change. For what is implied in the word "recollection," but the departure of knowledge, which is ever being forgotten, and is renewed and preserved by recollection, and appears to be the same although in reality new, according to that law of succession by which all mortal things are preserved, not absolutely the same, but by substitution, the old worn-out mortality leaving another new and similar existence behind—unlike the divine, which is always the same and not another? And in this way, Socrates, the mortal body, or mortal anything, partakes of immortality; but the immortal in another way. Marvel not then at the love which all men have of their offspring; for that universal love and interest is for the sake of immortality.'

I was astonished at her words, and said: 'Is this really true, O thou wise Diotima?' And she answered with all the authority of an accomplished sophist: 'Of that, Socrates, you may be assured;—think only of the ambition of men, and you will wonder at the senselessness of their ways, unless you consider how they are stirred by the love of an immortality of fame. They are ready to run all risks greater far than they would have run for their children, and to spend money and undergo any sort of toil, and even to die, for the sake of leaving behind them a name which shall be eternal. Do you imagine that Alcestis would have died to save Admetus, or Achilles to avenge Patroclus, or your own Codrus in order to preserve the kingdom for his sons, if they had not imagined that the memory of their virtues, which still survives among us, would be immortal? Nay,' she said, 'I am persuaded that all men do all things, and the better they are the more they do them, in hope of the glorious fame of immortal virtue; for they desire the immortal.

'Those who are pregnant in the body only, betake themselves to women and beget children—this is the character of their love; their offspring, as they hope, will preserve their memory and giving them the blessedness and immortality which they desire in the future. But souls which are pregnant—for there certainly are men who are more creative in their souls than in their bodies—conceive that which is proper for the soul to conceive or contain. And what are these conceptions?—wisdom and virtue in general. And such creators are poets and all artists who are deserving of the name inventor. But the greatest and fairest sort of wisdom by far is that which is concerned with the ordering of states and families, and which is called temperance and justice. And he who in youth has the seed of these implanted in him and is himself inspired, when he comes to maturity desires to beget and generate. He wanders about seeking beauty that he may beget offspring—for in deformity he will beget nothing—and naturally embraces the beautiful rather than the deformed body; above all when he finds a fair and noble and well-nurtured soul, he embraces the two in one person, and to such an one he is full of speech about virtue and the nature and pursuits of a good man; and he tries to educate him; and at the touch of the beautiful which is ever present to his memory, even when absent, he brings forth that which he had conceived long before, and in company with him tends that which he brings forth; and they are married by a far nearer tie and have a closer friendship than those who beget mortal children, for the children who are their common offspring are fairer and more immortal. Who, when he thinks of Homer and Hesiod and other great poets, would not rather have their children than ordinary human ones? Who would not emulate them in the creation of children such as theirs, which have preserved their memory and given them everlasting glory? Or who would not have such children as Lycurgus left behind him to be the saviours, not only of Lacedaemon, but of Hellas, as one may say? There is Solon, too, who is the revered father of Athenian laws; and many others there are in many other places, both among Hellenes and barbarians, who have given to the world many noble works, and have been the parents of virtue of every kind; and many temples have been raised in their honour for the sake of children such as theirs; which were never raised in honour of any one, for the sake of his mortal children.

These are the lesser mysteries of love, into which even you, Socrates, may enter; to the greater and more hidden ones which are the crown of these, and to which, if you pursue them in a right spirit, they will lead, I know not whether you will be able to attain. But I will do my utmost to inform you, and do you follow if you can. For he who would proceed aright in this matter should begin in youth to visit beautiful forms; and first, if he be guided by his instructor aright, to love one such form only—out of that he should create fair thoughts; and soon he will of himself perceive that the beauty of one form is akin to the beauty of another; and then if beauty of form in general is his pursuit, how foolish would he be not to recognize that the beauty in every form is one and the same! And when he perceives this he will abate his violent love of the one, which he will despise and deem a small thing, and will become a lover of all beautiful forms; in the next stage he will consider that the beauty of the mind is more honourable than the beauty of the outward form. So that if a virtuous soul have but a little comeliness, he will be content to love and tend him, and will search out and bring to the birth thoughts which may improve the young, until he is compelled to contemplate and see the beauty of institutions and laws, and to understand that the beauty of them all is of one family, and that personal beauty is a trifle; and after laws and institutions he will go on to the sciences, that he may see their beauty, being not like a servant in love with the beauty of one youth or man or institution, himself a slave mean and narrow-minded, but drawing towards and contemplating the vast sea of beauty, he will create many fair and noble thoughts and notions in boundless love of wisdom; until on that shore he grows and waxes strong, and at last the vision is revealed to him of a single science, which is the science of beauty everywhere. To this I will proceed; please to give me your very best attention:

'He who has been instructed thus far in the things of love, and who has learned to see the beautiful in due order and succession, when he comes toward the end will suddenly perceive a nature of wondrous beauty (and this, Socrates, is the final cause of all our former toils)—a nature which in the first place is everlasting, not growing and decaying, or waxing and waning; secondly, not fair in one point of view and foul in another, or at one time or in one relation or at one place fair, at another time or in another relation or at another place foul, as if fair to some and foul to others, or in the likeness of a face or hands or any other part of the bodily frame, or in any form of speech or knowledge, or existing in any other being, as for example, in an animal, or in heaven, or in earth, or in any other place; but beauty absolute, separate, simple, and everlasting, which without diminution and without increase, or any change, is imparted to the ever-growing and perishing beauties of all other things. He who from these ascending under the influence of true love, begins to perceive that beauty, is not far from the end. And the true order of going, or being led by another, to the things of love, is to begin from the beauties of earth and mount upwards for the sake of that other beauty, using these as steps only, and from one going on to two, and from two to all fair forms, and from fair forms to fair practices, and from fair practices to fair notions, until from fair notions he arrives at the notion of absolute beauty, and at last knows what the essence of beauty is. This, my dear Socrates,' said the stranger of Mantineia, 'is that life above all others which man should live, in the contemplation of beauty absolute; a beauty which if you once beheld, you would see not to be after the measure of gold, and garments, and fair boys and youths, whose presence now entrances you; and you and many a one would be content to live seeing them only and conversing with them without meat or drink, if that were possible—you only want to look at them and to be with them. But what if man had eyes to see the true beauty—the divine beauty, I mean, pure and clear and unalloyed, not clogged with the pollutions of mortality and all the colours and vanities of human life—thither looking, and holding converse with the true beauty simple and divine? Remember how in that communion only, beholding beauty with the eye of the mind, he will be enabled to bring forth, not images of beauty, but realities (for he has hold not of an image but of a reality), and bringing forth and nourishing true virtue to become the friend of God and be immortal, if mortal man may. Would that be an ignoble life?'

Such, Phaedrus—and I speak not only to you, but to all of you—were the words of Diotima; and I am persuaded of their truth. And being persuaded of them, I try to persuade others, that in the attainment of this end human nature will not easily find a helper better than love: And therefore, also, I say that every man ought to honour him as I myself honour him, and walk in his ways, and exhort others to do the same, and praise the power and spirit of love according to the measure of my ability now and ever.

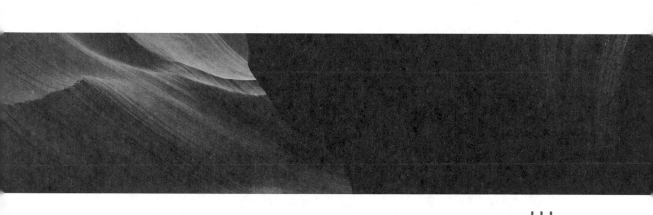

III

The Bhagavadgītā (Selections)

Editors' Introduction

The selected chapters from the *Bhagavad Gita* that you are about to read are drawn from one of the most popular spiritual classics of the Hindu tradition. Often translated as "The Song of God" or "The Song Celestial," the *Gita*, an abbreviated title for the more formal *Bhagavad Gita*, is part of one of the most popular epics of Indian culture, the *Mahābhārata* (the *Ramayana* being the other). Mistakenly, most Westerners think that both the *Gita* and the *Mahābhārata* are sacred scriptures of the Hindu tradition, but this is in fact not the case. Rather, the *Mahābhārata* is one of India's great epics, not unlike the *Iliad* or the *Odyssey* are for ancient Greece and subsequently for Western culture in general, in which are embodied in mythological and symbolic form the history, culture and spiritual values that are the foundation of India's rich and diverse religious heritage. While not a scripture per se, the *Gita* is more properly classified as bhaktic or "devotional" literature. Along with teaching religious moral values, the *Gita* is designed to inspire the reader to strive for moksha or "spiritual liberation" from the world of *maya* or illusion. As part of its classification as bhaktic literature, Hindus all over the world chant from the *Gita* during religious ceremonies often called *puja*, which means "worship" in Sanskrit, the sacred language of many Hindu doctrinal and liturgical texts.

Even though the *Gita* is not a scripture, its eighteen chapters are replete with the theology and worldview of Hinduism as most specifically embodied in the *Vedas*, the oldest of the Hindu scriptures, and the *Upanishads*, a corpus of metaphysical and theological writings of later development that are also classified as "scripture" in the Hindu tradition. In terms of the *Bhagavad Gita*, while the ideas and values drawn from the Vedas are included in its chapters, it is really the *Upanishads* that are its main source of theological and cosmological inspiration. Also included are some metaphysical ideas mutually shared with Buddhism, which developed out of its mother tradition Hinduism in the same way that Christianity developed out of Judaism, its mother tradition.

Though the *Gita* contains much theology, its essence is ethical and the truths it seeks to impart are presented in the form of an ethical dilemma set within the context of war fought on a vast battlefield, all of which can be taken as metaphors or symbols for the spiritual journey and the perils that come along with the quest for Ultimate Reality or *Brahman*, a word which comes close to the concept of "God" in the Abrahamic traditions of Judaism, Christianity, or Islam. However, unlike the one God of the Abrahamic faiths, *Brahman* is not conceived of in Hinduism as a personal God but more as the impersonal ground or source of all existence and life or as unconditioned Absolute Truth with a capital "T" that is ultimately beyond all human conception. Yet, this does not mean that in Hinduism there is no concept of a personal God who enters into relationship with human beings and who communicates with them intimately through visions, dreams, ritual and devotional practices, and in response to prayer. Rather, *Brahman*, the impersonal absolute, does in fact relate to human beings in very personal ways through the avatars or divine incarnations that appear on Earth as needed in the form of various male, female, and androgynous deities, and sometimes even as half-human, half-animal incarnations. The half-human, half-elephant god *Ganesha* is a perfect example of the latter. It is as Lord Krishna, an avatar of *Vishnu*, a hypostasis of *Brahman* that God relates personally with Arjuna, the chief protagonist of the *Bhagavad Gita*.

If asked to sum up the teachings of the *Gita* in one simple maxim, it is "your business is with the deed not with the result." This is the primary lesson about the spiritual quest and about life in general that is taught through the chapters of the *Gita*. It is this maxim that Lord Krishna teaches to Arjuna, the third son of King Pându, of the Pāṇḍavas dynasty when he is about to begin a war that was precipitated when Arjuna's one hundred cousins, who belonged to the Kaurava dynasty, refused to return even a few villages to the five Pāṇḍava brothers after their return from enforced exile. Standing on his side of the battlefield with Lord Krishna beside him as his chief advisor, Arjuna looks at his uncles, cousins, and friends standing on the other side of the battlefield. At that crucial moment, Arjuna wonders whether or not he is "morally prepared or justified in killing his blood relations" despite the fact that it was Arjuna and his brother Bhīma who had courageously prepared for this war. One way or the other, Arjuna was certain that he would be victorious in this war since he had Lord Krishna, one of the incarnations of *Vishnu*, on his side. Yet, just as the battle is about to begin, Arjuna puts it on hold to have a conversation with Krishna about the battle he is about to begin and whether or not it is the right thing to do. The conversation ends with Krishna convincing Arjuna that in the grand scheme of things, he is nothing but a pawn and the best that Arjuna can do is his duty and not to question God's will. In so doing, Lord Krishna provides a philosophy of life that gives Arjuna the courage to begin the battle that had become temporarily stalled because he (Arjuna) had lost his nerve.

The spiritual and moral teachings that undergird this story of war are what you are about to read in the eleven chapters that follow and as you enter into the drama of the *Gita*.

By way of cultural background, the *Bhagavad Gita* was first translated into English and published by Charles Wilkins in November of 1784. An improvement of the original translation from the Sanskrit was subsequently done by Frederich Max Mueller (1823–1900), the German Sanskrit scholar, who included the updated translation in his *Sacred Books of the East* series published by Oxford University Press. The *Bhagavad Gita* is one of the most widely read texts of the world. It has inspired many prominent Americans, among them, Henry David Thoreau, Ralph Waldo Emerson, Walt Whitman, and, in the twentieth century, Martin Luther King, Jr.

Along with the *Bible*, specifically the Beatitudes attributed to Jesus in the Synoptic Gospels of Matthew and Luke, the *Bhagavad Gita* was the other main spiritual source that inspired Mohandas K. Gandhi's Satyagraha (soul force) movement of non-violent resistance that played a major role in India's struggle for independence from the British Empire. The *Gita* was also a main source of inspiration for the twentieth century Indian poet, philosopher, and Nobel Peace Prize laureate Rabindranath Tagore. In the second half of the twentieth century, the *Gita* exerted an immense influence, especially in the 1950s, on such Beat poets and writers as Allen Ginsberg, Jack Kerouac, and Gary Snyder. In the 1960s, the *Bhagavad Gita* played a major role among the American counterculture, mostly through the *Hare Krishna* movement. Chiefly through the writings of Christopher Isherwood and Alan Watts, the *Bhagavad Gita* introduced Indian religious values and Vedanta philosophy to generations of artists, poets, political activists and religious seekers of all stripes.

THE BHAGAVADGĪTĀ IN THE MAHĀBHĀRATA

Dhṛtarāṣṭra said:

Whose warriors, Saṃjaya, were the first to give battle exultantly? Who were in cheerful spirits there? Who lost heart and wits? Who were the first to strike in that heart-shattering war, my men or the Pāṇḍavas'? Saṃjaya, tell me! In whose multitudinous army was there a smell of fragrant flowers, and was the speech of the thunderous warriors devout?

Saṃjaya said:

20   The warriors in both armies exulted, and in both rose a fragrance of flowers and incense. The first clash of the massed, marshaled troops that slowly and proudly advanced was magnificent, and the sound of music mixed with peals of conches and drums and the noise of roaring elephants and churning troops were deafening.

Dhṛtarāṣṭra said:

23[1].1   When in the Field of the Kurus, the Field of the Law, my troops and the Pāṇḍavas had massed belligerently, what did they do, Saṃjaya?

Saṃjaya said:

When King Duryodhana saw the Pāṇḍava's army arrayed, he approached the Teacher and said, "Look at that mighty host of the sons of Pāṇḍu, marshaled by Drupada's son,[1] your sagacious student! There are champions there, great archers, the likes of Bhīma and Arjuna in battle—Yuyudhāna, Virāṭa, the great warrior Drupada, Dhṛṣṭaketu, Cekitāna, the gallant king of the Kāśis, Purujit Kuntibhoja, and the Śaibya, a bull among men, valiant Yudhāmanyu and gallant Uttamaujas, Saubhadra and the Draupadeyas, all good warriors. But now hear, best of brahmins, about our outstanding men, the leaders of my army, I mention them by name: yourself, Bhīṣma, Karṇa, Kṛpa, Samitiṃjaya, Aśvatthāman, Vikarṇa, the son of Somadatta, and many other heroes who are laying down their lives for me, all experienced fighters with many kinds of weapons. Their army, protected by Bhīma, is no match for us, but this army, protected by Bhīṣma, is a match for them. All of you, stationed at your positions, must defend Bhīṣma at all passages!"

Then grandfather, the majestic elder of the Kurus, roared loud his lion's roar, bringing joy to Duryodhana, and blew his conch. On a sudden, thereupon, conches, kettledrums, cymbals, drums and clarions were sounded, and there was a terrifying noise. The Mādhava and Pāṇḍava, standing on their chariot yoked with the four white horses, both blew their conches—Hṛṣīkeśa[2] his Pāñcajanya, Dhanaṃjaya his Devadatta. Wolf-Belly of the terrible deeds blew his great conch Pauṇḍra, Nakula and Sahadeva their Sughoṣa and Maṇipuṣpaka. The Kāśi king, a great archer, the mighty warrior

Śikhaṇḍin, Dhṛṣṭadyumna, Virāṭa and the undefeated Sātyaki, Drupada and all the Draupadeyas, O king of the earth, and strong-armed Saubhadra, each blew his conch. The sound rent the hearts of the Dhārtarāṣṭras and reverberated fearfully through sky and earth.

20   The ape-bannered Pāṇḍava, seeing the Dhārtarāṣṭras in position, lifted his bow when the clash of arms began, O king, and said to Hṛṣīkeśa, "Acyuta, station my chariot in between the two armies, far enough for me to see the eager warriors in position—for, whom am I to fight in this enterprise of war? I want to see the men who are about to give battle, who have come together here to do a favor to the evil-spirited Duryodhana."

At Guḍākeśa's words, O Bhārata, Hṛṣīkeśa stationed the fine chariot between the two
25   armies, before Bhīṣma, Droṇa and all the kings, and he said to the Pārtha, "Behold the Kurus assembled!" The Pārtha saw them stand there, fathers, grandfathers, teachers, maternal uncles, brothers, sons, grandsons, friends, fathers-in-law, and good companions, in both armies. Watching all his relatives stand arrayed, he was overcome with the greatest compassion, and he said despairingly, "Kṛṣṇa, when I see all my family poised for war, my limbs falter and my mouth goes dry. There is a tremor in my body
30   and my hairs bristle. Gāṇḍīva is slipping from my hand and my skin is burning, I am not able to hold my ground and my mind seems to whirl. And I see contrary portents, Keśava, but I see no good to come from killing my family in battle! I do not wish victory, Keśava, nor kingship and pleasures. What use is kingship to us, Govinda? What use are comforts and life? The very men for whose sake we want kingship, comforts, and joy, stand in line to battle us, forfeiting their hard-to-relinquish lives! Teachers, fathers, sons, grandfathers,
35   maternal uncles, fathers-in-law, grandsons, brothers-in-law, and other relatives-in-law—I do not want to kill them, though they be killers, Madhusūdana, even for the sovereignty of the three worlds, let alone earth!

"What joy is left, Janārdana, after we have killed the Dhārtarāṣṭras? Nothing but guilt will accrue to us if we kill these assassins! Therefore we must not kill the Dhārtarāṣṭras and our kin, for how can we be happy when we have killed family, Mādhava? Even if their minds are so sick with greed that they do not see the evil that is brought on by the destruction of family, and the crime that lurks in the betrayal of friendship, how can we fail to know enough to shrink from this crime, we who do see the evil brought on by the destruction of family, Janārdana?

40   "With the destruction of family the eternal family Laws are destroyed. When Law is destroyed, lawlessness besets the entire family. From the prevalence of lawlessness the women of the family become corrupt, Kṛṣṇa; when the women are corrupt, there is class miscegenation, and miscegenation leads to hell for family killers and family. Their ancestors tumble, their rites of riceball and water disrupted. These evils of family killers that bring about class miscegenation cause the sempiternal class Laws and family Laws

to be cast aside. For men who have cast aside their family Laws a place in hell is assured, as we have been told.

45   "Woe! We have resolved to commit a great crime as we stand ready to kill family out of greed for kingship and pleasures! It were healthier for me if the Dhārtarāṣṭras, weapons in hand, were to kill me, unarmed and defenseless, on the battlefield!"

Having spoken thus, on that field of battle, Arjuna sat down in the chariot pit, letting go of arrows and bow, his heart anguished with grief.

Saṃjaya said:

24[2].1   Then, to this Arjuna who was so overcome with compassion, despairing, his troubled eyes filled with tears, Madhusūdana said—

The Lord said:

Why has this mood come over you at this bad time, Arjuna, this cowardice unseemly to the noble, not leading to heaven, dishonorable? Do not act like a eunuch, Pārtha, it does not become you! Rid yourself of this vulgar weakness of heart, stand up, enemy-burner!

Arjuna said:

How can I fight back at Bhīṣma with my arrows in battle, or at Droṇa, Madhusūdana? Both deserve my homage, enemy-slayer!

It were better that without slaying my gurus
I went begging instead for alms in this land
Than that I by slaying my covetous gurus
Indulge in the joys that are dipped in their blood.

And we do not know what is better for us:
That we defeat them or they defeat us;
Dhārtarāṣṭra's men are positioned before us,
After killing whom we have nothing to live for.

My nature afflicted with the vice of despair,
My mind confused over what is the Law,
I ask, what is better? Pray tell me for sure,
Pray guide me, your student who asks for your help!

There is nothing I see that might dispel
This sorrow that desiccates my senses,
If on earth I were to obtain without rivals
A kingdom, nay even the reign of the Gods!

Saṃjaya said:

10   Having spoken thus to Hṛṣīkeśa, enemy-burner Guḍākeśa said to Govinda, "I will not fight!" and fell silent. And with a hint of laughter Hṛṣīkeśa spoke to him who sat forlorn between the two armies, O Bhārata—

The Lord said:

You sorrow over men you should not be sorry for, and yet you speak to sage issues. The wise are not sorry for either the living or the dead. Never was there a time when I did not exist, or you, or these kings, nor shall any of us cease to exist hereafter. Just as creatures with bodies pass through childhood, youth, and old age in their bodies, so there is a passage to another body, and a wise man is not confused about it. The contacts of the senses with their objects, which produce sensations of cold and heat, comfort and discomfort, come and go without staying, Kaunteya. Endure them, Bhārata. The wise

15   man whom they do not trouble, for whom happiness and unhappiness are the same, is fit for immortality.

There is no becoming of what did not already exist, there is no unbecoming of what does exist: those who see the principles see the boundary between the two.[1] But know that that on which all this world is strung is imperishable: no one can bring about the destruction of this indestructible. What ends of this unending embodied, indestructible, and immeasurable being is just its bodies—therefore fight, Bhārata! He who thinks that this being is a killer and he who imagines that it is killed do neither of them know. It is not killed nor does it kill.

20   It is never born nor does it die;
Nor once that it is will it ever not be;
Unborn, unending, eternal, and ancient
It is not killed when the body is killed.

The man who knows him for what he is—indestructible, eternal, unborn, without end—how does he kill whom or have whom killed, Pārtha?

As a man discards his worn-out clothes
And puts on different ones that are new,
So the one in the body discards aged bodies
And joins with other ones that are new.

Swords do not cut him, fire does not burn him, water does not wet him, wind does not parch him. He cannot be cut, he cannot be burned, wetted, or parched, for he is eternal,

25   ubiquitous, stable, unmoving, and forever. He is the unmanifest, beyond thought, he is said to be beyond transformation; therefore if you know him as such, you have no cause for grief.

Or suppose you hold that he is constantly born and constantly dead, you still have no cause to grieve over him, strong-armed prince, for to the born death is assured, and birth is assured to the dead; therefore there is no cause for grief, if the matter is inevitable. Bhārata, with creatures their beginnings are unclear, their middle periods are clear, and their ends are unclear—why complain about it?

> It is by a rare chance that a man does see him,
> It's a rarity too if another proclaims him,
> A rare chance that someone else will hear him,
> And even if hearing him no one knows him.

30   This embodied being is in anyone's body forever beyond killing, Bhārata; therefore you have no cause to sorrow over any creatures. Look to your Law and do not waver, for there is nothing more salutary for a baron than a war that is lawful. It is an open door to heaven, happily happened upon; and blessed are the warriors, Pārtha, who find a war like that!

Or suppose you will not engage in this lawful war: then you give up your Law and honor, and incur guilt. Creatures will tell of your undying shame, and for one who has

35   been honored dishonor is worse than death. The warriors will think that you shrank from the battle out of fear, and those who once esteemed you highly will hold you of little account. Your ill-wishers will spread many unspeakable tales about you, condemning your skill—and what is more miserable than that?

Either you are killed and will then attain to heaven, or you triumph and will enjoy the earth. Therefore rise up, Kaunteya, resolved upon battle! Holding alike happiness and unhappiness, gain and loss, victory and defeat, yoke yourself to the battle, and so do not incur evil.

This is the spirit[2] according to theory;[3] now hear how this spirit applies in practice,[4]

40   yoked with which you will cut away the bondage of the act. In this there is no forfeiture of effort, nor an obstacle to completion;[5] even very little of *this* Law[6] saves from great peril. This one spirit is defined here as singleness of purpose, scion of Kuru, whereas the spirits of those who are not purposeful are countless and many-branched.[7] This flowering language which the unenlightened expound,[8] they who delight in the disputations[9] on the Veda, holding that there is nothing more, Pārtha, inspired by desires, set upon heaven— this language that brings on rebirth as the result of acts and abounds in a variety of rituals aimed at the acquisition of pleasures and power, robs those addicted to pleasures and power of their minds; and on them this spirit, this singleness of purpose in concentration, is not enjoined.[10] The domain of the Vedas is the world of the three *guṇas*:[11] transcend

45   that domain, Arjuna, beyond the pairs of opposites, always abiding in purity, beyond acquisition and conservation, the master of yourself. As much use as there is in a well

when water overflows on all sides,[12] so much use is there in all Vedas for the enlightened brahmin.

Your entitlement is only to the rite, not ever at all to its fruits.[13] Be not motivated by the fruits of acts, but also do not purposely seek to avoid acting.[14] Abandon self-interest, Dhanaṃjaya, and perform the acts while applying this singlemindedness. Remain equable in success and failure—this equableness is called the application;[15] for the act as such is far inferior to the application of singleness of purpose to it, Dhanaṃjaya. Seek shelter in this singlemindedness—pitiful are those who are motivated by fruits! Armed with this singleness of purpose, a man relinquishes here both good and evil *karman*.[16] Therefore yoke yourself to this application—this application is the capacity to act.[17] The enlightened who are armed with this singleness of purpose rid themselves of the fruits that follow upon acts; and, set free from the bondage of rebirth,[18] go on to a state of bliss. When you have the desire to cross over this quagmire of delusion, then you will become disenchanted with what is supposed to be revealed, and the revealed itself.[19] When your spirit of purposiveness stands unshaken at cross-purposes with the revealed truth, and immobile in concentration, then you will have achieved the application.

Arjuna said:

What describes the man who stands in concentration, Keśava? What does the one whose insight is firm say? How does he sit? How does he walk?

The Lord said:

A man is called one whose insight is firm when he forsakes all the desirable objects that come to his mind, Pārtha, and is sufficient unto himself. Not distressed in adversities, without craving for pleasures, innocent of passion, fear and anger, he is called a sage whose insight is firm. Firm stands the insight of him who has no preference for anything, whether he meets good or evil, and neither welcomes nor hates either one. When he entirely withdraws his senses from their objects[20] as a tortoise withdraws its limbs, his insight stands firm. For an embodied man who does not eat,[21] the sense objects fade away, except his taste for them; his taste, too, fades when he has seen the highest.

Even of a wise man who tries, Kaunteya, the whirling senses carry off the mind by force. One should sit down, controlling one's senses, *yoked*, and intent on me, for firm stands the insight of him who has his senses under control. When a man thinks about sense objects, an interest in them develops. From this interest grows desire, from desire anger; from anger rises delusion, from delusion loss of memory, from loss of memory the death of the spirit, and from the death of the spirit one perishes. When he experiences the objects with senses that neither love nor hate and are under his control, and thus has himself under control, he attains to serenity. In a state of serenity all his

65 sufferings cease, for in one whose mind is serene, singleness of purpose is soon fixed. The one who is not yoked has no singleness of purpose; the one who is not yoked has no power to bring things about; and he who does not bring things about knows no serenity—and how can a man without serenity know happiness? For a mind that is amenable to the ranging senses carries off a man's capacity for insight, as the wind a ship at sea. Therefore the insight of him is firm who keeps his senses entirely away from their objects, strong-armed prince. The controlled man wakes in what is night for all creatures, as it is night for the seer of vision when the other creatures are awake.

70
> If all objects of wishes flow into a man
> As rivers flow into the ocean bed
> Which, while being filled, stays unmoved to its depths,
> He becomes serene, not the one who desires them.

The man who forsakes all objects of desire and goes about without cravings, possessiveness, and self-centeredness becomes serene.

This is the stance on *brahman*, Pārtha: having achieved it one is not deluded. Maintaining this stance even in his last hour, he attains to the *nirvāṇa* that is *brahman*.[22]

Arjuna said:

25[3].1 If you hold that insight is superior to action, Janārdana, why then do you urge me on to fearful action? With quite contradictory words you seem to confuse my own insight. Therefore tell me definitively which is the course by which I will attain to the supreme good.

The Lord said:

I have of old propounded, prince sans blame, that in this world there is a twofold position to take: for those who uphold insight through a discipline of knowledge, for those who uphold action through a discipline of action. A person does not avoid incurring *karman* just by not performing acts,[1] nor does he achieve success by
5 giving up acts. For no one lives even for a moment without doing *some* act, for the three forces[2] of nature cause everyone to act, willy-nilly. He who, while curbing the faculties of action, yet in his mind indulges his memories of sense objects is called a self-deceiving hypocrite. But he who curbs his senses with his mind, Arjuna, and then disinterestedly undertakes the discipline of action with his action faculties, stands out. Carry out the fixed acts, for action is better than failure to act: even the mere maintenance of your body does not succeed without acting.

All the world is in bondage to the *karman*[3] of action, except for action for purposes
10 of sacrifice:[4] therefore engage in action for that purpose, disinterestedly, Kaunteya. Prajāpati, after creating creatures and sacrifice together, said in the beginning: "Ye shall multiply by it, it shall be the cow that yields your desires. Give ye the Gods being with it,

and the Gods shall give ye being. And thus giving each other being ye shall attain to the highest good. Themselves enhanced in their being with sacrifice, the Gods shall give ye the pleasures ye desire: he who enjoys their gifts without return to them is but a thief." The strict who eat only what is left over after sacrificing are cleansed of all taints, while the wicked who cook for themselves alone eat filth.

15   Creatures exist by food, food grows from rain, rain springs from sacrifice, sacrifice arises from action. This ritual action, you must know, originates from the *brahman* of the Veda,[5] and this *brahman* itself issues from the Syllable *OM*.[6] Therefore the ubiquitous *brahman*[7] is forever based upon sacrifice. He who does not keep rolling the wheel that has been set in motion, indulging his senses in a lifespan of evil, lives for nothing, Pārtha. On the other hand, a man who delights in the self, is satiated with the self, is completely contented with the self alone, has nothing left to do. He has no reason at all to do anything or not to do anything, nor does he have any incentive of personal interest in any creature at all. Therefore pursue the daily tasks disinterestedly, for, while performing his acts without self-interest, a person obtains the highest good. For it was

20   by acting alone[8] that Janaka and others achieved success, so you too must act while only looking to what holds together the world.[9] People do whatever the superior man does: people follow what he sets up as the standard.

I have no task at all to accomplish in these three worlds, Pārtha. I have nothing to obtain that I do not have already. Yet I move in action. If I were not to move in action, untiringly, at all times, Pārtha, people all around would follow my lead. These people would collapse if I did not act; I would be the author of miscegenation; I would assas-

25   sinate these creatures. The wise, disinterested man should do his acts in the same way as the ignorant do, but only to hold the world together, Bhārata. One should not sow dissension in the minds of the ignorant, who are interested in their actions: the wise man should take kindly to all acts, but himself do them in a disciplined fashion.

At any rate, actions are performed by the three forces of nature, but, deluded by self-attribution, one thinks: "I did it!" But he who knows the principles that govern the distribution of those forces and their actions knows that the forces are operating on the forces, and he takes no interest in actions. Because they are confused about these forces of nature, people identify with the actions of these forces, and he who knows it all has no reason to upset the slow-witted who do not.[10]

30   Leaving all actions to me,[11] with your mind intent upon the universal self, be without personal aspirations or concern for possessions, and fight unconcernedly. They who always follow this view of mine, believing it without disputing it, are freed from their *karman*. But those who do dispute and fail to follow my view, deluded in all they know, they, to be sure, are witless and lost.

Even the man of knowledge behaves according to his nature—creatures follow their natures: who will stop them? Love and hatred lie waiting in the sense and its object: one should not fall into their power, for they ambush one.

35 It is more salutary to carry out your own Law poorly than another's Law well; it is better to die in your own Law than to prosper in another's.

Arjuna said:

What is it that drives a man to commit evil, Vārṣṇeya, however reluctantly, as though propelled by force?

The Lord said:

It is desire, it is anger, which springs from the force of *rajas*, the great devourer, the great evil: know that that is the enemy here. This world is clouded by it as fire by smoke, as a mirror by dust, as an embryo by the caul. The knowledge of the conscient is covered by this eternal enemy desire, Kaunteya, as by an insatiable fire. The senses,

40 the mind, and the spirit are said to be its lair: by means of them it clouds knowledge and leads into delusion the one within the body. Therefore, bull of the Bharatas, first control your senses, then kill off that evil which destroys insight and knowledge.

The senses, they say, are superior to their objects; the mind is higher than the senses; the spirit is higher than the mind; and beyond the spirit is he. Thus knowing the one beyond the spirit, pull yourself together and kill desire, your indomitable enemy, strong-armed prince!

The Lord said:

26[4].1 I propounded this imperishable Yoga to Vivasvat. Vivasvat transmitted it to Manu; Manu told it to Ikṣvāku. Thus came down the tradition of Yoga which the royal seers knew. Over a long span of time this Yoga was lost on earth, enemy-burner. What I have propounded to you today is this same ancient Yoga, treating you in so doing as my loyal follower and friend, for this is the ultimate mystery.

Arjuna said:

But your birth is recent; Vivasvat's birth belongs to the distant past! How am I to understand that you "propounded it in the beginning"?

The Lord said:

5 I have known many past births, and so have you, Arjuna. I remember them all, while you do not, enemy-burner. Although indeed I am unborn and imperishable, although I am the lord of the creatures, I do resort to nature, which is mine,[1] and take on birth by my own wizardry. For whenever the Law languishes, Bhārata, and lawlessness flourishes, I create myself. I take on existence from eon to eon, for the rescue of the good and the destruction of the evil, in order to reestablish the

10   Law. He who knows thus the divinity, as in fact it is, of my birth and work, no more returns to rebirth when he dies—he returns to me, Arjuna. There have been many who, rid of passions, fears, and angers, and made pure by the austerities of insight, have immersed themselves in me, resorted to me, and become of one being with me. I share in them in the manner in which they turn to me; for in all their various ways men do follow my trail, Pārtha.

People offer up sacrifices to deities when they want their actions to be crowned with success; for in this world of men the success that follows action follows swiftly. I have created the society of the four classes with due regard for the various distribution of the *guṇas* and the range of their workings: know that I am its author, and that I am forever without *karman*. Actions do not stick to me, for I have no yearning for the fruits of my actions: he who understands me in this

15   way is himself no longer bound by his own actions. The ancient aspirants to release also performed their acts in this same spirit; therefore you too must perform the same act which the ancients performed long ago.

Even wise men are confused about what is "action" and what is "nonaction"—let me tell you what "action" is, and when you know it you shall be free of evil. For one should know about action, know about misaction, and know about nonaction—the course of "action" *is* complex. He is possessed of the right spirit who is able to discern that there is no *karman* in action,[2] while there is *karman* in nonaction; if he among all men is yoked with this spirit[3] he can perform any act. The wise call that man a sage all of whose undertakings are devoid of the intention to achieve an object of desire,[4] for his *karman*[5] has

20   been burned off by the fire of insight. If one engages in an act while forgetting about its fruit, being already fully satisfied and in need of nothing, one does not incur any *karman* at all. He is not polluted when he does only bodily acts, without any expectations,[6] keeping mind and self controlled, and renounces all possessions. Contented with anything that comes his way,[7] beyond the pairs of opposites, without envy, and equable in success and failure, he is not bound, even though he acts.

All the *karman* of one who acts sacrificially dissolves when he is disinterested and freed, and has steadied his thoughts with insight. *Brahman*[8] is the offering, *brahman* is the oblation that is poured into the *brahman* fire by *brahman*: he who thus contemplates the act as

25   nothing but *brahman* must reach *brahman*. There are yogins[9] who regard sacrifice as directed to deities;[10] others offer up sacrifice by sacrificing into the fire that is *brahman*. Others offer the senses[11] of hearing and so forth into the fires of restraint, while others sacrifice the objects[12] of sound, etc., into the fires of the senses. Others again offer up all the actions of the senses and those of the vital faculties into the wisdom-kindled fire of the yoga of self-restraint. There are sacrificers who offer with substances, others with austerities, others with yoga, others with knowledge and Vedic study—ascetics all and strict in their vows. Some sacrifice *prāṇa* into *apāna*[13] and

30 *apāna* into *prāṇa*, blocking the passage of *prāṇa* and *apāna* as they practice breath control. Others limit their meals and offer *prāṇas* into *prāṇas*.[14] All of them know the meaning of sacrifice and destroy their evil with sacrifice. Living on the elixir that is the remnants of their sacrifice, they go to the eternal *brahman*. This world is not of him who fails to sacrifice—could then the higher world be his, best of Kurus?

Thus sacrifices of many kinds are strung in the mouth of *brahman*:[15] know that they all spring from action, and knowing this you shall be free. The sacrifice of knowledge[16] is higher than a sacrifice of substances, enemy-burner, but all action culminates in knowledge, Pārtha. Know this: The men of wisdom who see the truth shall teach you their knowledge, if you submit to them, put questions 35 to them and attend to them. Armed with their knowledge you will no more fall victim to confusion, and through it you will see all creatures without exception within yourself and then within me. Even if you are the worst criminal of them all, you will cross over all villainy with just your lifeboat of knowledge. Just as a blazing fire reduces its kindling to ashes, Arjuna, so the fire of knowledge makes ashes of all *karman*. For there is no means of purification the like of knowledge; and in time one will find that knowledge within oneself, when one is oneself perfected by yoga. The believer who is directed to it and has 40 mastered his senses obtains the knowledge; and having obtained it he soon finds the greatest peace. The ignorant and unbelieving man who is riven with doubts perishes: for the doubter there is neither this world nor the next; nor is there happiness.

Acts do not bind him who has renounced his *karman* through yoga, cut down his doubts with knowledge, and mastered himself, Dhanaṃjaya. Therefore cut away his doubt in your heart, which springs from ignorance, with the sword of knowledge: rise to this yoga and stand up, Bhārata!

Arjuna said:

27[5].1 You praise the relinquishment of acts[1] and at the same time the practice of them, Kṛṣṇa. Now tell me decidedly which is the better of the two.

The Lord said:

Both the renunciation and the practice of acts lead to the supreme good; but of these two the practice of acts is higher than the renunciation of acts. He is to be counted a perpetual renouncer[2] who neither hates nor desires, for, strong-armed prince, if one transcends the pairs of opposites, one is easily freed from bondage. Only fools propound that insight and the practice of acts are different things, not the wise: by undertaking one you find the full fruit of both.

5 The adepts of insight and the adepts of practice reach one and the same goal: he sees truly who sees that insight and practice are one and the same. True renunciation is hard to accomplish without the practice of yoga,[3] but armed with yoga the sage soon attains

to *brahman*. Armed with yoga, pure of soul, master of self and senses, identifying himself with the selves of all creatures, he is not tainted even though he acts. The man of yoga, knowing the truth, knows that while seeing, hearing, touching, smelling, eating, walking, sleeping, breathing, speaking, eliminating, grasping, opening and closing his eyes, he does in fact do nothing,[4] as he realizes that it is only the senses operating on their objects.

10   If one places all *karman*[5] on *brahman* and acts disinterestedly, he is no more stained by evil than a lotus petal by muddy water. Yogins do their acts with body, mind, spirit, and even the senses disengaged, in order to purify the self, without any interest in the acts themselves. The man of yoga, renouncing the fruits of his acts, reaches the peace of the ultimate foundation, while the undisciplined man, who acts on his desires because he is interested in fruits, is fettered by *karman*. Having renounced all *karman* with the mind, the soul dwells, happy and masterful, in its nine-gated fortress,[6] neither doing nor causing acts.

The Lord has not created into people either authorship of acts, or the acts themselves, 15   or the concatenation of act and fruit: that is the doing of Nature.[7] The lord[8] does not take on any act's evil or good *karman*; ignorance obscures insight—that is why people get confused.[9] Of those, however, who have destroyed this ignorance about the self with true knowledge, this knowledge illumines like a sun that supreme reality. Their spirits directed to it, their selves into it, founded on it, devoted to it, they no more go to return again, for their knowledge has cleansed away the taints.

Wise are they who see no difference between a learned, well-mannered brahmin, a cow, an elephant, a dog, and an eater of dogs. In this very world they have conquered creation whose minds are rooted in disinterest. For *brahman* is without flaws and indifferent,[10] and therefore they are rooted in *brahman*.

20   He should not rejoice upon finding pleasure, nor sadden when meeting the unpleasant: the knower of *brahman* who stands upon *brahman* is steady of spirit and harbors no delusions. Disinterested in outer sense impressions, he finds the happiness that is in himself; his spirit yoked with the yoga[11] of *brahman*, he tastes a happiness that is permanent. Indeed, the pleasures that spring from sense impressions are sources of unhappiness, because they have beginnings and ends, Kaunteya, so the wise man does not indulge in them. The man who in this very life, before he is freed from his body, is able to withstand the driving force that gathers from craving and anger, is yoked, is happy. When he finds happiness within, joy within, light within, this man of yoga becomes *brahman*, attains to the beatitude that is 25   *brahman*. This beatitude that is *brahman* is achieved by the seers whose evil has been cast off, whose doubts have been resolved, who have mastered themselves and are dedicated to the well being of all creatures. The beatitude that is *brahman* lies before the ascetics

who are rid of craving and anger, who have tamed their thinking and know themselves. Keeping outside the impressions from the outside world, centering the gaze between the eyebrows, evening out inhalation and exhalation within the nostrils, controlling senses, mind, and spirit, totally devoted to release, with no trace left of desire, fear, or anger, the seer is released forever. Knowing that I am the recipient of sacrifices and austerities, the great lord of all the world, the friend of all creatures, he attains serenity.

The Lord said:

28[6].1 He who performs the task set for him without interest in its fruit is the true renouncer and yogin, not the one who does not maintain the fire and fails to perform the rites.[1] Know, Pāṇḍava, that what they proclaim as "renunciation" is precisely this discipline,[2] for no one becomes a man of discipline without abandoning the intention of fruits. When a sage wishes to rise to this discipline, action is called his means; when he has risen to this discipline, serenity is called his means. For he is said to have risen to the discipline only when he is interested no longer in sense objects, no longer in his acts, but has renounced all intentions.[3] Let him by himself save himself and not lower himself, for oneself alone is one's friend, oneself alone one's enemy. To him his self is a friend who by himself has conquered himself;[4] but when the man who has not mastered himself is hostile, he acts as his own enemy. To him who has mastered himself and has become serene, the higher self is completely stable, in cold and heat, in happiness and unhappiness, in honor or abuse. Contented in his insight and knowledge, firm on his peak, master of his senses. Looking with the same eyes on a lump of clay, a rock, or a piece of gold, he is called a yogin who is truly "yoked." He is set apart by his equanimity before friends, allies, enemies, uninvolved parties, neutrals, hateful folk, and relatives, before good men and evil ones.

10 Let the yogin[5] yoke himself at all times, while remaining in retreat, solitary, in control of his thoughts, without expectations and without encumbrances. Let him set up for himself a firm stool in a pure spot, neither too high nor too low, with a cover of cloth, deerskin, or *kuśa* grass. As he sits on his seat, let him pinpoint his mind, so that the workings of mind and senses are under control, and yoke himself to yoga for the cleansing of his self. Holding body, head, and neck straight and immobile, let him steadily gaze at the tip of his nose, without looking anywhere else. Serene, fearless, faithful to his vow of chastity, and restraining his thinking, let him sit yoked, his thought on me, his intention focused on me. When he thus yokes himself continuously, the yogin of restrained thought attains to the peace that lies in me, beyond *nirvāṇa*.[6]

Yoga is neither for him who eats too much or not at all, nor for him who sleeps too much or keeps himself awake, Arjuna. Sorrow-dispelling yoga is his who has curbed his meals and diversions, curbed his motions in activities, curbed his sleeping and waking. He is called "yoked" when his restrained mind has come to rest upon his self alone and he is without craving for any object of desire. Just as a candle flame outside a draft does not flicker[7]—that is the well-known metaphor of a yogin of restrained mind who yokes himself to the yoga of the self.

20   When thought ceases, curbed by the practice of yoga, when he himself looks upon himself and is contented with himself, when he knows a total bliss beyond sensual pleasure, which can be grasped by the spirit alone, and when he knows it and, once fixed upon it, does not truly stray from it, when he has acquired it and can think of no greater acquisition, when firm on it he cannot be swayed even by profound grief—then he knows that this is the unbinding of his bond with sorrow, which is called "yoga," and that this yoga must be yoked on him decisively with undespairing heart.

25   Renouncing without exception all objects of desire that are rooted in intentions, taming the village of his senses all around with his mind, he should little by little *cease*, while he holds his spirit with fortitude, merges his mind in the self, and thinks of nothing at all. Wherever his volatile mind might stray unsteadily, he halts it and subdues it in the self. For a higher bliss engulfs the yogin whose mind is at peace, whose passions are appeased—who has become *brahman*, with no more taints.

Yoking himself always in this manner, the taintless yogin effortlessly savors the infinite bliss that is the touch of *brahman*. Yoked in yoga, he sees himself in all creatures, all creatures in himself—he sees everything the same.

30   When he sees me in everything and sees everything in me, I will not be lost to him and he will not be lost to me. He who shares in me as living in all creatures and thus becomes one with me, he is a yogin who, however he moves, moves in me. He is deemed the ultimate yogin, Arjuna, who, by comparing everything with himself, sees the same in everything, whether it be blissful or wretched.

Arjuna said:

Madhusūdana, this yoga you propound as equanimity, I cannot see how it would stay stable, because we are changeful: for, Kṛṣṇa, the mind is always changing, whirling, domineering, and tough—I see it as no more susceptible to control than wind itself!

The Lord said:

35   No doubt at all, strong-armed prince, the mercurial mind is hard to hold down. Yet, Kaunteya, it *can* be held, with tenacity and dispassion. While I agree that this yoga is hard to achieve for one who is not master of himself, it can be achieved with the right means by a self-controlled man who makes the effort.

Arjuna said:

Still, Kṛṣṇa, non-ascetic who, while having faith, allows his mind to stray from this yoga before he achieves the ultimate success of yoga—what becomes of him? Does he not, like a shredded cloud, fade away, a failure either way,[8] strong-armed lord, without foundation and astray on the path to *brahman*? Pray resolve this doubt of mine completely, Kṛṣṇa, for no one can resolve this doubt but you.

The Lord said:

40 No, Pārtha, neither here nor hereafter is he lost, for no one who does good can go wrong, my friend. He goes to the worlds which are gained by merit, and when he has dwelled there for years without end, this "failed yogin" is born high in the house of pure and prosperous folk, or in the family of wise yogins: indeed, such a birth is quite rare in this world. There he will recover the purposiveness of his previous life, scion of Kuru, and strive once more to perfect it. For a person is sustained, even involuntarily, by his previous application: desirous of knowing the yoga he proceeds beyond the *brahman* that is

45 the Veda. Then this vigorously striving yogin goes the ultimate journey, cleansed of evil and perfected in numerous lives. The yogin surpasses the ascetics, surpasses even the sages who know, surpasses the workers who merely act. Therefore, Arjuna, become a yogin. Him I deem the most accomplished man of yoga among all yogins who shares in me[9] in good faith, with his inner self absorbed in me.

The Lord said:

29[7].1 Hear how you, fixing your mind on me and finding shelter in me, shall know me entirely beyond doubt, while practicing this yoga, Pārtha. I shall propound to you fully that insight and knowledge, after acquiring which nothing more remains to be known in this world. Among thousands of people there is perhaps one who strives toward success, and even among those who have striven successfully, perhaps only one really knows me.

5 My material nature[1] is eightfold, comprising the order of earth, water, fire, wind, ether, mind, spirit, and ego. This is my lower nature, but know that I have another, higher nature[2] which comprises the order of souls: it is by the latter that this world is sustained, strong-armed prince. Realize that all creatures have their source therein: I am the origin of this entire universe and its dissolution. There is nothing at all that transcends me, Dhanaṃjaya: all this is strung on me as strands of pearls are strung on a string. In water I am the taste, Kaunteya, in sun and moon the light, in all the Vedas the syllable *OM*, in ether the sound,[3] in men their manhood. In earth I am its fragrance, in the sun its fire, in all creatures their vitality, in

10 the ascetics their austerity. Know, Pārtha, that I am the eternal seed of all beings, I am the thought of the thinkers, the splendor of the splendid. I am the strength of the strong, but strength without ambition and passion. In the beings I am that desire that does not run counter to the Law, bull of the Bharatas. Know that all conditions of being, whether influenced by *sattva*, *rajas*, and *tamas*, come from me; but I am not in them: they are in me.

This entire world is deluded by these three conditions of being which derive from the *guṇas*,[4] and thus it fails to recognize me who am in all eternity beyond the *guṇas*. For this miraculous world of my illusion which consists in the three *guṇas* is hard to escape: only those who resort to me overcome this illusion. The evil, deluded, vile men who do not resort to me lose their wits to this illusion, and they are reduced to the condition of demons.

15

Four kinds of good men seek my love,[5] Arjuna: the suffering, the seekers for knowledge, the seekers for wealth, and the adepts,[6] bull of the Bharatas. Among them stands out the adept, who is loyal to me exclusively[7] and is always yoked, for I am unutterably dear to him, and he is dear to me. All four are people of stature, but the adept I count as myself, for through his discipline he comes to me as his incomparable destination. Only after many a birth does the adept attain to me, knowing "Vāsudeva is everything," and a man of such great spirit is rare to find. Robbed of all true knowledge by this desire or that, the others resort to other deities, while observing this or that restraint but themselves remaining constrained only by their own natures. Yet, whatever may be the divine body that any loyal[8] person seeks to worship with faith, it is I who make his faith in that body unshakable. Armed with that faith he aspires to propitiate that deity and obtains from it his desires—desires for which I in fact provide. However, the rewards of those of little wit are ephemeral: God-worshipers go to the Gods, but my loyal followers go to me.

20

To the unenlightened I am some unseen entity that has become manifest, for they are ignorant of my transcendent being, which is eternal and incomparable. Since they are clouded by the illusion of my yoga, I am opaque to all, and the muddled world does not recognize me as unborn and immortal.

25

Arjuna, I know the creatures of past, present, and future, but no one knows me. Confused by the conflicts that spring from desire and hatred, all creatures in creation are duped into total delusion, Bhārata, enemy-burner. But when finally the evil *karman* of righteous men has faded away, and they arc freed from the confusions of conflict, they devote themselves to me, firm in their vows. They who strive toward freedom from old age and death by resorting to me, know that *brahman* which is universal as well as specific to every person: they know the act entire. They who know me as "elemental," as "divine," and as "sacrificial," until their final hour, know me truly, with their spirits yoked.

30

Arjuna said:

30[8].1 What is that *brahman*? What is the individual self? What is act, Supreme Person? What is called "elemental," and what "divine?" Who in this body is the "sacrificial" one, and how is he so, Madhusūdana? And how are you to be known by the disciplined in their final hour?

The Lord said:

The supreme *brahman* is the imperishable. The individual self is called nature.[1] And the outpouring that brings about the origination of the being of the creatures is called act.

5 The "elemental" is transitory being;[2] the spirit[3] is the "divine," and I myself am the "sacrificial"[4] here in this body, O best of the embodied. He who leaves his body and departs this life while thinking of me alone in his final hour, rejoins my being—of that there can be no doubt. A person always becomes whatever being he thinks of when he at last relinquishes the body, Kaunteya, for one is given being from its being.[5] Therefore think of me at all times and fight: with mind and spirit fixed on me you shall beyond a doubt come to me. While thinking of the divine Supreme Person with a mind that is yoked to a discipline of practice and does not stray away from him, he goes to him, Pārtha.

> The Sage and Preceptor primordial,
> More minute than an atom, creator of all,
> Of form unimaginable, hued like the sun
> At the back of the night—who thus thinks of him

10
> In his final hour with unshaken mind,
> Armed with his devotion and power of yoga,
> With his breath ensconced between his eyebrows,
> Attains to the Person Supreme and Divine.

> The abode that the Veda-wise call the eternal.
> And the aspirants enter with passions shed,
> And in search of which they practice the *brahman*.
> I shall now propound to you summarily.

Closing all the doors of the senses and blocking the mind in the heart and holding within the head the breath of the soul, one embarks upon the retention of yoga. He reaches the highest goal who relinquishes the body and departs life while uttering the one-syllabled *brahman* that is *OM* and thinking of me. He who thinks of me continuously without ever straying in thought to another, that ever-yoked yogin finds me easy to reach, Pārtha. When the great-spirited travelers to the ultimate perfection reach me, they do not return to rebirth, that impermanent domain of misery. All the worlds, as far as the World of Brahmā, return eternally,[6] but once I have been reached there is no more rebirth.

15

They know of days and nights who know the Day of Brahmā that lasts thousands of eons, and the Night that ends after thousands of eons. At the dawning of the Day all manifestations emerge from the unmanifest; at the falling of the Night they dissolve in that self-same unmanifest. This village of creatures helplessly comes into being again and again and dissolves at the fall of Night, Pārtha, only to be reborn again at the dawn of Day. But there is a being beyond that being, an eternal Unmanifest beyond the unmanifest,[7] which, while all beings perish, does not itself perish.

20

This Unmanifest, also called Akṣara, they declare to be that ultimate goal upon reaching which souls no more return—it is my supreme domain. It is the Supreme Person,[8] attainable only through exclusive devotion, Pārtha, in whom the creatures inhere, the one on whom all this is strung.

I shall set forth the times at which the yogins departing life return or do not return. The scholars of *brahman* who depart life by fire, by sunshine, by day, in the bright fortnight, and during the six months after the winter solstice go to *brahman*. The yogin who reaches the light of the moon by smoke, by night, in the dark fortnight, and during the six months after the summer solstice returns.[9] These two are considered to be the two routes of the world: the white and the black; by the former one does not return, by the latter one does return. No yogin who knows these two routes is confused about them, Pārtha; therefore be at all times yoked to yoga, Arjuna.

25

> What reward of merit has been assigned
> To rituals, Vedas, austerities, gifts,
> All that merit the yogin who knows transcends
> To attain the supreme, primordial place.

The Lord said:

31[9].1 I shall proclaim to you, who do not demur, this most mysterious insight accompanied by knowledge which will set you free of evil. It is the royal wisdom, the royal mystery, the ultimate purification, which is learned from immediate evidence, conforms to the Law, is easy to accomplish, and permanent. Men who do not believe in this doctrine of Law, enemy-burner, fail to reach me and they return to the runaround of deaths.

5 All this world is strung on me in the form of the Unmanifest; all creatures exist in me, but I do not exist in them.[1] And again, the creatures do not exist in me[2]—behold my supernal yoga![3] While sustaining the creatures and giving them being, my self does not exist in them. Just as the vast wind which goes everywhere is yet always contained within space, so, realize this, all creatures are contained in me. All creatures return to my nature at the end of the eon, Kaunteya, and at the beginning of the eon I create them again. Resting on my own nature I create, again and again, this entire aggregate of creatures involuntarily by the force of my nature.[4]

10 No acts bind me, Dhanaṃjaya, for I remain disinterested and detached from all acts. Nature gives birth to the standing and moving creatures under my tutelage, Kaunteya, and for that reason does the world revolve.

The deluded disregard me in my human form, being ignorant of my higher nature as the great lord of the creatures. Mindless and futile in their expectations, actions and knowledge, they abandon themselves to the deluding nature of Asuras and Rākṣasas. But men of great spirit who accept my divine nature venerate me uniquely, Pārtha, knowing that

15 I am the eternal source of the creatures. There are those who, always yoked to devotion, adore me and glorify me, while exerting themselves with fortitude, and pay homage to me. Others venerate me, while sacrificing to me with the sacrifice that is knowledge, as one, or several, or many, in my universal manifestations. I am the rite, I am the sacrifice, I am the libation to the ancestors, I am the herb,[5] I am the formula, I am the butter, I am the fire, I am the offering. I am the father of this world, its mother, the Placer and Grandfather, the object of knowledge, the strainer, the syllable *OM*, the *ṛc, sāman,* and *yajus*; goal, master, lord, witness, abode, refuge, friend, source and destruction and continuity, container, imperishable seed. I shine and withhold rain or pour it out, I am immortality and death, the existent and the nonexistent, Arjuna.

20 The purified Vedic drinkers of Soma
Seek me with oblations to win their heaven;
And on reaching the blessed domain of Indra
Enjoy the celestial joys of the Gods.

But upon enjoying the vast world of heaven,
Their merit exhausted, they rejoin the mortals;
Thus following devoutly the Law of the Vedas
And craving desires they come and they go.

But to those who serve me while thinking only of me and none other, who are always yoked, to them I bring felicity. Even they who in good faith devote themselves to other deities really offer up their sacrifices to me alone, Kaunteya, be it without proper rite.[6] For I am the recipient of all sacrifices and their master, though they do not really recog-
25 nize me and therefore slip. To the Gods go they who are avowed to the Gods, to the ancestors go they who are avowed to the ancestors, to the ghouls[7] go they who are avowed to the ghouls, to me go they who sacrifice to me.

If one disciplined soul proffers to me with love a leaf, a flower, fruit, or water,[8] I accept this offering of love from him. Whatever you do, or eat, or offer, or give, or mortify, Kaunteya, make it an offering to me, and I shall undo the bonds of *karman*, the good and evil fruits. He whose spirit is yoked to the yoga of renunciation shall come to me. I am equable to all creatures, no one is hateful to me or dear—but those who share
30 me with love are in me and I am in them. Even a hardened criminal who loves me and none other is to be deemed a saint, for he has the right conviction; he soon becomes Law-minded and finds peace forever. Understand this, Kaunteya: no servitor of mine is lost. Even people of low origins, women, *vaiśyas*, nay *śūdras*, go the highest course if they rely on me, Pārtha. So how much more readily holy brahmins and devoted royal seers! Reduced to this passing world of unhappiness, embrace me! May your thoughts be toward me, your love toward me, your sacrifice toward me, your homage toward me, and you shall come to me, having thus yoked yourself to me as your highest goal.

The Lord Said:

32[10].1 Again, strong-armed prince, listen to my supreme word which, for your benefit I shall pronounce to you who love me. Neither the hosts of Gods nor the great seers themselves know my origin, for I am the beginning of Gods and great seers all. He who knows me as the unborn, beginningless great lord of the world, he among mortals is undeluded and freed from all evil taints.

5   Insight, knowledge, lack of delusion, forbearance, veracity, self-control, serenity, happiness, unhappiness, becoming and unbecoming, fear and fearlessness, nonviolence, equableness, contentment, austerity, liberality, renown, and dishonor—all the creatures' various modes of life spring from me alone. The ancient seven seers and the four Manus[1] from whom the creatures in the world have issued were born of my being from my mind. He who truly knows this ubiquity and yoga[2] of mine is himself yoked to unshakable yoga, no doubt of that. The wise, who are filled with being, love me in the knowledge that I am the source of everything and that everything comes forth from me. With their thoughts on me, their very lives devoted to me, enlightening one another

10   and always recounting my stories, they are full of contentment and delight. To those who, always yoked, love me joyfully I grant the singleness of mind by which they attain to me. Residing in their own very being I compassionately dispel the darkness of their ignorance with the shining lamp of knowledge.

Arjuna said:

The divine seer Nārada[3] and all the seers declare that you are the supreme *brahman*, the supreme abode, the supreme means of sanctification, the divine and eternal Person, the primordial God, unborn and ubiquitous. So declare Asita Devala and Vyāsa,[4] and

15   you yourself tell me so, Keśava, I know that all this is true; indeed neither Gods nor Dānavas know your true manifestation, O lord. You yourself know yourself, Supreme Person, you who give being to the creatures, lord of the creatures, God of Gods, master of the world! Pray tell me of all your divine ubiquities,[5] by means of which you permeate these worlds. How may I know you, yogin, in my constant meditations? In what various modes of being may I meditate on you, my lord? Tell me again fully of your yoga and ubiquity, Janārdana, for I am not sated of listening to your Elixir!

The Lord said:

Well then, I shall recount to you my divine ubiquities, best of Kurus, the chief ones, for there is no end to my plenitude.

20   I am the self that dwells in all beings, Guḍākeśa, I am the beginning, the middle, and the end of the beings. Of the Ādityas I am Viṣṇu, of the celestial lights the shining sun, of the Maruts I am Marici, to the constellations I am the moon.[6] Of the Vedas, I am the Sāmaveda, of the Gods I am Vāsava, of the senses the mind, of the creatures the

consciousness. Of the Rudras I am Saṃkara, the God of Riches am I to Yakṣas and Rākṣasas, of the Vasus I am the fire, of the mountains the Meru. Know that of the priests I am their chief Bṛhaspati, Pārtha, of marshals Skanda,[7] of the waters I am the

25   ocean. Of the great seers I am Bhṛgu, of words the One Syllable, of sacrifices the prayer, of standing creatures the Himālaya.

Among all trees I am the Aśvattha, of the divine seers Nārada, of the Gandharvas Citraratha, of the Siddhas the hermit Kapila. Know that among horses I am Uccaiḥśravas born from the Elixir,[8] Airāvata among grand elephants, the king among his people. Of weapons I am the thunderbolt, of cows the Cow of Plenty, I am Kandarpa[9] in procreation. I am Vāsuki of the snakes. I am Ananta among the Serpents, Varuna among sea

30   creature, Aryaman among the Fathers, Yama among those who tame.[10] Of the Daityas I am Prahlāda, Kāla among things that count,[11] the lion among wild animals, Garuḍa among birds.

Of the means of purification I am the wind, among armsmen Rāma, among sea monsters the crocodile, among rivers the Ganges. I am the beginning, middle, and end of the creations, Arjuna, the wisdom of the self among all wisdom, the debate of the disputers. I am the *a* among syllables,[12] the *dvaṃdva*[13] among compounds, I am everlasting Time, the Placer who looks everywhere, I am all-snatching Death, and the Source of things yet

35   to be. Of feminines I am Fame, Beauty, Speech, Recollection, Wisdom, Fortitude, and Patience. Of the Sāmans I am the Bṛhat, of meters the Gāyatrī, of months Mārgaśīrṣa,[14] of seasons Spring. Of gamblers I am the dicing game, of the splendid the splendor; I am the victory, the resolution, the courage of the courageous.

Among the Vṛṣṇis I am Vāsudeva, among the Pāṇḍavas Arjuna, of the hermits I am Vyāsa, of sages Kavi Uśanas.[15] I am the stick of those who chastise, the statesmanship of those who seek to triumph, the taciturnity of the mysteries,[16] the wisdom of the wise.

I am whatever is the seed of all creatures, Arjuna. Not a being, standing or moving,

40   can exist without me. There is no limit to my divine ubiquities, enemy-burner: the full extent of my ubiquity I have here merely indicated. Whatever beings have transcending power, luster and might, know that each and every one of them has its source in a particle of my splendor. But what is the point to you of knowing this much, Arjuna? I support this entire universe with but a single portion of mine!

Arjuna said:

33[11].1   This ultimate mystery bearing upon the soul, which you have propounded to me as a favor, has dispelled my delusion. I have heard from you in all detail the becoming and unbecoming of the creatures, lotus-eyed one, and your own indestructible greatness. Now I wish to set eye on your real, supernal form, just as you have described yourself, sovereign lord, Supreme Person! If you think that I shall be able to look upon it, lord, master of Yoga,[1] display to me your imperishable person.

The Lord said:

5   Pārtha, behold my hundreds and thousands of shapes, of many kinds, divine, in manifold colors and figures. Behold the Ādityas, Vasus, Rudras, Aśvins, Maruts;[2] behold,
Bhārata, many marvels that have never been witnessed before. Behold the entire universe with standing and moving creatures centered here in this body of mine—and
whatever else you desire to see. But you shall not be able to look upon me with just your
ordinary eyes: I shall give you divine sight: behold my sovereign Yoga!

Saṃjaya said:

Having thus spoken, Hari, the great sovereign of Yoga, revealed to the Pārtha his su-
10   preme supernal form, with countless mouths and eyes, displaying multitudes of marvels, wearing numbers of divine ornaments, and raising divine weapons beyond count.
And this form wore celestial garlands and robes, it was anointed with the perfumes of
the Gods—it was God himself, infinite and universal, containing all miracles.[3]

If in the sky the light of a thousand suns were to rise at once, it would be the likeness of
the light of that great-spirited One. In that body of the God of Gods the Pāṇḍava saw
the entire universe centered, in its infinite differentiations. Dhanaṃjaya was stunned,
and he shivered. He folded his hands, bowed his head and said—

Arjuna said:

15   I see all Gods in your body, O God,
       And all creatures in all their varieties—
       On his lotus seat the sovereign Brahmā,
       The seers all and the snakes divine.

       Your own infinitude stretching away,
       Many arms, eyes, bellies, and mouths do I see,
       No end do I see, no beginning, no middle,
       In you, universal in power and form.

       With diadem, mace, and discus endowed,
       A mass of light ablaze on all sides,
       I see you, so rare to behold, all around
       Immeasurably burning like sun or the fire.

       You are *Akṣara*, highest of truths to be known,[4]
       The highest foundation of all this world,
       Undying protector of Law sempiternal,
       The Person Eternal I hold you to be,

Beginningless, middleless, endless, almighty,
Many-armed, with eyes that are sun and moon,
I see you with mouths that are blazing fires
Setting fire to this world with your incandescence.

20   All space that extends between heaven and earth,
All horizons are filled by you alone;
Having seen your dreadful and wondrous form
The three worlds shudder, great-spirited One!

For yonder the hosts of the Gods go into you—
Some laud you in fear with folded hands,
The throngs of the seers and Siddhas say Hail!
And sing your praise in long litanies.

Ādityas and Rudras, Vasus and Sādhyas,
The All-Gods, Asvins, Maruts and Fathers,
Gandharvas and Asuras, Yakṣas and Siddhas
Behold you amazed in all their numbers.

At the sight of your mass with its eyes and mouths.
Multitudinous arms, thighs, bellies, and feet,
Strong-armed One, and maws that are spiky with tusks
The worlds are in panic and so am I!

At the aspect of you who are brushing the sky,
Ablaze, many-hued, maws gaping, and eyes
Asparkle and wide, my innards are quaking,
And, Viṣṇu, I find neither firmness nor peace.

25   Just watching your mouths that bristle with fangs
And resemble the fire at the end of the eon,
I know no directions and find no shelter—
Have mercy, great God, repose of the world!

And yonder all sons of Dhṛtarāṣṭra
Along with the hosts of the kings of the earth,
Like Bhīṣma, Droṇa, that son of a *sūta*,[5]
Along with our own chief warriors too

Are hastening into your numerous mouths[6]
That are spiky with tusks and horrifying—
There are some who are dangling between your teeth,
Their heads already crushed to bits.

As many a river in spate ever faster
Streams oceanward in a headlong rush,
So yonder heroic rulers of earth
Are streaming into your flame-licked mouths.

As moths on the wing ever faster will aim
For a burning fire and perish in it,
Just so do these men increasing their speed
Make haste to your mouths to perish in them.

30   You are greedily licking your lips to devour
These worlds entire with your flickering mouths:
Your dreadful flames are filling with fire,
And burn to its ends this universe, Viṣṇu![7]

Reveal to me, who are you so dread?
Obeisance to you, have mercy, good God!
I seek to encompass you who are primeval,
For I comprehend not the course you are taking.

The Lord said:

I am Time grown old to destroy the world,
Embarked on the course of world annihilation:
Except for yourself none of these will survive.
Of these warriors arrayed in opposite armies.

Therefore raise yourself now and reap rich fame,
Rule the plentiful realm by defeating your foes!
I myself have doomed them ages ago:
Be merely my hand in this, Left-handed Archer!

Slay Droṇa and Bhīṣma and Jayadratha,
And Karṇa as well as other fine warriors—
My victims—destroy them and tarry not!
Wage war! You shall trounce your rivals in battle!

Saṃjaya said:

35   Upon hearing these words from Keśava
The Diademed Arjuna folded his hands,
And trembling he bowed and responded to Kṛṣṇa
In a stammer, prostrate, and terror-struck—

Arjuna said:

It is meet, Hṛṣīkeśa, that, hearing you praised,
The world is enraptured and flooded with love:
The terrified Rākṣasas flee to all regions,
The throngs of the Siddhas proffer their homage.

And why should they fail to bow down, great-souled One.
Creator more worthy of honor than Brahmā?
Unending Lord God, repose of the world,
You're what is and is not and what is beyond it.

The Original God, the Person Eternal,
You are of this world the ultimate support,
The knower, the known, the final abode—
All is strung upon you, of infinite form:

Moon, wind, fire, Varuṇa, Yama are you,
Prajāpati are you, the great-grandfather,
I praise thee, I praise thee a thousandfold,
Once more and again I praise thee, I praise thee,

I praise thee in front, I praise thee in back,
I praise thee on every side, O All!
Of infinite vigor, of measureless might,
You encompass it all and therefore are all.

If, thinking you friend, I have too boldly
Cried, "Yādava! Kṛṣṇa! Come here, my good friend!"[8]
Not knowing of this your magnificence,
Out of absence of mind or sheer affection,

If perchance I have slighted you—merely in jest—
In matters of sport, bed, seating, or meal,[9]
In privacy, Acyuta, or before others—
I ask your indulgence, immeasurable One!

Of the quick and the firm you are the begetter,
By all to be honored the worthiest guru;
No one is your equal, still less then your better.
For in all three worlds your might has no bounds.

Therefore I bow low, prostrating my body,
And ask your forgiveness, worshipful Lord!

Pray bear with me, God, as a father with son,
As a friend with friend, as a lover with loved one.

45   At the sight of this unwitnessed marvel I thrill
While a sense of dread unsettles my mind:
Please show me, O God, the body I've known.
Have mercy, Lord God, repose of the world!

I wish now to see you again as before,
With your diadem, mace, and discus in hand,
Assume once again your four-armed form.
O thousand-armed One, embodied in all!

The Lord said:

Out of grace for you, Arjuna, have I revealed
By my power of Yoga my highest form,
Full of fire, universal, primeval, unending,
Which no one but you has ever beheld.

Not with Veda or rites, not with study or gifts,
Not with sacrifice or with awesome *tapas*
Can I in this world be beheld in this form
By any but you, great hero of Kuru.

Have no more fear, be no longer bemused
By the sight of this form of me so awe-inspiring;
Your terror gone, your heart again pleased,
Set eyes once more on the body you know!

Saṃjaya said:

50   Quoth Vāsudeva to Arjuna
And showed him once more his form of before,
And put that terrified man to rest
By becoming again his gentle old self.

Arjuna said:

Now that I see your gentle human shape, Janārdana, I have come to my senses and my
normal tenor is restored!

The Lord said:

You have seen this rarely revealed form that is mine: even the Gods always yearn for a glimpse of this form. Thus, as I am and as you have seen me, I cannot be seen with the aid of the Vedas, austerities, gifts, and sacrifices. Only through exclusive *bhakti*[10] can I be seen thus, Arjuna, and known as I really am, and entered into, enemy-tamer. Only he comes to me, Pāṇḍava, who acts for me, who holds me as the highest, who is devoted to me without self-interest and without any animosity against any creature.

Arjuna said:

34[12].1   Who are the foremost adepts of yoga: those who attend on you with the devotion they constantly practice, or those who seek out the imperishable that is unmanifest?[1]

The Lord said:

Those I deem the most adept at yoga who fix their minds on me and in constant yoga and with complete faith attend on me. But those who attend on the inexpressible unmanifest Imperishable, omnipresent, inconceivable, standing on the peak,[2] immovable, and fixed, while they master their senses and remain equably disposed to everyone and everything and have the well-being of all creatures at heart, those reach me too. But it requires greater toil for those whose minds are directed to the Unmanifest, for their goal is not manifest and the embodied attain it with hardship. On the other hand, those who, absorbed in me, resign all their acts to me and contemplatively attend on me with exclusive yoga,[3] soon find in me their savior from the ocean that is the run around of deaths. Pārtha, for their minds are conducted to enter into me.

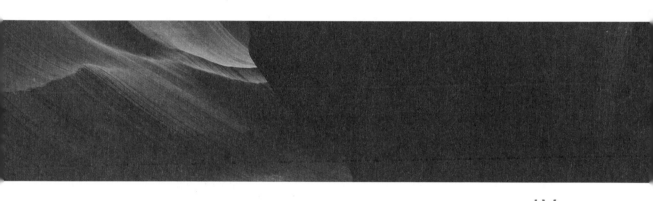

IV

St. Augustine

Editors' Introduction

While recognized as an extraordinary autobiographical account of conversion, the *Confessions* of St. Augustine can also be understood as an extended prayer to and before God. We tend to think of personal prayer as a private matter, but here Augustine invites us to reflect along with him as he reviews his life in the presence of the God to whom he is praying.

If we understand the book in this way, we can better grasp the meaning of its title. On one level, the *Confessions* embodies the common usage of the term "confession" as a statement of repentance for one's sins. There is certainly plenty of this in the text. In fact, some readers are mystified by the seemingly inordinate length with which the author decries the sins of his past—sins that do not strike at least some readers as being particularly egregious or harmful. (Here's a hint—pay attention to Augustine's story of the pears.) But this confession of sin is only one aspect of what Augustine wishes to convey to his readers through these reflections. "Confession" can also be understood as a form of praise, and this is perhaps the most important meaning it has for Augustine here. His confession of the bad deeds from his past is meant to illuminate the tremendous goodness and mercy of God—a God who he experiences as having freed him from his earlier, inauthentic ways of life. Augustine's prayer is a prayer of praise and thanksgiving to God for helping him to be free to become his true self. For Augustine, that true self cannot be understood apart from his relationship to the One who has freed and enlightened him.

Augustine was born in 354 A.D. in the northern African city of Thagaste (modern day Souk Ahras in Algeria). His mother, Monica, was a Christian, and his father, Patricius, was a pagan. At this time, northern Africa was part of the Roman Empire. Around the age of seventeen he was sent to Carthage (in what is now Tunisia) for higher studies in classical literature and rhetoric. While in Carthage he began to live with a woman (whose name we do not know) with whom he had a son, Adeodatus ("Godsend"). It appears that he and his companion loved one another deeply, and that they remained mutually faithful during the course of their fourteen-year relationship.

Although his mother was a Christian, Augustine was not baptized, and he seems to have been little affected by the Christian message during his youth and teenage years. While there is sometimes a tendency to focus on the misadventures and sins of his early years (an image he did much to perpetuate himself, in order to highlight the significance of his conversion), it is important to keep in mind that Augustine was someone who was always searching and who always thought seriously about philosophical, moral, and religious questions. When he was nineteen he came across a treatise called the *Hortensius* written by the Roman philosopher Cicero. This book inspired him with a desire to seek wisdom, and it can be truly said of Augustine that while this desire would sometimes be submerged by other concerns, it never left him. His was a probing intellect, and his life unfolded as a search for answers to the most serious questions. One episode in his ongoing intellectual journey occurred during his years in Carthage when he was attracted to a group called the Manichees. Manicheanism was a religious/philosophical system that originated in Persia. Manichean teaching was dualistic, believing that the world was the scene of a struggle between an evil power and a power of good. According to this view, God was good but incapable of conquering evil. Another dualistic feature of Manicheanism was a sharp contrast between matter and spirit. For seriously committed Manichees, this entailed a very negative view of the material world, and it was their belief that salvation involved freeing oneself as much as possible from the concerns of the flesh.

Having completed his education, Augustine found employment teaching rhetoric in Carthage. Dissatisfied with the behavior of his students, he made his way to Rome in 383, in the hope that education might be viewed more seriously there. Once again disappointed, he applied for and won a professorship in the northern Italian city of Milan. There he encountered two influences that would prove to be crucial in his process of conversion: Neo-Platonic philosophy and the preaching of St. Ambrose, bishop of Milan. Neo-Platonism is a complex philosophical teaching; some of what attracted Augustine to it was the idea of life as a journey of ascent toward union with divine reality and the idea of God as an entirely spiritual substance. With regard to this latter idea, the notion that "real" was not the same thing as "body" came as a tremendous intellectual breakthrough for him. Through Ambrose, Augustine came to appreciate the importance of the Bible, a book he had previously viewed as unsophisticated in comparison with philosophy.

Despite these movements of intellectual conversion, Augustine remained at this time an ambitious young man eager to make a name for himself in Milan. Whether at his mother's urging, by his own decision, or through a mutually agreed upon arrangement, it was decided that his longtime companion (the mother of his son) would return to Africa. If Augustine was going to move up in society he needed to contract a "proper" marriage, and he needed to marry someone with a substantial dowry. While Augustine's behavior toward his partner is hardly defensible, it should be kept in mind that in fourth century Roman society it was relatively common for a young man to live with a female companion for an extended period of time and then to leave her when he contracted a legal marriage. Marriage at this time was often entered into for financial reasons and as a way of joining two families together. Be careful not to read contemporary ideas about romantic love or Christian commitment into the practices of late Roman society. Augustine's mother Monica arranged a marriage, but since the promised bride was still too young to marry, Augustine would have to wait two years between the time of sending away his partner and his arranged marriage. This he found difficult to do, and he soon began to live with another woman.

Despite these circumstances, Augustine remained unsettled and searching morally, spiritually, and intellectually. His friend Alypius helped to convince him that he (Augustine) was not made for marriage, so he broke off the plan for the arranged marriage and ended the relationship with the woman with whom he was living. Through friends he also became acquainted with various accounts of personal conversion, including the story of St. Anthony of the Desert (an Egyptian saint/monk who lived from 251 to 356). Augustine found himself deeply moved by these conversion narratives. He was now on the verge of a decisive breakthrough. The moment came in the summer of 386. Highly agitated and suffering from a good deal of personal confusion and anguish, Augustine (along with Alypius) went out into the garden adjoining the place where he was living. There, coming from a nearby house, he heard the voice of a young child singing over and over again the words "Pick it up and read." Augustine picked up a volume containing the letters of St. Paul, opened it randomly to a page, and found there words that he took to be addressed to him by God. Augustine, his son Adeodatus, Alypius, and several other friends were baptized by St. Ambrose on Easter 387.

Within a year Augustine decided to return to Africa. On the way there, in the Italian city of Ostia, his mother died. Shortly after he returned to Africa, his son died at age seventeen. In 391, he was ordained a priest in Hippo Regius (present day Annaba in Algeria), and in 395 he was named bishop of the city. He served as bishop until his death in 430. Intense and energetic as always, he immersed himself in the pastoral care of his people, wrote voluminously, and preached with great effectiveness. He died as the Vandals (a Germanic tribe) were laying siege to his city. The Roman world that had shaped him in so many ways was, if not disappearing, about to be deeply transformed. Through the *Confessions* and his other writings he would exert a profound influence on the new world that would emerge from the ruins of Rome.

CONFESSIONS (SELECTIONS)

Book I

Early Years

i (1)   'You are great, Lord, and highly to be praised (Ps. 47: 2): great is your power and your wisdom is immeasurable' (Ps. 146:5). Man, a little piece of your creation, desires to praise you, a human being 'bearing his mortality with him' (2 Cor. 4: 10), carrying with him the witness of his sin and the witness that you 'resist the proud' (1 Pet. 5:5). Nevertheless, to praise you is the desire of man, a little piece of your creation. You stir man to take pleasure in praising you, because you have made us for yourself, and our heart is restless until it rests in you.[1]

'Grant me Lord to know and understand' (Ps. 118: 34, 73, 144) which comes first—to call upon you or to praise you, and whether knowing you precedes calling upon you. But who calls upon you when he does not know you? For an ignorant person might call upon someone else instead of the right one. But surely you may be called upon in prayer that you may be known. Yet 'how shall they call upon him in whom they have not believed? and how shall they believe without a preacher?' (Rom. 10: 14). 'They will praise the Lord who seek for him' (Ps. 21: 27).

In seeking him they find him, and in finding they will praise him. Lord, I would seek you, calling upon you—and calling upon you is an act of believing in you. You have been preached to us. My faith, Lord, calls upon you. It is your gift to me. You breathed it into me by the humanity of your Son, by the ministry of your preacher.[2]

ii (2)   How shall I call upon my God, my God and Lord? Surely when I call on him, I am calling on him to come in to me. But what place is there in me where my God can enter into me? 'God made heaven and earth' (Gen. 1: 1). Where may he come to me? Lord my God, is there any room in me which can contain you? Can heaven and earth, which you have made and in which you have made me, contain you? Without you, whatever exists would not exist. Then can what exists contain you? I also have being. So why do I request you to come to me when, unless you were within me, I would have no being at all? I am not now possessed by Hades; yet even there are you (Ps. 138: 8): for 'even if I were to go down to Hades, you would be present'. Accordingly, my God, I would have no being, I would not have any existence, unless you were in me. Or rather, I would have no being if I were not in you 'of whom are all things, through whom are all things, in whom are all things' (Rom. 11: 36). Even so, Lord, even so. How can I call on you to come if I am already in you? Or where can you come from so as to be in me? Can I move outside heaven and earth so that my God may come to me from there? For God has said 'I fill heaven and earth' (Jer. 23: 24).

---

1   For Plotinus (6. 7. 23. 4) the soul finds rest only in the One. Augustine's sentence announces a major theme of his work.

2   Probably Ambrose (as in Augustine 's letter 147. 52) rather than Christ; i.e. the two phrases are contrasting, not parallel and equivalent. That the humanity of Christ is an example of faith is common in Augustine. See below, X. xliii (68).

Book II

Adolescence

i (1)   I intend to remind myself of my past foulnesses and carnal corruptions, not because I love them but so that I may love you, my God. It is from love of your love that I make the act of recollection. The recalling of my wicked ways is bitter in my memory, but I do it so that you may be sweet to me, a sweetness touched by no deception, a sweetness serene and content. You gathered me together from the state of disintegration in which I had been fruitlessly divided. I turned from unity in you to be lost in multiplicity.[1]

At one time in adolescence I was burning to find satisfaction in hellish pleasures. I ran wild in the shadowy jungle of erotic adventures. 'My beauty wasted away and in your sight I became putrid' (Dan. 10: 8), by pleasing myself and by being ambitious to win human approval.

ii (2)   The single desire that dominated my search for delight was simply to love and to be loved. But no restraint was imposed by the exchange of mind with mind, which marks the brightly lit pathway of friendship. Clouds of muddy carnal concupiscence filled the air. The bubbling impulses of puberty befogged and obscured my heart so that it could not see the difference between love's serenity and lust's darkness. Confusion of the two things boiled within me. It seized hold of my youthful weakness sweeping me through the precipitous rocks of desire to submerge me in a whirlpool of vice.[2] Your wrath was heavy upon me and I was unaware of it. I had become deafened by the clanking chain[3] of my mortal condition, the penalty of my pride. I travelled very far from you, and you did not stop me. I was tossed about and spilt, scattered and boiled dry in my fornications. And you were silent. How slow I was to find my joy! At that time you said nothing, and I travelled much further away from you into more and more sterile things productive of unhappiness, proud in my self-pity, incapable of rest in my exhaustion.

(3)   If only someone could have imposed restraint on my disorder. That would have transformed to good purpose the fleeting experiences of beauty in these lowest of things, and fixed limits to indulgence in their charms. Then the stormy waves of my youth would have finally broken on the shore of marriage. Even so, I could not have been wholly content to confine sexual union to acts intended to procreate children, as your law prescribes, Lord. For you shape the propagation of our mortal race, imposing your gentle hand to soften the brambles which were excluded from your paradise.[4] Your

---

1   The language here is characteristic of Porphyry (e.g. *ep.ad Marcellam 10*, p. 280, 25 Nauck) and Plotinus 6. 6. 1. 5. See below XI. xxix (39).
2   Echo of Virgil, *Aeneid* 3. 422 (Scylla and Charybdis).
3   Virgil, *Aeneid* 6. 558.
4   Augustine's vision of the sex-life of Adam and Eve before the Fall passed from belief that their union was wholly spiritual (below XIII. xx (28)) to a conviction that it was both spiritual and physical, but controlled by reason and will, never by unreasoning passion, and wholly free of the thorny problems that beset sexuality in common experience.

omnipotence is never far from us, even when we are far from you.[5] Alternatively, I ought to have paid more vigilant heed to the voice from your clouds: 'Nevertheless those who are married shall have trouble in the flesh, and I would spare you' (Cor. 7: 28), and 'It is good for a man not to touch a woman' (1 Cor. 7: 1), and 'He who has no wife thinks on the things of God, how he can please God. But he who is joined in marriage thinks on the affairs of the world, how he can please his wife' (1 Cor. 7: 32–3). Had I paid careful attention to these sayings and 'become a eunuch for the sake of the kingdom of heaven' (Matt. 19: 12), I would have been happier finding fulfilment in your embraces.

(4)   But I in my misery seethed and followed the driving force of my impulses, abandoning you. I exceeded all the bounds set by your law, and did not escape your chastisement-indeed no mortal can do so. For you were always with me, mercifully punishing me, touching with a bitter taste all my illicit pleasures. Your intention was that I should seek delights unspoilt by disgust and that, in my quest where I could achieve this, I should discover it to be in nothing except you Lord, nothing but you. You 'fashion pain to be a lesson' (Ps. 93: 20 LXX), you 'strike to heal', you bring death upon us so that we should not die apart from you (Deut. 32: 39).[6]

Where was I in the sixteenth year of the age of my flesh? 'Far away in exile from the pleasures of your house' (Mic. 2: 9). Sensual folly assumed domination over me, and I gave myself totally to it in acts allowed by shameful humanity but under your laws illicit. My family did not try to extricate me from my headlong course by means of marriage. The only concern was that I should learn to speak as effectively as possible and carry conviction by my oratory.

iii (5)   During my sixteenth year there was an interruption in my studies. I was recalled from Madauros, the nearby town where I had first lived away from home to learn literature and oratory. During that time funds were gathered in preparation for a more distant absence at Carthage, for which my father had more enthusiasm than cash, since he was a citizen of Thagaste with very modest resources.[7] To whom do I tell these things? Not to you, my God. But before you I declare this to my race, to the human race, though only a tiny part can light on this composition of mine. And why do I include this episode? It is that I and any of my readers may reflect on the great depth from which we have to cry to you (Ps. 129: 1). Nothing is nearer to your ears than a confessing heart and a life grounded in faith (cf. Rom. 10: 9). At that time everybody was full of praise

---

5   The Neoplatonist Porphyry wrote: 'He who knows God has God present to him, and he who does not know him is absent from him who is everywhere present.' (*Ad Gauron* 12. 3). Cf. above, II. ii (3).

6   Cf. above I. v. (6). The beneficence of punishment is affirmed in 2 Macc. 6: 12–16.

7   Augustine's biographer, Possidius, records that his father Patrick sat on the town council or *curia* of Thagaste, a position bringing social credit and financial burdens. The estate was not large, and in relative terms the family was reckoned 'poor', i.e. it possessed only a few slaves for the housework and the land, which in one letter Augustine describes as 'a few acres'. Naturally Augustine's family was not poor in an absolute sense; they were far from being destitute. But 'pauper' is once defined by Ovid as 'a man who knows how many sheep he has'. Patrick is likely to have known how many he had.

for my father because he spent money on his son beyond the means of his estate, when that was necessary to finance an education entailing a long journey. Many citizens of far greater wealth did nothing of the kind for their children. But this same father did not care what character before you I was developing, or how chaste I was so long as I possessed a cultured tongue—though my culture really meant a desert uncultivated by you, God. You are the one true and good lord of your land, which is my heart.

(6)   In my sixteenth year idleness interposed because of my family's lack of funds. I was on holiday from all schooling and lived with my parents. The thorns of lust rose above my head, and there was no hand to root them out. Indeed, when at the bathhouse my father saw that I was showing signs of virility and the stirrings of adolescence, he was overjoyed to suppose that he would now be having grandchildren, and told my mother so. His delight was that of the intoxication which makes the world oblivious of you, its Creator, and to love your creation instead of you. He was drunk with the invisible wine of his perverse will directed downwards to inferior things.[8] But in my mother's heart you had already begun your temple and the beginning of your holy habitation (Ecclus. 24: 14). My father was still a catechumen and had become that only recently. So she shook with a pious trepidation and a holy fear (2 Cor. 7: 15). For, although I had not yet become a baptized believer, she feared the twisted paths along which walk those who turn their backs and not their face towards you (Jer. 2: 27).

(7)   Wretch that I am, do I dare to say that you, my God, were silent when in reality I was travelling farther from you? Was it in this sense that you kept silence to me? Then whose words were they but yours which you were chanting in my ears through my mother, your faithful servant? But nothing of that went down into my heart to issue in action. Her concern (and in the secret of my conscience I recall the memory of her admonition delivered with vehement anxiety) was that I should not fall into fornication, and above all that I should not commit adultery with someone else's wife. These warnings seemed to me womanish advice which I would have blushed to take the least notice of. But they were your warnings and I did not realize it. I believed you were silent, and that it was only she who was speaking, when you were speaking to me through her. In her you were scorned by me, by me her son, the son of your handmaid, your servant (Ps. 115: 16). But I did not realize this and went on my way headlong with such blindness that among my peer group I was ashamed not to be equally guilty of shameful behaviour when I heard them boasting of their sexual exploits. Their pride was the more aggressive, the more debauched their acts were; they derived pleasure not merely from the lust of the act but also from the admiration it evoked. What is more worthy of censure than vice? Yet I went deeper into vice to avoid being despised, and when there was no act by admitting to which I could rival my depraved companions, I used to pretend I had

---

8   Augustine's father celebrated the signs of his son's virility by becoming inebriated. The implications of this passage on Patrick's hopes for a grandchild appear the only evidence to suggest that Augustine was the eldest of the children.

done things I had not done at all, so that my innocence should not lead my companions to scorn my lack of courage, and lest my chastity be taken as a mark of inferiority.[9]

(8)   Such were the companions with whom I made my way through the streets of Babylon.[10] With them I rolled in its dung as if rolling in spices and precious ointments (S. of S. 5. 4: 14). To tie me down the more tenaciously to Babylon's belly, the invisible enemy trampled on me (Ps. 55: 3) and seduced me because I was in the mood to be seduced. The mother of my flesh already had fled from the centre of Babylon (Jer. 51: 6), but still lingered in the outskirts of the city. Although she had warned me to guard my virginity, she did not seriously pay heed to what her husband had told her about me, and which she felt to hold danger for the future: for she did not seek to restrain my sexual drive within the limit of the marriage bond, if it could not be cut back to the quick. The reason why she showed no such concern was that she was afraid that the hope she placed in me could be impeded by a wife. This was not the hope which my mother placed in you for the life to come, but the hope which my parents entertained for my career that I might do well out of the study of literature. Both of them, as I realized, were very ambitious for me: my father because he hardly gave a thought to you at all, and his ambitions for me were concerned with mere vanities; my mother because she thought it would do no harm and would be a help to set me on the way towards you, if I studied the traditional pattern of a literary education. That at least is my conjecture as I try to recall the characters of my parents.

The reins were relaxed to allow me to amuse myself. There was no strict discipline to keep me in check, which led to an unbridled dissoluteness in many different directions. In all of this there was a thick mist shutting me off from the brightness of your face, my God, and my iniquity as it were 'burst out from my fatness' (Ps. 72: 7).

iv (9)   Theft receives certain punishment by your law (Exod. 20: 15), Lord, and by the law written in the hearts of men (Rom. 2: 14) which not even iniquity itself destroys. For what thief can with equanimity endure being robbed by another thief? He cannot tolerate it even if he is rich and the other is destitute. I wanted to carry out an act of theft and did so, driven by no kind of need other than my inner lack of any sense of, or feeling for, justice. Wickedness filled me. I stole something which I had in plenty and of much better quality. My desire was to enjoy not what I sought by stealing but merely the excitement of thieving and the doing of what was wrong. There was a pear tree near our vineyard laden with fruit, though attractive in neither colour nor taste. To shake the fruit off the tree and carry off the pears, I and a gang of naughty adolescents set off late at night after (in our usual pestilential way) we had continued our game in the streets. We carried off a huge

---

9   The theme of this paragraph is found in Ambrose, *Noah* 22, 81.

10   Augustine's portrait of his wild years may be compared with the savage contemporary portrait of the riff-raff of Rome about 380 by the pagan historian Ammianus Marcellinus, who speaks of people spending their entire lives on alcohol, gambling brothels, and public shows (28. 4. 28).

load of pears. But they were not for our feasts but merely to throw to the pigs. Even if we ate a few, nevertheless our pleasure lay in doing what was not allowed.

Such was my heart, O God, such was my heart. You had pity on it when it was at the bottom of the abyss. Now let my heart tell you what it was seeking there in that I became evil for no reason.[11] I had no motive for my wickedness except wickedness itself. It was foul, and I loved it. I loved the self-destruction, I loved my fall, not the object for which I had fallen but my fall itself. My depraved soul leaped down from your firmament to ruin.[12] I was seeking not to gain anything by shameful means, but shame for its own sake.

v (10)   There is beauty in lovely physical objects, as in gold and silver and all other such things. When the body touches such things, much significance attaches to the rapport of the object with the touch. Each of the other senses has its own appropriate mode of response to physical things. Temporal honour and the power of giving orders and of being in command have their own kind of dignity, though this is also the origin of the urge to self-assertion. Yet in the acquisition of all these sources of social status, one must not depart from you, Lord, nor deviate from your law. The life which we live in this world has its attractiveness because of a certain measure in its beauty and its harmony with all these inferior objects that are beautiful. Human friendship is also a nest of love and gentleness because of the unity it brings about between many souls. Yet sin is committed for the sake of all these things and others of this kind when, in consequence of an immoderate urge towards those things which are at the bottom end of the scale of good,[13] we abandon the higher and supreme goods, that is you, Lord God, and your truth and your law (Ps. 118: 142). These inferior goods have their delights, but not comparable to my God who has made them all. It is in him that the just person takes delight; he is the joy of those who are true of heart (Ps. 63: 11).

(11)   When a crime is under investigation to discover the motive for which it was done, the accusation is not usually believed except in cases where the appetite to obtain (or the fear of losing) one of those goods which we have called inferior appears a plausible possibility. They are beautiful and attractive even if, in comparison with the higher goods which give true happiness, they are mean and base. A man committed murder. Why? Because he loved another's wife or his property; or he wanted to acquire money to live on by plundering his goods; or he was afraid of losing his own property by the action of his victim; or he had suffered injury and burned with desire for revenge. No one would commit murder without a motive, merely because he took pleasure in killing. Who would believe that? It was said of one brutal and cruel man [Catiline] that he was

---

11   Echo of Sallust's language about Catiline. Augustine presents himself as a new Catiline.

12   Like Lucifer.

13   Throughout his writings Augustine holds to a doctrine of gradations of goodness. The good of the body is inferior to that of the soul; the will, in itself midway, may turn to higher or to lower things, and may err by preferring inferior goods to superior.

evil and savage without reason.[14] Yet the preceding passage gave the motive: 'lest disuse might make his hand or mind slow to react'. Why did he wish for that? Why so? His objective was to capture the city by violent crimes to obtain honours, government, and wealth; to live without fear of the laws and without the difficulty of attaining his ambitions because of the poverty of his family estate and his known criminal record. No, not even Catiline himself loved his crimes; something else motivated him to commit them.

vi (12)   Wretch that I was, what did I love in you, my act of theft, that crime which I did at night in the sixteenth year of my life? There was nothing beautiful about you, my thieving. Indeed do you exist at all for me to be addressing you?

The fruit which we stole was beautiful because it was your creation, most beautiful of all Beings, maker of all things, the good God, God the highest good and my true good. The fruit was beautiful, but was not that which my miserable soul coveted. I had a quantity of better pears. But those I picked solely with the motive of stealing. I threw away what I had picked. My feasting was only on the wickedness which I took pleasure in enjoying. If any of those pears entered my mouth, my criminality was the piquant sauce. And now, Lord my God, I inquire what was the nature of my pleasure in the theft. The act has nothing lovely about it, none of the loveliness found in equity and prudence, or in the human mind whether in the memory or in the senses or in physical vitality. Nor was it beautiful in the way the stars are, noble in their courses, or earth and sea full of newborn creatures which, as they are born, take the place of those which die;[15] not even in the way that specious vices have a flawed reflection of beauty.

(13)   Pride imitates what is lofty; but you alone are God most high above all things. What does ambition seek but honour and glory? Yet you alone are worthy of honour and are glorious for eternity. The cruelty of powerful people aims to arouse fear. Who is to be feared but God alone? What can be seized or stolen from his power? When or where or how or by whom? Soft endearments are intended to arouse love. But there are no caresses tenderer than your charity, and no object of love is more healthy than your truth, beautiful and luminous beyond all things. Curiosity appears to be a zeal for knowledge; yet you supremely know all. Ignorance and stupidity are given the names of simplicity and innocence; but there is no greater simplicity than in you. And what greater innocence than yours, whereas to evil men their own works are damaging? Idleness appears as desire for a quiet life; yet can rest be assured apart from the Lord? Luxury wants to be called abundance and satiety; but you are fullness and the inexhaustible treasure of incorruptible pleasure. Prodigality presents itself under the shadow of generosity; but you are the rich bestower of all good things. Avarice wishes to have large possessions; you possess everything. Envy contends about excellence; but what is more excellent than you? Anger seeks revenge; who avenges with greater justice than you? Fear quails before

---

14   Sallust, *Catiline* 16 (also cited by Augustine, *Sermon on Ps. 108*, 3).

15   Augustine regarded the cycle of birth and death as 'beautiful'; i.e. death is evil to the individual, not to the race.

sudden and unexpected events attacking things which are loved, and takes precautions for their safety; to you is anything unexpected or sudden? Or who can take away from you what you love? There is no reliable security except with you. Regret wastes away for the loss of things which cupidity delighted in. Its wish would be that nothing be taken away, just as nothing can be taken from you.

(14)   So the soul fornicates (Ps. 72: 27) when it is turned away from you and seeks outside you the pure and clear intentions which are not to be found except by return- ing to you. In their perverted way all humanity imitates you. Yet they put themselves at a distance from you and exalt themselves against you. But even by thus imitating you they acknowledge that you are the creator of all nature and so concede that there is no place where one can entirely escape from you. Therefore in that act of theft what was the object of my love, and in what way did I viciously and perversely imitate my Lord? Was my pleasure to break your law, but by deceit since I had not the power to do that by force? Was I acting like a prisoner with restricted liberty who does without punishment what is not permitted, thereby making an assertion of possessing a dim resemblance to omnipotence? Here is a runaway slave fleeing his master and pursuing a shadow (Job 7: 2). What rottenness! What a monstrous life and what an abyss of death! Was it possible to take pleasure in what was illicit for no reason other than that it was not allowed?

vii (15)   'What shall I render to the Lord?' (Ps. 115: 2) who recalls these things to my memory, but my soul feels no fear from the recollection. I will love you, Lord, and I will give thanks and confession to your name because you have forgiven me such great evils and my nefarious deeds. I attribute to your grace and mercy that you have melted my sins away like ice (Ecclus. 3: 17). I also attribute to your grace whatever evil acts I have not done. What could I not have done when I loved gratuitous crime? I confess that everything has been forgiven, both the evil things I did of my own accord, and those which I did not do because of your guidance.

No one who considers his frailty would dare to attribute to his own strength his chastity and innocence, so that he has less cause to love you—as if he had less need of your mercy by which you forgive the sins of those converted to you. If man is called by you, follows your voice, and has avoided doing those acts which I am recalling and avowing in my own life, he should not mock the healing of a sick man by the Physician, whose help has kept him from falling sick, or at least enabled him to be less gravely ill. He should love you no less, indeed even more; for he sees that the one who delivered me from the great sicknesses of my sins is also he through whom he may see that he himself has not been a victim of the same great sicknesses.

viii (16)   'What fruit had I', wretched boy, in these things (Rom. 6: 21) which I now blush to recall, above all in that theft in which I loved nothing but the theft itself? The theft itself was a nothing, and for that reason I was the more miserable. Yet had I been alone I would not have done it—I remember my state of mind to be thus at the time—alone I would never have done it. Therefore my love in that act was to be associated with the gang in whose company I did it. Does it follow that I loved something other than the theft? No, nothing else in reality because association with the gang is also a nothing. What is it in reality? Who can teach me that, but he who 'illuminates my heart' (Ecclus. 2: 10) and disperses the shadows in it? What else has stirred my mind to ask and discuss and consider this question? If I had liked the pears which I stole and actually desired to enjoy them, I could by myself have committed that wicked act, had it been enough to attain the pleasure which I sought. I would not have needed to inflame the itch of my cupidity through the excitement generated by sharing the guilt with others. But my pleasure was not in the pears; it was in the crime itself, done in association with a sinful group.

ix (17)   What was my state of mind? It is quite certain that it was utterly shameful and a disgrace to me that I had it. Yet what was it? 'Who understands his sins?' (Job 10: 15). It was all done for a giggle, as if our hearts were tickled to think we were deceiving those who would not think us capable of such behaviour and would have profoundly disapproved. Why then did I derive pleasure from an act I would not have done on my own? Is it that nobody can easily laugh when alone? Certainly no one readily laughs when alone; yet sometimes laughter overcomes individuals when no one else is present if their senses or their mind perceive something utterly absurd. But alone I would not have done it, could not conceivably have done it by myself. See, before you, my God, the living memory of my soul. Alone I would not have committed that crime, in which my pleasure lay not in what I was stealing but in the act of theft. But had I been alone, it would have given me absolutely no pleasure, nor would I have committed it. Friendship can be a dangerous enemy, a seduction of the mind lying beyond the reach of investigation.[16] Out of a game and a jest came an avid desire to do injury and an appetite to inflict loss on someone else without any motive on my part of personal gain, and no pleasure in settling a score. As soon as the words are spoken 'Let us go and do it', one is ashamed not to be shameless.

x (18)   Who can untie this extremely twisted and tangled knot? It is a foul affair, I have no wish to give attention to it; I have no desire to contemplate it. My desire is for you, justice and innocence, you are lovely and splendid to honest eyes; the satiety of your love is insatiable. With you is utter peace and a life immune from disturbance. The person who enters into you 'enters into the joy of the Lord' (Matt. 25: 21), and will not be afraid; he will find himself in the supreme Good where it is supremely good to be. As an adolescent I went astray from you (Ps. 118: 76), my God, far from your unmoved stability. I became to myself a region of destitution.[17]

---

16   Similarly IX. ii. (2).

17   The Prodigal Son is fused with a Neoplatonic theme of the soul's destitution without God, which is taken up at the beginning of book III and again in VII. x (16). Destitution in the soul distant from God is a theme in Porphyry (*De abstinentia* 3. 27 and *Sententiae* 40), based on Plato's *Symposium*.

Book III

Student at Carthage

i (I)   I came to Carthage and all around me hissed a cauldron of illicit loves. As yet I had never been in love and I longed to love; and from a subconscious poverty of mind I hated the thought of being less inwardly destitute. I sought an object for my love; I was in love with love, and I hated safety and a path free of snares (Wisd. 14: 11; Ps. 90: 3). My hunger was internal, deprived of inward food, that is of you yourself, my God. But that was not the kind of hunger I felt. I was without any desire for incorruptible nourishment, not because I was replete with it, but the emptier I was, the more unappetizing such food became. So my soul was in rotten health. In an ulcerous condition it thrust itself to outward things, miserably avid to be scratched by contact with the world of the senses. Yet physical things had no soul. Love lay outside their range. To me it was sweet to love and to be loved, the more so if I could also enjoy the body of the beloved. I therefore polluted the spring water of friendship with the filth of concupiscence. I muddied its clear stream by the hell of lust, and yet, though foul and immoral, in my excessive vanity, I used to carry on in the manner of an elegant man about town. I rushed headlong into love, by which I was longing to be captured. 'My God, my mercy' (Ps. 58: 18) in your goodness you mixed in much vinegar with that sweetness. My love was returned and in secret I attained the joy that enchains. I was glad to be in bondage, tied with troublesome chains, with the result that I was flogged with the red-hot iron rods of jealousy, suspicion, fear, anger, and contention.[1]

ii (2)   I was captivated by theatrical shows. They were full of representations of my own miseries and fuelled my fire. Why is it that a person should wish to experience suffering by watching grievous and tragic events which he himself would not wish to endure? Nevertheless he wants to suffer the pain given by being a spectator of these sufferings, and the pain itself is his pleasure. What is this but amazing folly? For the more anyone is moved by these scenes, the less free he is from similar passions. Only, when he himself suffers, it is called misery; when he feels compassion for others, it is called mercy.[2] But what quality of mercy is it in fictitious and theatrical inventions? A member of the audience is not excited to offer help, but invited only to grieve. The greater his pain, the greater his approval of the actor in these representations. If the human calamities, whether in ancient histories or fictitious myths, are so presented that the theatregoer is not caused pain, he walks out of the theatre disgusted and highly critical. But if he feels pain, he stays riveted in his seat enjoying himself.[3]

---

1   Beating with red-hot rods was part of the standard arsenal of the torturer, normally employed in Roman lawcourts on naked bodies in criminal cases to secure evidence, especially from slaves.

2   Echo of Cicero, *Pro Ligorio* 38.

3   This passage is the most extended ancient discussion of tragic pity and catharsis, a theme famous since Aristotle, whose texts on this theme were not read by Augustine and his contemporaries. Augustine is closer to Plato, *Republic* 10 606–7, and *Philebus* 48ab. As bishop, Augustine knew many of his people liked going to the theatre, and deplored it (*De catechizandis rudibus* 11 and 48) largely because of the frequently erotic content of the shows, but also because of the fictional character of the plays, fiction being, to his mind, a form of mendacity.

(3)   Tears and agonies, therefore, are objects of love. Certainly everyone wishes to enjoy himself. Is it that while no one wants to be miserable, yet it is agreeable to feel merciful? Mercy cannot exist apart from suffering. Is that the sole reason why agonies are an object of love? This feeling flows from the stream of friendship;[4] but where does it go? Where does it flow to? Why does it run down into the torrent of boiling pitch, the monstrous heats of black desires into which it is transformed? From a heavenly serenity it is altered by its own consent into something twisted and distorted. Does this mean mercy is to be rejected? Not in the least. At times, therefore, sufferings can be proper objects of love. But, my soul, be on your guard against uncleanness, under the protection of my God, 'the God of our fathers, to be praised and exalted above all for all ages' (Dan. 3: 52–5); be on your guard against uncleanness. Even today I am not unmoved to pity. But at that time at the theatres I shared the joy of lovers when they wickedly found delight in each other, even though their actions in the spectacle on the stage were imaginary; when, moreover, they lost each other, I shared their sadness by a feeling of compassion. Nevertheless, in both there was pleasure. Today I have more pity for a person who rejoices in wickedness than for a person who has the feeling of having suffered hard knocks by being deprived of a pernicious pleasure or having lost a source of miserable felicity. This is surely a more authentic compassion; for the sorrow contains no element of pleasure.

Even if we approve of a person who, from a sense of duty in charity, is sorry for a wretch, yet he who manifests fraternal compassion would prefer that there be no cause for sorrow. It is only if there could be a malicious good will (which is impossible) that someone who truly and sincerely felt compassion would wish wretches to exist so as to be objects of compassion. Therefore some kind of suffering is commendable, but none is lovable. You, Lord God, lover of souls, show a compassion far purer and freer of mixed motives than ours; for no suffering injures you. 'And who is sufficient for these things?' (2 Cor. 2: 16).

(4)   But at that time, poor thing that I was, I loved to suffer and sought out occasions for such suffering. So when an actor on stage gave a fictional imitation of someone else's misfortunes, I was the more pleased; and the more vehement the attraction for me, the more the actor compelled my tears to flow. There can be no surprise that an unhappy sheep wandering from your flock[5] and impatient of your protection was infected by a disgusting sore. Hence came my love for sufferings, but not of a kind that pierced me very deeply; for my longing was not to experience myself miseries such as I saw on stage. I wanted only to hear stories and imaginary legends of sufferings which, as it were, scratched me on the surface. Yet like the scratches of fingernails, they produced inflamed spots, pus, and repulsive sores. That was my kind of life. Surely, my God, it was no real life at all?

---

4   On tension between sex and friendship cf. IV. ix (14).
5   Reminiscence of Virgil, *Eclogue* 3. 3; cf. Luke 15: 4 ff.

iii (5)   Your mercy faithfully hovered over me from afar. In what iniquities was I wasting myself! I pursued a sacrilegious quest for knowledge, which led me, a deserter from you, down to faithless depths and the fraudulent service of devils. The sacrifices I offered them were my evil acts. And in all this I experienced your chastisement. During the celebration of your solemn rites within the walls of your Church, I even dared to lust after a girl and to start an affair that would procure the fruit of death.[6] So you beat me with heavy punishments, but not the equivalent of my guilt; O my God, my great mercy, my refuge (Ps. 58: 18, 143: 2) from the terrible dangers in which I was wandering. My stiff neck took me further and further away from you. I loved my own ways, not yours. The liberty I loved was merely that of a runaway.[7]

(6)   My studies which were deemed respectable had the objective of leading me to distinction as an advocate in the lawcourts,[8] where one's reputation is high in proportion to one's success in deceiving people. The blindness of humanity is so great that people are actually proud of their blindness. I was already top of the class in the rhetor's school, and was pleased with myself for my success and was inflated with conceit. Yet I was far quieter than the other students[9] (as you know, Lord), and had nothing whatever to do with the vandalism which used to be carried out by the Wreckers. This sinister and diabolical self-designation was a kind of mark of their urbane sophistication. I lived among them shamelessly ashamed of not being one of the gang. I kept company with them and sometimes delighted in their friendship, though I always held their actions in abhorrence. The Wreckers used wantonly to persecute shy and unknown freshmen. Their aim was to persecute them by mockery and so to feed their own malevolent amusement. Nothing more resembles the behaviour of devils than their manner of carrying on. So no truer name could be given them than the Wreckers. Clearly they are themselves wrecked first of all and perverted by evil spirits, who are mocking them and seducing them in the very acts by which they love to mock and deceive others.

iv (7)   This was the society in which at a vulnerable age I was to study the textbooks on eloquence. I wanted to distinguish myself as an orator for a damnable and conceited purpose, namely delight in human vanity. Following the usual curriculum I had already come across a book by a certain Cicero,[10] whose language (but not his heart) almost everyone admires. That book of his contains an exhortation to study philosophy and

---

6   That is, sin: Rom. 7: 5.

7   Runaway slaves in antiquity were rigorously pursued. Churches provided temporary asylum in cases where inhuman maltreatment was the cause of flight. But to take in a runaway was possible only for the rich and powerful. The liberty enjoyed, therefore, was that of an escaped prisoner, hunted by the authorities.

8   Echo of Ovid, *Fasti* 4. 188.

9   A contemporary student later recalled the young Augustine as being a quiet and bookish man (*ep.* 93. 51).

10   'A certain Cicero' might seem cold and distant were it not that the same idiom is used for the apostle Paul in XII. xv (20); i.e. it is a rhetorical convention of the time. The antithesis between Cicero's style and his heart (*pectus*) is genuinely negative: to a Christian, Cicero belonged to another culture.

is entitled *Hortensius*.[11] The book changed my feelings. It altered my prayers, Lord, to be towards you yourself. It gave me different values and priorities. Suddenly every vain hope became empty to me, and I longed for the immortality of wisdom with an incredible ardour in my heart. I began to rise up to return to you. For I did not read the book for a sharpening of my style, which was what I was buying with my mother's financial support now that I was 18 years old and my father had been dead for two years. I was impressed not by the book's refining effect on my style and literary expression but by the content.[12]

(8)   My God, how I burned, how I burned with longing to leave earthly things and fly back to you. I did not know what you were doing with me. For 'with you is wisdom' (Job 12: 13, 16). 'Love of wisdom' is the meaning of the Greek word *philosophia*.[13] This book kindled my love for it. There are some people who use philosophy to lead people astray. They lend colour to their errors and paint them over by using a great and acceptable and honourable name. Almost all those who in the author's times and earlier behaved in this way are noted in that book and refuted. That text is a clear demonstration of the salutary admonition given by your Spirit through your good and devoted servant (Paul): 'See that none deceives you by philosophy and vain seduction following human tradition; following the elements of this world and not following Christ; in him dwells all the fullness of divinity in bodily form' (Col. 2: 8–9). At that time, as you know, light of my heart, I did not yet know these words of the apostle. Nevertheless, the one thing that delighted me in Cicero's exhortation was the advice 'not to study one particular sect but to love and seek and pursue and hold fast and strongly embrace wisdom itself, wherever found'. One thing alone put a brake on my intense enthusiasm—that the name of Christ was not contained in the book. This name, by your mercy Lord (Ps. 24: 7), this name of my Saviour your Son, my infant heart had piously drunk in with my mother's milk, and at a deep level I retained the memory. Any book which lacked this name, however well written or polished or true, could not entirely grip me.

v (9)   I therefore decided to give attention to the holy scriptures and to find out what they were like. And this is what met me: something neither open to the proud nor laid bare to mere children; a text lowly to the beginner but, on further reading, of mountainous difficulty and enveloped in mysteries. I was not in any state to be able to enter into that, or to bow my head to climb its steps. What I am now saying did not then enter my

---

11   Cicero's *Hortensius*, composed in 45 BC near the end of his life, is lost except for quotations (many in Augustine). The work rebutted Hortensius' opinion that philosophical study has no social utility and does not contribute to human happiness. Cicero depended much on Aristotle's *Protreptikos* (also extant only in fragments), notably for the argument that only a philosopher can judge the truth of Hortensius' opinion, which is itself a philosophical statement. As book X of *Confessions* shows, Augustine was influenced by Cicero's analysis of the sources of happiness.

12   Among Augustine's sharp criticisms of contemporary culture of his time is the proposition that it valued form far higher than content.

13   This sentence comes from Cicero's *Hortensius*.

mind when I gave my attention to the scripture. It seemed to me unworthy in comparison with the dignity of Cicero.[14] My inflated conceit shunned the Bible's restraint, and my gaze never penetrated to its inwardness. Yet the Bible was composed in such a way that as beginners mature, its meaning grows with them. I disdained to be a little beginner. Puffed up with pride, I considered myself a mature adult.

vi (10)   That explains why I fell in with men proud of their slick talk, very earthly-minded and loquacious. In their mouths were the devil's traps and a birdlime compounded of a mixture of the syllables of your name, and that of the Lord Jesus Christ, and that of the Paraclete, the Comforter, the Holy Spirit.[15] These names were never absent from their lips; but it was no more than sound and noise with their tongue. Otherwise their heart was empty of truth. They used to say 'Truth, truth', and they had a lot to tell me about it; but there was never any truth in them. They uttered false statements not only about you who really are the Truth, but also about the elements of the world, your creation. On that subject the philosophers have said things which are true, but even them I would think to be no final authority for love of you, my supremely good Father, beauty of all things beautiful. Truth, truth: how in my inmost being the very marrow of my mind sighed for you! Those people used to sound off about you to me frequently and repeatedly with mere assertions and with the support of many huge tomes.[16] To meet my hunger, instead of you they brought me a diet of the sun and moon, your beautiful works—but they are your works, not you yourself, nor indeed the first of your works. For priority goes to your spiritual creation rather than the physical order, however heavenly and full of light.[17] But for myself, my hunger and thirst were not even for the spiritual creation but for you yourself, the truth 'in whom there is no changing nor shadow caused by any revolving' (Jas. 1: 17). The dishes they placed before me contained splendid hallucinations. Indeed one would do better to love this visible sun, which at least is truly evident to the eyes, than those false mythologies which use the eyes to deceive the mind. Nevertheless, because I took them to be you, I ate—not indeed with much of an appetite, for the taste in my mouth was not that of yourself. You were not those empty fictions, and I derived no nourishment from them but was left more exhausted than before.

---

14   The humble style of the Bible, together with a concern for maintaining the family property, is mentioned by Augustine as a major deterrent to conversion for the educated and well-to-do classes (*De catechizandis rudibus* 13). The second-century Old Latin (i.e. pre-Jerome) version was painfully close to translationese for large parts of the Old Testament. On the other hand, the sublimity of Genesis I and the prologue of St John's Gospel moved some non-Christian readers to deep admiration.

15   The Manichees claimed to be authentic Christians, orthodox church members having in their view only half the truth, and taught a version of the doctrine of the Trinity, a Christology which excluded the reality of the humanity of Christ but spoke of Jesus as redeemer, and a doctrine that the Paraclete is the other self of Mani.

16   Manichees had exquisitely decorated liturgical books, finely bound, as orthodox Churches outside great cities, had not. Sun and moon they venerated as divine, or at least as residences for divine beings in transit in the celestial realm.

17   That God first created a spiritual creation called 'heaven' in Gen. 1: 1, and unformed matter called 'earth' which was then given form, is a theme of book XII and of the contemporary *De Genesi contra Manichaeos* 1. 7. 11.

Food pictured in dreams[18] is extremely like food received in the waking state; yet sleepers receive no nourishment, they are simply sleeping. But those fantasies had not the least resemblance to you as you have now told me, because they were physical images, fictional bodily shapes. But more certain objects of knowledge are the actually existing bodies which we see with our physical sight, whether they are celestial or earthly. We see them just as beasts and birds do, and they are more certain than the images we form of them. And yet again the pictures of these realities which our imagination forms are more reliable than the mythological pictures of vast and unlimited entities whose being, by an extension of our image-making of real objects, we may postulate, but which do not exist at all. Such were the empty phantoms with which I was fed or rather was not fed.

But you, my love, for whom I faint that I may receive strength (2 Cor. 11: 10), you are not the bodies which we see, though they be up in heaven, nor even any object up there lying beyond our sight. For you have made these bodies, and you do not even hold them to be among the greatest of your creatures. How far removed you are from those fantasies of mine, fantasies of physical entities which have no existence! We have more reliable knowledge in our images of bodies which really exist, and the bodies are more certain than the images. But you are no body. Nor are you soul, which is the life of bodies; for the life of bodies is superior to bodies themselves, and a more certain object of knowledge.[19] But you are the life of souls, the life of lives. You live in dependence only on yourself, and you never change, life of my soul.

(11)   At that time where were you in relation to me? Far distant. Indeed I wandered far away, separated from you, not even granted to share in the husks of the pigs, whom I was feeding with husks.[20] How superior are the fables of the masters of literature and poets to these deceptive traps! For verses, poems, and 'the flight of Medea'[21] are certainly more useful than the Five Elements which take on different colours, each in accordance with one of the Five Caverns of Darkness[22]—things which have no reality whatever and kill anyone who believes they have. Verses and poetry I can transform into real nourishment. 'Medea flying through the air' I might recite, but would not assert to be fact. Even if I heard someone reciting the passage, I would not believe it. Yet the other [Manichee]

---

18   Dreams were a lifelong interest for Augustine; see X. xxx (41) below. The vividness of dreams, indistinguishable from actuality, he regarded as deceptive. On the other hand, he knew of many converted to God through dreams, or guided in decisions. The subject was associated with the ancient discussions of the nature of inspiration.

19   It is axiomatic for Augustine that what the mind knows by discernment of eternal, metaphysical truth is more certain than its judgement of the perceptions of the five senses, which are unreliable.

20   The husks of Luke 15: 16 are for Jerome (*ep.* 21. 13.4) pagan literature. Apparently Augustine had become bored by the texts he had to teach his pupils (the pigs!).

21   Medea's flight (cf. Ovid, *Metamorphoses* 7. 219–36), also mentioned elsewhere in Augustine's early writings (*Solil.* 2. 29; *ep.* 7. 4; *De moribus ecclesiae* 2. 14), was probably a standard subject for rhetorical exercises.

22   In Manichee myth the Five Elements dwell in caverns of darkness, water, wind, fire, and smoke, productive respectively of reptiles, fish, birds, quadrupeds, and bipeds (Augustine, *De moribus* 2. .9. 14; Simplicius, *Commentary on Epictetus* 34).

myths I did believe. Wretched man that I was, by what steps was I brought down to the depths of hell, there to toil and sweat from lack of truth! For I sought for you, my God (I confess to you who took pity on me even when I did not yet confess). In seeking for you I followed not the intelligence of the mind, by which you willed that I should surpass the beasts, but the mind of the flesh. But you were more inward than my most inward part and higher than the highest element within me.

I had stumbled on that bold-faced woman, lacking in prudence, who in Solomon's allegory sits on a chair outside her door and says 'Enjoy a meal of secret bread and drink sweet stolen water' (Prov. 9: 17). She seduced me; for she found me living outside myself, seeing only with the eye of the flesh, and chewing over in myself such food as I had devoured by means of that eye.

vii (12)   I was unaware of the existence of another reality, that which truly is,[23] and it was as if some sharp intelligence were persuading me to consent to the stupid deceivers when they asked me: 'Where does evil come from? and is God confined within a corporeal form? has he hair and nails? and can those be considered righteous who had several wives at the same time and killed people and offered animals in sacrifice?'[24] In my ignorance I was disturbed by these questions, and while travelling away from the truth I thought I was going towards it. I did not know that evil has no existence except as a privation of good, down to that level which is altogether without being. How could I see this when for me 'to see' meant a physical act of looking with the eyes and of forming an image in the mind? I had not realized God is a Spirit (John 4: 24), not a figure whose limbs have length and breadth and who has a mass. For mass is less in a part than in its whole, and if it is unlimited, it is less in a part defined within a given space than in its unlimited extension.[25] It is not everywhere entire as a Spirit and as God. Moreover, I was wholly ignorant of what it is in ourselves which gives us being, and how scripture is correct in saying that we are 'in God's image' (Gen. 1: 27).

(13)   I also did not know that true inward justice which judges not by custom but by the most righteous law of almighty God. By this law the moral customs of different regions and periods were adapted to their places and times, while that law itself remains unaltered everywhere and always.[26] It is not one thing at one place or time, another thing at another. Accordingly Abraham and Isaac and Jacob and Moses and David, and

---

23   The Platonic notion of degrees of being-and-goodness, a hierarchy in which every existent is good in its own order, made possible the relativization of evil central to Plato's vindication of divine power and goodness. Cf. II. v. (10) above.

24   Manichees strongly attacked the book of Genesis (that 'man is made in God's image' assumes God to have human physical characteristics?), the polygamy of the patriarchs, and the character of Moses for his murder of the Egyptian (Exod. 2: 12). They thought the Old Testament animal sacrifices indistinguishable from paganism.

25   Plotinus (6; 4–5) has two intricate tracts arguing (in commentary on Plato, *Parmenides* 131B) that omnipresence is a distinct concept from that of a universal physical diffusion of something with material magnitude. Augustine's language here (and in VII. i. (I)) is close to Plotinus 6. 5. 4. 5 ff.

26   The argument here about the relativity of positive laws is akin to that in Cicero's *Republic* III xi, 18–19; xxii, 33.

all those praised by the mouth of God were righteous. When untrained minds judge them wicked, they judge 'by man's day' (1 Cor. 4: 3) and assess the customs of the entire race by the criterion of their own moral code. It is as if a man, ignorant of which piece of armour is designed for which part of the body, should want to cover the head with a greave or put on his leg a helmet, and then complain that it is not a good fit. Or it is as if on a public holiday when trading is prohibited after noon, someone is furious not to be allowed to sell in the afternoon something which he was at liberty to sell in the morning. Or as if in a house one sees something being touched with the hands by a particular slave, which the waiter who serves the wine cups is not allowed to do; or as if something is allowed to happen behind the stables which is not permitted in the dining-room, and a man is indignant on the ground that, though it is one house and one family, the same liberties are not given to all members to do what they please anywhere they like.

This is the style of those who are irate when they hear that something was allowed to the just in that age which is not granted to the just now, and that God gave one command to the former and another to the latter for reasons of a change in historical circumstances, though both ancient and modern people are bound to submit to the same justice. Yet in one and the same person on a single day and in the same house they may see one action fitting for one member to perform, another action fitting for another. What has been allowed during a long period is not permitted one hour later. An act allowed or commanded in one corner is forbidden and subject to punishment if done in an adjacent corner. Does that mean that justice is 'liable to variation and change'?[27] No. The times which it rules over are not identical, for the simple reason that they are times. But the grasp of human beings, 'whose life on earth is short' (Wisd. 15: 9), is not competent to harmonize cause and effect valid in earlier ages and among other nations of which they have no experience, in relation to the times and peoples of whom they have direct knowledge. Yet they can easily observe in a single body or at one time or in one house what is fitting for one member, at what moments, and for which parts or persons. By the one variation they are outraged, with the other they see no difficulty.

(14)   At that time I did not know these things or give any thought to them. On all sides they hit me in the eye, and I failed to see them. When I wrote poetry,[28] I was not allowed to place a foot where I wished, but had to use different kinds of feet at different points in different metres. Even in the same verse one could not put the same foot in any and every place. The art of poetic composition did not have different rules in different places, but had all the same rules at all times. I had not the insight to see how the justice, to which good and holy people were obliged to submit, embraces within its principles all

27   Echo of Virgil, *Aeneid* 4. 569 (of woman).

28   Augustine was soon to win a public poetry competition (IV. iii (5)). The first five books of his work *On Music* are devoted to metre. The only surviving verse from his pen is three lines of an evening hymn sung at the lighting of the candle (*City of God* 15. 22).

that it prescribes for all times in a far more excellent and sublime way, and, although it is in no respect subject to variation, yet it is not given all at once, but at various times it prescribed in differing contexts what is proper for the circumstances.[29] In my blindness I reprehended the holy fathers not only for acting at the time as God commanded and inspired them, but also for predicting the future as God revealed it to them.[30]

29   Augustine's ethic regards the Golden Rule as absolute, its application being relative to the situation and to the motive or intention of the doer. The criterion of every moral precept is love (*Enchiridion* 121). Nakedness is right in the baths, wrong at a dinner-party or lawcourt (*De natura boni* 23; *De doctrina christiana* 3. 12. 18). Nevertheless, no circumstances or intentions could make unnatural sexual acts acceptable. (Rom. 1: 24–8).

30   The Manichees entirely rejected the orthodox belief that the Hebrew prophets predicted gospel events and the mission of the Church. Augustine answered at length in *Contra Faustum* 12–13, written at the same time as the *Confessions*.

Book IV

Manichee and Astrologer

i (1)   During this same period of nine years, from my nineteenth to my twenty-eighth year, our life was one of being seduced and seducing, being deceived and deceiving (2 Tim. 3: 13), in a variety of desires. Publicly I was a teacher of the arts which they call liberal;[1] privately I professed a false religion—in the former role arrogant, in the latter superstitious, in everything vain. On the one side we pursued the empty glory of popularity, ambitious for the applause of the audience at the theatre when entering for verse competitions to win a garland of mere grass, concerned with the follies of public entertainments and unrestrained lusts. On the other side, we sought to purge ourselves of that filth by supplying food to those whose title was the Elect and Holy, so that in the workshop of their stomach they could manufacture for us angels and gods to bring us liberation.[2] This was how my life was spent, and these were the activities of myself and my friends who had been deceived through me and with me.

Proud people may laugh at me. As yet they have not themselves been prostrated and brought low for their soul's health by you, my God. But I shall nevertheless confess to you my shame, since it is for your praise (Ps. 105: 47). Allow me, I pray you, grant me leave to run through my memory, as it is in the present, of the past twistings of my mistaken life and to sacrifice to you 'a victim of jubilation' (Ps. 26: 6). Without you, what am I to myself but a guide to my own self-destruction? When all is well with me, what am I but an infant sucking your milk and feeding on you, 'the food that is incorruptible' (John 6: 27)? What is a human being (name anyone you may please) when he is merely a man? So let the mighty and powerful laugh at our expense. In our weakness and indigence (Ps. 73: 21), we may make our confession to you.

ii (2)   In those years I used to teach the art of rhetoric. Overcome by greed myself, I used to sell the eloquence that would overcome an opponent. Nevertheless, Lord, as you know (Ps. 68: 6), I preferred to have virtuous students (virtuous as they are commonly called). Without any resort to a trick I taught them the tricks of rhetoric, not that they should use them against the life of an innocent man, but that sometimes they might save the life of a guilty person.[3] God, from far off you saw me falling about on slippery

---

1   Literature, rhetoric and dialectic, leading on to the mathematical studies of arithmetic, geometry, music, and astronomy; called 'liberal' because they were the mark of a cultivated gentleman.

2   In Manichee texts, every meal of the Elect is a holy feeding on particles of light concealed in fruits and plants, helping to gain remission of sins for those Hearers who prepare it. Above, III. x (18).

3   Augustine formulates the principle that an advocate should not throw dust in the eyes of the court, but is entitled to require that the prosecution prove their case, even when he may think his client guilty. He holds that it is worse for an innocent person to be condemned than for a guilty person to be acquitted. The theme is already in Cicero, *De officiis* 2. 51.

ground and in the midst of much smoke (Isa. 42: 3) discerned the spark of my integrity which in my teaching office I manifested to people who 'loved vanity and sought after a lie' (Ps. 4: 3).

In those years I had a woman. She was not my partner in what is called lawful marriage. I had found her in my state of wandering desire and lack of prudence. Nevertheless, she was the only girl for me, and I was faithful to her. With her I learnt by direct experience how wide a difference there is between the partnership of marriage entered into for the sake of having a family and the mutual consent of those whose love is a matter of physical sex, and for whom the birth of a child is contrary to their intention—even though, if offspring arrive, they compel their parents to love them.

(3)   I also recall how, when I had decided to enter for a poetry competition at the theatre, a soothsayer of some sort sent to ask what fee I would give him to ensure victory. But I replied that I hated and abominated those vile mysteries, and that even if the crown were immortal and made of gold, I would not allow a fly to be killed to bring about my success.[4] For in his mysteries he would be going to kill animals, and by offering these creatures in honour of daemons, his intention was to gain their support for my winning. Yet my rejection of this evil proposition was not motivated by respect for the purity which you enjoin, 'God of my heart' (Ps. 72: 26). I knew nothing about love for you, of whom I had no conception other than of physical objects luminous with light. In sighing after such fictions does not the soul 'commit fornication against you' (Ps. 72: 27) and 'trust in lies and feed the winds' (Prov. 10: 4)? I refused sacrifice to daemons on my behalf; yet by adherence to that superstition I sacrificed myself to them. What is it to 'feed the winds' if not to feed the spirits, that is, by one's errors to become an object of delight and derision to them?...

iv (7)   During those years when first I began to teach in the town where I was born, I had come to have a friend who because of our shared interests was very close. He was my age, and we shared the flowering of youth. As a boy he had grown up with me, and we had gone to school together and played with one another. He was then not yet my friend, and when he did become so, it was less than a true friendship which is not possible unless you bond together those who cleave to one another by the love which 'is poured into our hearts by the Holy Spirit who is given to us' (Rom. 5: 5). Nevertheless, it was a very sweet experience, welded by the fervor of our identical interests. For I had turned him away from the true faith, to which, being only young, he had no strong or profound allegiance, towards those superstitions and pernicious mythologies which were the reason for my mother's tears over me. So under my influence this man's mind

---

4   Manichees wholly rejected animal sacrifices, and regarded the Old Testament requirement of such sacrifices as one of the stronger arguments against its authority.

was wandering astray, and my soul could not endure to be without him. But you were present, immediately at the back of those who flee from you, at once both 'God of vengeances' (Ps. 93: I) and fount of mercies: you turn us to yourself in wonderful ways. You took the man from this life when our friendship had scarcely completed a year. It had been sweet to me beyond all the sweetnesses of life that I had experienced.

(8)   Who on his own can recount your praises for the experiences of his life alone (cf. Ps. 105: 2)? At that time what did you do, my God? 'How unsearchable is the abyss of your judgements' (Ps. 35: 7; Rom. 11: 33)! When he was sick with fever, for a long time he lay unconscious in a mortal sweat, and when his life was despaired of, he was baptized without his knowing it. To me this was a matter of no interest.[5] I assumed that his soul would retain what it had received from me, not what had happened to his body while he was unconscious. But it turned out quite differently. For he recovered and was restored to health, and at once, as soon as I could speak with him (and I was able to do so as soon as he could speak, since I never left his side, and we were deeply dependent on one another), I attempted to joke with him, imagining that he too would laugh with me about the baptism which he had received when far away in mind and sense. But he had already learnt that he had received the sacrament. He was horrified at me as if I were an enemy, and with amazing and immediate frankness advised me that, if I wished to be his friend, I must stop saying this kind of thing to him. I was dumbfounded and perturbed; but I deferred telling him of all my feelings until he should get better and recover his health and strength. Then I would be able to do what I wished with him. But he was snatched away from my lunacy, so that he might be preserved with you for my consolation. After a few days, while I was absent, the fever returned, and he died.

(9)   'Grief darkened my heart' (Lam. 5: 17). Everything on which I set my gaze was death. My home town became a torture to me; my father's house a strange world of unhappiness; all that I had shared with him was without him transformed into a cruel torment. My eyes looked for him everywhere, and he was not there. I hated everything because they did not have him, nor could they now tell me 'look, he is on the way', as used to be the case when he was alive and absent from me. I had become to myself a vast problem,[6] and I questioned my soul 'Why are you sad, and why are you very distressed?' But my soul did not know what reply to give. If I had said to my soul 'Put your trust in God' (Ps. 41: 6, 12), it would have had good reason not to obey. For the very dear friend I had lost was a better and more real person than the [Manichee] phantom in which I would have been telling my soul to trust. Only tears were sweet to me, and in my 'soul's delights' (Ps. 138: 11) weeping had replaced my friend.

---

5   Augustine's unnamed friend came of a Catholic family, evidently responsible for his baptism. To baptize an unconscious sick person (if a catechumen) was accepted in the North African Churches. Manichees rejected baptism as a superfluous and useless external act.

6   Repeated X. xxxiii (50).

v (10)   Now, Lord, all that belongs to the past, and with time my wound is less pain-ful.[7] Can I hear from you who are the truth, and move the ear of my heart close to your mouth, so that you can explain to me why weeping is a relief to us when unhappy? Or, although present everywhere, have you thrust our misery far from you and remain in yourself (Wisd. 7: 27) while we are tossed about by successive trials? Yet if our tearful entreaties did not reach your ears, no remnant of hope would remain for us. How does it come about that out of the bitterness of life sweet fruit is picked by groaning and weeping and sighing and mourning? Does the sweetness lie in the hope that you hear us? That is certainly the case in our prayers which express the longing to reach their object. But surely that is not true of sadness and grief for what has been lost, such as overwhelmed me at that time. I had no hope that he would come back to life, and my tears did not petition for this. I merely grieved and wept. I was in misery and had lost the source of my joy. Or is weeping really a bitter thing which gives relief only when we cannot bear to think of the things which formerly we enjoyed, and which is pleasurable at the moments when we shrink from the memory of them?

Book V

Carthage, Rome and Milan

viii (14)   You were at work in persuading me to go to Rome and to do my teaching there rather than at Carthage. The consideration which persuaded me I will not omit to confess to you because in this also your profoundly mysterious providence and your mercy very present to us are proper matters for reflection and proclamation. My motive in going to Rome was not that the friends who urged it on me promised higher fees and a greater position of dignity, though at that time these considerations had an influence on my mind. The principal and almost sole reason was that I had heard how at Rome the young men went quietly about their studies and were kept in order by a stricter imposition of discipline. They did not rush all at once and in a mob into the class of a teacher with whom they were not enrolled, nor were pupils admitted at all unless the teacher gave them leave. By contrast at Carthage the licence of the students is foul and uncontrolled. They impudently break in and with almost mad behaviour disrupt the order which each teacher has established for his pupils' benefit. They commit many acts of vandalism with an astonishing mindlessness, which would be punished under the law were it not that custom protects them. Thereby their wretched self-delusion is shown up. They act as if they were allowed to do what would never be permitted by your eternal law. They think they are free to act with impunity when by the very blindness of their behaviour they are being punished, and inflict on themselves incomparably worse

---

7   Echo of Ovid, *Remedium Amoris* 131.

damage than on others.[8] When I was a student, I refused to have anything to do with these customs; as a professor I was forced to tolerate them in outsiders who were not my own pupils. So I decided to go where all informed people declared that such troubles did not occur. But it was you, 'my hope and my portion in the land of the living' (Ps. 141: 6) who wished me to change my earthly home for 'the salvation of my soul' (Ps. 34: 3). You applied the pricks which made me tear myself away from Carthage, and you put before me the attractions of Rome to draw me there, using people who love a life of death, committing insane actions in this world, promising vain rewards in the next.[9] To correct my 'steps' (Ps. 36: 23; Prov. 20: 20) you secretly made use of their and my perversity. For those who disturbed my serenity were blinded with a disgraceful frenzy. Those who invited me to go elsewhere had a taste only for this earth. I myself, while I hated a true misery here, pursued a false felicity there.

(15) But you knew, God, why I left Carthage and went to Rome, and of that you gave no hint either to me or to my mother, who was fearfully upset at my going and followed me down to the sea. But as she vehemently held on to me calling me back or saying she would come with me, I deceived her. I pretended I had a friend I did not want to leave until the wind was right for him to sail. I lied to my mother—to such a mother—and I gave her the slip. Even this you forgave me, mercifully saving me from the waters of the sea, when I was full of abominable filth, so as to bring me to the water of your grace [in baptism]. This water was to wash me clean, and to dry the rivers flowing from my mother's eyes which daily before you irrigated the soil beneath her face.

Nevertheless since she refused to return home without me, with difficulty I persuaded her to stay that night in a place close to our ship, the memorial shrine to blessed Cyprian.[10] But that night I secretly set out; she did not come, but remained praying and weeping. By her floods of tears what was she begging of you, my God, but that you would not allow me to sail? Yet in your deep counsel you heard the central point of her longing, though not granting her what she then asked, namely that you would make me what she continually prayed for. The wind blew and filled our sails and the shore was lost to our sight. There, when morning came, she was crazed with grief, and with recriminations and groans she filled your ears. But you paid no heed to her cries. You were using my ambitious desires as a means towards putting an end to those desires, and the longing she felt for her own flesh and blood was justly chastised by the whip of sorrows. As mothers do, she loved to have me with her, but much more than most mothers; and she did not understand that you were to use my absence as a means of bringing

---

8   Plotinus (3. 2. 8. 26–31) similarly comments that ruffians and hoodlums do themselves much injury.

9   Augustine's appointment to Rome was facilitated by his Manichee connections.

10   Cyprian, bishop of Carthage martyred in 258, was for the African Churches their outstanding hero, the vigil of whose feast day (14 September) was marked by all-night dancing.

her joy. She did not know that. So she wept and lamented, and these agonies proved that there survived in her the remnants of Eve, seeking with groaning for the child she had brought forth in sorrow (Gen. 3: 16). And yet after accusing me of deception and cruelty, she turned again to pray for me and to go back to her usual home. Meanwhile I came to Rome.

ix (16)   At Rome my arrival was marked by the scourge of physical sickness, and I was on the way to the underworld, bearing all the evils I had committed against you, against myself, and against others—sins both numerous and serious, in addition to the chain of original sin[11] by which 'in Adam we die' (1 Cor. 15: 22). You had not yet forgiven me in Christ for any of them, nor had he by his cross delivered me from the hostile disposition towards you which I had contracted by my sins. How could he deliver me from them if his cross was, as I had believed, a phantom?[12] Insofar as the death of his flesh was in my opinion unreal, the death of my soul was real. And insofar as the death of his flesh was authentic, to that extent the life of my soul, which disbelieved that, was inauthentic. The fevers became worse, and I was on my way out and dying. If at that time I had died, where was I going but into the fire and to the torments which, by your true order of justice, my deeds deserved? My mother did not know I was ill, but she was praying for me, though not beside me. But you are present everywhere. Where she was, you heard her, and where I was, you had mercy on me so that I recovered the health of my body. I still remained sick in my sacrilegious heart, for though in such great danger, I had no desire for your baptism. I did better as a boy when I begged for it from my devout mother, as I have recalled and confessed.[13] But I had grown in shame and in my folly used to laugh at the counsels of your medicine: Yet you did not allow me to die in this sad condition of both body and soul. If my mother's heart had suffered that wound, she would never have recovered. I cannot speak enough of the love she had for me. She suffered greater pains in my spiritual pregnancy than when she bore me in the flesh.

(17)   I do not see how she could have recovered if my death in those circumstances had like a scourge struck across the compassion of her love. Where would have been all her prayers, so frequent as to be ceaseless? Nowhere except with you. But, God of mercies, would you despise the contrite and humble heart of a chaste and sober widow (cf. 1 Tim. 5: 10), liberal in almsgiving, obedient and helpful in serving your saints, letting no day pass without making an oblation at your altar, twice a day at morning and at evening coming to your Church with unfailing regularity, taking no part in vain gossip and old wives' chatter, but wanting to hear you in your words[14] and to speak

---

11   This is the earliest occurrence of this phrase to describe inherent human egotism, the inner condition contrasted with overt actions.

12   Manichees disbelieved the reality of the crucifixion, for them a symbol of universal human suffering.

13   II. xi (17).

14   i.e. through the Bible.

to you in her prayers? Could you, who gave her this character, despise and repel from your assistance tears by which she sought of you, not gold and silver nor any inconstant or transitory benefit, but the salvation of her son's soul? No indeed, Lord, of course you were there and were hearing her petition, and were following through the order of events that you had predestinated. You could not have misled her in those visions and your responses, both those which I have already mentioned, and those which I have omitted. At her faithful breast she held on to them, and in her unceasing prayer she as it were presented to you your bond of promises. For your mercy is for ever (Ps. 117: 1; 137: 8), and you deign to make yourself a debtor obliged by your promises to those to whom you forgive all debts.

x (18)   You healed my sickness, and at that time made 'the son of your maidservant' (Ps. 115: 16) whole in body as an interim step towards giving him a better and more certain health. Even during this period at Rome I was associated with those false and deceiving Saints—not only with their Hearers, one of whom was the man in whose house I had lain sick and recovered health, but also with those whom they call Elect. I still thought that it is not we who sin, but some alien nature which sins in us. It flattered my pride to be free of blame and, when I had done something wrong, not to make myself confess to you that you might heal my soul; for it was sinning against you (Ps. 40: 5). I liked to excuse myself and to accuse some unidentifiable power which was with me and yet not I. But the whole was myself and what divided me against myself was my impiety. That was a sin the more incurable for the fact that I did not think myself a sinner. My execrable wickedness preferred the disastrous doctrine that in me you, almighty God, suffer defeat rather than that, to be saved, I needed to surrender to you.

You had not yet 'put a guard on my mouth and a gate of continence about my lips' (Ps. 140: 2) to prevent my heart slipping into evil words to find excuses for sinning with 'people who do iniquity' (Ps. 140: 3). That is why I was still in close association 'with their Elect' (Ps. 140: 4), even though I had already lost hope of being able to advance higher in that false doctrine. I had decided to be content to remain with them if I should find nothing better; but my attitude was increasingly remiss and negligent.

(19)   The thought had come into my mind that the philosophers whom they call Academics were shrewder than others. They taught that everything is a matter of doubt, and that an understanding of the truth lies beyond human capacity. For to me that seemed clearly to be their view, and so they are popularly held to think. I did not yet understand their intention.[15]

I did not neglect to tell my host that he should not put the excessive trust, which I perceived him to have, in the fabulous matters of which Manichee books are full. But I was

---

15   Augustine (*Against the Academics* III) accepted from Porphyry the opinion that the scepticism of the ancient Academy about the possibility of assured knowledge about anything went with an esoteric positive doctrine. Their intention was to safeguard Plato's spiritual metaphysic from the materialism of Stoics and Epicureans.

in more intimate friendship with them than with others who were not in that heresy. I did not defend it with the zest that at one time I had. Nevertheless my close association with them (the number of them secretly living in Rome was large) made me reluctant to look elsewhere. In particular I had no hope that truth could be found in your Church, Lord of heaven and earth (Gen. 24: 3), maker of all things visible and invisible (Col. 1: 16). The Manichees had turned me away from that. I thought it shameful to believe you to have the shape of the human figure, and to be limited by the bodily lines of our limbs.[16] When I wanted to think of my God, I knew of no way of doing so except as a physical mass. Nor did I think anything existed which is not material. That was the principal and almost sole cause of my inevitable error.

(20)   For the same reason I also believed that evil is a kind of material substance with its own foul and misshapen mass, either solid which they used to call earth, or thin and subtle, as is the body of air. They imagine it to be a malignant mind creeping through the earth. And since piety (however bizarre some of my beliefs were) forbade me to believe that the good God had created an evil nature, I concluded that there are two opposed masses, both infinite, but the evil rather smaller, the good larger;[17] and of this pestilential beginning other blasphemous notions were the corollary. When my mind attempted to return to the Catholic faith, it was rebuffed because the Catholic faith is not what I thought. My God, to whom your mercies make it possible for me to make confession, I felt it more reverent to believe you infinite in all respects but one, namely the mass of evil opposed to you, than to think you in all parts limited to the shape of the human body. I thought it better to believe that you had created no evil—which in my ignorance I thought not merely some sort of substance but even corporeal, since I did not know how to think of mind except as a subtle physical entity diffused through space—rather than to believe that the nature of evil, as I understood it, came from you. Our Saviour himself, your only Son, I imagined emerging from the mass of your dazzling body of light for our salvation. I could believe of him only what my vain imagination could picture. I thought a nature such as his could not be born of the Virgin Mary without being mingled with flesh. That he could be mixed with us and not polluted I did not see, because my mental picture was what it was. I was afraid to believe him incarnate lest I had to believe him to be defiled by the flesh. Today your spiritual believers will kindly and lovingly laugh at me when they read these my confessions. Nevertheless that was the state of my mind.

xi (21)   I did not think there was any defence against the Manichees' criticisms of your scriptures. Sometimes, however, I desired to debate particular points with someone very learned in those books, and to discover what he thought about these questions. At Carthage the lectures of a certain Elpidius, who publicly spoke and debated against

16   Manichee attacks on Genesis 1 especially scorned the notion that man is in God's image.
17   Manichees did not hold the area of Darkness to be equal to that of Light, but to be a black 'wedge' cutting into the Light.

the Manichees, began to disturb me, when he cited matter from the scriptures to which there was no easy reply. The Manichee answer seemed to me weak. They did not easily produce their response before the public but did so to us in private. They asserted that the scriptures of the New Testament had been tampered with by persons unknown, who wanted to insert the Jews' law into the Christian faith. They were incapable of producing any uncorrupted copies. But the principal things which held me captive and somehow suffocated me, as long as I thought only in physical terms, were those vast masses. Gasping under their weight I could not breathe the pure and simple breeze of your truth.

xii (22)   I began to be busy about the task of teaching the art of rhetoric for which I had come to Rome. I first gathered some pupils at my lodging, and with them and through them I began to be known. I quickly discovered that at Rome students behaved in a way which I would never have had to endure in Africa. Acts of vandalism, it was true, by young hooligans did not occur at Rome; that was made clear to me. But, people told me, to avoid paying the teacher his fee, numbers of young men would suddenly club together and transfer themselves to another tutor,[18] breaking their word and out of love of money treating fairness as something to be flouted. I cordially detested them, but not 'with a perfect hatred' (Ps. 138: 22); for I probably felt more resentment for what I personally was to suffer from them than for the wrong they were doing to anyone and everyone. Certainly such people are a disgrace and 'commit fornication against you' (Ps. 72: 27). They love the passing, transient amusements and the filthy lucre which dirties the hand when it is touched. They embrace a world which is fleeing away. They despise you, though you abide and call the prodigal back and pardon the human soul for its harlotry when it returns to you. Today too I hate such wicked and perverted people, though I love them as people in need of correction, so that instead of money they may prefer the doctrine which they learn and, above the doctrine, may prefer you, God, the truth, the abundant source of assured goodness and most chaste peace. But at that time I was determined not to put up with badly behaved people more out of my own interest than because I wanted them to become good for your sake.

xiii (23)   So after a notification came from Milan to Rome to the city prefect saying that at Milan a teacher of rhetoric was to be appointed with his travel provided by the government service, I myself applied through the mediation of those intoxicated with Manichee follies. My move there was to end my association with them, but neither of

18   Augustine's contemporary, a pagan Alexandrian schoolmaster named Palladas, has the identical complaint about his pupils, who would leave him for another teacher just as they were due to pay the annual fee of one gold *solidus* (*The Greek Anthology* 9, 174). At Antioch Libanius circumvented pupils' dishonesty by making a contract with their parents (*oratio* 43). A teacher with 40 pupils would be doing reasonably well, but was not wealthy; moreover, he had to pay something to an usher to guard the entrance veil. Salaries and fees would be higher in larger cities (see above, I. xvi (26)). Elsewhere Augustine says that in small towns there was only a single teacher; the market perhaps would not have supported a second.

us knew that. An oration I gave on a prescribed topic was approved by the then prefect Symmachus[19] who sent me to Milan.

And so I came to Milan to Ambrose the bishop, known throughout the world as among the best of men, devout in your worship. At that time his eloquence valiantly ministered to your people 'the abundance of your sustenance' and 'the gladness of oil' (Ps. 44: 8; So: 17; 147:14), and the sober intoxication of your wine.[20] I was led to him by you, unaware that through him, in full awareness, I might be led to you. That 'man of God' (2 Kgs. 1: 9) received me like a father and expressed pleasure at my coming with a kindness most fitting in a bishop. I began to like him, at first indeed not as a teacher of the truth, for I had absolutely no confidence in your Church, but as a human being who was kind to me. I used enthusiastically to listen to him preaching to the people, not with the intention which I ought to have had, but as if testing out his oratorical skill to see whether it merited the reputation it enjoyed or whether his fluency was better or inferior than it was reported to be. I hung on his diction in rapt attention, but remained bored and contemptuous of the subject-matter. My pleasure was in the charm of his language. It was more learned than that of Faustus, but less witty and entertaining, as far as the manner of his speaking went. But in content there could be no comparison. Through Manichee deceits Faustus wandered astray. Ambrose taught the sound doctrine of salvation. From sinners such as I was at that time, salvation is far distant. Nevertheless, gradually, though I did not realize it, I was drawing closer.

xiv (24)   I was not interested in learning what he was talking about. My ears were only for his rhetorical technique; this empty concern was all that remained with me after I had lost any hope that a way to you might lie open for man. Nevertheless together with the words which I was enjoying, the subject matter, in which I was unconcerned, came to make an entry into my mind. I could not separate them. While I opened my heart in noting the eloquence with which he spoke, there also entered no less the truth which he affirmed, though only gradually. First what he said began to seem defensible, and I did not now think it impudent to assert the Catholic faith, which I had thought defenceless against Manichee critics. Above all, I heard first one, then another, then many difficult passages in the Old Testament scriptures figuratively interpreted, where I, by taking them literally, had found them to kill (2 Cor. 3: 6). So after several passages in the Old Testament had been expounded spiritually, I now found fault with that despair of mine,

---

19   Symmachus, a prominent and opulent pagan, became prefect of Rome in September 384. Augustine's arrival at Milan was probably in October.

20   'Sober intoxication', describing the ecstasy of a knowledge of God lying beyond reason, occurs in Ambrose and, before him, in the Jewish theologian Philo of Alexandria. Also Plotinus 6. 7. 35. 27.

caused by my belief that the law and the prophets could not be defended at all against the mockery of hostile critics. However, even so I did not think the Catholic faith something I ought to accept. Granted it could have educated people who asserted its claims and refuted objections with abundant argument and without absurdity. But that was not sufficient ground to condemn what I was holding. There could be an equally valid defence for both. So to me the Catholic faith appeared not to have been defeated but also not yet to be the conqueror.

(25)   I then energetically applied my critical faculty to see if there were decisive arguments by which I could somehow prove the Manichees wrong. If I had been able to conceive of spiritual substance, at once all their imagined inventions would have collapsed and my mind would have rejected them. But I could not. However, in regard to the physical world and all the natural order accessible to the bodily senses, consideration and comparison more and more convinced me that numerous philosophers held opinions much more probable than theirs. Accordingly, after the manner of the Academics, as popularly understood, I doubted everything, and in the fluctuating state of total suspense of judgement I decided I must leave the Manichees, thinking at that period of my skepticism that I should not remain a member of a sect to which I was now preferring certain philosophers. But to these philosophers, who were without Christ's saving name, I altogether refused to entrust the healing of my soul's sickness. I therefore decided for the time being to be a catechumen in the Catholic Church, which the precedent of my parents recommended to me, until some clear light should come by which I could direct my course.

Book VII

A Neoplatonic Quest

i (1)   By now my evil and wicked youth was dead. I was becoming a grown man. But the older I became, the more shameful it was that I retained so much vanity as to be unable to think any substance possible other than that which the eyes normally perceive. From the time that I began to learn something of your wisdom, I did not conceive of you, God, in the shape of the human body. I always shunned this, and was glad when I found the same concept in the faith of our spiritual mother, your Catholic Church. But how otherwise to conceive of you I could not see. I a mere man, and a man with profound defects, was trying to think of you the supreme, sole and true God. With all my heart I believed you to be incorruptible, immune from injury, and unchangeable. Although I did not know why and how, it was clear to me and certain that what is corruptible is inferior to that which cannot be corrupted; what is immune from injury I unhesitatingly put above that which is not immune; what suffers no change is better than that which can change. My heart vehemently protested against all the physical images in my mind, and by this single blow I attempted to expel from my mind's eye the swarm of unpurified notions flying about there.[1] Hardly had they been dispersed when in the flash of an eye (1 Cor. 15: 52) they had regrouped and were back again. They attacked my power of vision and clouded it. Although you were not in the shape of the human body, I nevertheless felt forced to imagine something physical occupying space diffused either in the world or even through infinite space outside the world.[2] Admittedly I thought of this as incorruptible and inviolable and unchangeable, which I set above what is corruptible, violable, and changeable. But I thought that anything from which space was abstracted was non-existent, indeed absolutely nothing, not even a vacuum, as when a body is removed from a place, and the space remains evacuated of anything physical, whether earthly, watery, airy or heavenly, but is an empty space—like a mathematical concept of space without content.

(2)   So my heart had become gross (Matt. 13: 15), and I had no clear vision even of my own self. I thought simply non-existent anything not extended in space or diffused or concentrated or expanding, which does not possess, or is incapable of possessing, such qualities. My eyes are accustomed to such images. My heart accepted the same structure. I did not see that the mental power by which I formed these images does not occupy any space, though it could not form them unless it were some great thing.[3] I conceived even you, life of my life, as a large being, permeating infinite space on every side, penetrating the entire mass of the world, and outside this extending in all directions for immense distances without end; so earth had you, heaven had you, everything had you, and in relation to you all was finite; but you not so. Just as the sunlight meets no obstacle in the body of the air (this air which is above the earth) to stop it from passing through and penetrating it without breaking it up or splitting it, but fills it entirely: so I thought that you permeate not only the body of heaven and air and sea but even earth, and that in everything, both the greatest and the smallest things, this physical frame is open to receive your presence, so that by a secret breath of life you govern all things which you created, both inwardly and outwardly. This was my conjecture, for I was incapable of thinking otherwise; but it was false. For on that hypothesis a larger part of the earth would possess more of you and a smaller part less, and all things would be full of you in the sense that more of you would be contained by an elephant's body than a sparrow's to the degree that it is larger and occupies more space; so, piece by piece, you would be making different parts of yourself present to parts of the world, much of you in large parts, little of you in small parts. And that is not the case. But you had not yet 'lightened my darkness' (Ps. 17: 29).

---

1   Echo of Virgil, *Aeneid* 3. 233.
2   Similarly Plotinus 6. 5. 2.
3   Similarly Plotinus 4. 2. 1.

Book VIII

The Birthpangs of Conversion

i (1)   My God, in my thanksgiving I want to recall and confess your mercies over me. Let my bones be penetrated by your love (Ps. 85: 13) and say, 'Lord who is like you?' (Ps. 34: 10). 'You have broken my chains, I will sacrifice to you the sacrifice of praise' (Ps. 115: 16-17). I will tell how you broke them. Let all who adore you say when they hear these things: 'Blessed is the Lord in heaven and in earth; great and wonderful is his name' (Ps. 71: 18–19; 134: 6).

Your words stuck fast in my heart and on all sides I was defended by you. Of your eternal life I was certain, though I saw it 'in an enigma and as if in a mirror' (1 Cor. 13: 12). All doubt had been taken from me that there is indestructible substance from which comes all substance. My desire was not to be more certain of you but to be more stable in you. But in my temporal life everything was in a state of uncertainty, and my heart needed to be purified from the old leaven (1 Cor. 5: 7 f.). I was attracted to the way, the Saviour himself, but was still reluctant to go along its narrow paths. And you put into my heart, and it seemed good in my sight (Ps. 18: 15), that I should visit Simplicianus.[1] It was evident to me that he was a good servant of yours; your grace shone in him. I had also heard that from his youth he had lived a life dedicated to you. By this time he had become an old man, and after a long life of saintly zeal in pursuing your way he appeared to me a man of much experience and much learning. So indeed he was. Accordingly, I wanted to consult with him about my troubles, so that he could propose a method fitted for someone in my disturbed condition, whereby I could learn to walk in your way.

(2)   I saw the Church full, with one going this way, another a different way.[2] My secular activity I held in disgust, and now that I was not burning with my old ambitions in hope of honour and money it was burdensome to me to tolerate so heavy a servitude. By now those prizes gave me no pleasure in comparison with your gentleness and 'the beauty of your house which I loved' (Ps. 25: 8). But I was still firmly tied by woman. The apostle did not forbid me to marry, though he exhorted me to something better and very much wished that all men were as unattached as he himself. But I being weaker chose a softer option, and because of this one factor I was inconstant in other respects and was wasting away with nagging anxieties. Moreover, there were other matters which were a tiresome distraction to me, but which I was compelled to put up with because they go with married life; once tied by that, I was restricted. From the mouth of truth I had heard that there are 'eunuchs who have castrated themselves for the kingdom of heaven's sake'. But, he says, 'let him who can accept this accept it' (Matt. 19: 12).

---

1   Simplicianus succeeded Ambrose as bishop of Milan in 397 and died c.400; so he was still living when the *Confessions* were published.

2   1 Cor. 7: 7 (of married and unmarried). Augustine means that the Church included both married and unmarried believers (a marked difference from Manicheism).

'Assuredly all men are vain in whom there is no knowledge of God; not even from the things which appear good can they find him who is' (Wisd. 13: 1). But now I was not in vanity of that kind. I had climbed beyond it, and by the witness of all creation I had found you our Creator and your Word who is God beside you and with you is one God, by whom you created all things (John 1: 1–3).

There are impious people of another sort who 'not knowing God, have not glorified him as God nor given thanks' (Rom. 1: 21). In this respect also I had fallen; but 'your right hand sustained me' (Ps. 17: 36). You took me thence and placed me where I could recover my strength. For you said to man 'Behold piety is wisdom', and 'Do not wish to appear wise' (Job 28: 28; Prov. 26: 5). 'Those who asserted themselves to be wise have been made foolish' (Rom. 1: 22).

And now I had discovered the good pearl. To buy it I had to sell all that I had; and I hesitated (Matt. 13: 46).

ii (3)   So I visited Simplicianus, father to the then bishop Ambrose in the receiving of grace.[3] Ambrose truly loved him as one loves a father. I told him the story of my wanderings in error. But when I mentioned that I had read some books of the Platonists, which had been translated into Latin by Victorinus, at one time rhetor in the city of Rome who had, I had heard, died a Christian, he congratulated me that I had not fallen in with the writings of other philosophers full of fallacies and deceptions 'according to the elements of this world' (Col. 2: 8), whereas in all the Platonic books God and his Word keep slipping in. Then, to exhort me to the humility of Christ hidden from the wise and revealed to babes (Matt. 11: 25) he recalled his memory of Victorinus himself, whom he had known intimately when he was at Rome. He told me a story about him which I will not pass over in silence. For the story gives occasion for me to confess to you in great praise for your grace.

Victorinus was extremely learned and most expert in all the liberal disciplines. He had read and assessed many philosophers' ideas, and was tutor to numerous noble senators. To mark the distinguished quality of his teaching he was offered and accepted a statue in the Roman forum, an honour which the citizens of this world think supreme.[4] Until he was of advanced years, he was a worshipper of idols and took part in sacrilegious rites.

---

3   Simplicianus, at one time in Rome, moved to Milan and was the senior priest responsible for baptizing Ambrose when he, the provincial governor, in 374 was suddenly nominated to be bishop of Milan. In Rome Simplicianus knew Marius Victorinus, a rhetor of African origin, who embodied the ideal of high culture, writing (extant) books on grammar, rhetoric, and dialectic, translating some of Aristotle's logic, and presenting to Latin readers works by Porphyry and Plotinus. Victorinus read Neoplatonism into the prologue to St John's gospel; and could count himself a Christian fellow-traveller. After conversion in his seventies, his writings on Christian theology tend to present the faith as a kind of Platonism for the masses.

4   Jerome says the statue was in the Forum of Trajan.

At that time almost all the Roman nobility was enthusiastic for the cult of Osiris[5] and 'Monstrous gods of every kind and Anubis the barking dog, Monsters who once bore arms against Neptune and Venus and against Minerva' (Virgil, *Aeneid* 8. 698 f.), gods that Rome once conquered but then implored for aid. The old Victorinus had defended these cults for many years with a voice terrifying to opponents. Yet he was not ashamed to become the servant of your Christ, and an infant born at your font, to bow his head to the yoke of humility and to submit his forehead to the reproach of the cross.[6]

(4)   Lord God, 'you have inclined the heavens and come down, you have touched the mountains and they have smoked' (Ps. 143: 5).[7] By what ways did you make an opening into that heart? Simplicianus said Victorinus read holy scripture, and all the Christian books he investigated with special care. After examining them he said to Simplicianus, not openly but in the privacy of friendship, 'Did you know that I am already a Christian?' Simplicianus replied: 'I shall not believe that or count you among the Christians unless I see you in the Church of Christ.' Victorinus laughed and said: 'Then do walls make Christians?' He used frequently to say 'I am a Christian already', and Simplicianus would give the same answer, to which he equally often repeated his joke about walls. He was afraid to offend his friends, proud devil-worshippers. He thought that from the height of Babylonish dignity, as if from the cedars of Lebanon which the Lord had not yet broken (Ps. 28: 5), the full weight of their hostility would land on him. But after his reading, he began to feel a longing and drank in courage. He was afraid he would be 'denied' by Christ 'before the holy angels' (Luke 12: 9). He would have felt guilty of a grave crime if he were ashamed of the mysteries of the humility of your Word and were not ashamed of the sacrilegious rites of proud demons, whose pride he imitated when he accepted their ceremonies. He became ashamed of the emptiness of those rites and felt respect for the truth. Suddenly and unexpectedly he said to Simplicianus (as he told me): 'Let us go to the Church; I want to become a Christian.' Simplicianus was unable to contain himself for joy and went with him. Not long after he had received his instructions in the first mysteries, he gave in his name for baptism that he might be reborn, to the amazement of Rome and the joy of the Church. The proud 'saw and were angry. They gnashed with their teeth and were sick at heart' (Ps. 111: 10). But the Lord God was the hope of his servant; 'he paid no regard to vanities and lying follies' (Ps. 39. 5).

(5)   Finally the hour came for him to make the profession of faith which is expressed in set form. At Rome these words are memorized and then by custom recited from an elevated place before the baptized believers by those who want to come to your grace.

---

5   The Latin text has a corruption here; the translation above has a little manuscript support, but cannot claim to offer more than a guess at the general sense.

6   The sign of the cross on the forehead in baptism.

7   Augustine (*Sermon on Ps. 143*) interprets the 'inclined heavens' to mean the apostles who, when people wanted to honour them as gods, humbly pointed them to the true God; the 'mountains' are the proud, and 'smoke' when, at God's touch, they confess their sins (like Victorinus).

Simplicianus used to say that the presbyters offered him the opportunity of affirming the creed in private, as was their custom to offer to people who felt embarrassed and afraid. But he preferred to make profession of his salvation before the holy congregation. For there was no salvation in the rhetoric which he had taught; yet his profession of that had been public. How much less should he be afraid in proclaiming your word, when he used to feel no fear in using his own words before crowds of frenzied pagans. When he mounted the steps to affirm the confession of faith, there was a murmur of delighted talk as all the people who knew him spoke his name to one another. And who there did not know him? A suppressed sound came from the lips of all as they rejoiced, 'Victorinus, Victorinus!' As soon as they saw him, they suddenly murmured in exaltation and equally suddenly were silent in concentration to hear him. He proclaimed his unfeigned faith with ringing assurance. All of them wanted to clasp him to their hearts, and the hands with which they embraced him were their love and their joy.

iii (6)   God of goodness, what causes man to be more delighted by the salvation of a soul who is despaired of but is then liberated from great danger than if there has always been hope or if the danger has only been minor? You also, merciful Father, rejoice 'more over one penitent than over ninety-nine just persons who need no penitence' (Luke 15: 4). We too experience great pleasure when we hear how the shepherd's shoulders exult when they carry the lost sheep, and as we listen to the story of the drachma restored to your treasuries while the neighbours rejoice with the woman who found it. Tears flow at the joy of the solemnities of your house (Ps. 25: 8) when in your house the story is read of your younger son 'who was dead and is alive again, was lost and has been found' (Luke 15: 32). You rejoice indeed in us and in your angels who are holy in holy love. You are always the same, and you always know unchangeably the things which are not always the same.[8]

(7)   What then is it in the soul which causes it to take more pleasure in things which it loves when they are found and recovered than if it has always had them? There are other examples which attest this fact, and everyday life is full of instances where the evidence cries out: 'That is the case.' A victorious emperor celebrates a triumph. He would not have conquered if he had not fought. The greater the danger in the battle, the greater the joy in the triumph. A storm throws people about on a voyage and threatens shipwreck. All grow pale at the imminence of death. Sky and sea become calm, and the relief is great because the fear has been great. A dear person is sick, and his pulse reveals he is in a serious condition. All who wish him to recover his health feel sick in mind at the same time. He takes a turn for the better and, although he may not walk with his former strength, yet now there is joy as there was not before when he walked in good health and strength. Human beings obtain normal pleasures of human life not as they

8   It is a Neoplatonic axiom that the immutable and eternal deity knows mutable and temporal things with a transcendent and immutable knowing.

come on us unexpectedly and against our will, but after discomforts which are planned and accepted by deliberate choice. There is no pleasure in eating and drinking unless they are preceded by the unpleasant sensation of hunger and thirst. Drunkards eat salty things to make their desire uncomfortable. As drinking extinguishes the desire, there is delightful sensation. It is established custom that betrothed girls are not immediately handed over, lest the husband hold the bride being given to him to be cheaply gained if he has not sighed after her, impatient at the delay.

(8)   The same phenomenon appears in acts which are demeaning and execrable, in acts which are allowed and lawful, in the sincerest expressions of honourable friendship, and in the case of the one 'who was dead and is alive again, was lost and is found' (Luke 15: 32). In every case the joy is greater, the worse the pain which has preceded it. Why is this, Lord my God? You are eternal to yourself, you are your own joy; and beings round you continually rejoice in your society. Why is it that this part of the creation alternates between regress and progress, between hostilities and reconciliations? Or is that a restriction placed on them, a limit you have imposed, when 'from the highest heaven' (Ps. 112: 4) down to the lowest things on earth, from the beginning to the end of the ages, from an angel down to a worm, from the first movement down to the last, you have assigned to its proper place and time all kinds of good things and all your just works?

You are so high among the highest, and I am low among the lowest, a mean thing. You never go away from us. Yet we have difficulty in returning to you.

iv (9)   Come Lord, stir us up and call us back, kindle and seize us, be our fire and our sweetness. Let us love, let us run. Surely many return to you from a deeper hell of blindness than Victorinus. They approach and are illuminated as they receive light. Those who receive it obtain from you 'power to become your sons' (John 1: 9, 12). But if they are less well known to the people, there is less rejoicing over them even among those who know them. When many share in the joy, individuals also feel a richer delight. They kindle excitement among themselves and are inflamed by one another. Then those who are known to many are to many a personal influence towards salvation. Where they lead, many will follow. That is why on their account even those who have preceded them feel great joy; for their rejoicing is not only for them.

But God forbid that in your tabernacle the rich be preferred to the poor or the noble to those of low origin. You have chosen in preference the weak things of the world to confound the powerful, and you have chosen the low of this world and things that are despised and things which have no existence as if they had being, to bring to nothing things which have being. (1 Cor. 1: 27 f.). Yet the very same writer, the least of your apostles (1 Cor. 15: 9), by whose tongue you uttered those words, was the person who by combat humbled the pride of Paul the proconsul under the gentle yoke of your Christ, and commissioned him as a provincial governor of the great king (Acts 13:

7–12). Thereafter he himself, formerly named Saul, loved to be called Paul as a reminder of that great victory. The enemy suffers a severer defeat when he is overcome in a man upon whom he has a greater hold and by whose influence he dominates many. Pride in aristocratic nobility enables him to hold sway especially over the upper class, and by their title and authority he dominates many more. Special pleasure, therefore, was felt at the conversion of Victorinus' heart in which the devil had an impregnable fortress, and of Victorinus' tongue which he had used as a mighty and sharp dart to destroy many. Your children had good reason to rejoice the more jubilantly because our king had bound the strong man (Matt. 12: 29), and they saw his vessels being snatched away to be cleaned and made fit for your honour to be 'useful to the Lord for every good work' (2 Tim. 2: 21).

v (10)   As soon as your servant Simplicianus told me this story about Victorinus, I was ardent to follow his example. He had indeed told it to me with this object in view. Later on, he added, in the time of the emperor Julian when a law was promulgated forbidding Christians to teach literature and rhetoric,[9] Victorinus welcomed the law and preferred to abandon the school of loquacious chattering rather than your word, by which you make 'skilled the tongues of infants' (Wisd. 10: 21). I felt that he was not so much courageous as fortunate to find occasion for dedicating all his time to you. I sighed after such freedom, but was bound not by an iron imposed by anyone else but by the iron of my own choice. The enemy had a grip on my will and so made a chain for me to hold me a prisoner. The consequence of a distorted will is passion. By servitude to passion, habit is formed, and habit to which there is no resistance becomes necessity. By these links, as it were, connected one to another (hence my term a chain), a harsh bondage held me under restraint. The new will, which was beginning to be within me a will to serve you freely and to enjoy you, God, the only sure source of pleasure, was not yet strong enough to conquer my older will, which had the strength of old habit. So my two wills, one old, the other new, one carnal, the other spiritual, were in conflict with one another, and their discord robbed my soul of all concentration.

(11)   In this way I understood through my own experience what I had read, how 'the flesh lusts against the spirit and the spirit against the flesh' (Gal. 5: 17). I was split between them, but more of me was in that which I approved in myself than in that which I disapproved. In the latter case it was 'no more I' (Rom. 7: 17), since in large part I was passive and unwilling rather than active and willing. But I was responsible for the fact that habit had become so embattled against me; for it was with my consent that I came

---

9   Julian's edict of 17 June 362 was based on the presupposition (shared by puritan Christians) that pagan literature and pagan religion are indissoluble. Christians such as Gregory of Nazianzus resented it. The admiring pagan Ammianus Marcellinus thought it should be condemned to everlasting silence as disgraceful. At Athens the famous sophist Prohaeresius declined to accept the special exemption granted him by Julian and, like Victorinus at Rome, resigned. Augustine himself (*City of God* 18, 52) thought the edict an act of persecuting intolerance.

to the place in which I did not wish to be. Who has the right to object if a just penalty pursues a sinner? I no longer had my usual excuse to explain why I did not yet despise the world and serve you, namely, that my perception of the truth was uncertain. By now I was indeed quite sure about it. Yet I was still bound down to the earth. I was refusing to become your soldier,[10] and I was as afraid of being rid of all my burdens as I ought to have been at the prospect of carrying them.

(12)   The burden of the world weighed me down with a sweet drowsiness such as commonly occurs during sleep. The thoughts with which I meditated about you were like the efforts of those who would like to get up but are overcome by deep sleep and sink back again. No one wants to be asleep all the time, and the sane judgement of everyone judges it better to be awake. Yet often a man defers shaking off sleep when his limbs are heavy with slumber. Although displeased with himself he is glad to take a bit longer, even when the time to get up has arrived. In this kind of way I was sure it was better for me to render myself up to your love than to surrender to my own cupidity. But while the former course was pleasant to think about and had my notional assent, the latter was more pleasant and overcame me. I had no answer to make to you when you said to me 'Arise, you who are asleep, rise from the dead, and Christ shall give you light' (Eph. 5: 14). Though at every point you showed that what you were saying was true, yet I, convinced by that truth, had no answer to give you except merely slow and sleepy words: 'At once'—'But presently'—'Just a little longer, please'. But 'At once, at once' never came to the point of decision, and 'Just a little longer, please' went on and on for a long while. In vain, I 'delighted in your law in respect of the inward man; but another law in my members fought against the law of my mind and led me captive in the law of sin which was in my members' (Rom. 7: 22). The law of sin is the violence of habit by which even the unwilling mind is dragged down and held, as it deserves to be, since by its own choice it slipped into the habit. 'Wretched man that I was, who would deliver me from this body of death other than your grace through Jesus Christ our Lord?' (Rom. 7: 24–5).

vi (13)   Lord, my helper and redeemer, I will now tell the story, and confess to your name, of the way in which you delivered me from the chain of sexual desire, by which I was tightly bound, and from the slavery of worldly affairs. I went about my usual routine in a state of mental anxiety. Every day I sighed after you. I used to frequent your Church whenever I had time off from the affairs under whose weight I was groaning. With me was Alypius, unemployed in his work as a lawyer after a third period as assessor and waiting for someone else to whom he could again sell his advice, just as I was selling the art of public speaking—if oratory is something that can be conveyed by teaching. Nebridius, however, had yielded to the pressure of his friendship with us and was assistant teacher to Verecundus, a close friend to all of us, a citizen of Milan and

---

10   From Tertullian on (AD 200), Latin Christians spoke of baptism in military terms as enlistment in Christ's army by an oath (*sacramemtum*) with the cross as the standard (*vexillum, signum*) and the sign of the cross over the forehead.

instructor in literature there. Verecundus was in urgent need of reliable assistance, and by right of friendship claimed from our group the supply he badly wanted. So Nebridius was not attracted to this work by desire for the profits; for had he so wished, he could have made more money on his own as teacher of literature. He was a most gentle and kind friend, and recognizing the duty of generosity would not scorn our request. He performed his task most prudently, and took care not to become known to important people, as this world reckons them, so avoiding anything likely to distract his mind. He wanted to keep his mind free and to devote as many hours as possible to the pursuit of wisdom by investigating some problem or listening to conversation.

(14)   One day when Nebridius was absent for a reason I cannot recall, Alypius and I received a surprise visit at home from a man named Ponticianus, a compatriot in that he was an African, holding high office at the court. He wanted something or other from us. We sat down together to converse. By chance he noticed a book on top of a gaming table which lay before us. He picked it up, opened it, and discovered, much to his astonishment, that it was the apostle Paul. He had expected it to be one of the books used for the profession which was wearing me out. But then he smiled and looked at me in a spirit of congratulation. He was amazed that he had suddenly discovered this book and this book alone open before my eyes. He was a Christian and a baptized believer. He often prostrated himself before you, our God, at the Church with frequent and long times of prayer. When I had indicated to him that those scriptures were the subject of deep study for me, a conversation began in which he told the story of Antony the Egyptian monk, a name held in high honour among your servants, though up to that moment Alypius and I had never heard of him. When he discovered this, he dwelt on the story instilling in us who were ignorant an awareness of the man's greatness, and expressing astonishment that we did not know of him. We were amazed as we heard of your wonderful acts very well attested and occurring so recently, almost in our own time, done in orthodox faith and in the Catholic Church. All of us were in a state of surprise, we because of the greatness of the story, he because we had not heard about it.

(15)   From there his conversation moved on to speak of the flocks in the monasteries and their manner of life well pleasing to you and the fertile deserts of the wilderness. Of these we knew nothing. There was a monastery full of good brothers at Milan outside the city walls, fostered by Ambrose, and we had not known of it. He developed the theme and talked on while we listened with rapt silence. Then it occurred to him to mention how he and three of his colleagues (the date I do not know but it was at Trier), when the emperor was detained by a circus spectacle in the forenoon, went out for a walk in the gardens adjacent to the walls. There they strolled in couples, one as it turned out with Ponticianus, the other two separately wandering off on their own. In their wanderings they happened on a certain house where there lived some of your servants, poor in spirit: 'of such is the kingdom of heaven' (Matt. 5: 3). They found there a

book in which was written the Life of Antony.[11] One of them began to read it. He was amazed and set on fire, and during his reading began to think of taking up this way of life and of leaving his secular post in the civil service to be your servant. For they were agents in the special branch.[12] Suddenly he was filled with holy love and sobering shame. Angry with himself, he turned his eyes on his friend and said to him: 'Tell me, I beg of you, what do we hope to achieve with all our labours? What is our aim in life? What is the motive of our service to the state? Can we hope for any higher office in the palace than to be Friends of the Emperor? And in that position what is not fragile and full of dangers? How many hazards must one risk to attain to a position of even greater danger? And when will we arrive there? Whereas, if I wish to become God's friend, in an instant I may become that now.' So he spoke, and in pain at the coming to birth of new life, he returned his eyes to the book's pages. He read on and experienced a conversion inwardly where you alone could see and, as was soon evident, his mind rid itself of the world. Indeed, as he read and turned over and over in the turbulent hesitations of his heart, there were some moments when he was angry with himself. But then he perceived the choice to be made and took a decision to follow the better course. He was already yours, and said to his friend: 'As for myself, I have broken away from our ambition, and have decided to serve God, and I propose to start doing that from this hour in this place. If it costs you too much to follow my example, do not turn against me.' His friend replied that he would join him and be associated with him for such great reward and for so great a service. And both men, already yours, were building their tower at the right cost of forsaking all their property and following you (Luke 14: 28). Then Ponticianus and his companion who were walking through other parts of the garden in search of them, came to the same place and, on finding them, suggested returning home since the daylight had already begun to fade. But they told him of their decision and purpose, and how this intention had started and had become a firm resolve. They begged the others, if they did not wish to be associated with them, not to obstruct them. Ponticianus and his friend, however, did not change from their old career; nevertheless, as he told us, they wept for themselves. They offered their friends devout congratulations, and commended themselves to their prayers. Then, dragging their hearts along the ground, they went off into the palace. The others fixed their hearts on heaven and stayed at the house. Both had fiancées. When later their fiancées heard this, they also dedicated their virginity to you.

---

11   Antony's Life by Athanasius of Alexandria was translated into Latin by Evagrius of Antioch, a friend of Jerome, about 371; an earlier version was also in circulation.

12   *Agentes in rebus* were an inspectorate of the imperial bureaucracy, sometimes used as intelligence gatherers and secret police, but mainly responsible to the Master of the Offices (who was among other things head of the intelligence service) for the operation of the *cursus publicus* or government communications system. Promotion in this department could lead as high as a provincial governorship, though this was rare. 'Friends of the Emperor' were not a branch of the civil service, but honoured individuals in high office; in the later Roman Empire all high office holders were vulnerable to palace revolutions and conspiracies.

vii (16)   This was the story Ponticianus told. But while he was speaking, Lord, you turned my attention back to myself. You took me up from behind my own back where I had placed myself because I did not wish to observe myself (Ps. 20: 13), and you set me before my face (Ps. 49: 21) so that I should see how vile I was, how twisted and filthy, covered in sores and ulcers.[13] And I looked and was appalled, but there was no way of escaping from myself. If I tried to avert my gaze from myself, his story continued relentlessly, and you once again placed me in front of myself; you thrust me before my own eyes so that I should discover my iniquity and hate it. I had known it, but deceived myself, refused to admit it, and pushed it out of my mind.

(17)   But at that moment the more ardent my affection for those young men of whom I was hearing, who for the soul's health had given themselves wholly to you for healing, the more was the detestation and hatred I felt for myself in comparison with them. Many years of my life had passed by—about twelve—since in my nineteenth year I had read Cicero's *Hortensius*, and had been stirred to a zeal for wisdom. But although I came to despise earthly success, I put off giving time to the quest for wisdom. For 'it is not the discovery but the mere search for wisdom which should be preferred even to the discovery of treasures and to ruling over nations and to the physical delights available to me at a nod.'[14] But I was an unhappy young man, wretched as at the beginning of my adolescence when I prayed you for chastity and said: 'Grant me chastity and continence, but not yet.' I was afraid you might hear my prayer quickly, and that you might too rapidly heal me of the disease of lust which I preferred to satisfy rather than suppress. I had gone along 'evil ways' (Ecclus. 2: 10) with a sacrilegious superstition, not indeed because I felt sure of its truth but because I preferred it to the alternatives, which I did not investigate in a devout spirit but opposed in an attitude of hostility.

(18)   I supposed that the reason for my postponing 'from day to day' (Ecclus. 5: 8) the moment when I would despise worldly ambition and follow you was that I had not seen any certainty by which to direct my course. But the day had now come when I stood naked to myself, and my conscience complained against me: 'Where is your tongue? You were saying that, because the truth is uncertain, you do not want to abandon the burden of futility. But look, it is certain now, and the burden still presses on you. Yet wings are won by the freer shoulders of men who have not been exhausted by their searching and have not taken ten years or more to meditate on these matters.' This is how I was gnawing at my inner self. I was violently overcome by a fearful sense of shame during the time that Ponticianus was telling his story. When he had ended his talk and settled the matter for which he came, he went home and I was left to myself. What accusations against myself did I not bring? With what verbal rods did I not scourge my soul so that it would follow me in my attempt to go after you! But my soul hung back.

13   Echo of Seneca, *De Ira* 2. 36. 1.
14   A quotation or at least paraphrase of Cicero (*Hortensius*, fragment 106 Grilli). Cf. XII. i (1) below.

It refused, and had no excuse to offer. The arguments were exhausted, and all had been refuted. The only thing left to it was a mute trembling, and as if it were facing death it was terrified of being restrained from the treadmill of habit by which it suffered 'sickness unto death' (John 11: 4).

viii (19)   Then in the middle of that grand struggle in my inner house, which I had vehemently stirred up with my soul in the intimate chamber of my heart, distressed not only in mind but in appearance, I turned on Alypius and cried out: 'What is wrong with us? What is this that you have heard? Uneducated people are rising up and capturing heaven (Matt. 11: 12), and we with our high culture without any heart—see where we roll in the mud of flesh and blood. Is it because they are ahead of us that we are ashamed to follow? Do we feel no shame at making not even an attempt to follow?' That is the gist of what I said, and the heat of my passion took my attention away from him as he contemplated my condition in astonished silence. For I sounded very strange. My uttered words said less about the state of my mind than my forehead, cheeks, eyes, colour, and tone of voice.

Our lodging had a garden. We had the use of it as well as of the entire house, for our host, the owner of the house, was not living there. The tumult of my heart took me out into the garden where no one could interfere with the burning struggle with myself in which I was engaged, until the matter could be settled. You knew, but I did not, what the outcome would be. But my madness with myself was part of the process of recovering health, and in the agony of death I was coming to life. I was aware how ill I was, unaware how well I was soon to be. So I went out into the garden. Alypius followed me step after step. Although he was present, I felt no intrusion on my solitude. How could he abandon me in such a state? We sat down as far as we could from the buildings. I was deeply disturbed in spirit, angry with indignation and distress that I was not entering into my pact and covenant with you, my God, when all my bones (Ps. 34: 10) were crying out that I should enter into it and were exalting it to heaven with praises. But to reach that destination one does not use ships or chariots or feet.[15] It was not even necessary to go the distance I had come from the house to where we were sitting. The one necessary condition, which meant not only going but at once arriving there, was to have the will to go—provided only that the will was strong and unqualified, not the turning and twisting first this way, then that, of a will half-wounded, struggling with one part rising up and the other part falling down.

(20)   Finally in the agony of hesitation I made many physical gestures of the kind men make when they want to achieve something and lack the strength, either because they lack the actual limbs or because their limbs are fettered with chains or weak with sickness or in some way hindered. If I tore my hair, if I struck my forehead, if I intertwined

---

15   Echo of Plotinus I. 6. 8. 21.

my fingers and clasped my knee, I did that because to do so was my will. But I could have willed this and then not done it if my limbs had not possessed the power to obey. So I did many actions in which the will to act was not equalled by the power. Yet I was not doing what with an incomparably greater longing I yearned to do, and could have done the moment I so resolved. For as soon as I had the will, I would have had a wholehearted will. At this point the power to act is identical with the will. The willing itself was performative of the action. Nevertheless, it did not happen. The body obeyed the slightest inclination of the soul to move the limbs at its pleasure more easily than the soul obeyed itself, when its supreme desire could be achieved exclusively by the will alone.

ix (21)   What is the cause of this monstrous situation? Why is it the case? May your mercy illuminate me as I ask if perhaps an answer can be found in the hidden punishments and secret tribulations that befall the sons of Adam? What causes this monstrous fact? and why is it so? The mind commands the body and is instantly obeyed. The mind commands itself and meets resistance. The mind commands the hand to move, and it is so easy that one hardly distinguishes the order from its execution. Yet mind is mind, and hand is body. The mind orders the mind to will. The recipient of the order is itself, yet it does not perform it. What causes this monstrosity and why does this happen? Mind commands, I say, that it should will, and would not give the command if it did not will, yet does not perform what it commands. The willing is not wholehearted, so the command is not wholehearted. The strength of the command lies in the strength of will, and the degree to which the command is not performed lies in the degree to which the will is not engaged. For it is the will that commands the will to exist, and it commands not another will but itself. So the will that commands is incomplete, and therefore what it commands does not happen. If it were complete, it would not need to command the will to exist, since it would exist already. Therefore there is no monstrous split between willing and not willing. We are dealing with a morbid condition of the mind which, when it is lifted up by the truth, does not unreservedly rise to it but is weighed down by habit. So there are two wills. Neither of them is complete, and what is present in the one is lacking to the other.

x (22)   'Let them perish from your presence' (Ps. 67: 3) O God, as do 'empty talkers and seducers' of the mind (Titus 1: 10)[16] who from the dividing of the will into two in the process of deliberation, deduce that there are two minds with two distinct natures, one good, the other bad. They really are evil themselves when they entertain these evil doctrines. Yet the very same people would be good if they held to the true doctrines and assented to the truth. As your apostle says to them 'You were at one time darkness, but now are light in the Lord' (Eph. 5: 8). But they wish to be light not in the Lord but in themselves because they hold that the nature of the soul is what God is. They have in fact become a thicker darkness in that by their horrendous arrogance they have

---

16   Manichees.

withdrawn further away from you—from you who are 'the true light illuminating every man coming into this world' (John 1: 9). They should give heed to what you say and blush: 'Come to him and be illuminated, and your faces will not blush' (Ps. 33: 6).

In my own case, as I deliberated about serving my Lord God (Jer. 30: 9) which I had long been disposed to do, the self which willed to serve was identical with the self which was unwilling. It was I. I was neither wholly willing nor wholly unwilling. So I was in conflict with myself and was dissociated from myself. The dissociation came about against my will. Yet this was not a manifestation of the nature of an alien mind but the punishment suffered in my own mind. And so it was 'not I' that brought this about 'but sin which dwelt in me' (Rom. 7: 17, 20), sin resulting from the punishment of a more freely chosen sin, because I was a son of Adam.

(23)   If there are as many contrary natures as there are wills in someone beset by in-decision, there will be not two wills but many. If a person is deliberating whether to go to the Manichees' conventicle or to the theatre, they cry: 'Here are two natures, a good one leads one way, a bad one leads the other way. How otherwise explain the opposition of two wills to one another?' But I affirm that they are both evil, both the will to attend their meeting and the will to go to the theatre. They think that the intention to go along to them can only be good. What then? If one of us Catholic Christians were deliberat-ing and, with two wills quarrelling with one another, fluctuated between going to the theatre or to our Church, surely the Manichees would be quite undecided what to say about that. Either they will have to concede that to go to our Church is an act of good will, as is the case with those worshippers who are initiated into its sacraments and feel the obligation thereby imposed, or they will have to think two evil natures and two evil minds are in conflict within a single person. This argument will prove untrue their usual assertion that one is good, the other bad. The alternative for them will be to be converted to the true view and not to deny that in the process of deliberation a single soul is wavering between different wills.

(24)   Accordingly, when they note two wills in one person in conflict with each other, let them no more say that two conflicting minds are derived from two rival substances, and that two conflicting principles are in contention, one good, the other evil. God of truth, you condemn them and refute and confound them. For both wills are evil when someone is deliberating whether to kill a person by poison or by a dagger; whether to encroach on one estate belonging to someone else or a different one, when he cannot do both; whether to buy pleasure by lechery or avariciously to keep his money; whether to go to the circus or the theatre if both are putting on a performance on the same day, or (I add a third possibility) to steal from another person's house if occasion offers, or (I add a fourth option) to commit adultery if at the same time the chance is available. Suppose that all these choices are confronted at one moment of time, and all are equally desired, yet they cannot all be done simultaneously. They tear the mind apart by the mutual

incompatibility of the wills—four or more according to the number of objects desired. Yet they do not usually affirm that there is such a multiplicity of diverse substances.

The same argument holds for good wills. For I ask them whether it is good to delight in a reading from the apostle, or if it is good to take pleasure in a sober psalm, or if it is good to discourse upon the gospel. In each case they will reply 'good'. What then? If all these offer equal delight at one and the same time, surely the divergent wills pull apart the human heart while we are deliberating which is the most attractive option to take? All are good and yet are in contention with each other until the choice falls on one to which is then drawn the entire single will which was split into many. So also when the delight of eternity draws us upwards and the pleasure of temporal good holds us down, the identical soul is not wholehearted in its desire for one or the other. It is torn apart in a painful condition, as long as it prefers the eternal because of its truth but does not discard the temporal because of familiarity.

xi (25)   Such was my sickness and my torture, as I accused myself even more bitterly than usual. I was twisting and turning in my chain until it would break completely: I was now only a little bit held by it, but I was still held. You, Lord, put pressure on me in my hidden depths with a severe mercy wielding the double whip[17] of fear and shame, lest I should again succumb, and lest that tiny and tenuous bond which still remained should not be broken, but once more regain strength and bind me even more firmly. Inwardly I said to myself: Let it be now, let it be now. And by this phrase I was already moving towards a decision; I had almost taken it, and then I did not do so.[18] Yet I did not relapse into my original condition, but stood my ground very close to the point of deciding and recovered my breath. Once more I made the attempt and came only a little short of my goal; only a little short of it—yet I did not touch it or hold on to it. I was hesitating whether to die to death and to live to life. Ingrained evil had more hold over me than unaccustomed good. The nearer approached the moment of time when I would become different, the greater the horror of it struck me. But it did not thrust me back nor turn me away, but left me in a state of suspense.

(26)   Vain trifles and the triviality of the empty-headed, my old loves, held me back. They tugged at the garment of my flesh and whispered: 'Are you getting rid of us?' And 'from this moment we shall never be with you again, not for ever and ever'. And 'from this moment this and that are forbidden to you for ever and ever.' What they were suggesting in what I have called 'this and that'—what they were suggesting, my God, may your mercy avert from the soul of your servant! What filth, what disgraceful things they were suggesting! I was listening to them with much less than half my attention.

---

17   Virgil, *Aeneid* 5. 547.

18   Persius' fifth satire (quoted below VIII. xii (28)) portrays a lover who swears to give up his mistress but returns on her first appeal (5. 157). An epigram in the Greek Anthology (5. 24) concerns a lover whose conscience warns him to fly from his mistress but his will has not the strength.

They were not frankly confronting me face to face on the road, but as it were whispering behind my back, as if they were furtively tugging at me as I was going away, trying to persuade me to look back. Nevertheless they held me back. I hesitated to detach myself, to be rid of them, to make the leap to where I was being called. Meanwhile the overwhelming force of habit was saying to me: 'Do you think you can live without them?'

(27)   Nevertheless it was now putting the question very halfheartedly. For from that direction where I had set my face and towards which I was afraid to move, there appeared the dignified and chaste Lady Continence, serene and cheerful without coquetry, enticing me in an honourable manner to come and not to hesitate. To receive and embrace me she stretched out pious hands, filled with numerous good examples for me to follow. There were large numbers of boys and girls, a multitude of all ages, young adults and grave widows and elderly virgins. In every one of them was Continence herself, in no sense barren but 'the fruitful mother of children' (Ps. 112: 9), the joys born of you, Lord, her husband. And she smiled on me with a smile of encouragement as if to say: 'Are you incapable of doing what these men and women have done? Do you think them capable of achieving this by their own resources and not by the Lord their God? Their Lord God gave me to them. Why are you relying on yourself, only to find yourself unreliable? Cast yourself upon him, do not be afraid. He will not withdraw himself so that you fall. Make the leap without anxiety; he will catch you and heal you.'

I blushed with embarrassment because I was still listening to the mutterings of those vanities, and racked by hesitations I remained undecided. But once more it was as if she said: "Stop your ears to your impure members on earth and mortify them" (Col. 3: 5). They declare delights to you, but "not in accord with the law of the Lord your God" (Ps. 118: 85). This debate in my heart was a struggle of myself against myself. Alypius stood quite still at my side, and waited in silence for the outcome of my unprecedented state of agitation.

xii (28)   From a hidden depth a profound self-examination had dredged up a heap of all my misery and set it 'in the sight of my heart' (Ps. 18: 15). That precipitated a vast storm bearing a massive downpour of tears. To pour it all out with the accompanying groans, I got up from beside Alypius (solitude seemed to me more appropriate for the business of weeping), and I moved further away to ensure that even his presence put no inhibition upon me. He sensed that this was my condition at that moment. I think I may have said something which made it clear that the sound of my voice was already choking with tears. So I stood up while in profound astonishment he remained where we were sitting. I threw myself down somehow under a certain figtree,[19] and let my tears flow freely. Rivers streamed from my eyes, a sacrifice acceptable to you (Ps. 50: 19), and (though not in these words, yet in this sense) I repeatedly said to you: 'How long,

---

19   Perhaps a symbolic reference to the fig tree of Adam (Gen. 3: 7; cf. John 1: 48).

O Lord? How long, Lord, will, you be angry to the uttermost? Do not be mindful of our old iniquities.' (Ps. 6: 4). For I felt my past to have a grip on me. It uttered wretched cries: 'How long, how long is it to be?' 'Tomorrow, tomorrow.'[20] 'Why not now? Why not an end to my impure life in this very hour?'

(29)   As I was saying this and weeping in the bitter agony of my heart, suddenly I heard a voice from the nearby house[21] chanting as if it might be a boy or a girl (I do not know which), saying and repeating over and over again 'Pick up and read, pick up and read.' At once my countenance changed, and I began to think intently whether there might be some sort of children's game in which such a chant is used. But I could not remember having heard of one. I checked the flood of tears and stood up. I interpreted it solely as a divine command to me to open the book and read the first chapter I might find. For I had heard how Antony happened to be present at the gospel reading, and took it as an admonition addressed to himself when the words were read: 'Go, sell all you have, give to the poor, and you shall have treasure in heaven; and come, follow me' (Matt. 19: 21).[22] By such an inspired utterance he was immediately 'converted to you' (Ps. 50: 15). So I hurried back to the place where Alypius was sitting. There I had put down the book of the apostle when I got up. I seized it, opened it and in silence read the first passage on which my eyes lit: 'Not in riots and drunken parties, not in eroticism and indecencies, not in strife and rivalry, but put on the Lord Jesus Christ and make no provision for the flesh in its lusts' (Rom. 13: 13–14).

I neither wished nor needed to read further. At once, with the last words of this sentence, it was as if a light of relief from all anxiety flooded into my heart. All the shadows of doubt were dispelled.

(30)   Then I inserted my finger or some other mark in the book and closed it. With a face now at peace I told everything to Alypius. What had been going on in his mind, which I did not know, he disclosed in this way. He asked to see the text I had been reading. I showed him, and he noticed a passage following that which I had read. I did not know how the text went on; but the continuation was 'Receive the person who is weak in faith' (Rom. 14: 1). Alypius applied this to himself, and he made that known to me. He was given confidence by this admonition. Without any agony of hesitation he joined me in making a good resolution and affirmation of intention, entirely congruent with his moral principles in which he had long been greatly superior to me. From there

---

20   Persius, *Satires* 5. 66.

21   The oldest manuscript reads here 'from the house of God'. The child's voice is in any event a divine oracle to Augustine. The variant may echo Ps. 41: 5.

22   Athanasius, *Life of Antony* 2.

we went in to my mother, and told her. She was filled with joy. We told her how it had happened. She exulted, feeling it to be a triumph, and blessed you who 'are powerful to do more than we ask or think' (Eph. 3: 20). She saw that you had granted her far more than she had long been praying for in her unhappy and tearful groans.

The effect of your converting me to yourself was that I did not now seek a wife and had no ambition for success in this world. I stood firm upon that rule of faith on which many years before you had revealed me to her.[23] You 'changed her grief into joy' (Ps. 29: 12) far more abundantly than she desired, far dearer and more chaste than she expected when she looked for grandchildren begotten of my body.

---

23   See above, III, xi (19–20).

Selections from *Confessions* by St. Augustine, trans. Henry Chadwick. (1991): pp. 3–4, 24–34, 35–45, 52–54, 56–58, 80–111, 111–112, 133–154. Translation © Henry Chadwick 1991. By permission of Oxford University Press.

V

Dante Alighieri

Editors' Introduction

From the tortures of hell, through the painful process of purification in purgatory, to a vision of paradise that tests the limits of what can be expressed in language, Dante's poem has left a lasting imprint on the imagination of western culture.

It is likely that Dante would have found this to be entirely appropriate. He was not a man given to modesty with regard to his talent. He believed that he had something important to say about the human condition, something that transcended the circumstances of his particular time and place. Even though many of the characters we encounter in *Inferno*, *Purgatory*, and *Paradise* may be unfamiliar to us due to the fact that they are figures from the ancient and medieval worlds, or because they are associated with events taking place on the Italian peninsula during Dante's lifetime, he believed that his readers could draw important lessons from the situations he described, lessons applicable to people at all times. While there is no doubt that he was addressing the circumstances of his time, he also understood himself as having a prophetic role, offering wisdom to the world on matters of religion, politics, culture, philosophy, and society. To understand how he came to take this role upon himself, we need to know something about his earlier life.

At the time Dante was born (1265) in Florence, there was no single nation known as Italy. The Italian peninsula consisted of various territories and city-states, many of which were frequently being fought over by kings, popes, and the townspeople themselves. Dante would have considered himself primarily a citizen of Florence; this city-state was his "homeland." As a child he followed a normal course of education for the time, studying grammar, rhetoric, and classical and medieval literature. The most influential event of his childhood was his encounter with Beatrice Portinari. He first met her when they were both eight years old, and he became smitten by her. When he saw her nine years later, she became even more firmly ensconced in his imagination as the epitome of grace and beauty. Beatrice's death in 1290 grieved Dante deeply, and as a distraction from grief he busied himself with the study of philosophy and theology. In *The Divine Comedy* Beatrice will appear as one of the primary agents of Dante's salvation, a virtual female Christ figure.

As a young man Dante had already begun to study and write poetry. He married Gemma Donati when he was twenty, and together they had four children. With the death of his father in 1285, Dante became responsible for his entire family, leading him to take a more public and political role in the life of his city. This involvement was to have significant and ultimately, unfortunate consequences for him. The two predominant political factions in Florence were the Guelfs and the Ghibellines; the Guelfs were further divided into the Black and the White factions ("Black" and "White" having nothing to do with race or color here). Dante became a prominent White Guelf, reaching the height of his influence in 1300, when he was elected one of the seven priors (basically a councilman/

leader) of Florence. It was a time of tremendous violence and strife. In 1302, while on a diplomatic mission to Rome to dissuade the pope from inviting French troops to enter Tuscany (the region in which Florence is located), the Black Guelf party came to power in Florence, and Dante was condemned to exile on the basis of trumped up charges of political corruption. If he had ever returned to Florence, he would have been executed.

Dante never again returned to the city he loved, remaining in exile until his death in 1321. At first he found it difficult to adjust to life away from Florence. He moved from place to place, eventually settling in the Italian city of Ravenna, where he died and was buried. Exile forced Dante to think more deeply about his life and to reflect upon the disorders of his time. Out of these reflections came the work we know as *The Divine Comedy*. He began the work around 1308 and completed it shortly before his death. Dante called his work *Commedia*; the adjective "Divine" was suggested later by the Italian Renaissance writer Boccaccio. The title "Commedia" does not mean that the poem is funny ("funny" is not a word that normally comes to mind when thinking about the *Commedia*); rather it indicates that the poem ends happily, as Dante the pilgrim is caught up in his vision of God.

For those with just a passing familiarity with Dante, there is sometimes a tendency to reduce his understanding of life to that which is presented in *Inferno*. That would be a serious mistake. Always bear in mind that two thirds of the work is about conversion and salvation. Dante was well acquainted with human sin and evil, but he was able to look beyond these realities and to offer hope for the redemption of the world. Nor is there anything escapist about Dante's message. When, in *Paradise*, he ascends to his final vision of God, it is not with the intention of fleeing from the world; rather, the vision will become the guiding principle for the transformed perspective that he will now bring to his life. He very much believed in God's victory over sin and death, and he insisted that with divine help the world could become a place of order and harmony, far removed from the petty and destructive internecine conflicts that so marred the society in which he lived. For those accustomed to thinking of poetry as an art form with only peripheral relevance to what we consider the "real world," Dante's conception of his mission may seem odd. Yet it was precisely as a poet that he took upon himself the mantle of a prophet. He used his unsurpassed imaginative powers to create a work in which he recounted his own painful process of conversion and challenged his readers both then and now to change their lives—not out of fear of divine punishment (in Dante, people are punished by their sins rather than *for* their sins), but out of the conviction that the final word about human affairs is a word of grace.

THE DIVINE COMEDY

Inferno (Selections)

Inferno is the first and most widely read of the three works that comprise *The Divine Comedy*. Its geography can be imagined as a funnel lined with various concentric circles in which sins of ever increasing severity are punished. There are three major divisions within *Inferno*, based upon the three different types of sins. After Limbo, Circles Two through Five are reserved for those who have sinned due to some form of incontinence or lack of self-restraint with regard to something that in itself is a good. For example, food is something natural and healthy for people, but indulged in to excess it becomes the sin of gluttony. Canto V (included below) describes the fate of those who suffer from the sin of lust, which, in Dante's view, is an excess of a desire natural to human beings.

Circle Six is a place of transition in which heretics dwell. The Seventh Circle is inhabited by those who have committed sins of violence. In Circles Eight and Nine Dante writes of those who are guilty of various forms of fraud, including flatterers, grafters, hypocrites, thieves, and traitors. Always bear in mind that for Dante sin is understood to be not only damaging to the person it infects, but also (and in some ways more importantly) to the community to which the sinner belongs. This is one of the reasons why Dante views sins of fraud to be so serious—the dishonesty of the fraudulent makes genuine community impossible, since once the bond of trust is broken, society deteriorates.

Canto I

Halfway through his life, Dante the Pilgrim wakes to find himself lost in a dark wood. Terrified at being alone in so dismal a valley, he wanders until he comes to a hill bathed in sunlight, and his fear begins to leave him. But when he starts to climb the hill his path is blocked by three fierce beasts: first a Leopard, then a Lion, and finally a She-Wolf. They fill him with fear and drive him back down to the sunless wood. At that moment the figure of a man appears before him; it is the shade of Virgil, and the Pilgrim begs for help. Virgil tells him that he cannot overcome the beasts which obstruct his path; they must remain until a "Greyhound" comes who will drive them back to Hell. Rather by another path will the Pilgrim reach the sunlight, and Virgil promises to guide him on that path through Hell and Purgatory, after which another spirit, more fit than Virgil, will lead him to Paradise. The Pilgrim begs Virgil to lead on, and the Guide starts ahead. The Pilgrim follows.

>   Midway along the journey of our life
>   I woke to find myself in a dark wood,
>   for I had wandered off from the straight path.   3

How hard it is to tell what it was like,
    this wood of wilderness, savage and stubborn
    (the thought of it brings back all my old fears),   6

a bitter place! Death could scarce be bitterer. But
    if I would show the good that came of it
    I must talk about things other than the good.   9

How I entered there I cannot truly say,
    I had become so sleepy at the moment
    when I first strayed, leaving the path of truth;   12

but when I found myself at the foot of a hill,
    at the edge of the wood's beginning, down in the valley,
    where I first felt my heart plunged deep in fear,   15

I raised my head and saw the hilltop shawled in
    morning rays of light sent from the planet
    that leads men straight ahead on every road.   18

And then only did terror start subsiding
    in my heart's lake, which rose to heights of fear
    that night I spent in deepest desperation.   21

Just as a swimmer, still with panting breath, now
    safe upon the shore, out of the deep,
    might turn for one last look at the dangerous waters,   24

so I, although my mind was turned to flee,
    turned round to gaze once more upon the pass
    that never let a living soul escape.   27

I rested my tired body there awhile
    and then began to climb the barren slope
    (I dragged my stronger foot and limped along).   30

Beyond the point the slope begins to rise
    sprang up a leopard, trim and very swift!
    It was covered by a pelt of many spots.   33

31–51   The three beasts that block the Pilgrim's path could symbolize the three major divisions of Hell. The spotted Leopard
        (32) represents Fraud (cf. Canto XVI, 106–108) and reigns over the Eighth and Ninth Circles where the Fraudulent
        are punished (Cantos XVIII–XXXIV). The Lion (45) symbolizes all forms of Violence that are punished in the
        Seventh Circle (XII–XVII). The She-Wolf (49) represents the different types of Concupisence or Incontinence that
        are punished in Circles Two to Five (V–VIII).

And, everywhere I looked, the beast was there
    blocking my way, so time and time again
    I was about to turn and go back down.   36

The hour was early in the morning then,
    the sun was climbing up with those same stars
    that had accompanied it on the world's first day,   39

the day Divine Love set their beauty turning;
    so the hour and sweet season of creation
    encouraged me to think I could get past   42

that gaudy beast, wild in its spotted pelt,
    but then good hope gave way and fear returned
    when the figure of a lion loomed up before me,   45

and he was coming straight toward me, it seemed,
    with head raised high, and furious with hunger
    the air around him seemed to fear his presence.   48

And now a she-wolf came, that in her leanness
    seemed racked with every kind of greediness
    (how many people she has brought to grief!).   51

This last beast brought my spirit down so low
    with fear that seized me at the sight of her,
    I lost all hope of going up the hill.   54

As a man who, rejoicing in his gains,
    suddenly seeing his gain turn into loss,
    will grieve as he compares his then and now,   57

so she made me do, that relentless beast;
    coming toward me, slowly, step by step,
    she forced me back to where the sun is mute.   60

While I was rushing down to that low place,
    my eyes made out a figure coming toward me
    of one grown faint, perhaps from too much silence. 63

62   The approaching figure represents (though not exclusively, for he has other meanings) Reason or Natural Philosophy. The Pilgrim cannot proceed to the light of Divine Love (the mountaintop) until he has overcome the three beasts of his sin; and because it is impossible for man to cope with the beasts unaided, Virgil has been summoned to guide the Pilgrim.

63   The voice of Reason has been silent in the Pilgrim's ear for a long time.

And when I saw him standing in this wasteland,
 "Have pity on my soul," I cried to him,
 "whichever you are, shade or living man!" 66

"No longer living man, though once I was,"
 he said, "and my parents were from Lombardy,
 both of them were Mantuans by birth. 69

I was born, though somewhat late, *sub Julio*,
 and lived in Rome when good Augustus reigned,
 when still the false and lying gods were worshipped. 72

I was a poet and sang of that just man,
 son of Anchises, who sailed off from Troy
 after the burning of proud Ilium. 75

But why retreat to so much misery?
 Why not climb up this blissful mountain here,
 the beginning and the source of all man's joy?" 78

"Are you then Virgil, are you then that fount
 from which pours forth so rich a stream of words?"
 I said to him, bowing my head modestly. 81

"O light and honor of the other poets,
 may my long years of study, and that deep love
 that made me search your verses, help me now! 84

You are my teacher, the first of all my authors,
 and you alone the one from whom I took
 the noble style that was to bring me honor. 87

You see the beast that forced me to retreat;
 save me from her, I beg you, famous sage,
 she makes me tremble, the blood throbs in my veins." 90

"But you must journey down another road,"
 he answered, when he saw me lost in tears,
 "if ever you hope to leave this wilderness; 93

this beast, the one you cry about in fear,
 allows no soul to succeed along her path,
 she blocks his way and puts an end to him. 96

---

91 Dante must choose another road because, in order to arrive at the Divine Light, it is necessary first to recognize the true nature of sin, renounce it, and pay penance for it.

She is by nature so perverse and vicious,
    her craving belly is never satisfied,
        still hungering for food the more she eats.   99

She mates with many creatures, and will go on
    mating with more until the greyhound comes
        and tracks her down to make her die in anguish.   102

He will not feed on either land or money:
    his wisdom, love, and virtue shall sustain him;
        he will be born between Feltro and Feltro.   105

He comes to save that fallen Italy
    for which the maid Camilla gave her life
        and Turnus, Nisus, Euryalus died of wounds.   108

And he will hunt for her through every city
    until he drives her back to Hell once more,
        whence Envy first unleashed her on mankind.   111

And so, I think it best you follow me
    for your own good, and I shall be your guide
        and lead you out through an eternal place   114

where you will hear desperate cries, and see
    tormented shades, some old as Hell itself,
        and know what second death is, from their screams.   117

And later you will see those who rejoice
    while they are burning, for they have hope of coming,
        whenever it may be, to join the blessed—   120

101–111   The Greyhound has been identified with Henry VII, Charles Martel, and even Dante himself. It seems more plausible that the Greyhound represents Can Grande della Scala, the ruler of Verona from 1308 to 1329, whose "wisdom, love, and virtue" (104) were certainly well-known to Dante. Whoever the Greyhound may be, the prophecy would seem to indicate in a larger sense the establishment of a spiritual kingdom on earth in which "wisdom, love, and virtue" will replace the bestial sins of the world. Perhaps Dante had no specific person in mind.

107   Camilla was the valiant daughter of King Metabus, who was slain while fighting against the Trojans (*Aeneid* XI).

108   Turnus was the king of the Rutulians. Nisus and Euryalus were young Trojan warriors slain during a nocturnal raid on the camp of the Rutulians.

117   The "second" death is that of the soul, which occurs when the soul is damned.

122   Just as Virgil, the pagan Roman poet, cannot enter the Christian Paradise because he lived before the birth of Christ and lacks knowledge of Christian salvation, so Reason can only guide the Pilgrim to a certain point: In order to enter Paradise, the Pilgrim's guide must be Christian Grace or Revelation (Theology) in the figure of Beatrice.

to whom, if you too wish to make the climb,
  a spirit, worthier than I, must take you;
  I shall go back, leaving you in her care,   123

because that Emperor dwelling on high
  will not let me lead any to His city,
  since I in life rebelled against His law.   126

Everywhere He reigns, and there He rules;
  there is His city, there is His high throne.
  Oh, happy the one He makes His citizen!"   129

And I to him: "Poet, I beg of you,
  in the name of God, that God you never knew,
  save me from this evil place and worse,   132

lead me there to the place you spoke about
  that I may see the gate Saint Peter guards
  and those whose anguish you have told me of."   135

Then he moved on, and I moved close behind him.

Canto II

But the pilgrim begins to waver; he expresses to Virgil his misgivings about his ability
to undertake the journey proposed by Virgil. His predecessors have been Aeneas and
Saint Paul, and he feels unworthy to take his place in their company. But Virgil rebukes
his cowardice, and relates the chain of events that led him to come to Dante. The Virgin
Mary took pity on the Pilgrim in his despair and instructed Saint Lucia to aid him. The
Saint turned to Beatrice because of Dante's great love for her, and Beatrice in turn went
down to Hell, into Limbo, and asked Virgil to guide her friend until that time when
she herself would become his guide. The Pilgrim takes heart at Virgil's explanation and
agrees to follow him.

The day was fading and the darkening air
  was releasing all the creatures on our earth
  from their daily tasks, and I, one man alone,   3

was making ready to endure the battle
  of the journey, and of the pity it involved,
  which my memory, unerring, shall now retrace.   6

---

124 Note the pagan terminology of Virgil's reference to God: It expresses, as best it can, his unenlightened conception of the
     Supreme Authority.

O Muses! O high genius! Help me now!
    O memory that wrote down what I saw,
    here your true excellence shall be revealed!   9

Then I began: "O poet come to guide me,
    tell me if you think my worth sufficient
    before you trust me to this arduous road.   12

You wrote about young Sylvius's father,
    who went beyond, with flesh corruptible,
    with all his senses, to the immortal realm;   15

but if the Adversary of all evil
    was kind to him, considering who he was,
    and the consequence that was to come from him,   18

this cannot seem, to thoughtful men, unfitting,
    for in the highest heaven he was chosen
    father of glorious Rome and of her empire,   21

and both the city and her lands, in truth,
    were established as the place of holiness
    where the successors of great Peter sit.   24

And from this journey you celebrate in verse,
    Aeneas learned those things that were to bring
    victory for him, and for Rome, the Papal seat;   27

then later the Chosen Vessel, Paul, ascended
    to ring back confirmation of that faith
    which is the first step on salvation's road.   30

But why am I to go? Who allows me to?
    I am not Aeneas, I am not Paul,
    neither I nor any man would think me worthy;   33

and so, if I should undertake the journey,
    I fear it might turn out an act of folly—
    you are wise, you see more than my words express."   36

As one who unwills what he willed, will change
    his purpose with some new second thought,
    completely quitting what he first had started,   39

28–30   In his Second Epistle to the Corinthians (12:2–4), the apostle Paul alludes to his mystical elevation to the third
         heaven and to the arcane messages pronounced there.

so I did, standing there on that dark slope,
    thinking, ending the beginning of that venture
    I was so quick to take up at the start.   42

"If I have truly understood your words,"
    that shade of magnanimity replied,
    "your soul is burdened with that cowardice   45

which often weighs so heavily on man,
    it turns him from a noble enterprise
    like a frightened beast that shies at its own shadow,   48

To free you from this fear, let me explain
    the reason I came here, the words I heard
    that first time I felt pity for your soul: 51

I was among those dead who are suspended,
    when a lady summoned me. She was so blessed
    and beautiful, I implored her to command me.   54

With eyes of light more bright than any star,
    in low, soft tones she started to address me
    in her own language, with an angel's voice: 57

'O noble soul, courteous Mantuan,
    whose fame the world continues to preserve
    and will preserve as long as world there is,   60

my friend, who is no friend of Fortune's, strays
    on a desert slope; so many obstacles
    have crossed his path, his fright has turned him back   63

I fear he may have gone so far astray,
    from what report has come to me in Heaven,
    that I may have started to his aid too late.   66

Now go, and with your elegance of speech,
    with whatever may be needed for his freedom,
    give him your help, and thereby bring me solace.   69

I am Beatrice, who urges you to go;
    I come from the place I am longing to return to;
    love moved me, as it moves me now to speak.   72

When I return to stand before my Lord,
    often I shall sing your praises to Him.'
    And then she spoke no more. And I began,   75

'O Lady of Grace, through whom alone mankind
    may go beyond all worldly things contained
    within the sphere that makes the smallest round,   78

your plea fills me with happy eagerness
    to have obeyed already would still seem late!
    You needed only to express your wish.   81

But tell me how you dared to make this journey
    all the way down to this point of spacelessness,
    away from your spacious home that calls you back.'   84

'Because your question searches for deep meaning,
    I shall explain in simple words,' she said,
    'just why I have no fear of coming here.   87

A man must stand in fear of just those things
    that truly have the power to do us harm,
    of nothing else, for nothing else is fearsome.   90

God gave me such a nature through His Grace,
    the torments you must bear cannot affect me,
    nor are the fires of Hell a threat to me.   93

A gracious lady sits in Heaven grieving
    for what happened to the one I send you to,
    and her compassion breaks Heaven's stern decree.   96

She called Lucia and making her request,
    she said, "Your faithful one is now in need
    of you, and to you I now commend his soul."   99

Lucia, the enemy of cruelty,
    hastened to make her way to where I was,
    sitting by the side of ancient Rachel,   102

and said to me: "Beatrice, God's true praise,
    will you not help the one whose love was such
    it made him leave the vulgar crowd for you?   105

---

94   The lady is the Virgin Mary.

102   In the Dantean Paradise Rachel is seated by Beatrice.

Do you not hear the pity of his weeping,
    do you not see what death it is that threatens him
    along that river the sea shall never conquer?"   108

There never was a wordly person living
    more anxious to promote his selfish gains
    than I was at the sound of words like these—   111

to leave my holy seat and come down here
    and place my trust in you, in your noble speech'
    that honors you and all those who have heard it!   114

When she had finished reasoning, she turned
    her shining eyes away, and there were tears.
    How eager then I was to come to you!   117

And I have come to you just as she wished,
    and I have freed you from the beast that stood
    blocking the quick way up the mount of bliss.   120

So what is wrong? Why, why do you delay?
    Why are you such a coward in your heart,
    why aren't you bold and free of all your fear,   123

when three such gracious ladies, who are blessed,
    watch out for you up there in Heaven's court,
    and my words, too, bring promise of such good?"   126

As little flowers from the frosty night
    are closed and limp, and when the sun shines down
    on them, they rise to open on their stem,   129

my wilted strength began to bloom within me,
    and such warm courage flowed into my heart
    that I spoke like a man set free of fear.   132

"O she, compassionate, who moved to help me!
    And you, all kindness, in obeying quick
    those words of truth she brought with her for you—   135

you and the words you spoke have moved my heart
    with such desire to continue onward
    that now I have returned to my first purpose.   138

Let us start, for both our wills, joined now, are one.
　　You are my guide, you are my lord and teacher."
　　These were my words to him and, when he moved,　　　　141

I entered on that deep and rugged road.

Canto III

As the two poets enter the vestibule that leads to Hell itself, Dante sees the inscription above the gate, and he hears the screams of anguish from the damned souls. Rejected by God and not accepted by the powers of Hell, the first group of souls are "nowhere," because of their cowardly refusal to make a choice in life. Their punishment is to follow a banner at a furious pace forever, and to be tormented by flies and hornets. The Pilgrim recognizes several of these shades but mentions none by name. Next they come to the River Acheron, where they are greeted by the infernal boatman, Charon. Among those doomed souls who are to be ferried across the river, Charon sees the living man and challenges him, but Virgil lets it be known that his companion must pass. Then across the landscape rushes a howling wind, which blasts the Pilgrim out of his senses, and he falls to the ground.

I AM THE WAY INTO THE DOLEFUL CITY,
　　I AM THE WAY INTO ETERNAL GRIEF,
　　I AM THE WAY TO A FORSAKEN RACE.　　　　3

JUSTICE IT WAS THAT MOVED MY GREAT CREATOR;
　　DIVINE OMNIPOTENCE CREATED ME,
　　AND HIGHEST WISDOM JOINED WITH PRIMAL LOVE.　　　　6

BEFORE ME NOTHING BUT ETERNAL THINGS
　　WERE MADE, AND I SHALL LAST ETERNALLY.
　　ABANDON EVERY HOPE, ALL YOU WHO ENTER.　　　　9

I saw these words spelled out in somber colors
　　inscribed along the ledge above a gate;
　　"Master," I said, "these words I see are cruel."　　　　12

He answered me, speaking with experience:
　　"Now here you must leave all distrust behind;
　　let all your cowardice die on this spot.　　　　15

5–6　Divine Omnipotence, Highest Wisdom, and Primal Love are, respectively, the Father, the Son, and the Holy Ghost. Thus, the gate of Hell was created by the Trinity moved by Justice.

We are at the place where earlier I said
　　you could expect to see the suffering race
　　of souls who lost the good of intellect."   18

Placing his hand on mine, smiling at me
　　in such a way that I was reassured,
　　he led me in, into those mysteries.   21

Here sighs and cries and shrieks of lamentation
　　echoed throughout the starless air of Hell;
　　at first these sounds resounding made me weep: 24

tongues confused, a language strained in anguish
　　with cadences of anger, shrill outcries
　　and raucous groans that joined with sounds of hands,   27

raising a whirling storm that turns itself
　　forever through that air of endless black,
　　like grains of sand swirling when a whirlwind blows.   30

And I, in the midst of all this circling horror,
　　began, "Teacher, what are these sounds I hear?
　　What souls are these so overwhelmed by grief?"   33

And he to me: "This wretched state of being
　　is the fate of those sad souls who lived a life
　　but lived it with no blame and with no praise.   36

They are mixed with that repulsive choir of angels
　　neither faithful nor unfaithful to their God,
　　who undecided stood but for themselves.   39

Heaven, to keep its beauty, cast them out,
　　but even Hell itself would not receive them,
　　for fear the damned might glory over them."   42

And I. "Master, what torments do they suffer
　　that force them to lament so bitterly?"
　　He answered: "I will tell you in few words: 45

these wretches have no hope of truly dying,
　　and this blind life they lead is so abject
　　it makes them envy every other fate.   48

---

18   Souls who have lost sight of God.

The world will not record their having been there;
    Heaven's mercy and its justice turn from them.
    Let's not discuss them; look and pass them by."   51

And so I looked and saw a kind of banner
    rushing ahead, whirling with aimless speed
    as though it would not ever take a stand;   54

behind it an interminable train
    of souls pressed on, so many that I wondered
    how death could have undone so great a number.   57

When I had recognized a few of them,
    I saw the shade of the one who must have been
    the coward who had made the great refusal.   60

At once I understood, and I was sure
    this was that sect of evil souls who were
    hateful to God and to His enemies.   63

These wretches, who had never truly lived,
    went naked, and were stung and stung again
    by the hornets and the wasps that circled them   66

and made their faces run with blood in streaks;
    their blood, mixed with their tears, dripped to their feet,
    and disgusting maggots collected in the pus.   69

And when I looked beyond this crowd I saw
    a throng upon the shore of a wide river,
    which made me ask, "Master, I would like to know: 72

who are these people, and what law is this
    that makes those souls so eager for the crossing
    as I can see, even in this dim light?"   75

And he: "All this will be made plain to you
    as soon as we shall come to stop awhile
    upon the sorrowful shore of Acheron."   78

52–69   In the *Inferno* divine retribution assumes the form of the *contrapasso*, i.e., the just punishment of sin, effected by a process either resembling or contrasting to the sin itself. In this canto the *contrapasso* opposes the sin of neutrality, or inactivity: The souls who in their early lives had no banner, no leader to follow, now run forever after one.

60   The coward could be Pontius Pilate, who refused to pass sentence on Christ.

And I, with eyes cast down in shame, for fear
    that I perhaps had spoken out of turn,
    said nothing more until we reached the river.   81

And suddenly, coming toward us in a boat,
    a man of years whose ancient hair was white
    shouted at us, "Woe to you, perverted souls!   84

Give up all hope of ever seeing Heaven:
    I come to lead you to the other shore,
    into eternal darkness, ice, and fire.   87

And you, the living soul, you over there,
    get away from all these people who are dead."
    But when he saw I did not move aside,   90

he said, "Another way, by other ports,
    not here, shall you pass to reach the other shore;
    a lighter skiff than this must carry you."   93

And my guide, "Charon, this is no time for anger!
    It is so willed, there where the power is
    for what is willed; that's all you need to know."   96

These words brought silence to the woolly cheeks
    of the ancient steersman of the livid marsh,
    whose eyes were set in glowing wheels of fire.   99

But all those souls there, naked, in despair,
    changed color and their teeth began to chatter
    at the sound of his announcement of their doom.   102

They were cursing God, cursing their own parents,
    the human race, the time, the place, the seed
    of their beginning, and their day of birth.   105

Then all together, weeping bitterly,
    they packed themselves along the wicked shore
    that waits for every man who fears not God.   108

The devil, Charon, with eyes of glowing coals,
    summons them all together with a signal,
    and with an oar he strikes the laggard sinner.   111

As in autumn when the leaves begin to fall,
 one after the other (until the branch
 is witness to the spoils spread on the ground),   114

so did the evil seed of Adam's Fall
 drop from that shore to the boat, one at a time,
 at the signal, like the falcon to its lure.   117

Away they go across the darkened waters,
 and before they reach the other side to land,
 a new throng starts collecting on this side.   120

"My son," the gentle master said to me,
 "all those who perish in the wrath of God
 assemble here from all parts of the earth;   123

they want to cross the river, they are eager;
 it is Divine Justice that spurs them on,
 turning the fear they have into desire.   126

A good soul never comes to make this crossing,
 so, if Charon grumbles at the sight of you,
 you see now what his words are really saying."   129

He finished speaking, and the grim terrain
 shook violently; and the fright it gave me
 even now in recollection makes me sweat.   132

Out of the tear-drenched land a wind arose
 which blasted forth into a reddish light,
 knocking my senses out of me completely,   135

and I fell as one falls tired into sleep.

Canto IV

Waking from his swoon, the Pilgrim is led by Virgil to the First Circle of Hell, known as Limbo, where the sad shades of the virtuous non-Christians dwell. The souls here, including Virgil, suffer no physical torment, but they must live, in desire, without hope of seeing God. Virgil tells about Christ's descent into Hell and His salvation of several Old Testament figures.

124–126 It is perhaps a part of the punishment that the souls of all the damned are eager for their punishment to begin; those who were so willing to sin on earth, are in hell damned with a willingness to receive their just retribution.

A heavy clap of thunder! I awoke
    from the deep sleep that drugged my mind—startled,
    the way one is when shaken out of sleep.   3

I turned my rested eyes from side to side,
    already on my feet and, staring hard,
    I tried my best to find out where I was,   6

and this is what I saw: I found myself
    upon the brink of grief's abysmal valley
    that collects the thunderings of endless cries.   9

So dark and deep and nebulous it was,
    try as I might to force my sight below,
    I could not see the shape of anything.   12

"Let us descend into the sightless world,"
    began the poet (his face was deathly pale):
    "I will go first, and you will follow me."   15

And I, aware of his changed color, said:
    "But how can I go on if you are frightened?
    You are my constant strength when I lose heart."   18

And he to me: "The anguish of the souls
    that are down here paints my face with pity
    which you have wrongly taken to be fear.   21

Let us go, the long road urges us."
    He entered then, leading the way for me
    down to the first circle of the abyss.   24

Down there, to judge only by what I heard,
    there were no wails but just the sounds of sighs
    rising and trembling through the timeless air,   27

the sounds of sighs of untormented grief
    burdening these groups, diverse and teeming,
    made up of men and women and of infants.   30

Then the good master said, "You do not ask
    what sort of souls are these you see around you.
    Now you should know before we go on farther,   33

they have not sinned. But their great worth alone
    was not enough, for they did not know Baptism,
    which is the gateway to the faith you follow,   36

and if they came before the birth of Christ,
    they did not worship God the way one should;
    I myself am a member of this group.   39

For this defect, and for no other guilt,
    we here are lost. In this alone we suffer:
    cut off from hope, we live on in desire."   42

The words I heard weighed heavy on my heart;
    to think that souls as virtuous as these
    were suspended in that limbo, and forever!   45

"Tell me, my teacher, tell me, O my master,"
    I began (wishing to have confirmed by him
    the teachings of unerring Christian doctrine),   48

"did any ever leave here, through his merit
    or with another's help, and go to bliss?"
    And he, who understood my hidden question,   51

answered: "I was a novice in this place
    when I saw a mighty lord descend to us
    who wore the sign of victory as his crown.   54

He took from us the shade of our first parent,
    of Abel, his good son, of Noah, too,
    and of obedient Moses, who made the laws;   57

Abram, the Patriarch, David the King,
    Israel with his father and his children,
    with Rachel, whom he worked so hard to win;   60

and many more he chose for blessedness;
    and you should know, before these souls were taken,
    no human soul had ever reached salvation."   63

Canto V

From limbo Virgil leads his ward down to the threshold of the Second Circle of Hell, where for the first time he will see the damned in Hell being punished for their sins. There, barring their way, is the hideous figure of Minòs, the bestial judge of Dante's underworld; but after strong words from Virgil, the poets are allowed to pass into the dark space of this circle, where can be heard the wailing voices of the Lustful, whose punishment consists in being forever whirled about in a dark, stormy wind. After seeing a thousand or more famous lovers—including Semiramis, Dido, Helen, Achilles, and Paris—the Pilgrim asks to speak to two figures he sees together. They are Francesca da

Rimini and her lover, Paolo, and the scene in which they appear is probably the most famous episode of the *Inferno*. At the end of the scene, the Pilgrim, who has been overcome by pity for the lovers, faints to the ground.

This way I went, descending from the first
    into the second round, that holds less space
    but much more pain—stinging the soul to wailing.   3

There stands Minòs grotesquely, and he snarls,
    examining the guilty at the entrance;
    he judges and dispatches, tail in coils.   6

By this I mean that when the evil soul
    appears before him, it confesses all,
    and he, who is the expert judge of sins,   9

knows to what place in Hell the soul belongs;
    the times he wraps his tail around himself
    tell just how far the sinner must go down.   12

The damned keep crowding up in front of him:
    they pass along to judgment one by one;
    they speak, they hear, and then are hurled below.   15

"O you who come to the place where pain is host,"
    Minòs spoke out when he caught sight of me,
    putting aside the duties of his office,   18

"be careful how you enter and whom you trust
    it's easy to get in, but don't be fooled!"
    And my guide said to him: "Why keep on shouting?   21

Do not attempt to stop his fated journey; it
    is so willed there where the power is
    for what is willed; that's all you need to know."   24

And now the notes of anguish start to play
    upon my ears; and now I find myself
    where sounds on sounds of weeping pound at me.   27

---

4   Minòs was the son of Zeus and Europa. As king of Crete he was revered for his wisdom and judicial gifts. For these qualities he became chief magistrate of the underworld in classical literature. (See Virgil, *Aeneid* VI, 432–433.) Although Dante did not alter Minòs' official function, he transformed him into a demonic figure, both in his physical characteristics and in his bestial activity.

I came to a place where no light shone at all,
    bellowing like the sea racked by a tempest,
    when warring winds attack it from both sides.   30

The infernal storm, eternal in its rage,
    sweeps and drives the spirits with its blast:
    it whirls them, lashing them with punishment.   33

When they are swept back past their place of judgment,
    then come the shrieks, laments, and anguished cries;
    there they blaspheme God's almighty power.   36

I learned that to this place of punishment
    all those who sin in lust have been condemned,
    those who make reason slave to appetite;   39

and as the wings of starlings in the winter
    bear them along in wide-spread, crowded flocks,
    so does that wind propel the evil spirits: 42

now here, then there, and up and down, it drives them
    with never any hope to comfort them
    hope not of rest but even of suffering less.   45

And just like cranes in flight, chanting their lays,
    stretching an endless line in their formation,
    I saw approaching, crying their laments,   48

spirits carried along by the battling winds.
    And so I asked, "Teacher, tell me, what souls
    are these punished in the sweep of the black wind?"   51

"The first of those whose story you should know,"
    my master wasted no time answering,
    "was empress over lands of many tongues;   54

her vicious tastes had so corrupted her
    she licensed every form of lust with laws
    to cleanse the stain of scandal she had spread;   57

she is Semiramis, who, legend says,
    was Ninus' wife as well as his successor;
    she governed all the land the Sultan rules.   60

31–32   The *contrapasso* or punishment suggests that lust (the "infernal storm") is pursued without the light of reason (in the darkness).

The next is she who killed herself for love
    and broke faith with the ashes of Sichaeus;
    and there is Cleopatra, who loved men's lusting.   63

See Helen there, the root of evil woe
    lasting long years, and see the great Achilles,
    who lost his life to love, in final combat;   66

see Paris, Tristan"—then, more than a thousand
    he pointed out to me, and named them all,
    those shades whom love cut off from life on earth.   69

After I heard my teacher call the names
    of all these knights and ladies of ancient times,
    pity confused my senses, and I was dazed.   72

I began: "Poet, I would like, with all my heart,
    to speak to those two there who move together
    and seem to be so light upon the winds."   75

And he: "You'll see when they are closer to us;
    if you entreat them by that love of theirs
    that carries them along, they'll come to you."   78

When the winds bent their course in our direction
    I raised my voice to them, "O wearied souls,
    come speak with us if it be not forbidden."   81

As doves, called by desire to return
    to their sweet nest, with wings raised high and poised,
    float downward through the air, guided by will,   84

---

64   Helen of Troy.

65–66   Enticed by the beauty of Polyxena, a daughter of the Trojan king, Achilles desired her to be his wife, but Hecuba, Polyxena's mother, arranged a counterplot with Paris so that when Achilles entered the temple for his presumed marriage, he was treacherously slain by Paris.

67   Paris was the son of Priam, king of Troy, whose abduction of Helen ignited the Trojan War. Tristan was the central figure of numerous medieval French, German, and Italian romances. Sent as a messenger by his uncle, King Mark of Cornwall, to obtain Isolt for him in marriage, Tristan became enamored of her, and she of him. After Isolt's marriage to Mark, the lovers continued their love affair, and in order to maintain its secrecy they necessarily employed many deceits and ruses. According to one version, Mark, increasingly suspicious of their attachment, finally discovered them together and ended the incestuous relationship by mortally wounding Tristan with a lance.

74   The two are Francesca, daughter of Guido Vecchio da Polenta, lord of Ravenna; and Paolo Malatesta, third son of Malatesta da Verrucchio, lord of Rimini. Around 1275 the aristocratic Francesca was married for political reasons to Gianciotto, the physically deformed second son of Malatesta da Verrucchio. In time a love affair developed between Francesca and Gianciotto's younger brother, Paolo. One day the betrayed husband discovered them in an amorous embrace and slew them both.

so these two left the flock where Dido is
    and came toward us through the malignant air,
    such was the tender power of my call.   87

"O living creature, gracious and so kind,
    who makes your way here through this dingy air
    to visit us who stained the world with blood,   90

if we could claim as friend the King of Kings,
    we would beseech him that he grant you peace,
    you who show pity for our atrocious plight.   93

Whatever pleases you to hear or speak
    we will hear and we will speak about with you
    as long as the wind, here where we are, is silent.   96

The place where I was born lies on the shore
    where the river Po with its attendant streams
    descends to seek its final resting place.   99

Love, quick to kindle in the gentle heart,
    seized this one for the beauty of my body,
    torn from me. (How it happened still offends me!)   102

Love, that excuses no one loved from loving,
    seized me so strongly with delight in him
    that, as you see, he never leaves my side.   105

Love led us straight to sudden death together.
    Caïna awaits the one who quenched our lives."
    These were the words that came from them to us.   108

When those offended souls had told their story,
    I bowed my head and kept it bowed until
    the poet said, "What are you thinking of?"   111

When finally I spoke, I sighed, "Alas,
    all those sweet thoughts, and oh, how much desiring
    brought these two down into this agony."   114

And then I turned to them and tried to speak;
    I said, "Francesca, the torment that you suffer
    brings painful tears of pity to my eyes.   117

---

107   Caïna was one of the four divisions of Cocytus, the lower part of Hell, wherein those souls who treacherously betrayed their kin are tormented.

But tell me, in that time of your sweet sighing
    how, and by what signs, did love allow you
    to recognize your dubious desires?"   120

And she to me: "There is no greater pain
    than to remember, in our present grief,
    past happiness (as well your teacher knows)!   123

But if your great desire is to learn
    the very root of such a love as ours,
    I shall tell you, but in words of flowing tears.   126

One day we read, to pass the time away,
    of Lancelot, of how he fell in love;
    we were alone, innocent of suspicion.   129

Time and again our eyes were brought together
    by the book we read; our faces flushed and paled.
    To the moment of one line alone we yielded: 132

it was when we read about those longed-for lips
    now being kissed by such a famous lover,
    that this one (who shall never leave my side)   135

then kissed my mouth, and trembled as he did.
    Our Galehot was that book and he who wrote it.
    That day we read no further." And all the while   138

the one of the two spirits spoke these words,
    the other wept, in such a way that pity
    blurred my senses; I swooned as though to die,   141

and fell to Hell's floor as a body, dead, falls.

Canto XIX deals with a form of fraud known as simony. Simony is a sin in which an individual tries to make money by selling or profiting from the exercise of church offices. Consequently, we find reference in this canto to several popes Dante considered guilty of this crime. His attitude toward them is quite harsh, since he believed that the corruption of the church had terrible consequences for the good of society. You will notice that the sinners we encounter in Cantos XIX and XXI are found in concentric ditches called bolgia (from the Italian word for pouch). In various places there are stone bridges over the bolgia over which Dante and Virgil can cross as they descend deeper into hell.

Canto XIX

From the bridge above the Third *Bolgia* can be seen a rocky landscape below filled with holes, from each of which protrude a sinner's legs and feet; flames dance across their soles. When the Pilgrim expresses curiosity about a particular pair of twitching legs, Virgil carries him down into the *bolgia* so that the Pilgrim himself may question the sinner. The legs belong to Pope Nicholas III, who astounds the Pilgrim by mistaking him for Boniface VIII, the next pope, who, as soon as he dies, will fall to the same hole, thereby pushing Nicholas farther down. He predicts that soon after Boniface, Pope Clement V will come, stuffing both himself and Boniface still deeper. To Nicholas's rather rhetoric-filled speech the Pilgrim responds with equally high language, inveighing against the Simonists, the evil churchmen who are punished here. Virgil is much pleased with his pupil and, lifting him in an affectionate embrace, he carries him to the top of the arch above the next *bolgia*.

> O Simon Magus! O scum that followed him!
>> Those things of God that rightly should be wed
>> to holiness, you, rapacious creatures,   3

> for the price of gold and silver, prostitute.
>> Now, in your honor, I must sound my trumpet
>> for here in the third pouch is where you dwell.   6

> We had already climbed to see this tomb,
>> and were standing high above it on the bridge,
>> exactly at the mid-point of the ditch.   9

> O Highest Wisdom, how you demonstrate
>> your art in Heaven, on earth, and here in Hell!
>> How justly does your power make awards!   12

1–6   As related in Acts (8:9–24), Simon the magician, having observed the descent of the Holy Spirit upon the apostles John and Peter, desired to purchase this power for himself, whereupon Peter harshly admonished him for even thinking that the gift of God might be bought. Derived from this sorcerer's name, the word "simony" (74) refers to those offenses involving the sale or fraudulent possession of ecclesiastical offices.

I saw along the sides and on the bottom
    the livid-colored rock all full of holes;
    all were the same in size, and each was round.   15

To me they seemed no wider and no deeper
    than those inside my lovely San Giovanni,
    in which the priest would stand or baptize from;   18

and one of these, not many years ago,
    I smashed for someone who was drowning in it:
    let this be mankind's picture of the truth!   21

From the mouth of every hole were sticking out
    a single sinner's feet, and then the legs
    up to the calf—the rest was stuffed inside.   24

The soles of every sinner's feet were flaming; their
    naked legs were twitching frenziedly
    they would have broken any chain or rope.   27

Just as a flame will only move along
    an object's oily outer peel, so here
    the fire slid from heel to toe and back.   30

"Who is that one, Master, that angry wretch,
    who is writhing more than any of his comrades,"
    I asked, "the one licked by a redder flame?"   33

And he to me, "If you want to be carried down
    along that lower bank to where he is,
    you can ask him who he is and why he's here."   36

And I, "My pleasure is what pleases you:
    you are my lord, you know that from your will
    I would not swerve. You even know my thoughts."   39

When we reached the fourth bank, we began to turn
    and, keeping to the left, made our way down
    to the bottom of the holed and narrow ditch.   42

The good guide did not drop me from his side
    until he brought me to the broken rock
    of that one who was fretting with his shanks.   45

---

25   Just as the Simonists' perversion of the Church is symbolized by their "perverted" immersion in holes resembling baptis-
mal fonts, so their "baptism" is perverted: instead of the head being moistened with water, the feet are "baptized" with
oil and fire.

"Whatever you are, holding your upside down,
   O wretched soul, stuck like a stake in ground,
   make a sound or something," I said, "if you can."   48

I stood there like a priest who is confessing
   some vile assassin who, fixed in his ditch,
   has called him back again to put off dying.   51

He cried: "Is that you, here, already, upright?
   Is that you here already upright, Boniface?
   By many years the book has lied to me!   54

Are you fed up so soon with all that wealth
   for which you did not fear to take by guile
   the Lovely Lady, then tear her asunder?"   57

I stood there like a person just made fun of,
   dumbfounded by a question for an answer,
   not knowing how to answer the reply.   60

Then Virgil said: "Quick, hurry up and tell him:
   'I'm not the one, I'm not the one you think!'"
   And I answered just the way he told me to.   63

The spirit heard, and twisted both his feet,
   then, sighing with a grieving, tearful voice,
   he said: "Well then, what do you want of me?   66

If it concerns you so to learn my name
   that for this reason you came down the bank,
   know that I once was dressed in the great mantle.   69

---

53   From the foreknowledge granted to the infernal shades, the speaker shows that Pope Boniface VIII, upon his death in 1303, will take his place in that very receptacle wherein he himself is now being tormented. The Pilgrim's voice, so close at hand, has caused the sinner to believe that his successor has arrived unexpectedly before his time (three years, in fact) and, consequently, that the Divine Plan of Events, the Book of Fate (54), has lied to him.

Having obtained the abdication of Pope Celestine V, Boniface gained the support of Charles II of Nantes and thus was assured of his election to the papacy (1294). In addition to misusing the Church's influence in his dealings with Charles, Boniface VIII freely distributed ecclesiastical offices among his family and confidants. As early as 1300 he was plotting the destruction of the Whites, the Florentine political faction to which Dante belonged.

57   The "Lovely Lady" is the Church.

67–72   Gian Gaetano degli Orsini (lit. "of the little bears," hence the designation "she-bear's son" and the reference to "my cubs") became Pope Nicholas III in 1277. As a cardinal he won renown for his integrity; however, in the short three years between ascent to the papal throne and his death he became notorious for his simoniacal practices.

But actually I was the she-bear's son,
    so greedy to advance my cubs, that wealth
    I pocketed in life, and here, myself.   72

Beneath my head are pushed down all the others
    who came, sinning in simony, before me,
    squeezed tightly in the fissures of the rock.   75

I, in my turn, shall join the rest below
    as soon as he comes, the one I thought you were
    when, all too quick, I put my question to you.   78

But already my feet have baked a longer time
    (and I have been stuck upside-down like this)
    than he will stay here planted with feet aflame: 81

soon after him shall come one from the West,
    a lawless shepherd, one whose fouler deeds
    make him a fitting cover for us both.   84

He shall be another Jason, like the one
    in Maccabees: just as his king was pliant,
    so France's king shall soften to this priest."   87

I do not know, perhaps I was too bold here,
    but I answered him in tune with his own words:
    "Well, tell me now: what was the sum of money   90

that holy Peter had to pay our Lord
    before He gave the keys into his keeping?
    Certainly He asked no more than 'Follow me.'   93

Nor did Peter or the rest extort gold coins
    or silver from Matthias when he was picked
    to fill the place the evil one had lost.   96

---

77   The man still to come is Boniface VIII. (See above, note on line 53)

82–84   The "lawless shepherd" is Pope Clement V of Gascony, who, upon his death in 1314, will join Nicholas and Boniface in eternal torment.

85–87   Having obtained the high priesthood of the Jews by bribing King Antiochus of Syria, Jason neglected the sacrifices and sanctuary of the temple and introduced Greek modes of life into his community. As Jason had fraudulently acquired his position, so had Menelaus, who offered more money to the king, supplanted Jason (2 Maccabees 47:7–27). As Jason obtained office from King Antiochus fraudulently, so shall Clement acquire his from Philip.

94–96   After the treachery and subsequent expulsion of Judas, the apostles cast lots in order to replenish their number. Thus, by the will of God, not through monetary payment, was Matthias elected to the vacated post (Acts 1:15–26).

So stay stuck there, for you are rightly punished,
    and guard with care the money wrongly gained
    that made you stand courageous against Charles.   99

And were it not for the reverence I have
    for those highest of all keys that you once held
    in the happy life—if this did not restrain me,   102

I would use even harsher words than these,
    for your avarice brings grief upon the world,
    crushing the good, exalting the depraved.   105

You shepherds it was the Evangelist had in mind
    when the vision came to him of her who sits
    upon the waters playing whore with kings: 108

that one who with the seven heads was born
    and from her ten horns managed to draw strength
    so long as virtue was her bridegroom's joy.   111

You have built yourselves a God of gold and silver!
    How do you differ from the idolator,
    except he worships one, you worship hundreds?   114

O Constantine, what evil did you sire,
    not by your conversion, but by the dower
    that the first wealthy Father got from you!"   117

And while I sang these very notes to him,
    his big flat feet kicked fiercely out of anger,
    —or perhaps it was his conscience gnawing him.   120

I think my master liked what I was saying,
    for all the while he smiled and was intent
    on hearing the ring of truly spoken words.   123

106–111   St. John the Evangelist relates his vision of the dissolute Imperial City of Rome. To Dante, she "who sits / upon the waters" represents the Church, which has been corrupted by the simoniacal activities of many popes (the "shepherds" of the Church). The seven heads symbolize the seven Holy Sacraments; the ten horns represent the Ten Commandments.

115–117   Constantine the Great, emperor of Rome (306–387), was converted to Christianity in the year 312. Having conquered the eastern Mediterranean lands, he transferred the capital of the Roman Empire to Constantinople (360). This move, according to tradition, stemmed from Constantine's decision to place the western part of the empire under the jurisdiction of the Church in order to repay Pope Sylvester ("the first wealthy Father") for healing him of leprosy. The so-called "Donation of Constantine," though it was proved in the fifteenth century to be a complete fabrication on the part of the clergy, was universally accepted as the truth in the Middle Ages. Dante the Pilgrim reflects this tradition in his sad apostrophe to the individual who first would have introduced wealth to the Church and who, unknowingly, would be ultimately responsible for its present corruption.

Then he took hold of me with both his arms,
    and when he had me firm against his breast,
    he climbed back up the path he had come down.   126

He did not tire of the weight clasped tight to him,
    but brought me to the top of the bridge's arch,
    the one that joins the fourth bank to the fifth.   129

And here he gently set his burden down
    gently, for the ridge, so steep and rugged,
    would have been hard even for goats to cross.   132

From there another valley opened to me.

Canto XXI

When the two reach the summit of the arch over the Fifth *Bolgia*, they see in the ditch below the bubbling of boiling pitch. Virgil's sudden warning of danger frightens the Pilgrim even before he sees a black devil rushing toward them, with a sinner slung over his shoulder. From the bridge the devil flings the sinner into the pitch, where he is poked at and tormented by the family of Malebranche devils. Virgil, advising his ward to hide behind a rock, crosses the bridge to face the devils alone. They threaten him with their pitchforks, but when he announces to their leader, Malacoda, that Heaven has willed that he lead another through Hell, the devil's arrogance collapses. Virgil calls the Pilgrim back to him. Scarmiglione, who tries to take a poke at him, is rebuked by his leader, who tells the travelers that the sixth arch is broken here but farther on they will find another bridge to cross. He chooses a squad of his devils to escort them there: Alichino, Calcabrina, Cagnazzo, Barbariccia, Libicocco, Draghignazzo, Ciriatto, Graffiacane, Farfarello, and Rubicante. The Pilgrim's suspicion about their unsavory escorts is brushed aside by his guide, and the squad starts off, giving an obscene salute to their captain, who returns their salute with a fart.

From this bridge to the next we walked and talked
    of things my Comedy does not care to tell;
    and when we reached the summit of the arch,   3

we stopped to see the next fosse of Malebolge
    and to hear more lamentation voiced in vain:
    I saw that it was very strangely dark!   6

In the vast and busy shipyard of the Venetians
    there boils all winter long a tough, thick pitch
    that is used to caulk the ribs of unsound ships.   9

Since winter will not let them sail, they toil:
    some build new ships, others repair the old ones,
    plugging the planks come loose from many sailings;   12

some hammer at the bow, some at the stern,
    one carves the oars while others twine the ropes,
    one mends the jib, one patches up the mainsail;   15

here, too, but heated by God's art, not fire,
    a sticky tar was boiling in the ditch
    that smeared the banks with viscous residue.   18

I saw it there, but I saw nothing in it,
    except the rising of the boiling bubbles
    breathing in air to burst and sink again.   21

I stood intently gazing there below,
    my guide, shouting to me: "Watch out, watch out!"
    took hold of me and drew me to his side.   24

I turned my head like one who can't resist
    looking to see what makes him run away
    (his body's strength draining with sudden fear),   27

but, looking back, does not delay his flight;
    and I saw coming right behind our backs,
    rushing along the ridge, a devil, black!   30

His face, his look, how frightening it was!
    With outstretched wings he skimmed along the rock,
    and every single move he made was cruel;   33

on one of his high-hunched and pointed shoulders
    he had a sinner slung by both his thighs,
    held tightly clawed at the tendons of his heels.   36

He shouted from our bridge: "Hey, Malebranche,
    here's one of Santa Zita's elders for you!
    You stick him under—I'll go back for more;   39

I've got that city stocked with the likes of him,
    they're all a bunch of grafters, save Bonturo!
    You can change a 'no' to 'yes' for cash in Lucca."   42

7–15 During the Middle Ages the shipyard at Venice, built in 1104, was one of the most active and productive in all Europe. The image of the busy shipyard with its activity revolving around a vat of viscous pitch establishes the tone for this canto (and the next) as one of tense and excited movement.

He flung him in, then from the flinty cliff
    sprang off. No hound unleashed to chase a thief
    could have taken off with greater speed than he.   45

That sinner plunged, then floated up stretched out,
    and the devils underneath the bridge all shouted:
    "You shouldn't imitate the Holy Face!   48

The swimming's different here from in the Serchio!
    We have our grappling-hooks along with us—
    don't show yourself above the pitch, or else!"   51

With a hundred prongs or more they pricked him, shrieking:
    "You've got to do your squirming under cover,
    try learning how to cheat beneath the surface."   54

They were like cooks who make their scullery boys
    poke down into the caldron with their forks
    to keep the meat from floating to the top.   57

My master said: "We'd best not let them know that
    you are here with me; crouch down behind
    some jutting rock so that they cannot see you;   60

whatever insults they may hurl at me,
    you must not fear, I know how things are run here;
    I have been caught in as bad a fix before."   63

He crossed the bridge and walked on past the end;
    as soon as he set foot on the sixth bank
    he forced himself to look as bold as possible.   66

With all the sound and fury that breaks loose
    when dogs rush out at some poor begging tramp,
    making him stop and beg from where he stands,   69

the ones who hid beneath the bridge sprang out
    and blocked him with a flourish of their pitchforks,
    but he shouted: "All of you behave yourselves!   72

46–51   The "Holy Face" was a wooden crucifix at Lucca. The sinner surfaces stretched out (46) on his back with arms flung
        wide like the figure on a crucifix—and this gives rise to the devil's remark that here in Hell one does not swim the
        same way as in the Serchio (a river near Lucca). In other words, in the Serchio people swim for pleasure, often floating
        on their backs (in the position of a crucifix).

Before you start to jab me with your forks,
    let one of you step forth to hear me out,
        and then decide if you still care to grapple."   75

They all cried out: "Let Malacoda go!"
    One stepped forward—the others stood their ground
        and moving, said, "What good will this do him?"   78

"Do you think, Malacoda," said my master,
    "that you would see me here, come all this way,
        against all opposition, and still safe,   81

without propitious fate and God's permission?
    Now let us pass, for it is willed in Heaven
        that I lead another by this savage path."   84

With this the devil's arrogance collapsed,
    his pitchfork, too, dropped right down to his feet,
        as he announced to all: "Don't touch this man!"   87

"You, hiding over there," my guide called me,
    "behind the bridge's rocks, curled up and quiet,
        come back to me, you may return in safety.   90

At his words I rose and then I ran to him
    and all the devils made a movement forward;
        I feared they would not really keep their pact.   93

(I remember seeing soldiers under truce,
    as they left the castle of Caprona, frightened
        to be passing in the midst of such an enemy.)   96

I drew up close to him, as close as possible,
    and did not take my eyes from all those faces
        that certainly had nothing good about them.   99

Their prongs were aimed at me, and one was saying:
    "Now do I let him have it in the rump?"
        They answered all for one: "Sure, stick him good!"   102

---

76   Malacoda is the leader of the devils in this *bolgia*. It is significant that a devil whose name means "evil tail" ends this canto
        with a fart (139).

94–96   Dante's personal recollection concerns the siege of Caprona (a fortress on the Arno River near Pisa) by Guelph troops
        from Lucca and Florence in 1289.

But the devil who had spoken with my guide
    was quick to spin around and scream an order:
    "At ease there, take it easy, Scarmiglione!"   105

Then he said to us: "You cannot travel straight
    across this string of bridges, for the sixth arch
    lies broken at the bottom of its ditch;   108

if you have made your mind up to proceed,
    you must continue on along this ridge;
    not far, you'll find a bridge that crosses it.   111

Five hours more and it will be one thousand,
    two hundred sixty-six years and a day
    since the bridge-way here fell crumbling to the ground.   114

I plan to send a squad of mine that way
    to see that no one airs himself down there;
    go along with them, they will not misbehave.   117

Front and center, Alichino, Calcabrina,"
    he shouted his commands, "you too, Cagnazzo;
    Barbariccia, you be captain of the squad.   120

Take Libicocco with you and Draghignazzo,
    toothy Ciriatto and Graffiacane,
    Farfarello and our crazy Rubicante.   123

Now tour the ditch, inspect the boiling tar;
    these two shall have safe passage to the bridge
    connecting den to den without a break."   126

"O master, I don't like the looks of this,"
    I said, "let's go, just you and me, no escort,
    you know the way. I want no part of them!   129

If you're observant, as you usually are,
    why is it you don't see them grind their teeth
    and wink at one another?—we're in danger!"   132

112–114   Christ's death on Good Friday, A.D. 34, would in five hours, according to Malacoda, have occurred 1266 years
        ago yesterday—"today" being the morning of Holy Saturday, 1300. Although the bridge across the next *bolgia*
        was shattered by the earthquake following Christ's crucifixion, Malacoda tells Virgil and the Pilgrim that there is
        another bridge that crosses this *bolgia*. This lie, carefully contrived by the spokesman for the devils, sets the trap for
        the overly confident, trusting Virgil and his wary charge.

And he to me: "I will not have you frightened;
>> let them do all the grinding that they want,
>> they do it for the boiling souls, not us."   135

Before they turned left-face along the bank
>> each one gave their good captain a salute
>> with farting tongue pressed tightly to his teeth,   138

and he blew back with his bugle of an ass-hole.

Circle IX (also known as Cocytus) is reserved for traitors. It has four subdivisions: Caïna, which contains traitors against kin; Antenora, for those who betray their homeland; Ptolomea, where we find those who violate the bond between host and guest; and Judecca, the eternal home of those who betray their benefactors. It is here, at the very bottom of hell, that we come across Lucifer.

Canto XXXII

They descend farther down into the darkness of the immense plain of ice in which shades of Traitors are frozen. In the outer region of the ice-lake, Caïna, are those who betrayed their kin in murder; among them, locked in a frozen embrace, are Napoleone and Alessandro of Mangona, and others are Mordred, Focaccia, Sassol Mascheroni, and Camicion de'pazzi.

If I had words grating and crude enough
>> that really could describe this horrid hole
>> supporting the converging weight of Hell,   3

I could squeeze out the juice of my memories
>> to the last drop. But I don't have these words,
>> and so I am reluctant to begin.   6

To talk about the bottom of the universe
>> the way it truly is, is no child's play,
>> no task for tongues that gurgle baby-talk.   9

But may those heavenly ladies aid my verse
>> who aided Amphion to wall-in Thebes,
>> that my words may tell exactly what I saw.   12

O misbegotten rabble of all rabble,
>> who crowd this realm, hard even to describe,
>> it were better you had lived as sheep or goats!   15

When we reached a point of darkness in the well
    below the giant's feet, farther down the slope,
      and I was gazing still at the high wall,   18

I heard somebody say: "Watch where you step!
    Be careful that you do not kick the heads
      of this brotherhood of miserable souls."   21

At that I turned around and saw before me
    a lake of ice stretching beneath my feet,
      more like a sheet of glass than frozen water.   24

In the depths of Austria's wintertime, the Danube
    never in all its course showed ice so thick,
      nor did the Don beneath its frigid sky,   27

as this crust here; for if Mount Tambernic
    or Pietrapana would crash down upon it,
      not even at its edges would a crack creak.   30

The way the frogs (in the season when the harvest
    will often haunt the dreams of the peasant girl)
      sit croaking with their muzzles out of water,   33

so these frigid, livid shades were stuck in ice
    up to where a person's shame appears;
      their teeth clicked notes like storks' beaks snapping shut. 36

And each one kept his face bowed toward the ice:
    the mouth bore testimony to the cold,
      the eyes, to sadness welling in the heart.   39

I gazed around awhile and then looked down,
    and by my feet I saw two figures clasped
      so tight that one's hair could have been the other's.   42

"Tell me, you two, pressing your chests together,"
    I asked them, "who are you?" Both stretched their necks
      and when they had their faces raised toward me,   45

their eyes, which had before been only glazed,
    dripped tears down to their lips, and the cold froze
      the tears between them, locking the pair more tightly.   48

Wood to wood with iron was never clamped
    so firm! And the two of them like billy-goats
      were butting at each other, mad with anger.   51

Another one with both ears frozen off,
    and head still bowed over his icy mirror,
    cried out: "What makes you look at us so hard?   54

If you're interested to know who these two are:
    the valley where Bisenzio's waters flow
    belonged to them and to their father, Albert;   57

the same womb bore them both, and if you scour
    all of Caïna, you will not turn up one
    who's more deserving of this frozen aspic—   60

not him who had his breast and shadow pierced
    with one thrust of the lance from Arthur's hand;
    not Focaccia; not even this one here,   63

whose head gets in my way and blocks my view,
    known in the world as Sassol Mascheroni,
    and if you're Tuscan you must know who he was.   66

To save me from your asking for more news:
    I was Camicion de' Pazzi, and I await
    Carlin, whose guilt will make my own seem less."   69

Farther on I saw a thousand doglike faces,
    purple from the cold. That's why I shudder,
    and always will, when I see a frozen pond.   72

55–58   The two brothers were Napoleone and Alessandro, sons of Count Alberto of Mangona, who owned part of the valley of the Bisenzio near Florence. The two quarreled often and eventually killed each other in a fight concerning their inheritance.

59   The icy ring of Cocytus is named Caïna after Cain, who slew his brother Abel. Thus, in the first division of this, the Ninth Circle, are punished those treacherous shades who murderously violated family bonds.

61–62   Mordred, the wicked nephew of King Arthur, tried to kill the king and take his kingdom. But Arthur pierced him with such a mighty blow that when the lance was pulled from the dying traitor a ray of sunlight traversed his body and interrupted Mordred's shadow. The story is told in the Old French romance *Lancelot du Lac*, the book that Francesca claims led her astray with Paolo in Canto V, 127.

63   Focaccia was one of the Cancellieri family of Pistoia and a member of the White parry. His treacherous murder of his cousin, Detto de' Cancellieri (a Black), was possibly the act that led to the Florentine intervention in Pistoian affairs.

65   The early commentators say that Sassot Mascheroni was a member of the Toschi family in Florence who murdered his nephew in order to gain his inheritance.

68–69   Nothing is known of Camicion de' Pazzi except that he murdered one Umbertino, a relative. Another of Camicion's kin, Carlino de' Pazzi (69) from Valdarno, was still alive when the Pilgrim's conversation with Camicion was taking place. But Camicion already knew that Carlino, in July 1302, would accept a bribe to surrender the castle of Piantravigne to the Blacks of Florence.

Canto XXXIV

Far across the frozen ice can be seen the gigantic figure of Lucifer, who appears from this distance like a windmill seen through fog; and as the two travelers walk on toward that terrifying sight, they see the shades of sinners totally buried in the frozen water. At the center of the earth Lucifer stands frozen from the chest downward, and his horrible ugliness (he has three faces) is made more fearful by the fact that in each of his three mouths he chews on one of the three worst sinners of all mankind, the worst of those who betrayed their benefactors: Judas Iscariot, Brutus, and Cassius. Virgil, with the Pilgrim on his back, begins the descent down the shaggy body of Lucifer. They climb down through a crack in the ice, and when they reach the Evil One's thighs, Virgil turns and begins to struggle upward (because they have passed the center of the earth), still holding on to the hairy body of Lucifer, until they reach a cavern, where they stop for a short rest. Then a winding path brings them eventually to the earth's surface, where they see the stars.

"*Vexilla regis prodeunt Inferni,*"
    my master said, "closer to us, so now
    look ahead and see if you can make him out."   3

A far-off windmill turning its huge sails
    when a thick fog begins to settle in,
    or when the light of day begins to fade,   6

that is what I thought I saw appearing.
    And the gusts of wind it stirred made me shrink back
    behind my guide, my only means of cover.   9

Down here, I stood on souls fixed under ice
    (I tremble as I put this into verse);
    to me they looked like straws worked into glass.   12

Some lying flat, some perpendicular,
    either with their heads up or their feet,
    and some bent head to foot, shaped like a bow.   15

When we had moved far enough along the way
    that my master thought the time had come to show me
    the creature who was once so beautiful,   18

---

1   The opening lines of the hymn "*Vexilla regis prodeunt*"—"The banners of the King advance"—(written by Venantius Fortunatus, sixth-century bishop of Poitiers; this hymn belongs to the liturgy of the Church) are here parodied by the addition of the word *Inferni*, "of Hell," to the word *regis*, "of the King." Sung on Good Friday, the hymn anticipates the unveiling of the Cross; Dante, who began his journey on the evening of Good Friday, is prepared by Virgil's words for the sight of Lucifer, who will appear like a "windmill" in a "thick fog." The banners referred to are Lucifer's wings.

he stepped aside, and stopping is announced:
    "This is he, this is Dis; this is the place
    that calls for all the courage you have in you."   21

How chilled and nerveless, Reader, I felt then;
    do not ask me—I cannot write about it—
    there are no words to tell you how I felt.   24

I did not die—I was not living either!
    Try to imagine, if you can imagine,
    me there, deprived of life and death at once.   27

The king of the vast kingdom of all grief
    stuck out with half his chest above the ice;
    my height is closer to the height of giants   30

than theirs is to the length of his great arms;
    consider now how large all of him was:
    this body in proportion to his arms.   33

If once he was as fair as now he's foul
    and dared to raise his brows against his Maker,
    it is fitting that all grief should spring from him.   36

Oh, how amazed I was when I looked up
    and saw a head—one head wearing three faces!
    One was in front (and that was a bright red),   39

the other two attached themselves to this one
    just above the middle of each shoulder,
    and at the crown all three were joined in one: 42

The right face was a blend of white and yellow,
    the left the color of those people's skin
    who live along the river Nile's descent.   45

Beneath each face two mighty wings stretched out,
    the size you might expect of this huge bird
    (I never saw a ship with larger sails):   48

38–45   Dante presents Lucifer's head as a perverted parallel of the Trinity. The colors of the three single faces (red, yellow, black) are probably antithetically analogous to the qualities attributed to the Trinity (see Canto III, 5–6). Thereore, Highest Wisdom would be opposed by ignorance (black). Divine Omnipotence by impotence (yellow), Primal Love by hatred or envy (red).

not feathered wings but rather like the ones
    a bat would have. He flapped them constantly,
    keeping three winds continuously in motion 51

to lock Cocytus eternally in ice.
    He wept from his six eyes, and down three chins
    were dripping tears all mixed with bloody slaver. 54

In each of his three mouths he crunched a sinner,
    with teeth like those that rake the hemp and flax,
    keeping three sinners constantly in pain; 57

the one in front—the biting he endured
    was nothing like the clawing that he took:
    sometimes his back was raked clean of its skin. 60

"That soul up there who suffers most of all,"
    my guide explained, "is Judas Iscariot:
    the one with head inside and legs out kicking. 63

As for the other two whose heads stick out,
    the one who hangs from that black face is Brutus
    see how he squirms in silent desperation; 66

the other one is Cassius, he still looks sturdy.
    But soon it will be night. Now is the time
    to leave this place, for we have seen it all." 69

I held on to his neck, as he told me to,
    while he watched and waited for the time and place,
    and when the wings were stretched out just enough, 72

he grabbed on to the shaggy sides of Satan;
    then downward, tuft by tuft, he made his way
    between the tangled hair and frozen crust. 75

61–63   Having betrayed Christ for thirty pieces of silver, Judas endures greater punishment than the other two souls.

65   Marcus Brutus, who was deceitfully persuaded by Cassius (67) to join the conspiracy, aided in the assassination of Julius Caesar. It is fitting that in his final vision of the Inferno the Pilgrim should see those shades who committed treacherous acts against Divine and worldly authorities: the Church and the Roman Empire. This provides the culmination, at least in this canticle, of these basic themes: Church and Empire.

67   Caius Cassius Longinus was another member of the conspiracy against Caesar. By describing Cassius as "still look[ing] sturdy," Dante shows he has evidently confused him with Lucius Cassius, whom Cicero calls *adeps*, "corpulent."

When we had reached the point exactly where
    the thigh begins, right at the haunch's curve,
    my guide, with strain and force of every muscle,   78

turned his head toward the shaggy shanks of Dis
    and grabbed the hair as if about to climb—
    I thought that we were heading back to Hell.   81

"Hold tight, there is no other way," he said,
    panting, exhausted, "only by these stairs
    can we leave behind the evil we have seen."   84

When he had got me through the rocky crevice,
    he raised me to its edge and set me down,
    then carefully he climbed and joined me there.   87

I raised my eyes, expecting I would see
    the half of Lucifer I saw before.
    Instead I saw his two legs stretching upward.   90

If at that sight I found myself confused,
    so will those simple-minded folk who still
    don't see what point it was I must have passed.   93

"Get up," my master said, "get to your feet,
    the way is long, the road a rough climb up,
    already the sun approaches middle tierce!"   96

It was no palace promenade we came to,
    but rather like some dungeon Nature built:
    it was paved with broken stone and poorly lit.   99

"Before we start to struggle out of here,
    O master," I said when I was on my feet,
    "I wish you would explain some things to me.   102

Where is the ice? And how can he be lodged
    upside-down? And how, in so little time,
    could the sun go all the way from night to day?"   105

---

96   The time is approximately halfway between the canonical hours of Prime and Tierce, i.e., 7:30 A.M. The rapid change from night ("But soon it will be night," 68) to day (96) is the result of the travelers' having passed the earth's center, thus moving into the Southern Hemisphere, which is twelve hours ahead of the Northern.

"You think you're still on the center's other side,"
    he said, "where I first grabbed the hairy worm
    of rottenness that pierces the earth's core;   108

and you were there as long as I moved downward
    but, when I turned myself, you passed the point
    to which all weight from every part is drawn.   111

Now you are standing beneath the hemisphere
    which is opposite the side covered by land,
    where at the central point was sacrificed   114

the Man whose birth and life were free of sin.
    You have both feet upon a little sphere
    whose other side Judecca occupies;   117

when it is morning here, there it is evening.
    And he whose hairs were stairs for our descent
    has not changed his position since his fall.   120

When he fell from the heavens on this side,
    all of the land that once was spread out here,
    alarmed by his plunge, took cover beneath the sea   123

and moved to our hemisphere; with equal fear
    the mountain-land, piled up on this side, fled
    and made this cavern here when it rushed upward.   126

Below somewhere there is a space, as far
    from Beelzebub as the limit of his tomb,
    known not by sight but only by the sound   129

of a little stream that makes its way down here
    through the hollow of a rock that it has worn,
    gently winding in gradual descent."   132

My guide and I entered that hidden road
    to make our way back up to the bright world.
    We never thought of resting while we climbed.   135

127–132   Somewhere below the land that rushed upward to form the Mount of Purgatory "there is a space" (127) through
    which a stream runs, and it is through this space that Virgil and Dante will climb to reach the base of the Mount.
    The "space" is at the edge of the natural dungeon that constitutes Lucifer's "tomb," and serves as the entrance to the
    passage from the earth's center to its circumference, created by Lucifer in his fall from Heaven to Hell.

We climbed, he first and I behind, until,
>through a small round opening ahead of us
>I saw the lovely things the heavens hold,   138

and we came out to see once more the stars.

Purgatory (Selections)

Purgatory is depicted by Dante as a mountain that one ascends by circling around, beginning from the plain at its base. The sins represented in *Purgatory* are not different from those we saw in *Inferno*. What distinguishes the punishment of sin in purgatory is that the sinners desire to change their ways and are now engaged in a process of purification and conversion. Once in purgatory there is no turning back; eventually they will be in paradise. However, as we see in Canto II below, those who are in the process of being saved do not necessarily realize how strenuous this process of conversion will be—they prefer to congregate at the foot of the mountain, catching up on the latest news from home and singing songs from the good old days. In order to get them to appreciate the seriousness of what lies ahead for them and to get them to begin to ascend the mountain, Dante employs the Roman statesman and philosopher, Cato, a figure noted for his integrity and no-nonsense ways.

Canto II

As the sun rises, Dante and Virgil are still standing at the water's edge and wondering which road to take in order to ascend the mountain of Purgatory, when the Pilgrim sees a reddish glow moving across the water. The light approaches at an incredible speed, and eventually they are able to discern the wings of an angel. The angel is the miraculous pilot of a ship containing souls of the Redeemed, who are singing the psalm *In exitu Israel de Aegypto*. At a sign from the angel boatsman, these souls disembark, only to roam about on the shore. Apparently, they are strangers, and, mistaking Virgil and Dante for familiars of the place, they ask them which road leads up the mountainside. Virgil answers that they, too, are pilgrims, only recently arrived. At this point some of the souls realize that the Pilgrim is still alive, and they stare at him in fascination. Recognizing a face that he knows in this crowd of souls, Dante tries three times in vain to embrace the shade of his old friend Casella, a musician; then he asks Casella for a song and, as he sings, all the souls are held spellbound. Suddenly the Just Old Man, Cato, appears to disperse the rapt crowd, sternly rebuking them for their negligence and exhorting them to run to the mountain to begin their ascent.

The sun was touching the horizon now,
    the highest point of whose meridian arc
    was just above Jerusalem; and Night,   3

revolving always opposite to him,
    rose from the Ganges with the Scales that fall
    out of her hand when she outweighs the day.   6

Thus, where we were, Aurora's lovely face
    with a vermilion flush on her white cheeks
    was aging in a glow of golden light.   9

We were still standing at the water's edge,
    wondering about the road ahead, like men
    whose thoughts go forward while their bodies stay,   12

when, suddenly, I saw, low in the west
    (like the red glow of Mars that burns at dawn
    through the thick haze that hovers on the sea),   15

a light—I hope to see it come again!—
    moving across the waters at a speed
    faster than any earthly flight could be.   18

I turned in wonder to my guide, and then,
    when I looked back at it again, the light
    was larger and more brilliant than before,   21

and there appeared, on both sides of this light,
    a whiteness indefinable, and then,
    another whiteness grew beneath the shape.   24

My guide was silent all the while, but when
    the first two whitenesses turned into wings,
    and he saw who the steersman was, he cried: 27

"Fall to your knees, fall to your knees! Behold
    the angel of the Lord! And fold your hands.
    Expect to see more ministers like him.   30

See how he scorns to use man's instruments;
    he needs no oars, no sails, only his wings
    to navigate between such distant shores.   33

1–6   At the time the canto opens, it is midnight at the Ganges, sunset at Jerusalem, noon at the Pillars of Hercules, and dawn at Purgatory.

See how he has them pointing up to Heaven:
    he fans the air with these immortal plumes
    that do not moult as mortal feathers do."   36

Closer and closer to our shore he came,
    brighter and brighter shone the bird of God,
    until I could no longer bear the light,   39

and bowed my head. He steered straight to the shore,
    his boat so swift and light upon the wave,
    it left no sign of truly sailing there;   42

and the celestial pilot stood astern
    with blessedness inscribed upon his face.
    More than a hundred souls were in his ship: 45

In exitu Israël de Aegypto,
    they all were singing with a single voice,
    chanting it verse by verse until the end.   48

The angel signed them with the holy cross,
    and they rushed from the ship onto the shore;
    he disappeared, swiftly, as he had come.   51

The souls left there seemed strangers to this place:
    they roamed about, while looking all around,
    endeavoring to understand new things.   54

The sun, which with its shafts of light had chased
    the Goat out of the heavens' highest field,
    was shooting rays of day throughout the sky,   57

when those new souls looked up to where we were,
    and called to us: "If you should know the road
    that leads up to the mountainside, show us."   60

---

42   The boat draws no water because the souls of the Saved have no weight.

46   "*In exitu Israël de Aegypto*"—"When Israel came out of Egypt" (Psalm 113)—is a song of thanksgiving to God for freeing the nation of Israel from the bondage of Egypt. For Christians the Exodus, or liberation of the Jews, prefigures Christ's Resurrection from the dead. In turn, his death and Resurrection served to free each individual Christian soul from the slavery of sin. Since at this point in the action of the poem it is Easter Sunday morning, the very day of the Resurrection, the singing of this psalm is particularly appropriate, and the connection between the Exodus and Resurrection is thus reinforced.

55–57   At dawn the constellation Capricorn lies on the meridian, ninety degrees from the horizon. Because of the sun's ever-increasing light, Capricorn is now invisible. In other words, the daylight is getting stronger.

And Virgil answered them: "You seem to think
    that we are souls familiar with this place,
    but we, like all of you, are pilgrims here;   63

we just arrived, not much ahead of you,
    but by a road which was so rough and hard
    to climb this mountain now will be like play."   66

Those souls who noticed that my body breathed,
    and realized that I was still alive,
    in their amazement turned a deathly pale.   69

Just as a crowd, greedy for news, surrounds
    the messenger who bears the olive branch,
    and none too shy to elbow-in his way,   72

so all the happy souls of these Redeemed
    stared at my face, forgetting, as it were,
    the way to go to make their beauty whole.   75

One of these souls pushed forward, arms outstretched,
    and he appeared so eager to embrace me
    that his affection moved me to show mine.   78

O empty shades, whose human forms seem real!
    Three times I clasped my hands around his form,
    as many times they came back to my breast.   81

I must have been the picture of surprise,
    for he was smiling as he drew away,
    and I plunged forward still in search of him.   84

Then, gently, he suggested I not try,
    and by his voice I knew who this shade was;
    I begged him stay and speak to me awhile.   87

"As once I loved you in my mortal flesh,
    without it now I love you still," he said.
    "Of course I'll stay. But tell me why you're here."   90

"I make this journey now, O my Casella,
    hoping one day to come back here again,"
    I said. "But how did you lose so much time?"   93

---

91   Casella, a musician and singer, was a friend of Dante's and very likely set to music Dante's *canzone* "Amor che ne la mente mi ragiona," if not others as well.

He answered: "I cannot complain if he
    who, as he pleases, picks his passengers,
    often refused to take me in his boat,   96

for that Just Will is always guiding his.
    But for the last three months, indulgently,
    he has been taking all who wish to cross;   99

so when I went to seek the shore again,
    where Tiber's waters turn to salty sea,
    benignly, he accepted me aboard.   102

Now, back again he flies to Tiber's mouth,
    which is the meeting place of all the dead,
    except for those who sink to Acheron's shore."   105

"If no new law prevents remembering
    or practicing those love songs that once brought
    peace to my restless longings in the world,"   108

I said, "pray sing, and give a little rest
    to my poor soul which, burdened by my flesh,
    has climbed this far and is exhausted now."   111

Amor che ne la mente mi ragiona.
    began the words of his sweet melody—
    their sweetness still is sounding in my soul.   114

My master and myself and all those souls
    that came with him were deeply lost in joy,
    as if that sound were all that did exist.   117

And while we stood enraptured by the sound
    of those sweet notes—a sudden cry: "What's this,
    you lazy souls?" It was the Just Old Man.   120

"What negligence to stand around like this!
    Run to the mountain, shed that slough which still
    does not let God be manifest to you!"   123

---

101   Ostia, where the Tiber River enters the sea, is the place where souls departing for Purgatory gather to await transport.

112   *"Amor che ne la mente mi ragiona"* ("Love that speaks to me in my mind") is the first verse of the second *canzone*, which Dante comments on in the third book of his *Convivio*.

Just as a flock of pigeons in a field
    peacefully feeding on the grain and tares,
      no longer strutting proud of how they look,   126

immediately abandon all their food,
    flying away, seized by a greater need
      if something should occur that startles them—   129

so did that new-formed flock of souls give up
    their feast of song, and seek the mountainside,
      rushing to find a place they hoped was there.   132

And we were just as quick to take to flight.

> Having climbed the mountain of Purgatory, Dante and Virgil must pass through a purifying wall of flame before they can enter the earthly paradise, otherwise known as the Garden of Eden. Dante is fearful, but with Virgil's encouragement he proceeds through the flames. Standing within the Garden, Dante witnesses a heavenly procession leading the way toward Paradise. He desires nothing more than to ascend to the heavenly realm, but suddenly Beatrice appears and reminds him rather sternly that his conversion is not yet complete.

Canto XXVII

The sun is near setting when the poets leave the souls of the Lustful and encounter the angel of Chastity, singing the beatitude "Blessed are the Pure of Heart." The angel tells them that they can go no farther without passing through the flames, but, numbed with fear, the Pilgrim hesitates for a long time. Finally Virgil prevails upon him and they make the crossing through the excruciating heat. As they emerge on the other side, they hear the invitation "Come O ye blessed of my Father," and an angel exhorts them to climb as long as there is still daylight. But soon the sun sets and the poets are overcome by sleep. Toward morning the Pilgrim dreams of Leah and Rachel, who represent the active and contemplative lives, respectively. When he awakes, he is refreshed and eager and races up the remaining steps. In the last few lines Virgil describes the moral development achieved by the Pilgrim—such that he no longer needs his guidance. These are the last words that Virgil will speak in the poem.

It was the hour the sun's first rays shine down
    upon the land where its Creator shed
      his own life's blood, the hour the Ebro flows   3

1–6   The hour is six o'clock in the morning at Jerusalem, midnight at Spain (where the Ebro River is located), noon at India (through which the Ganges flows), and six o'clock in the evening at Purgatory.

beneath high Scales, and Ganges' waters boil
    in noonday heat: so day was fading, then,
    when God's angel of joy appeared to us.   6

Upon the bank beyond the fire's reach
    he stood, singing *Beati mundo corde!*
    The living beauty of his voice rang clear.   9

Then: "Holy souls, no farther can you go
    without first suffering fire. So, enter now,
    and be not deaf to what is sung beyond,"   12

he said to us as we came up to him.
    I, when I heard these words, felt like a man
    who is about to be entombed alive.   15

Gripping my hands together, I leaned forward
    and, staring at the fire, I recalled
    what human bodies look like burned to death.   18

Both of my friendly guides turned toward me then,
    and Virgil said to me: "O my dear son,
    there may be pain here, but there is no death.   21

Remember all your memories! If I
    took care of you when we rode Geryon,
    shall I do less when we are nearer God?   24

Believe me when I say that if you spent
    a thousand years within the fire's heart,
    it would not singe a single hair of yours;   27

and if you still cannot believe my words,
    approach the fire and test it for yourself
    on your own robe: just touch it with the hem.   30

It's time, high time, to put away your fears;
    turn towards me, come, and enter without fear!"
    But I stood there, immobile—and ashamed.   33

He said, somewhat annoyed to see me fixed
    and stubborn there, "Now, don't you see, my son:
    only this wall keeps you from Beatrice."   36

---

8   *"Beati mundo corde"* begins the last beatitude (Matthew 5:8), "Blessed are the pure of heart, for they shall see God."

As Pyramus, about to die, heard Thisbe
    utter her name, he raised his eyes and saw
    her there, the day mulberries turned blood red—   39

just so, my stubbornness melted away:
    hearing the name which blooms eternally
    within my mind, I turned to my wise guide.   42

He shook his head and smiled, as at a child
    won over by an apple, as he said:
    "Well, then, what are we doing on this side?"   45

"That precious fruit which all men eagerly
    go searching for on many different boughs
    will give, today, peace to your hungry soul."   117

These were the words that Virgil spoke to me,
    and never was a more auspicious gift
    received, or given, with more joyfulness.   120

Growing desire, desire to be up there,
    was rising in me: with every step I took
    I felt my wings were growing for the flight.   123

Once the stairs, swiftly climbed, were all behind
    and we were standing on the topmost step,
    Virgil addressed me, fixing his eyes on mine: 126

You now have seen, my son, the temporal
    and the eternal fire, you've reached the place
    where my discernment now has reached its end.   129

I led you here with skill and intellect;
    from here on, let your pleasure be your guide:
    the narrow ways, the steep, are far below.   132

Behold the sun shining upon your brow,
    behold the tender grass, the flowers, the trees,
    which, here, the earth produces of itself.   135

---

115   The fruit, which grows on many different branches, is the ideal happiness that mankind seeks in various ways.

127–128   The temporal fire is the fire of Purgatory: the purifying punishments of the mountain, including the wall of fire on
        the Seventh Terrace, which will disappear on the Judgment Day. The eternal fire is the fire of Hell.

Until those lovely eyes rejoicing come,
>   which, tearful, once urged me to come to you,
>   you may sit here, or wander, as you please.   138

Expect no longer words or signs from me.
>   Now is your will upright, wholesome and free,
>   and not to heed its pleasure would be wrong: 141

I crown and miter you lord of yourself!"

Canto XXX

One hundred singing angels appear in the sky overhead; they fill the air with a rain of flowers. Through the flowers, Beatrice appears. The Pilgrim turns to Virgil to confess his overpowering emotions, only to find that Virgil has disappeared! Beatrice speaks sternly to Dante, calling him by name and reprimanding him for having wasted his God-given talents, wandering from the path that leads to Truth. So hopeless, in fact, was his case, to such depths did he sink, that the journey to see the souls of the Damned in Hell was the only way left of setting him back on the road to salvation.

When the Septentrion of the First Heaven
>   (which never sets nor rises nor has known
>   any cloud other than the veil of sin),   3

which showed to everyone his duty there
>   (just as our lower constellation guides
>   the helmsman on his way to port on earth),   6

stopped short, that group of prophets of the truth
>   who were between the griffin and those lights
>   turned to the car as to their source of peace;   9

then, one of them, as sent from Heaven, sang
>   *Veni, sponsa, de Libano*, three times,
>   and all the other voices followed his.   12

---

1   The constellation sometimes called Septentrion is probably the Little Dipper (Ursa Minor), which contains seven stars, including the North Star. Thus the "Septentrion of the First Heaven" (the Empyrean) must be the seven blazing candlesticks that direct the procession.

11 "*Veni, sponsa, de Libano*" ("Come, bride, from Lebanon") is taken from the Song of Solomon (4:8), where the bride is interpreted as the soul wedded to Christ. Here the song has to do with the advent of Beatrice, one of whose allegorical meanings is *Sapientia*, or the wisdom of God.

As at the Final Summons all the blest
    will rise out of their graves, ready to raise
    new-bodied voices singing 'Hallelujah!'   15

just so rose up above the heavenly cart
    a hundred spirits *ad vocem tanti senis*,
    eternal heralds, ministers of God,   18

all shouting: *Benedictus qui venis!* then,
    tossing a rain of flowers in the air,
    Manibus, O, date lilia plenis!   21

Sometimes, as day approaches, I have seen
    all of the eastern sky a glow of rose,
    the rest of heaven beautifully clear,   24

the sun's face rising in a misty veil
    of tempering vapors that allow the eye
    to look straight at it for a longer time: 27

even so, within a nebula of flowers
    that flowed upward from angels' hands and then
    poured down, covering all the chariot,   30

appeared a lady—over her white veil
    an olive crown and, under her green cloak,
    her gown, the color of eternal flame.   33

And instantly—though many years had passed
    since last I stood trembling before her eyes,
    captured by adoration, stunned by awe—   36

my soul, that could not see her perfectly,
    still felt, succumbing to her mystery
    and power, the strength of its enduring love.   39

---

17   *"Ad vocem tanti senis"* translates as "At the voice of so great an elder."

19   *"Benedictus qui venis"* ("Blessed are Thou that comest") is a slightly modified version of Matthew 21:9, *Benedictus qui venit* ("Blessed is He who cometh"). Note that while Dante felt free to shift from the third to the second person in quoting this line, he left intact *Benedictus*, with its masculine form. In this way the word, though applied to Beatrice, who is about to appear, retains its original reference to Christ.

21   "O give us lilies with full hands." This quotation from the *Aeneid* (VI, 883) is surely intended as high tribute to Virgil, the Pilgrim's guide, since his words are placed on the same level as verses from the Bible.

31–33 The lady is Beatrice, and the colors she wears are those of the three theological virtues: Faith, Hope, and Charity.

No sooner were my eyes struck by the force
    of the high, piercing virtue I had known
    before I quit my boyhood years, than I   42

turned to the left—with all the confidence
    that makes a child run to its mother's arms,
    when he is frightened or needs comforting—   45

to say to Virgil: "Not one drop of blood
    is left inside my veins that does not throb:
    I recognize signs of the ancient flame."   48

But Virgil was not there. We found ourselves
    without Virgil, sweet father, Virgil to whom
    for my salvation I gave up my soul.   51

All the delights around me, which were lost
    by our first mother, could not keep my cheeks,
    once washed with dew, from being stained with tears.   54

"Dante, though Virgil leaves you, do not weep,
    not yet, that is, for you shall have to weep
    from yet another wound. Do not weep yet."   57

Just as an admiral, from bow or stern,
    watches his men at work on other ships,
    encouraging their earnest labors—so,   60

rising above the chariot's left rail
    (when I turned round, hearing my name called out,
    which of necessity I here record),   63

I saw the lady who had first appeared
    beneath the angelic festival of flowers
    gazing upon me from beyond the stream.   66

Although the veil that flowed down from her head,
    fixed by the crown made of Minerva's leaves,
    still kept me from a perfect view of her,   69

I sensed the regal sternness of her face,
    as she continued in the tone of one
    who saves the sharpest words until the end: 72

---

55   This is the first time that the Pilgrim hears his own name during his journey.

"Yes, look at me! Yes, I am Beatrice!
      So, you at last have deigned to climb the mount?
      You learned at last that here lies human bliss?"   78

I lowered my head and looked down at the stream,
      but, filled with shame at my reflection there,
      I quickly fixed my eyes upon the grass.   78

I was the guilty child facing his mother,
      abject before her harshness: harsh, indeed,
      is unripe pity not yet merciful.   81

As she stopped speaking, all the angels rushed
      into the psalm *In te, Domine, speravi,*
      but did not sing beyond *pedes meos.*   84

As snow upon the spine of Italy,
      frozen among the living rafters there,
      blown and packed hard by wintry northeast winds,   87

will then dissolve, dripping into itself,
      when, from the land that knows no noonday shade,
      there comes a wind like flame melting down wax;   90

so tears and sighs were frozen hard in me,
      until I heard the song of those attuned
      forever to the music of the spheres;   93

but when I, sensed in their sweet notes the pity
      they felt for me (it was as if they said:
      "Lady, why do you shame him so?"), the bonds   96

of ice packed tight around my heart dissolved,
      becoming breath and water: from my breast,
      through mouth and eyes, anguish came pouring forth.   99

Still on the same side of the chariot
      she stood immobile; then she turned her words
      to that compassionate array of beings: 102

83–84   The angels are singing the first part of the thirty-first psalm, which begins, "In Thee, O lord, have I put my trust." They continue through line 8 (*pedes meos*), "Thou hast set my feet in a spacious place"—which is precisely the place where the Pilgrim is standing at this moment.

89   The land is equatorial Africa, where the sun is often directly overhead, sending its rays straight down so that objects cast no shadow.

"With your eyes fixed on the eternal day,
    darkness of night or sleep cannot conceal
    from you a single act performed on earth;   105

and though I speak to you, my purpose is
    to make the one who weeps on that far bank
    perceive the truth and match his guilt with grief.   108

Not only through the working of the spheres,
    which brings each seed to its appropriate end
    according as the stars keep company,   111

but also through the bounty of God's grace,
    raining from vapors born so high above
    they cannot be discerned by human sight,   114

was this man so endowed, potentially,
    in early youth—had he allowed his gifts
    to bloom, he would have reaped abundantly.   117

But the more vigorous and rich the soil,
    the wilder and the weedier it grows
    when left untilled, its bad seeds flourishing.   120

There was a time my countenance sufficed,
    as I let him look into my young eyes
    for guidance on the straight path to his goal;   123

but when I passed into my second age
    and changed my life for Life, that man you see
    strayed after others and abandoned me;   126

when I had risen from the flesh to spirit,
    become more beautiful, more virtuous,
    he found less pleasure in me, loved me less,   129

and wandered from the path that leads to truth,
    pursuing simulacra of the good,
    which promise more than they can ever give.   132

I prayed that inspiration come to him
    through dreams and other means: in vain I tried
    to call him back, so little did he care.   135

To such depths did he sink that, finally,
    there was no other way to save his soul
    except to have him see the Damned in Hell.   138

That this might be, I visited the Dead,
   and offered my petition and my tears
   to him who until now has been his guide.   141

The highest laws of God would be annulled
   if he crossed Lethe, drinking its sweet flow,
   without having to pay at least some scot   144

of penitence poured forth in guilty tears."

Paradise (Selections)

Having led Dante into Paradise, the guidance of Beatrice eventually yields to that of St. Bernard of Clairvaux (1090–1153). Bernard was one of the great monastic reformers of the Middle Ages, a driving force in the development and spread of the Cistercian order of monks. He was also a renowned theologian and a mystic. His appearance as the one who will lead Dante to his final vision of heaven is entirely appropriate. For Dante, Bernard would have represented an ideal of what leadership within the church is meant to be—leadership that he found so frequently lacking in the church authorities of his own time. Bernard combined spiritual depth, an impressive intellect, and great ability as an organizer. The combination of these qualities would have placed him high in Dante's esteem. *The Divine Comedy* concludes with Dante caught up within the celestial Rose, at one with those saints who line its interior, overcome with the love of God.

Canto XXXII

Rapt in love's Bliss, that contemplative soul
   generously assumed the role of guide
   as he began to speak these holy words: 3

"The wound which Mary was to close and heal
   she there, who sits so lovely at her feet,
   would open wider then and prick the flesh.   6

And sitting there directly under her
   among the thrones of the third tier is Rachel,
   and, there, see Beatrice by her side.   9

4–6 When Mary gave birth to Christ she provided the means of healing the wound of original sin. She "who sits so lovely at her feet" (5) is Eve, who disobeyed God and surrendered to the serpent.

Sarah, Rebecca, Judith, and then she,
    who was the great-grandmother of the singer
    who cried for his sin: '*Miserere mei*,'   12

you see them all as I go down from tier
    to tier and name them in their order,
    petal by petal, downward through the Rose.   15

Down from the seventh row, as up to it,
    was a descending line of Hebrew women
    that parted all the petals of the Rose;   18

according to the ways in which the faith
    viewed Christ, these women constitute the wall
    dividing these ranks down the sacred stairs.   21

On this side where the flower is full bloomed
    to its last petal, sit the souls of those
    who placed their faith upon Christ yet to come;   24

on that side where all of the semi-circles
    are broken by the empty seats, sit those
    who turned their face to Christ already come.   27

And just as on this side the glorious throne
    of Heaven's lady with the other seats
    below it form this great dividing wall,   30

so, facing her, the throne of the great John
    who, ever holy, suffered through the desert,
    and martyrdom, then Hell for two more years,   33

and under him, chosen to mark the line,
    Francis, Benedict, Augustine and others
    descend from round to round as far as here.   36

Now marvel at the greatness of God's plan:
    this garden shall be full in equal number
    of this and that aspect of the one faith.   39

---

10   Sarah was Abraham's wife and the mother of Isaac. Rebecca was the daughter of Bethuel and the sister of Laban. She was married to Isaac and bore Esau and Jacob. Judith was the daughter of Meraris. She murdered Holofernes (Nebuchadnezzar's general) while he slept and thus saved Bethulia, which was under siege by the Assyrians. After the Assyrians fled the city Judith was celebrated by the Jews as their deliverer.

11–12 Ruth was the wife of Boaz and great-grandmother of David (the "singer"), author of the psalm of penitence, the *Miserere mei* ("have mercy on me," Psalm 51).

And know that downward from the center row
    which cuts the two dividing walls midway,
      no soul through his own merit earned his seat,   42

but through another's, under fixed conditions,
    for all these spirits were absolved of sin
      before they reached the age to make free choice.   45

You need only to look upon their faces
    and listen to the young sound of their voices
      to see and hear this clearly for yourself.   48

But you have doubts, doubts you do not reveal,
    so now I will untie the tangled knot
      in which your searching thoughts have bound you tight.   51

Within the vastness of this great domain
    no particle of chance can find a place
      no more than sorrow, thirst, or hunger can—   54

for all that you see here has been ordained
    by the eternal law with such precision
      that ring and finger are a perfect fit.   57

And, therefore, all these souls of hurried comers
    to the true life are not ranked *sine causa*
      some high, some low, according to their merit.   60

The King, through whom this kingdom is at rest
    in so much love and in so much delight
      that no will dares to wish for any more,   63

creating all minds in His own mind's bliss,
    endows each with as much grace as He wishes,
      at His own pleasure—let this fact suffice.   66

And Holy Scriptures set this down for you
    clear and expressly, speaking of those twins
      whose anger flared while in their mother's womb;   69

---

59   *Sine causa* is a Latin legal expression meaning "without cause."

68–69   Jacob and Esau were the twin sons of Rebecca and Isaac (see Genesis 25:21–34). St. Bernard mentions them as an example of the mystery of Divine Grace.

so, it is fitting that God's lofty light
        crown them with grace, as much as each one merits,
        according to the color of their hair.   72

Thus, through no merit of their own good works
        are they ranked differently; the difference is
        only in God's gift of original grace.   75

During mankind's first centuries on earth
        for innocent children to achieve salvation,
        only the faith of parents was required;   78

but then, when man's first age came to an end,
        all males had to be circumcised to give
        innocent wings the strength to fly to Heaven;   81

but when the age of grace came down to man,
        then, without perfect baptism in Christ,
        such innocence to Limbo was confined.   84

Now look at that face which resembles Christ
        the most, for only in its radiance
        will you be made ready to look at Christ."   87

I saw such bliss rain down upon her face,
        bestowed on it by all those sacred minds
        created to fly through those holy heights,   90

that of all things I witnessed to this point
        nothing had held me more spellbound than this,
        nor shown a greater likeness unto God;   93

and that love which had once before descended
        now sang, *Ave, Maria, gratia plena*,
        before her presence there with wings spread wide.   96

Response came to this holy prayer of praise
        from all directions of the Court of Bliss
        and every face grew brighter with that joy.   99

"O holy father, who for my sake deigns
        to stand down here, so far from the sweet throne
        destined for you throughout eternity,   102

---

79   Man's "first age" is from the time of Abraham until the birth of Christ.

who is that angel who so joyously
    looks straight into the eyes of Heaven's Queen,
    so much in love he seems to burn like fire?"   105

Thus, I turned for instruction once again
    to that one who in Mary's beauty glowed
    as does the morning star in fresh sunlight.   108

And he: "All loving pride and gracious joy,
    as much as soul or angel can possess,
    is all in him, and we would have it so,   111

for he it is who bore the palm below
    to Mary when the Son of God had willed
    to bear the weight of man's flesh on Himself.   114

Now let your eyes follow my words as I
    explain to you, and note the great patricians
    of this most just and pious of all realms.   117

Those two who sit most blest in their high thrones
    because they are the closest to the Empress
    are, as it were, the two roots of our Rose: 120

he, sitting on her left side, is that father,
    the one through whose presumptuous appetite
    mankind still tastes the bitterness of shame;   123

and on her right, you see the venerable
    Father of Holy Church to whom Christ gave
    the keys to this beautiful Rose of joy.   126

And he who prophesied before he died
    the sad days destined for the lovely Bride
    whom Christ won for himself with lance and nails   129

---

108   Reference to the morning star, Venus, is made in the litany to the Blessed Virgin.

120   Adam is one root of the Rose because from him sprung those who believed in Christ to come; St. Peter is the other because from him sprung those who believed in Christ who had already come.

127–130   St. John the Evangelist, author of the *Apocalypse*, foretold the adversity that would befall the Church. (Cf. *Purgatory* XXIX, 143–144.) The "lance and nails" (129) refers to the Crucifixion.

sits at his side. Beside the other sits
    the leader of those nurtured on God's manna,
    who were a fickle, ingrate, stubborn lot.   132

Across from Peter, see there, Anna sits,
    so happy to be looking at her daughter,
    she does not move an eye singing Hosanna;   135

facing the head of mankind's family
    sits Lucy, who first sent your lady to you
    when you were bent, headlong, on your own ruin.   138

But since the time left for your journey's vision
    grows short, let us stop here—like the good tailor
    who cuts the gown according to his cloth,   141

and turn our eyes upon the Primal Love
    so that, looking toward Him, you penetrate
    His radiance as deep as possible.   144

But lest you fall backwards beating your wings,
    believing to ascend on your own power,
    we must offer a prayer requesting grace,   147

grace from the one who has power to help you.
    Now, follow me, with all of your devotion,
    and do not let your heart stray from my words."   150

And he began to say this holy prayer:

Canto XXXIII

    "Oh Virgin Mother, daughter of your son,
        most humble, most exalted of all creatures
        chosen of God in His eternal plan,   3

you are the one who ennobled human nature
    to the extent that He did not disdain,
    Who was its Maker, to make Himself man.   6

Within your womb rekindled was the love
    that gave the warmth that did allow this flower
    to come to bloom within this timeless peace.   9

---

130   The "other" is Adam.

For all up here you are the noonday torch
    of charity, and down on earth, for men,
    the living spring of their eternal hope.   12

Lady, you are so great, so powerful,
    that who seeks grace without recourse to you
    would have his wish fly upward without wings.   15

Not only does your loving kindness rush
    to those who ask for it, but often times
    it flows spontaneously before the plea.   18

In you is tenderness, in you is pity,
    in you munificence—in you unites
    all that is good in God's created beings.   21

This is a man who from the deepest pit
    of all the universe up to this height
    has witnessed, one by one, the lives of souls, 24

who begs you that you grant him through your grace
    the power to raise his vision higher still
    to penetrate the final blessedness.   27

And I who never burned for my own vision
    more than I burn for his, with all my prayers
    I pray you—and I pray they are enough—   30

that you through your own prayers dispel the mist
    of his mortality, that he may have
    the Sum of Joy revealed before his eyes.   33

I pray you also, Queen who can achieve
    your every wish, keep his affections sound
    once he has had the vision and returns.   36

Protect him from the stirrings of the flesh:
    you see, with Beatrice, all the Blest,
    hands clasped in prayer, are praying for my prayer. 39

Those eyes so loved and reverenced by God,
    now fixed on him who prayed, made clear to us
    how precious true devotion is to her;   42

then she looked into the Eternal Light,
    into whose being, we must believe, no eyes
    of other creatures pierce with such insight.   45

And I who was approaching now the end
    of all man's yearning, strained with all the force
    in me to raise my burning longing high.   48

Bernard then gestured to me with a smile
    that I look up, but I already was
    instinctively what he would have me be: 51

for now my vision as it grew more clear
    was penetrating more and more the Ray
    of that exalted Light of Truth Itself.   54

And from then on my vision rose to heights
    higher than words, which fail before such sight,
    and memory fails, too, at such extremes.   57

As he who sees things in a dream and wakes to
    feel the passion of the dream still there
    although no part of it remains in mind,   60

just such am I: my vision fades and all
    but ceases, yet the sweetness born of it
    I still can feel distilling in my heart: 63

so imprints on the snow fade in the sun,
    and thus the Sibyl's oracle of leaves
    was swept away and lost into the wind.   66

O Light Supreme, so far beyond the reach
    of mortal understanding, to my mind
    relend now some small part of Your own Self,   69

and give to my tongue eloquence enough
    to capture just one spark of all Your glory
    that I may leave for future generations;   72

for, by returning briefly to my mind
    and sounding, even faintly, in my verse,
    more of Your might will be revealed to men.   75

If I had turned my eyes away, I think,
    from the sharp brilliance of the living Ray
    which they endured, I would have lost my senses   78

And this, as I recall, gave me more strength
    to keep on gazing till I could unite
    my vision with the Infinite Worth I saw.   81

O grace abounding and allowing me to dare
    to fix my gaze on the Eternal Light,
    so deep my vision was consumed in It!   84

I saw how it contains within its depths
    all things bound in a single book by love
    of which creation is the scattered leaves: 87

how substance, accident, and their relation
    were fused in such a way that what I now
    describe is but a glimmer of that Light.   90

I know I saw the universal form,
    the fusion of all things, for I can feel,
    while speaking now, my heart leap up in joy.   93

One instant brings me more forgetfulness
    than five and twenty centuries brought the quest
    that stunned Neptune when he saw Argo's keel.   96

And so my mind was totally entranced
    in gazing deeply, motionless, intent;
    the more it saw the more it burned to see.   99

And one is so transformed within that Light
    that it would be impossible to think
    of ever turning one's eyes from that sight,   102

because the good which is the goal of will
    is all collected there, and outside it
    all is defective that is perfect there.   105

Now, even in the things I do recall
    my words have no more strength than does a babe
    wetting its tongue, still at its mother's breast.   108

Not that within the Living Light there was
    more than a sole aspect of the Divine
    which always is what It has always been,   111

yet as I learned to see more, and the power
    of vision grew in me, that single aspect
    as I changed, seemed to me to change Itself.   114

91–93 The conjoining of substance and accident in God and the union of the temporal and the eternal is what Dante saw at
    that moment.

Within Its depthless clarity of substance
    I saw the Great Light shine into three circles
    in three clear colors bound in one same space;   117

the first seemed to reflect the next like rainbow on rainbow,
    and the third was like a flame
    equally breathed forth by the other two.   120

How my weak words fall short of my conception,
    which is itself so far from what I saw
    that "weak" is much too weak a word to use!   123

O Light Eternal fixed in Self alone,
    known only to Yourself, and knowing Self,
    You love and glow, knowing and being known!   126

That circling which, as I conceived it, shone
    in You as Your own first reflected light
    when I had looked deep into It a while,   129

seemed in Itself and in Its own Self-color
    to be depicted with man's very image.
    My eyes were totally absorbed in It.   132

As the geometer who tries so hard
    to square the circle, but cannot discover,
    think as he may, the principle involved,   135

so did I strive with this new mystery:
    I yearned to know how could our image fit
    into that circle, how could it conform;   138

but my own wings could not take me so high—
    then a great flash of understanding struck
    my mind, and suddenly its wish was granted.   141

At this point power failed high fantasy
    but, like a wheel in perfect balance turning,
    I felt my will and my desire impelled   144

by the Love that moves the sun and the other stars.

VI

Charles Dickens

Editors' Introduction

"A squeezing, wrenching, grasping, scraping, clutching, covetous old sinner" is how Dickens describes Ebenezer Scrooge, the most famous miser in western literature. *A Christmas Carol* tells the tale of Scrooge's transformation from a solitary misanthrope to a paradigm of what it means to embody the spirit of Christmas. The story is without question Dickens's most well-known work, not only in its written form, but in its many adaptions for theater and film.

Financial concerns were certainly on Dickens's mind when in 1843 he set out to write *A Christmas Carol*. Although he was already a famous and popular author, he was at the time a married man with an immediate and an extended family in need of support. In addition, his previous novel, *Martin Chuzzlewit*, had not been selling very well, and his publishers threatened to reduce his share of the proceeds of his future work. But Dickens's reasons for writing *A Christmas Carol* were not solely financial; he was also motivated by a sense of responsibility to address some of the pressing social issues of his day. These motivations can be explained to a significant degree by the shape of his life up to this point.

Born in 1812 in the English city of Portsmouth, Dickens moved to London with his family in 1815. London was the city in which he would spend most of his life, the city whose character and whose characters he would so vividly convey to his readers. His father John was a naval clerk, an amiable, irresponsible spend-thrift whose free spending ways would eventually land him in debtors' prison in 1824. The Dickens family was forced to sell many of their prized possessions, including young Charles's beloved collection of books. But things would get worse. During this period families would sometimes move into the prison to be near their imprisoned relative, so with the exception of twelve-year-old Charles the rest of his family moved into the Marshalsea Prison to be with John Dickens. In the meantime, Charles was sent to work in Warren's Blacking Warehouse, a shoe polish factory that was dark, dingy, and rat-infested. He was seated next to a window that looked out onto the street, where passersby could look at him as he pasted labels on bottles of shoe polish. For a sensitive, intellectually precocious child who already viewed himself as belonging to a different class of people than those with whom he worked, this was a deeply humiliating and traumatic experience. Having been yanked out of school, here he was con-signed to do mindless work, and the thought that this might be his fate for the rest of his life made him despair. When John Dickens inherited some money a few months later, he was released from prison, but John and his wife Elizabeth decided that Charles would continue to work in the factory, a decision that wounded him deeply. After a relatively short time, his father, seeing how dam-aging this experience was to Charles, insisted (against his wife's objections, who wanted Charles to remain at work) that his son leave the factory and resume his studies. Dickens almost never spoke about this experience later in life—the thought of it filled him with a mixture of anger, fear, and shame. The experience left him with an abiding fear of poverty, which showed itself in his preoccupa-tion with money and financial security. It also made him acutely sensitive to the ways in which the social, economic, and political system could oppress and destroy people. He would remain attuned to social problems and speak out against them for the rest of his life. Dickens died in 1870.

Debt, poverty, heartlessness, cold, dark, the lack of generosity, the withholding of love, fear, and a feeling of isolation—these experiences from Dickens's early life would make their appearance in *A Christmas Carol*. However, these evils do not have the final word in the story. Scrooge changes; he is able to confront his past, and under the guidance of the three spirits of Christmas, he becomes a kind and generous benefactor to all those with whom he comes in contact. Dickens would refer to the ideas reflected in the story as his "Carol philosophy," and while he gave expression to this philosophy throughout the tale, the words of Scrooge's nephew Fred sum it up well:

> "But I am sure I have always thought of Christmas time...as a good time; a kind, forgiving, charitable, pleasant time: the only time I know of, in the long calendar of the year, when men and women seem by one consent to open their shut-up hearts freely, and to think of people below them as if they really were fellow-passengers to the grave, and not another race of creatures bound on other journeys."

With regard to the social, economic, and political implications of this "Carol philosophy," it should be noted that while Dickens was a social reformer, he was no revolutionary. He saw his role as moving people to change by moving them by his words. Both in his fiction and in his many speeches and articles, he addressed issues of poverty, education, and institutional reform. Throughout his life he gave public readings from his works, and *A Christmas Carol* was one of the works he read most frequently, in an attempt to bring about in his listeners a greater sense of charity and solidarity with the unfortunate.

Although it is probably going too far to claim that Dickens was alone responsible for the way in which we understand and celebrate Christmas today—getting together with family and friends, sharing food and drink around a table with those we love, giving gifts, being friendly and charitable to strangers—Dickens certainly did much to foster this conception of the feast. This way of understanding Christmas has occasionally led some readers to the conclusion that Dickens contributed to the secularization of the holiday. Such a conclusion, however, is hard to sustain once we have a sense of the role religion played in Dickens's life. As an infant, he had been baptized into the Anglican Church, and apart from a three- or four-year period during which he was attracted to Unitarianism (mainly because he admired the minister), he remained at least nominally a member of the Church of England. He was an irregular churchgoer, but from what we know he seems to have accepted the fundamental doctrines of Christianity, and he was known to have prayed daily in the morning and the evening. More specifically, he was quite clear that the teaching of the New Testament was very important to him, both personally and as an essential part of his writing. When his youngest son was about to depart to work in Australia, Dickens had this to say among his parting words: "[The New Testament is] the best book that ever was or will be known in the world. . .I now most solemnly impress upon you the truth and beauty of the Christian religion as it came from Christ himself. . ." With reference to the influence of the New Testament on his work, he wrote that "one of my most constant and most earnest endeavors has been to exhibit in all my good people some faint reflections of the teachings of our great Master. . . All my strongest illustrations are derived from the New Testament; all my social abuses are shown as departures from its spirit." He further insisted that in his Christmas Books (of which *A Christmas Carol* is the first) "there is an express text preached on, and that text is always taken from the lips of Christ."

Throughout his fiction Dickens can be scathing in his depictions of those he judges to be religious hypocrites, but this should not blind us to the ways in which a deep appreciation for the spirit of the New Testament animates his work. Dickens can at times be overly sentimental, but as far as his religious vision is concerned he is rarely heavy-handed or preachy. He prefers to allow his understanding of religion to emerge from the interactions among his characters. Because these characters are often so colorful and vivid, there can be a tendency to miss the psychological subtlety Dickens brings to his creations. This observation can be applied to his work as a whole and to *A Christmas Carol* in particular. In some ways, this story has become a victim of its own popularity, readily dismissed as "uplifting" or obvious. Scrooge's conversion is viewed by some as unconvincing and superficial. Readers will form their own judgments on these questions, but when read carefully, *A Christmas Carol* reveals Dickens as a writer who is not only entertaining, but profound, sensitive, and capable of deep insight into the human condition.

A CHRISTMAS CAROL

Stave 1: Marley's Ghost

Marley was dead: to begin with. There is no doubt whatever about that. The register of his burial was signed by the clergyman, the clerk, the undertaker, and the chief mourner. Scrooge signed it. And Scrooge's name was good upon 'Change, for anything he chose to put his hand to.

Old Marley was as dead as a door-nail.

Mind! I don't mean to say that I know, of my own knowledge, what there is particularly dead about a door-nail. I might have been inclined, myself, to regard a coffin-nail as the deadest piece of ironmongery in the trade. But the wisdom of our ancestors is in the simile; and my unhallowed hands shall not disturb it, or the Country's done for. You will therefore permit me to repeat, emphatically, that Marley was as dead as a door-nail.

Scrooge knew he was dead? Of course he did. How could it be otherwise? Scrooge and he were partners for I don't know how many years. Scrooge was his sole executor, his sole administrator, his sole assign, his sole residuary legatee, his sole friend, and sole mourner. And even Scrooge was not so dreadfully cut up by the sad event, but that he was an excellent man of business on the very day of the funeral, and solemnised it with an undoubted bargain. The mention of Marley's funeral brings me back to the point I started from. There is no doubt that Marley was dead. This must be distinctly understood, or nothing wonderful can come of the story I am going to relate. If we were not perfectly convinced that Hamlet's Father died before the play began, there would be nothing more remarkable in his taking a stroll at night, in an easterly wind, upon his own ramparts, than there would be in any other middle-aged gentleman rashly turning out after dark in a breezy spot—say Saint Paul's Churchyard for instance—literally to astonish his son's weak mind.

Scrooge never painted out Old Marley's name. There it stood, years afterwards, above the warehouse door: Scrooge and Marley. The firm was known as Scrooge and Marley. Sometimes people new to the business called Scrooge Scrooge, and sometimes Marley, but he answered to both names. It was all the same to him.

Oh! But he was a tight-fisted hand at the grindstone, Scrooge! a squeezing, wrenching, grasping, scraping, clutching, covetous, old sinner! Hard and sharp as flint, from which no steel had ever struck out generous fire; secret, and self-contained, and solitary as an oyster. The cold within him froze his old features, nipped his pointed nose, shrivelled his cheek, stiffened his gait; made his eyes red, his thin lips blue; and spoke out shrewdly in his grating voice. A frosty rime was on his head, and on his eyebrows, and his wiry chin. He carried his own low temperature always about with him; he iced his office in the dogdays; and didn't thaw it one degree at Christmas.

External heat and cold had little influence on Scrooge. No warmth could warm, no wintry weather chill him. No wind that blew was bitterer than he, no falling snow was more intent upon its purpose, no pelting rain less open to entreaty. Foul weather didn't know where to have him. The heaviest rain, and snow, and hail, and sleet, could boast of the advantage over him in only one respect. They often 'came down' handsomely, and Scrooge never did.

Nobody ever stopped him in the street to say, with gladsome looks, 'My dear Scrooge, how are you? When will you come to see me?' No beggars implored him to bestow a trifle, no children asked him what it was o'clock, no man or woman ever once in all his life inquired the way to such and such a place, of Scrooge. Even the blind men's dogs appeared to know him; and when they saw him coming on, would tug their owners into doorways and up courts; and then would wag their tails as though they said, 'No eye at all is better than an evil eye, dark master!'

But what did Scrooge care! It was the very thing he liked. To edge his way along the crowded paths of life, warning all human sympathy to keep its distance, was what the knowing ones call 'nuts' to Scrooge.

Once upon a time—of all the good days in the year, on Christmas Eve—old Scrooge sat busy in his counting-house. It was cold, bleak, biting weather: foggy withal: and he could hear the people in the court outside, go wheezing up and down, beating their hands upon their breasts, and stamping their feet upon the pavement stones to warm them. The city clocks had only just gone three, but it was quite dark already—it had not been light all day—and candles were flaring in the windows of the neighbouring offices, like ruddy smears upon the palpable brown air. The fog came pouring in at every chink and keyhole, and was so dense without, that although the court was of the narrowest, the houses opposite were mere phantoms. To see the dingy cloud come drooping down, obscuring everything, one might have thought that Nature lived hard by, and was brewing on a large scale.

The door of Scrooge's counting-house was open that he might keep his eye upon his clerk, who in a dismal little cell beyond, a sort of tank, was copying letters. Scrooge had a very small fire, but the clerk's fire was so very much smaller that it looked like one coal. But he couldn't replenish it, for Scrooge kept the coal-box in his own room; and so surely as the clerk came in with the shovel, the master predicted that it would be necessary for them to part. Wherefore the clerk put on his white comforter, and tried to warm himself at the candle; in which effort, not being a man of a strong imagination, he failed.

'A merry Christmas, uncle! God save you!' cried a cheerful voice. It was the voice of Scrooge's nephew, who came upon him so quickly that this was the first intimation he had of his approach.

'Bah!' said Scrooge, 'Humbug!'

He had so heated himself with rapid walking in the fog and frost, this nephew of Scrooge's, that he was all in a glow; his face was ruddy and handsome; his eyes sparkled, and his breath smoked again. 'Christmas a humbug, uncle!' said Scrooge's nephew. 'You don't mean that, I am sure?'

'I do,' said Scrooge. 'Merry Christmas! What right have you to be merry? What reason have you to be merry? You're poor enough.'

'Come, then,' returned the nephew gaily. 'What right have you to be dismal? What reason have you to be morose? You're rich enough.'

Scrooge having no better answer ready on the spur of the moment, said 'Bah!' again; and followed it up with 'Humbug.'

'Don't be cross, uncle!' said the nephew.

'What else can I be,' returned the uncle, 'when I live in such a world of fools as this? Merry Christmas! Out upon merry Christmas! What's Christmas time to you but a time for paying bills without money; a time for finding yourself a year older, but not an hour richer; a time for balancing your books and having every item in 'em through a round dozen of months presented dead against you? If I could work my will,' said Scrooge indignantly, 'every idiot who goes about with "Merry Christmas" on his lips, should be boiled with his own pudding, and buried with a stake of holly through his heart. He should!'

'Uncle!' pleaded the nephew.

'Nephew!' returned the uncle sternly, 'keep Christmas in your own way, and let me keep it in mine.'

'Keep it!' repeated Scrooge's nephew. 'But you don't keep it.'

'Let me leave it alone, then,' said Scrooge. 'Much good may it do you! Much good it has ever done you!'

'There are many things from which I might have derived good, by which I have not prof-ited, I dare say,' returned the nephew. 'Christmas among the rest. But I am sure I have always thought of Christmas time, when it has come round—apart from the veneration due to its sacred name and origin, if anything belonging to it can be apart from that—as a good time; a kind, forgiving, charitable, pleasant time: the only time I know of, in the long calendar of the year, when men and women seem by one consent to open their shut-up hearts freely, and to think of people below them as if they really were fellow-passengers to the grave, and not another race of creatures bound on other journeys. And therefore, uncle, though it has never put a scrap of gold or silver in my pocket, I believe that it has done me good, and will do me good; and I say, God bless it!'

The clerk in the tank involuntarily applauded. Becoming immediately sensible of the impropriety, he poked the fire, and extinguished the last frail spark for ever.

'Let me hear another sound from you,' said Scrooge, 'and you'll keep your Christmas by losing your situation! You're quite a powerful speaker, sir,' he added, turning to his nephew. 'I wonder you don't go into Parliament.'

'Don't be angry, uncle. Come! Dine with us tomorrow.'

Scrooge said that he would see him—yes, indeed he did. He went the whole length of the expression, and said that he would see him in that extremity first.

'But why?' cried Scrooge's nephew. 'Why?'

'Why did you get married?' said Scrooge.

'Because I fell in love.'

'Because you fell in love!' growled Scrooge, as if that were the only one thing in the world more ridiculous than a merry Christmas. 'Good afternoon!'

'Nay, uncle, but you never came to see me before that happened. Why give it as a reason for not coming now?'

'Good afternoon,' said Scrooge.

'I want nothing from you; I ask nothing of you; why cannot we be friends?'

'Good afternoon,' said Scrooge.

'I am sorry, with all my heart, to find you so resolute. We have never had any quarrel, to which I have been a party. But I have made the trial in homage to Christmas, and I'll keep my Christmas humour to the last. So A Merry Christmas, uncle!'

'Good afternoon,' said Scrooge.

'And A Happy New Year!'

'Good afternoon,' said Scrooge.

His nephew left the room without an angry word, notwithstanding. He stopped at the outer door to bestow the greetings of the season on the clerk, who cold as he was, was warmer than Scrooge; for he returned them cordially.

'There's another fellow,' muttered Scrooge; who overheard him: 'my clerk, with fifteen shillings a week, and a wife and family, talking about a merry Christmas. I'll retire to Bedlam.'

This lunatic, in letting Scrooge's nephew out, had let two other people in. They were portly gentlemen, pleasant to behold, and now stood, with their hats off, in Scrooge's office. They had books and papers in their hands, and bowed to him.

'Scrooge and Marley's, I believe,' said one of the gentlemen, referring to his list. 'Have I the pleasure of addressing Mr. Scrooge, or Mr. Marley?'

'Mr. Marley has been dead these seven years,' Scrooge replied. 'He died seven years ago, this very night.'

'We have no doubt his liberality is well represented by his surviving partner,' said the gentleman, presenting his credentials.

It certainly was; for they had been two kindred spirits. At the ominous word 'liberality,' Scrooge frowned, and shook his head, and handed the credentials back.

'At this festive season of the year, Mr. Scrooge,' said the gentleman, taking up a pen, 'it is more than usually desirable that we should make some slight provision for the Poor and Destitute, who suffer greatly at the present time. Many thousands are in want of common necessaries; hundreds of thousands are in want of common comforts, sir.'

'Are there no prisons?' asked Scrooge.

'Plenty of prisons,' said the gentleman, laying down the pen again.

'And the Union workhouses?' demanded Scrooge. 'Are they still in operation?'

'They are. Still,' returned the gentleman, 'I wish I could say they were not.'

'The Treadmill and the Poor Law are in full vigour, then?' said Scrooge.

'Both very busy, sir.'

'Oh! I was afraid, from what you said at first, that something had occurred to stop them in their useful course,' said Scrooge. 'I'm very glad to hear it.'

'Under the impression that they scarcely furnish Christian cheer of mind or body to the multitude,' returned the gentleman, 'a few of us are endeavouring to raise a fund to buy the Poor some meat and drink and means of warmth. We choose this time, because it is a time, of all others, when Want is keenly felt, and Abundance rejoices. What shall I put you down for?'

'Nothing!' Scrooge replied.

'You wish to be anonymous?'

'I wish to be left alone,' said Scrooge. 'Since you ask me what I wish, gentlemen, that is my answer. I don't make merry myself at Christmas and I can't afford to make idle people merry. I help to support the establishments I have mentioned—they cost enough; and those who are badly off must go there.'

'Many can't go there; and many would rather die.'

'If they would rather die,' said Scrooge, 'they had better do it, and decrease the surplus population. Besides—excuse me—I don't know that.'

'But you might know it,' observed the gentleman.

'It's not my business,' Scrooge returned. 'It's enough for a man to understand his own business, and not to interfere with other people's. Mine occupies me constantly. Good afternoon, gentlemen!'

Seeing clearly that it would be useless to pursue their point, the gentlemen withdrew. Scrooge returned his labours with an improved opinion of himself, and in a more facetious temper than was usual with him.

Meanwhile the fog and darkness thickened so, that people ran about with flaring links, proffering their services to go before horses in carriages, and conduct them on their way. The ancient tower of a church, whose gruff old bell was always peeping slily down at Scrooge out of a Gothic window in the wall, became invisible, and struck the hours and quarters in the clouds, with tremulous vibrations afterwards as if its teeth were chattering in its frozen head up there. The cold became intense. In the main street at the corner of the court, some labourers were repairing the gas-pipes, and had lighted a great fire in a brazier, round which a party of ragged men and boys were gathered: warming their hands and winking their eyes before the blaze in rapture. The water-plug being left in solitude, its overflowing sullenly congealed, and turned to misanthropic ice. The brightness of the shops where holly sprigs and berries crackled in the lamp heat of the windows, made pale faces ruddy as they passed. Poulterers' and grocers' trades became a splendid joke; a glorious pageant, with which it was next to impossible to believe that such dull principles as bargain and sale had anything to do. The Lord Mayor, in the stronghold of the mighty Mansion House, gave orders to his fifty cooks and butlers to keep Christmas as a Lord Mayor's household should; and even the little tailor, whom he had fined five shillings on the previous Monday for being drunk and bloodthirsty in the streets, stirred up to-morrow's pudding in his garret, while his lean wife and the baby sallied out to buy the beef.

Foggier yet, and colder! Piercing, searching, biting cold. If the good Saint Dunstan had but nipped the Evil Spirit's nose with a touch of such weather as that, instead of using his familiar weapons, then indeed he would have roared to lusty purpose. The owner of one scant young nose, gnawed and mumbled by the hungry cold as bones are gnawed by dogs, stooped down at Scrooge's keyhole to regale him with a Christmas carol: but at the first sound of

'God bless you, merry gentleman! May nothing you dismay!'

Scrooge seized the ruler with such energy of action, that the singer fled in terror, leaving the keyhole to the fog and even more congenial frost.

At length the hour of shutting up the counting-house arrived. With an ill-will Scrooge dismounted from his stool, and tacitly admitted the fact to the expectant clerk in the Tank, who instantly snuffed his candle out, and put on his hat.

'You'll want all day to-morrow, I suppose?' said Scrooge.

'If quite convenient, sir.'

'It's not convenient,' said Scrooge, 'and it's not fair. If I was to stop half-a-crown for it, you'd think yourself ill-used, I'll be bound?'

The clerk smiled faintly.

'And yet,' said Scrooge, 'you don't think me ill-used, when I pay a day's wages for no work.'

The clerk observed that it was only once a year.

'A poor excuse for picking a man's pocket every twenty-fifth of December!' said Scrooge, buttoning his great-coat to the chin. 'But I suppose you must have the whole day. Be here all the earlier next morning.'

The clerk promised that he would; and Scrooge walked out with a growl. The office was closed in a twinkling, and the clerk, with the long ends of his white comforter dangling below his waist (for he boasted no great-coat), went down a slide on Cornhill, at the end of a lane of boys, twenty times, in honour of its being Christmas Eve, and then ran home to Camden Town as hard as he could pelt, to play at blindman's-buff.

Scrooge took his melancholy dinner in his usual melancholy tavern; and having read all the newspapers, and beguiled the rest of the evening with his banker's-book, went home to bed. He lived in chambers which had once belonged to his deceased partner. They were a gloomy suite of rooms, in a lowering pile of building up a yard, where it had so little business to be, that one could scarcely help fancying it must have run there when it was a young house, playing at hide-and-seek with other houses, and forgotten the way out again. It was old enough now, and dreary enough, for nobody lived in it but Scrooge, the other rooms being all let out as offices. The yard was so dark that even Scrooge, who knew its every stone, was fain to grope with his hands. The fog and frost so hung about the black old gateway of the house, that it seemed as if the Genius of the Weather sat in mournful meditation on the threshold.

Now, it is a fact, that there was nothing at all particular about the knocker on the door, except that it was very large. It is also a fact, that Scrooge had seen it, night and morning, during his whole residence in that place; also that Scrooge had as little of what is called fancy about him as any man in the city of London, even including—which is a bold word—the corporation, aldermen, and livery. Let it also be borne in mind that Scrooge had not bestowed one thought on Marley, since his last mention of his seven years' dead partner that afternoon. And then let any man explain to me, if he can, how it happened that Scrooge, having his key in the lock of the door, saw in the knocker, without its undergoing any intermediate process of change—not a knocker, but Marley's face.

Marley's face. It was not in impenetrable shadow as the other objects in the yard were, but had a dismal light about it, like a bad lobster in a dark cellar. It was not angry or ferocious, but looked at Scrooge as Marley used to look: with ghostly spectacles turned up on its ghostly forehead. The hair was curiously stirred, as if by breath or hot air; and, though the eyes were wide open, they were perfectly motionless. That, and its livid colour, made it horrible; but its horror seemed to be in spite of the face and beyond its control, rather than a part or its own expression.

As Scrooge looked fixedly at this phenomenon, it was a knocker again.

To say that he was not startled, or that his blood was not conscious of a terrible sensation to which it had been a stranger from infancy, would be untrue. But he put his hand upon the key he had relinquished, turned it sturdily, walked in, and lighted his candle.

He did pause, with a moment's irresolution, before he shut the door; and he did look cautiously behind it first, as if he half-expected to be terrified with the sight of Marley's pigtail sticking out into the hall. But there was nothing on the back of the door, except the screws and nuts that held the knocker on, so he said 'Pooh, pooh!' and closed it with a bang.

The sound resounded through the house like thunder. Every room above, and every cask in the wine-merchant's cellars below, appeared to have a separate peal of echoes of its own. Scrooge was not a man to be frightened by echoes. He fastened the door, and walked across the hall, and up the stairs; slowly too: trimming his candle as he went.

You may talk vaguely about driving a coach-and-six up a good old flight of stairs, or through a bad young Act of Parliament; but I mean to say you might have got a hearse up that staircase, and taken it broadwise, with the splinter-bar towards the wall and the door towards the balustrades: and done it easy. There was plenty of width for that, and room to spare; which is perhaps the reason why Scrooge thought he saw a locomotive hearse going on before him in the gloom. Half a dozen gas-lamps out of the street wouldn't have lighted the entry too well, so you may suppose that it was pretty dark with Scrooge's dip.

Up Scrooge went, not caring a button for that. Darkness is cheap, and Scrooge liked it. But before he shut his heavy door, he walked through his rooms to see that all was right. He had just enough recollection of the face to desire to do that.

Sitting-room, bedroom, lumber-room. All as they should be. Nobody under the table, nobody under the sofa; a small fire in the grate; spoon and basin ready; and the little saucepan of gruel (Scrooge had a cold in his head) upon the hob. Nobody under the bed; nobody in the closet; nobody in his dressing-gown, which was hanging up in a suspicious attitude against the wall. Lumber-room as usual. Old fire-guards, old shoes, two fish-baskets, washing-stand on three legs, and a poker.

Quite satisfied, he closed his door, and locked himself in; double-locked himself in, which was not his custom. Thus secured against surprise, he took off his cravat; put on his dressing-gown and slippers, and his nightcap; and sat down before the fire to take his gruel.

It was a very low fire indeed; nothing on such a bitter night. He was obliged to sit close to it, and brood over it, before he could extract the least sensation of warmth from such a handful of fuel. The fireplace was an old one, built by some Dutch merchant long ago, and paved all round with quaint Dutch tiles, designed to illustrate the Scriptures. There were Cains and Abels, Pharaohs' daughters; Queens of Sheba, Angelic messengers descending through the air on clouds like feather-beds, Abrahams, Belshazzars, Apostles putting off to sea in butter-boats, hundreds of figures to attract his thoughts—and yet that face of Marley, seven years dead, came like the ancient Prophet's rod, and swallowed up the whole. If each smooth tile had been a blank at first, with power to shape some picture on its surface from the disjointed fragments of his thoughts, there would have been a copy of old Marley's head on every one.

'Humbug!' said Scrooge; and walked across the room.

After several turns, he sat down again. As he threw his head back in the chair, his glance happened to rest upon a bell, a disused bell, that hung in the room, and communicated for some purpose now forgotten with a chamber in the highest story of the building. It was with great astonishment, and with a strange, inexplicable dread, that as he looked, he saw this bell begin to swing. It swung so softly in the outset that it scarcely made a sound; but soon it rang out loudly, and so did every bell in the house.

This might have lasted half a minute, or a minute, but it seemed an hour. The bells ceased as they had begun, together. They were succeeded by a clanking noise, deep down below; as if some person were dragging a heavy chain over the casks in the wine merchant's cellar. Scrooge then remembered to have heard that ghosts in haunted houses were described as dragging chains.

The cellar-door flew open with a booming sound, and then he heard the noise much louder, on the floors below; then coming up the stairs; then coming straight towards his door.

'It's humbug still!' said Scrooge. 'I won't believe it.'

His colour changed though, when, without a pause, it came on through the heavy door, and passed into the room before his eyes. Upon its coming in, the dying flame leaped up, as though it cried 'I know him; Marley's Ghost!' and fell again.

The same face: the very same. Marley in his pigtail, usual waistcoat, tights and boots; the tassels on the latter bristling, like his pigtail, and his coat-skirts, and the hair upon his head. The chain he drew was clasped about his middle. It was long, and wound about him like a tail; and it was made (for Scrooge observed it closely) of cash-boxes, keys, padlocks, ledgers, deeds, and heavy purses wrought in steel. His body was transparent; so that Scrooge, observing him, and looking through his waistcoat, could see the two buttons on his coat behind.

Scrooge had often heard it said that Marley had no bowels, but he had never believed it until now.

No, nor did he believe it even now. Though he looked the phantom through and through, and saw it standing before him; though he felt the chilling influence of its death-cold eyes; and marked the very texture of the folded kerchief bound about its head and chin, which wrapper he had not observed before; he was still incredulous, and fought against his senses.

'How now!' said Scrooge, caustic and cold as ever. 'What do you want with me?'

'Much!'—Marley's voice, no doubt about it.

'Who are you?'

'Ask me who I was.'

'Who were you then?' said Scrooge, raising his voice. 'You're particular, for a shade.' He was going to say 'to a shade,' but substituted this, as more appropriate.

'In life I was your partner, Jacob Marley.'

'Can you—can you sit down?' asked Scrooge, looking doubtfully at him.

'I can.'

'Do it, then.'

Scrooge asked the question, because he didn't know whether a ghost so transparent might find himself in a condition to take a chair; and felt that in the event of its being impossible, it might involve the necessity of an embarrassing explanation. But the ghost sat down on the opposite side of the fireplace, as if he were quite used to it.

'You don't believe in me,' observed the Ghost.

'I don't,' said Scrooge.

'What evidence would you have of my reality beyond that of your senses?'

'I don't know,' said Scrooge.

'Why do you doubt your senses?'

'Because,' said Scrooge, 'a little thing affects them. A slight disorder of the stomach makes them cheats. You may be an undigested bit of beef, a blot of mustard, a crumb of cheese, a fragment of an underdone potato. There's more of gravy than of grave about you, whatever you are!'

Scrooge was not much in the habit of cracking jokes, nor did he feel, in his heart, by any means waggish then. The truth is, that he tried to be smart, as a means of distracting his own attention, and keeping down his terror; for the spectre's voice disturbed the very marrow in his bones.

To sit, staring at those fixed glazed eyes, in silence for a moment, would play, Scrooge felt, the very deuce with him. There was something very awful, too, in the spectre's being provided with an infernal atmosphere of its own. Scrooge could not feel it himself, but this was clearly the case; for though the Ghost sat perfectly motionless, its hair, and skirts, and tassels, were still agitated as by the hot vapour from an oven.

'You see this toothpick?' said Scrooge, returning quickly to the charge, for the reason just assigned; and wishing, though it were only for a second, to divert the vision's stony gaze from himself.

'I do,' replied the Ghost.

'You are not looking at it,' said Scrooge.

'But I see it,' said the Ghost, 'notwithstanding.'

'Well!' returned Scrooge, 'I have but to swallow this, and be for the rest of my days persecuted by a legion of goblins, all of my own creation. Humbug, I tell you! humbug!'

At this the spirit raised a frightful cry, and shook its chain with such a dismal and appalling noise, that Scrooge held on tight to his chair, to save himself from falling in a swoon. But how much greater was his horror, when the phantom taking off the bandage round its head, as if it were too warm to wear indoors, its lower jaw dropped down upon its breast!

Scrooge fell upon his knees, and clasped his hands before his face.

'Mercy!' he said. 'Dreadful apparition, why do you trouble me?'

'Man of the worldly mind!' replied the Ghost, 'do you believe in me or not?'

'I do,' said Scrooge. 'I must. But why do spirits walk the earth, and why do they come to me?'

'It is required of every man,' the Ghost returned, 'that the spirit within him should walk abroad among his fellowmen, and travel far and wide; and if that spirit goes not forth in life, it is condemned to do so after death. It is doomed to wander through the world—oh, woe is me!—and witness what it cannot share, but might have shared on earth, and turned to happiness!'

Again the spectre raised a cry, and shook its chain and wrung its shadowy hands.

'You are fettered,' said Scrooge, trembling. 'Tell me why?'

'I wear the chain I forged in life,' replied the Ghost. 'I made it link by link, and yard by yard; I girded it on of my own free will, and of my own free will I wore it. Is its pattern strange to you?'

Scrooge trembled more and more.

'Or would you know,' pursued the Ghost, 'the weight and length of the strong coil you bear yourself? It was full as heavy and as long as this, seven Christmas Eves ago. You have laboured on it, since. It is a ponderous chain!'

Scrooge glanced about him on the floor, in the expectation of finding himself surrounded by some fifty or sixty fathoms of iron cable: but he could see nothing.

'Jacob,' he said, imploringly. 'Old Jacob Marley, tell me more. Speak comfort to me, Jacob!'

'I have none to give,' the Ghost replied. 'It comes from other regions, Ebenezer Scrooge, and is conveyed by other ministers, to other kinds of men. Nor can I tell you what I would. A very little more, is all permitted to me. I cannot rest, I cannot stay, I cannot linger anywhere. My spirit never walked beyond our counting-house—mark me!—in life my spirit never roved beyond the narrow limits of our money-changing hole; and weary journeys lie before me!'

It was a habit with Scrooge, whenever he became thoughtful, to put his hands in his breeches pockets. Pondering on what the Ghost had said, he did so now, but without lifting up his eyes, or getting off his knees.

'You must have been very slow about it, Jacob,' Scrooge observed, in a business-like manner, though with humility and deference.

'Slow!' the Ghost repeated.

'Seven years dead,' mused Scrooge. 'And travelling all the time!'

'The whole time,' said the Ghost. 'No rest, no peace. Incessant torture of remorse.'

'You travel fast?' said Scrooge.

'On the wings of the wind,' replied the Ghost.

'You might have got over a great quantity of ground in seven years,' said Scrooge.

The Ghost, on hearing this, set up another cry, and clanked its chain so hideously in the dead silence of the night, that the Ward would have been justified in indicting it for a nuisance.

'Oh! captive, bound, and double-ironed,' cried the phantom, 'not to know, that ages of incessant labour, by immortal creatures, for this earth must pass into eternity before the good of which it is susceptible is all developed. Not to know that any Christian spirit working kindly in its little sphere, whatever it may be, will find its mortal life too short for its vast means of usefulness. Not to know that no space of regret can make amends for one life's opportunity misused! Yet such was I! Oh! such was I!'

'But you were always a good man of business, Jacob,' faltered Scrooge, who now began to apply this to himself.

'Business!' cried the Ghost, wringing its hands again. 'Mankind was my business. The common welfare was my business; charity, mercy, forbearance, and benevolence, were, all, my business. The dealings of my trade were but a drop of water in the comprehensive ocean of my business!'

It held up its chain at arm's length, as if that were the cause of all its unavailing grief, and flung it heavily upon the ground again.

'At this time of the rolling year,' the spectre said, 'I suffer most. Why did I walk through crowds of fellow-beings with my eyes turned down, and never raise them to that blessed Star which led the Wise Men to a poor abode? Were there no poor homes to which its light would have conducted me!'

Scrooge was very much dismayed to hear the spectre going on at this rate, and began to quake exceedingly.

'Hear me!' cried the Ghost. 'My time is nearly gone.'

'I will,' said Scrooge. 'But don't be hard upon me! Don't be flowery, Jacob! Pray!'

'How it is that I appear before you in a shape that you can see, I may not tell. I have sat invisible beside you many and many a day.'

It was not an agreeable idea. Scrooge shivered, and wiped the perspiration from his brow.

'That is no light part of my penance,' pursued the Ghost. 'I am here to-night to warn you, that you have yet a chance and hope of escaping my fate. A chance and hope of my procuring, Ebenezer.'

'You were always a good friend to me,' said Scrooge. 'Thank 'ee!'

'You will be haunted,' resumed the Ghost, 'by Three Spirits.'

Scrooge's countenance fell almost as low as the Ghost's had done.

'Is that the chance and hope you mentioned, Jacob?' he demanded, in a faltering voice.

'It is.'

'I—I think I'd rather not,' said Scrooge.

'Without their visits,' said the Ghost, 'you cannot hope to shun the path I tread. Expect the first tomorrow, when the bell tolls One.'

'Couldn't I take 'em all at once, and have it over, Jacob?' hinted Scrooge.

'Expect the second on the next night at the same hour. The third upon the next night when the last stroke of Twelve has ceased to vibrate. Look to see me no more; and look that, for your own sake, you remember what has passed between us!'

When it had said these words, the spectre took its wrapper from the table, and bound it round its head, as before. Scrooge knew this, by the smart sound its teeth made, when the jaws were brought together by the bandage. He ventured to raise his eyes again, and found his supernatural visitor confronting him in an erect attitude, with its chain wound over and about its arm.

The apparition walked backward from him; and at every step it took, the window raised itself a little, so that when the spectre reached it, it was wide open. It beckoned Scrooge to approach, which he did. When they were within two paces of each other, Marley's Ghost held up its hand, warning him to come no nearer. Scrooge stopped.

Not so much in obedience, as in surprise and fear: for on the raising of the hand, he became sensible of confused noises in the air; incoherent sounds of lamentation and regret; wailings inexpressibly sorrowful and self-accusatory. The spectre, after listening for a moment, joined in the mournful dirge; and floated out upon the bleak, dark night.

Scrooge followed to the window: desperate in his curiosity. He looked out.

The air was filled with phantoms, wandering hither and thither in restless haste, and moaning as they went. Every one of them wore chains like Marley's Ghost; some few (they might be guilty governments) were linked together; none were free. Many had been personally known to Scrooge in their lives. He had been quite familiar with one old ghost, in a white waistcoat, with a monstrous iron safe attached to its ankle, who cried piteously at being unable to assist a wretched woman with an infant, whom it saw below, upon a door-step. The misery with them all was, clearly, that they sought to interfere, for good, in human matters, and had lost the power for ever.

Whether these creatures faded into mist, or mist enshrouded them, he could not tell. But they and their spirit voices faded together; and the night became as it had been when he walked home.

Scrooge closed the window, and examined the door by which the Ghost had entered. It was double-locked, as he had locked it with his own hands, and the bolts were undisturbed. He tried to say 'Humbug!' but stopped at the first syllable. And being, from the emotion he had undergone, or the fatigues of the day, or his glimpse of the Invisible World, or the dull conversation of the Ghost, or the lateness of the hour, much in need of repose; went straight to bed, without undressing, and fell asleep upon the instant.

Stave 2: The First of the Three Spirits

When Scrooge awoke, it was so dark, that looking out of bed, he could scarcely distinguish the transparent window from the opaque walls of his chamber. He was endeavouring to pierce the darkness with his ferret eyes, when the chimes of a neighbouring church struck the four quarters. So he listened for the hour.

To his great astonishment the heavy bell went on from six to seven, and from seven to eight, and regularly up to twelve; then stopped. Twelve. It was past two when he went to bed. The clock was wrong. An icicle must have got into the works. Twelve.

He touched the spring of his repeater, to correct this most preposterous clock. Its rapid little pulse beat twelve: and stopped.

'Why, it isn't possible,' said Scrooge, 'that I can have slept through a whole day and far into another night. It isn't possible that anything has happened to the sun, and this is twelve at noon.'

The idea being an alarming one, he scrambled out of bed, and groped his way to the window. He was obliged to rub the frost off with the sleeve of his dressing-gown before he could see anything; and could see very little then. All he could make out was, that it was still very foggy and extremely cold, and that there was no noise of people running to and fro, and making a great stir, as there unquestionably would have been if night had beaten off bright day, and taken possession of the world. This was a great relief, because "Three days after sight of this First of Exchange pay to Mr. Ebenezer Scrooge on his order," and so forth, would have become a mere United States security if there were no days to count by.

Scrooge went to bed again, and thought, and thought, and thought it over and over, and could make nothing of it. The more he thought, the more perplexed he was; and, the more he endeavoured not to think, the more he thought.

Marley's Ghost bothered him exceedingly. Every time he resolved within himself, after mature inquiry that it was all a dream, his mind flew back again, like a strong spring released, to its first position, and presented the same problem to be worked all through, "Was it a dream or not?"

Scrooge lay in this state until the chime had gone three-quarters more, when he re-membered, on a sudden, that the Ghost had warned him of a visitation when the bell tolled one. He resolved to lie awake until the hour was passed; and, considering that he could no more go to sleep than go to heaven, this was, perhaps, the wisest resolution in his power.

The quarter was so long, that he was more than once convinced he must have sunk into a doze unconsciously, and missed the clock. At length it broke upon his listening ear.

"Ding, dong!"

"A quarter past," said Scrooge, counting.

"Ding, dong!"

"Half past," said Scrooge.

"Ding, dong!"

"A quarter to it," said Scrooge. "Ding, dong!"

"The hour itself," said Scrooge triumphantly, "and nothing else!"

He spoke before the hour bell sounded, which it now did with a deep, dull, hollow, melancholy ONE. Light flashed up in the room upon the instant, and the curtains of his bed were drawn.

The curtains of his bed were drawn aside, I tell you, by a hand. Not the curtains at his feet, nor the curtains at his back, but those to which his face was addressed. The curtains of his bed were drawn aside; and Scrooge, starting up into a half-recumbent attitude, found himself face to face with the unearthly visitor who drew them: as close to it as I am now to you, and I am standing in the spirit at your elbow.

It was a strange figure—like a child: yet not so like a child as like an old man, viewed through some supernatural medium, which gave him the appearance of having receded from the view, and being diminished to a child's proportions. Its hair, which hung about its neck and down its back, was white as if with age; and yet the face had not a wrinkle in it, and the tenderest bloom was on the skin. The arms were very long and muscular; the hands the same, as if its hold were of uncommon strength. Its legs and feet, most delicately formed, were, like those upper members, bare. It wore a tunic of the purest white, and round its waist was bound a lustrous belt, the sheen of which was beautiful. It held a branch of fresh green holly in its hand; and, in singular contradiction of that wintry emblem, had its dress trimmed with summer flowers. But the strangest thing about it was, that from the crown of its head there sprung a bright clear jet of light, by which all this was visible; and which was doubtless the occasion of its using, in its duller moments, a great extinguisher for a cap, which it now held under its arm.

Even this, though, when Scrooge looked at it with increasing steadiness, was not its strangest quality. For as its belt sparkled and glittered now in one part and now in another, and what was light one instant, at another time was dark, so the figure itself fluctuated in its distinctness: being now a thing with one arm, now with one leg, now with twenty legs, now a pair of legs without a head, now a head without a body: of which dissolving parts, no outline would be visible in the dense gloom wherein they melted away. And in the very wonder of this, it would be itself again; distinct and clear as ever.

'Are you the Spirit, sir, whose coming was foretold to me?' asked Scrooge.

'I am.'

The voice was soft and gentle. Singularly low, as if instead of being so close beside him, it were at a distance.

'Who, and what are you?' Scrooge demanded.

'I am the Ghost of Christmas Past.'

'Long Past?' inquired Scrooge: observant of its dwarfish stature.

'No. Your past.'

Perhaps, Scrooge could not have told anybody why, if anybody could have asked him; but he had a special desire to see the Spirit in his cap; and begged him to be covered.

'What!' exclaimed the Ghost, 'would you so soon put out, with worldly hands, the light I give? Is it not enough that you are one of those whose passions made this cap, and force me through whole trains of years to wear it low upon my brow!'

Scrooge reverently disclaimed all intention to offend or any knowledge of having wilfully bonneted the Spirit at any period of his life. He then made bold to inquire what business brought him there.

'Your welfare!' said the Ghost.

Scrooge expressed himself much obliged, but could not help thinking that a night of unbroken rest would have been more conducive to that end. The Spirit must have heard him thinking, for it said immediately:

'Your reclamation, then. Take heed!'

It put out its strong hand as it spoke, and clasped him gently by the arm.

'Rise! and walk with me!'

It would have been in vain for Scrooge to plead that the weather and the hour were not adapted to pedestrian purposes; that bed was warm, and the thermometer a long way below freezing; that he was clad but lightly in his slippers, dressing-gown, and nightcap; and that he had a cold upon him at that time. The grasp, though gentle as a woman's hand, was not to be resisted. He rose: but finding that the Spirit made towards the window, clasped his robe in supplication.

'I am mortal,' Scrooge remonstrated, 'and liable to fall.'

'Bear but a touch of my hand there,' said the Spirit, laying it upon his heart, 'and you shall be upheld in more than this!'

As the words were spoken, they passed through the wall, and stood upon an open country road, with fields on either hand. The city had entirely vanished. Not a vestige of it was to be seen. The darkness and the mist had vanished with it, for it was a clear, cold winter day, with snow upon the ground.

'Good Heaven!' said Scrooge, clasping his hands together, as he looked about him. 'I was bred in this place. I was a boy here!'

The Spirit gazed upon him mildly. Its gentle touch, though it had been light and instantaneous, appeared still present to the old man's sense of feeling. He was conscious of a thousand odours floating in the air, each one connected with a thousand thoughts, and hopes, and joys, and cares long, long, forgotten!

'Your lip is trembling,' said the Ghost. 'And what is that upon your cheek?'

Scrooge muttered, with an unusual catching in his voice, that it was a pimple; and begged the Ghost to lead him where he would.

'You recollect the way?' inquired the Spirit.

'Remember it!' cried Scrooge with fervour; 'I could walk it blindfold.'

'Strange to have forgotten it for so many years!' observed the Ghost. 'Let us go on.'

They walked along the road, Scrooge recognising every gate, and post, and tree; until a little market-town appeared in the distance, with its bridge, its church, and winding river. Some shaggy ponies now were seen trotting towards them with boys upon their backs, who called to other boys in country gigs and carts, driven by farmers. All these boys were in great spirits, and shouted to each other, until the broad fields were so full of merry music, that the crisp air laughed to hear it.

'These are but shadows of the things that have been,' said the Ghost. 'They have no consciousness of us.'

The jocund travellers came on; and as they came, Scrooge knew and named them every one. Why was he rejoiced beyond all bounds to see them! Why did his cold eye glisten, and his heart leap up as they went past! Why was he filled with gladness when he heard them give each other Merry Christmas, as they parted at cross-roads and bye-ways, for their several homes! What was merry Christmas to Scrooge? Out upon merry Christmas! What good had it ever done to him?

'The school is not quite deserted,' said the Ghost. 'A solitary child, neglected by his friends, is left there still.'

Scrooge said he knew it. And he sobbed.

They left the high-road, by a well-remembered lane, and soon approached a mansion of dull red brick, with a little weathercock-surmounted cupola, on the roof, and a bell hanging in it. It was a large house, but one of broken fortunes; for the spacious offices were little used, their walls were damp and mossy, their windows broken, and their gates decayed. Fowls clucked and strutted in the stables; and the coach-houses and sheds were over-run with grass. Nor was it more retentive of its ancient state, within; for entering the dreary hall, and glancing through the open doors of many rooms, they found them poorly furnished, cold, and vast. There was an earthy savour in the air, a chilly bareness in the place, which associated itself somehow with too much getting up by candle-light, and not too much to eat.

They went, the Ghost and Scrooge, across the hall, to a door at the back of the house. It opened before them, and disclosed a long, bare, melancholy room, made barer still by lines of plain deal forms and desks. At one of these a lonely boy was reading near a feeble fire; and Scrooge sat down upon a form, and wept to see his poor forgotten self as he used to be.

Not a latent echo in the house, not a squeak and scuffle from the mice behind the panelling, not a drip from the half-thawed water-spout in the dull yard behind, not a sigh among the leafless boughs of one despondent poplar, not the idle swinging of an empty store-house door, no, not a clicking in the fire, but fell upon the heart of Scrooge with a softening influence, and gave a freer passage to his tears.

The Spirit touched him on the arm, and pointed to his younger self, intent upon his reading. Suddenly a man, in foreign garments: wonderfully real and distinct to look at: stood outside the window, with an axe stuck in his belt, and leading by the bridle an ass laden with wood.

'Why, it's Ali Baba!' Scrooge exclaimed in ecstasy. 'It's dear old honest Ali Baba! Yes, yes, I know! One Christmas time, when yonder solitary child was left here all alone, he did come, for the first time, just like that. Poor boy! And Valentine,' said Scrooge,' and his wild brother, Orson; there they go! And what's his name, who was put down in his drawers, asleep, at the Gate of Damascus; don't you see him! And the Sultan's Groom turned upside down by the Genii; there he is upon his head! Serve him right. I'm glad of it. What business had he to be married to the Princess!'

To hear Scrooge expending all the earnestness of his nature on such subjects, in a most extraordinary voice between laughing and crying; and to see his heightened and excited face; would have been a surprise to his business friends in the city, indeed.

'There's the Parrot!' cried Scrooge. 'Green body and yellow tail, with a thing like a lettuce growing out of the top of his head; there he is! Poor Robin Crusoe, he called him, when he came home again after sailing round the island. 'Poor Robin Crusoe, where have you been, Robin Crusoe?' The man thought he was dreaming, but he wasn't. It was the Parrot, you know. There goes Friday, running for his life to the little creek! Halloa! Hoop! Hallo!'

Then, with a rapidity of transition very foreign to his usual character, he said, in pity for his former self, 'Poor boy!' and cried again.

'I wish,' Scrooge muttered, putting his hand in his pocket, and looking about him, after drying his eyes with his cuff: 'but it's too late now.'

'What is the matter?' asked the Spirit.

'Nothing,' said Scrooge. 'Nothing. There was a boy singing a Christmas Carol at my door last night. I should like to have given him something: that's all.'

The Ghost smiled thoughtfully, and waved its hand: saying as it did so, 'Let us see another Christmas!'

Scrooge's former self grew larger at the words, and the room became a little darker and more dirty. The panels shrunk, the windows cracked; fragments of plaster fell out of the ceiling, and the naked laths were shown instead; but how all this was brought about, Scrooge knew no more than you do. He only knew that it was quite correct; that everything had happened so; that there he was, alone again, when all the other boys had gone home for the jolly holidays.

He was not reading now, but walking up and down despairingly.

Scrooge looked at the Ghost, and with a mournful shaking of his head, glanced anxiously towards the door.

It opened; and a little girl, much younger than the boy, came darting in, and putting her arms about his neck, and often kissing him, addressed him as her 'Dear, dear brother.'

'I have come to bring you home, dear brother!' said the child, clapping her tiny hands, and bending down to laugh. 'To bring you home, home, home!'

'Home, little Fan?' returned the boy.

'Yes.' said the child, brimful of glee. 'Home, for good and all. Home, for ever and ever. Father is so much kinder than he used to be, that home's like Heaven. He spoke so gently to me one dear night when I was going to bed, that I was not afraid to ask him once more if you might come home; and he said Yes, you should; and sent me in a coach to bring you. And you're to be a man!' said the child, opening her eyes,' and are never to come back here; but first, we're to be together all the Christmas long, and have the merriest time in all the world.'

'You are quite a woman, little Fan!' exclaimed the boy.

She clapped her hands and laughed, and tried to touch his head; but being too little, laughed again, and stood on tiptoe to embrace him. Then she began to drag him, in her childish eagerness, towards the door; and he, nothing loth to go, accompanied her.

A terrible voice in the hall cried. 'Bring down Master Scrooge's box, there!' and in the hall appeared the schoolmaster himself, who glared on Master Scrooge with a ferocious condescension, and threw him into a dreadful state of mind by shaking hands with him. He then conveyed him and his sister into the veriest old well of a shivering best-parlour that ever was seen, where the maps upon the wall, and the celestial and terrestrial globes in the windows, were waxy with cold. Here he produced a decanter of curiously light wine, and a block of curiously heavy cake, and administered instalments of those dainties to the young people: at the same time, sending out a meagre servant to offer a glass of something to the postboy, who answered that he thanked the gentleman, but if it was the same tap as he had tasted before, he had rather not. Master Scrooge's trunk being by this time tied on to the top of the chaise, the children bade the schoolmaster goodbye right willingly; and getting into it, drove gaily down the garden-sweep: the quick wheels dashing the hoar-frost and snow from off the dark leaves of the evergreens like spray.

'Always a delicate creature, whom a breath might have withered,' said the Ghost. 'But she had a large heart!'

'So she had,' cried Scrooge. 'You're right. I will not gainsay it, Spirit. God forbid!'

'She died a woman,' said the Ghost, 'and had, as I think, children.'

'One child,' Scrooge returned.

'True,' said the Ghost. 'Your nephew.'

Scrooge seemed uneasy in his mind; and answered briefly, 'Yes.'

Although they had but that moment left the school behind them, they were now in the busy thoroughfares of a city, where shadowy passengers passed and repassed; where shadowy carts and coaches battle for the way, and all the strife and tumult of a real city were. It was made plain enough, by the dressing of the shops, that here too it was Christmas time again; but it was evening, and the streets were lighted up.

The Ghost stopped at a certain warehouse door, and asked Scrooge if he knew it.

'Know it!' said Scrooge. 'I was apprenticed here!'

They went in. At sight of an old gentleman in a Welsh wig, sitting behind such a high desk, that if he had been two inches taller he must have knocked his head against the ceiling, Scrooge cried in great excitement:

'Why, it's old Fezziwig! Bless his heart; it's Fezziwig alive again!'

Old Fezziwig laid down his pen, and looked up at the clock, which pointed to the hour of seven. He rubbed his hands; adjusted his capacious waistcoat; laughed all over himself, from his shows to his organ of benevolence; and called out in a comfortable, oily, rich, fat, jovial voice:

'Yo ho, there! Ebenezer! Dick!'

Scrooge's former self, now grown a young man, came briskly in, accompanied by his fellow-prentice.

'Dick Wilkins, to be sure!' said Scrooge to the Ghost. 'Bless me, yes. There he is. He was very much attached to me, was Dick. Poor Dick! Dear, dear!'

'Yo ho, my boys!' said Fezziwig. 'No more work to-night. Christmas Eve, Dick. Christmas, Ebenezer! Let's have the shutters up,' cried old Fezziwig, with a sharp clap of his hands,' before a man can say Jack Robinson!'

You wouldn't believe how those two fellows went at it! They charged into the street with the shutters—one, two, three—had them up in their places—four, five, six—barred them and pinned then—seven, eight, nine—and came back before you could have got to twelve, panting like race-horses.

'Hilli-ho!' cried old Fezziwig, skipping down from the high desk, with wonderful agility. 'Clear away, my lads, and let's have lots of room here! Hilli-ho, Dick! Chirrup, Ebenezer!'

Clear away. There was nothing they wouldn't have cleared away, or couldn't have cleared away, with old Fezziwig looking on. It was done in a minute. Every movable was packed off, as if it were dismissed from public life for evermore; the floor was swept and watered, the lamps were trimmed, fuel was heaped upon the fire; and the warehouse was as snug, and warm, and dry, and bright a ball-room, as you would desire to see upon a winter's night.

In came a fiddler with a music-book, and went up to the lofty desk, and made an orchestra of it, and tuned like fifty stomach-aches. In came Mr. Fezziwig, one vast substantial smile. In came the three Miss Fezziwigs, beaming and lovable. In came the six young followers whose hearts they broke. In came all the young men and women employed in the business. In came the housemaid, with her cousin, the baker. In came the cook, with her brother's particular friend, the milkman. In came the boy from over the way, who was suspected of not having board enough from his master; trying to hide himself behind the girl from next door but one, who was proved to have had her ears pulled by her mistress. In they all came, one after another; some shyly, some boldly, some gracefully, some awkwardly, some pushing, some pulling; in they all came, anyhow and everyhow. Away they all went, twenty couples at once; hands half round and back again the other way; down the middle and up again; round and round in various stages of affectionate grouping; old top couple always turning up in the wrong place; new top couple starting off again, as soon as they got there; all top couples at last, and not a bottom one to help them. When this result was brought about, old Fezziwig, clapping his hands to stop the dance, cried out,' Well done!' and the fiddler plunged his hot face into a pot of porter, especially provided for that purpose. But scorning rest, upon his reappearance, he instantly began again, though there were no dancers yet, as if the other fiddler had been carried home, exhausted, on a shutter, and he were a bran-new man resolved to beat him out of sight, or perish.

There were more dances, and there were forfeits, and more dances, and there was cake, and there was negus, and there was a great piece of Cold Roast, and there was a great piece of Cold Boiled, and there were mince-pies, and plenty of beer. But the great effect of the evening came after the Roast and Boiled, when the fiddler (an artful dog, mind. The sort of man who knew his business better than you or I could have told it him.) struck up Sir Roger de Coverley.' Then old Fezziwig stood out to dance with Mrs. Fezziwig. Top couple, too; with a good stiff piece of work cut out for them; three or four and twenty pair of partners; people who were not to be trifled with; people who would dance, and had no notion of walking.

But if they had been twice as many—ah, four times—old Fezziwig would have been a match for them, and so would Mrs. Fezziwig. As to her, she was worthy to be his partner in every sense of the term. If that's not high praise, tell me higher, and I'll use it. A positive light appeared to issue from Fezziwig's calves. They shone in every part of the dance like moons. You couldn't have predicted, at any given time, what would have become of them next. And when old Fezziwig and Mrs. Fezziwig had gone all through the dance; advance and retire, both hands to your partner, bow and curtsey, corkscrew, thread-the-needle, and back again to your place; Fezziwig cut—cut so deftly, that he appeared to wink with his legs, and came upon his feet again without a stagger.

When the clock struck eleven, this domestic ball broke up. Mr. and Mrs. Fezziwig took their stations, one on either side of the door, and shaking hands with every person individually as he or she went out, wished him or her a Merry Christmas. When everybody had retired but the two prentices, they did the same to them; and thus the cheerful voices died away, and the lads were left to their beds; which were under a counter in the back-shop.

During the whole of this time, Scrooge had acted like a man out of his wits. His heart and soul were in the scene, and with his former self. He corroborated everything, remembered everything, enjoyed everything, and underwent the strangest agitation. It was not until now, when the bright faces of his former self and Dick were turned from them, that he remembered the Ghost, and became conscious that it was looking full upon him, while the light upon its head burnt very clear.

'A small matter,' said the Ghost, 'to make these silly folks so full of gratitude.'

'Small!' echoed Scrooge.

The Spirit signed to him to listen to the two apprentices, who were pouring out their hearts in praise of Fezziwig: and when he had done so, said,

'Why! Is it not? He has spent but a few pounds of your mortal money: three or four perhaps. Is that so much that he deserves this praise?'

'It isn't that,' said Scrooge, heated by the remark, and speaking unconsciously like his former, not his latter, self. 'It isn't that, Spirit. He has the power to render us happy or unhappy; to make our service light or burdensome; a pleasure or a toil. Say that his power lies in words and looks; in things so slight and insignificant that it is impossible to add and count them up: what then? The happiness he gives, is quite as great as if it cost a fortune.'

He felt the Spirit's glance, and stopped.

'What is the matter?' asked the Ghost.

'Nothing in particular,' said Scrooge.

'Something, I think?' the Ghost insisted.

'No,' said Scrooge,' No. I should like to be able to say a word or two to my clerk just now! That's all.'

His former self turned down the lamps as he gave utterance to the wish; and Scrooge and the Ghost again stood side by side in the open air.

'My time grows short,' observed the Spirit. 'Quick!'

This was not addressed to Scrooge, or to any one whom he could see, but it produced an immediate effect. For again Scrooge saw himself. He was older now; a man in the prime of life. His face had not the harsh and rigid lines of later years; but it had begun to wear the signs of care and avarice. There was an eager, greedy, restless motion in the eye, which showed the passion that had taken root, and where the shadow of the growing tree would fall.

He was not alone, but sat by the side of a fair young girl in a mourning-dress: in whose eyes there were tears, which sparkled in the light that shone out of the Ghost of Christmas Past.

'It matters little,' she said, softly. 'To you, very little. Another idol has displaced me; and if it can cheer and comfort you in time to come, as I would have tried to do, I have no just cause to grieve.'

'What Idol has displaced you?' he rejoined.

'A golden one.'

'This is the even-handed dealing of the world!' he said. 'There is nothing on which it is so hard as poverty; and there is nothing it professes to condemn with such severity as the pursuit of wealth!'

'You fear the world too much,' she answered, gently. 'All your other hopes have merged into the hope of being beyond the chance of its sordid reproach. I have seen your nobler aspirations fall off one by one, until the master-passion, Gain, engrosses you. Have I not?'

'What then?' he retorted. 'Even if I have grown so much wiser, what then? I am not changed towards you.'

She shook her head.

'Am I?'

'Our contract is an old one. It was made when we were both poor and content to be so, until, in good season, we could improve our worldly fortune by our patient industry. You are changed. When it was made, you were another man.'

'I was a boy,' he said impatiently.

'Your own feeling tells you that you were not what you are,' she returned. 'I am. That which promised happiness when we were one in heart, is fraught with misery now that we are two. How often and how keenly I have thought of this, I will not say. It is enough that I have thought of it, and can release you.'

'Have I ever sought release?'

'In words. No. Never.'

'In what, then?'

'In a changed nature; in an altered spirit; in another atmosphere of life; another Hope as its great end. In everything that made my love of any worth or value in your sight. If this had never been between us,' said the girl, looking mildly, but with steadiness, upon him; 'tell me, would you seek me out and try to win me now? Ah, no!'

He seemed to yield to the justice of this supposition, in spite of himself. But he said with a struggle, 'You think not.'

'I would gladly think otherwise if I could,' she answered, 'Heaven knows! When I have learned a Truth like this, I know how strong and irresistible it must be. But if you were free to-day, to-morrow, yesterday, can even I believe that you would choose a dowerless girl—you who, in your very confidence with her, weigh everything by Gain: or, choosing her, if for a moment you were false enough to your one guiding principle to do so, do I not know that your repentance and regret would surely follow? I do; and I release you. With a full heart, for the love of him you once were.'

He was about to speak; but with her head turned from him, she resumed.

'You may—the memory of what is past half makes me hope you will—have pain in this. A very, very brief time, and you will dismiss the recollection of it, gladly, as an unprofitable dream, from which it happened well that you awoke. May you be happy in the life you have chosen.'

She left him, and they parted.

'Spirit!' said Scrooge, 'show me no more! Conduct me home. Why do you delight to torture me?'

'One shadow more!' exclaimed the Ghost.

'No more!' cried Scrooge. 'No more, I don't wish to see it. Show me no more!'

But the relentless Ghost pinioned him in both his arms, and forced him to observe what happened next.

They were in another scene and place; a room, not very large or handsome, but full of comfort. Near to the winter fire sat a beautiful young girl, so like that last that Scrooge believed it was the same, until he saw her, now a comely matron, sitting opposite her daughter. The noise in this room was perfectly tumultuous, for there were more children there, than Scrooge in his agitated state of mind could count; and, unlike the celebrated herd in the poem, they were not forty children conducting themselves like one, but every child was conducting itself like forty. The consequences were uproarious beyond belief; but no one seemed to care; on the contrary, the mother and daughter laughed heartily, and enjoyed it very much; and the latter, soon beginning to mingle in the sports, got pillaged by the young brigands most ruthlessly. What would I not have given to be one of them! Though I never could have been so rude, no, no! I wouldn't for the wealth of all the world have crushed that braided hair, and torn it down; and for the precious little shoe, I wouldn't have plucked it off, God bless my soul! to save my life. As to measuring her waist in sport, as they did, bold young brood, I couldn't have done it; I should have expected my arm to have grown round it for a punishment, and never come straight again. And yet I should have dearly liked, I own, to have touched her lips; to have questioned her, that she might have opened them; to have looked upon the lashes of her downcast eyes, and never raised a blush; to have let loose waves of hair, an inch of which would be a keepsake beyond price: in short, I should have liked, I do confess, to have had the lightest licence of a child, and yet to have been man enough to know its value.

But now a knocking at the door was heard, and such a rush immediately ensued that she with laughing face and plundered dress was borne towards it the centre of a flushed and boisterous group, just in time to greet the father, who came home attended by a man laden with Christmas toys and presents. Then the shouting and the struggling, and the onslaught that was made on the defenceless porter. The scaling him, with chairs for ladders to dive into his pockets, despoil him of brown-paper parcels, hold on tight by his cravat, hug him round his neck, pommel his back, and kick his legs in irrepressible affection. The shouts of wonder and delight with which the development of every package was received! The terrible announcement that the baby had been taken in the act of putting a doll's frying-pan into his mouth, and was more than suspected of having swallowed a fictitious turkey, glued on a wooden platter! The immense relief of finding this a false alarm! The joy, and gratitude, and ecstasy! They are all indescribable alike. It is enough that by degrees the children and their emotions got out of the parlour, and by one stair at a time, up to the top of the house; where they went to bed, and so subsided.

And now Scrooge looked on more attentively than ever, when the master of the house, having his daughter leaning fondly on him, sat down with her and her mother at his own fireside; and when he thought that such another creature, quite as graceful and as full of promise, might have called him father, and been a spring-time in the haggard winter of his life, his sight grew very dim indeed.

'Belle,' said the husband, turning to his wife with a smile, 'I saw an old friend of yours this afternoon.'

'Who was it?'

'Guess!'

'How can I? Tut, don't I know,' she added in the same breath, laughing as he laughed. 'Mr. Scrooge.'

'Mr. Scrooge it was. I passed his office window; and as it was not shut up, and he had a candle inside, I could scarcely help seeing him. His partner lies upon the point of death, I hear; and there he sat alone. Quite alone in the world, I do believe.'

'Spirit!' said Scrooge in a broken voice, 'remove me from this place.'

'I told you these were shadows of the things that have been,' said the Ghost. 'That they are what they are, do not blame me.'

'Remove me!' Scrooge exclaimed, 'I cannot bear it!'

He turned upon the Ghost, and seeing that it looked upon him with a face, in which in some strange way there were fragments of all the faces it had shown him, wrestled with it.

'Leave me! Take me back. Haunt me no longer!'

In the struggle, if that can be called a struggle in which the Ghost with no visible resistance on its own part was undisturbed by any effort of its adversary, Scrooge observed that its light was burning high and bright; and dimly connecting that with its influence over him, he seized the extinguisher-cap, and by a sudden action pressed it down upon its head.

The Spirit dropped beneath it, so that the extinguisher covered its whole form; but though Scrooge pressed it down with all his force, he could not hide the light, which streamed from under it, in an unbroken flood upon the ground.

He was conscious of being exhausted, and overcome by an irresistible drowsiness; and, further, of being in his own bedroom. He gave the cap a parting squeeze, in which his hand relaxed; and had barely time to reel to bed, before he sank into a heavy sleep.

Stave 3: The Second of the Three Spirits

Awaking in the middle of a prodigiously tough snore, and sitting up in bed to get his thoughts together, Scrooge had no occasion to be told that the bell was again upon the stroke of One. He felt that he was restored to consciousness in the right nick of time, for the especial purpose of holding a conference with the second messenger despatched to him through Jacob Marley's intervention. But, finding that he turned uncomfortably cold when he began to wonder which of his curtains this new spectre would draw back, he put them every one aside with his own hands, and lying down again, established a sharp look-out all round the bed. For, he wished to challenge the Spirit on the moment of its appearance, and did not wish to be taken by surprise, and made nervous.

Gentlemen of the free-and-easy sort, who plume themselves on being acquainted with a move or two, and being usually equal to the time-of-day, express the wide range of their capacity for adventure by observing that they are good for anything from pitch-and-toss to manslaughter; between which opposite extremes, no doubt, there lies a tolerably wide and comprehensive range of subjects. Without venturing for Scrooge quite as hardily as this, I don't mind calling on you to believe that he was ready for a good broad field of strange appearances, and that nothing between a baby and rhinoceros would have astonished him very much.

Now, being prepared for almost anything, he was not by any means prepared for nothing; and, consequently, when the bell struck One, and no shape appeared, he was taken with a violent fit of trembling. Five minutes, ten minutes, a quarter of an hour went by, yet nothing came. All this time, he lay upon his bed, the very core and centre of a blaze of ruddy light, which streamed upon it when the clock proclaimed the hour; and which, being only light, was more alarming than a dozen ghosts, as he was powerless to make out what it meant, or would be at; and was sometimes apprehensive that he might be at that very moment an interesting case of spontaneous combustion, without having the consolation of knowing it. At last, however, he began to think—as you or I would have thought at first; for it is always the person not in the predicament who knows what ought to have been done in it, and would unquestionably have done it too—at last, I say, he began to think that the source and secret of this ghostly light might be in the adjoining room, from whence, on further tracing it, it seemed to shine. This idea taking full possession of his mind, he got up softly and shuffled in his slippers to the door.

The moment Scrooge's hand was on the lock, a strange voice called him by his name, and bade him enter. He obeyed.

It was his own room. There was no doubt about that. But it had undergone a surprising transformation. The walls and ceiling were so hung with living green, that it looked a perfect grove; from every part of which, bright gleaming berries glistened. The crisp leaves of holly, mistletoe, and ivy reflected back the light, as if so many little mirrors had been scattered there; and such a mighty blaze went roaring up the chimney, as that dull petrification of a hearth had never known in Scrooge's time, or Marley's, or for many and many a winter season gone. Heaped up on the floor, to form a kind of throne, were turkeys, geese, game, poultry, brawn, great joints of meat, sucking-pigs, long wreaths of sausages, mince-pies, plum-puddings, barrels of oysters, red-hot chestnuts, cherry-cheeked apples, juicy oranges, luscious pears, immense twelfth-cakes, and seething bowls of punch, that made the chamber dim with their delicious steam. In easy state upon this couch, there sat a jolly Giant, glorious to see, who bore a glowing torch, in shape not unlike Plenty's horn, and held it up, high up, to shed its light on Scrooge, as he came peeping round the door.

'Come in!' exclaimed the Ghost. 'Come in, and know me better, man!'

Scrooge entered timidly, and hung his head before this Spirit. He was not the dogged Scrooge he had been; and though the Spirit's eyes were clear and kind, he did not like to meet them.

'I am the Ghost of Christmas Present,' said the Spirit. 'Look upon me!'

Scrooge reverently did so. It was clothed in one simple green robe, or mantle, bordered with white fur. This garment hung so loosely on the figure, that its capacious breast was bare, as if disdaining to be warded or concealed by any artifice. Its feet, observable beneath the ample folds of the garment, were also bare; and on its head it wore no other covering than a holly wreath, set here and there with shining icicles. Its dark brown curls were long and free; free as its genial face, its sparkling eye, its open hand, its cheery voice, its unconstrained demeanour, and its joyful air. Girded round its middle was an antique scabbard; but no sword was in it, and the ancient sheath was eaten up with rust.

'You have never seen the like of me before!' exclaimed the Spirit.

'Never,' Scrooge made answer to it.

'Have never walked forth with the younger members of my family; meaning (for I am very young) my elder brothers born in these later years?' pursued the Phantom.

'I don't think I have,' said Scrooge. 'I am afraid I have not. Have you had many brothers, Spirit?'

'More than eighteen hundred,' said the Ghost.

'A tremendous family to provide for!' muttered Scrooge.

The Ghost of Christmas Present rose.

'Spirit,' said Scrooge submissively, 'conduct me where you will. I went forth last night on compulsion, and I learnt a lesson which is working now. To-night, if you have aught to teach me, let me profit by it.'

'Touch my robe!'

Scrooge did as he was told, and held it fast.

Holly, mistletoe, red berries, ivy, turkeys, geese, game, poultry, brawn, meat, pigs, sausages, oysters, pies, puddings, fruit, and punch, all vanished instantly. So did the room, the fire, the ruddy glow, the hour of night, and they stood in the city streets on Christmas morning, where (for the weather was severe) the people made a rough, but brisk and not unpleasant kind of music, in scraping the snow from the pavement in front of their dwellings, and from the tops of their houses, whence it was mad delight to the boys to see it come plumping down into the road below, and splitting into artificial little snow-storms.

The house fronts looked black enough, and the windows blacker, contrasting with the smooth white sheet of snow upon the roofs, and with the dirtier snow upon the ground; which last deposit had been ploughed up in deep furrows by the heavy wheels of carts and waggons; furrows that crossed and recrossed each other hundreds of times where the great streets branched off; and made intricate channels, hard to trace in the thick yellow mud and icy water. The sky was gloomy, and the shortest streets were choked up with a dingy mist, half thawed, half frozen, whose heavier particles descended in shower of sooty atoms, as if all the chimneys in Great Britain had, by one consent, caught fire, and were blazing away to their dear hearts' content. There was nothing very cheerful in the climate or the town, and yet was there an air of cheerfulness abroad that the clearest summer air and brightest summer sun might have endeavoured to diffuse in vain.

For, the people who were shovelling away on the housetops were jovial and full of glee; calling out to one another from the parapets, and now and then exchanging a facetious snowball—better-natured missile far than many a wordy jest— laughing heartily if it went right and not less heartily if it went wrong. The poulterers' shops were still half open, and the fruiterers' were radiant in their glory. There were great, round, pot-bellied baskets of chestnuts, shaped like the waistcoats of jolly old gentlemen, lolling at the doors, and tumbling out into the street in their apoplectic opulence. There were ruddy, brown-faced, broad-girthed Spanish onions, shining in the fatness of their growth like Spanish Friars, and winking from their shelves in wanton slyness at the girls as they went by, and glanced demurely at the hung-up mistletoe. There were pears and apples, clustered high in blooming pyramids; there were bunches of grapes, made, in the shopkeepers' benevolence to dangle from conspicuous hooks, that people's mouths might water gratis as they passed; there were piles of filberts, mossy and brown, recalling, in their fragrance, ancient walks among the woods, and pleasant shufflings ankle deep through withered leaves; there were Norfolk Biffins, squab and swarthy, setting off the yellow of the oranges and lemons, and, in the great compactness of their juicy persons, urgently entreating and beseeching to be carried home in paper bags and eaten after dinner. The very gold and silver fish, set forth among these choice fruits in a bowl, though members of a dull and stagnant-blooded race, appeared to know that there was something going on; and, to a fish, went gasping round and round their little world in slow and passionless excitement.

The Grocers'! oh the Grocers'! nearly closed, with perhaps two shutters down, or one; but through those gaps such glimpses! It was not alone that the scales descending on the counter made a merry sound, or that the twine and roller parted company so briskly, or that the canisters were rattled up and down like juggling tricks, or even that the blended scents of tea and coffee were so grateful to the nose, or even that the raisins were so plentiful and rare, the almonds so extremely white, the sticks of cinnamon so long and straight, the other spices so delicious, the candied fruits so caked and spotted with molten sugar as to make the coldest lookers-on feel faint and subsequently bilious. Nor was it that the figs were moist and pulpy, or that the French plums blushed in modest tartness from their highly-decorated boxes, or that everything was good to eat and in its Christmas dress; but the customers were all so hurried and so eager in the hopeful promise of the day, that they tumbled up against each other at the door, crashing their wicker baskets wildly, and left their purchases upon the counter, and came running back to fetch them, and committed hundreds of the like mistakes, in the best humour possible; while the Grocer and his people were so frank and fresh that the polished hearts with which they fastened their aprons behind might have been their own, worn outside for general inspection, and for Christmas daws to peck at if they chose.

But soon the steeples called good people all, to church and chapel, and away they came, flocking through the streets in their best clothes, and with their gayest faces. And at the same time there emerged from scores of bye-streets, lanes, and nameless turnings, innumerable people, carrying their dinners to the bakers' shops. The sight of these poor revellers appeared to interest the Spirit very much, for he stood with Scrooge beside him in a baker's doorway, and taking off the covers as their bearers passed, sprinkled incense on their dinners from his torch. And it was a very uncommon kind of torch, for once or twice when there were angry words between some dinner-carriers who had jostled each other, he shed a few drops of water on them from it, and their good humour was restored directly. For they said, it was a shame to quarrel upon Christmas Day. And so it was! God love it, so it was!

In time the bells ceased, and the bakers were shut up; and yet there was a genial shadowing forth of all these dinners and the progress of their cooking, in the thawed blotch of wet above each baker's oven; where the pavement smoked as if its stones were cooking too.

'Is there a peculiar flavour in what you sprinkle from your torch?' asked Scrooge.

'There is. My own.'

'Would it apply to any kind of dinner on this day?' asked Scrooge.

'To any kindly given. To a poor one most.'

'Why to a poor one most?' asked Scrooge.

'Because it needs it most.'

'Spirit,' said Scrooge, after a moment's thought, 'I wonder you, of all the beings in the many worlds about us, should desire to cramp these people's opportunities of innocent enjoyment.'

'I!' cried the Spirit.

'You would deprive them of their means of dining every seventh day, often the only day on which they can be said to dine at all,' said Scrooge. 'Wouldn't you?'

'I!' cried the Spirit.

'You seek to close these places on the Seventh Day?' said Scrooge. 'And it comes to the same thing.'

'*I* seek!' exclaimed the Spirit.

'Forgive me if I am wrong. It has been done in your name, or at least in that of your family,' said Scrooge.

'There are some upon this earth of yours,' returned the Spirit, 'who lay claim to know us, and who do their deeds of passion, pride, ill-will, hatred, envy, bigotry, and selfishness in our name, who are as strange to us and all our kith and kin, as if they had never lived. Remember that, and charge their doings on themselves, not us.'

Scrooge promised that he would; and they went on, invisible, as they had been before, into the suburbs of the town. It was a remarkable quality of the Ghost (which Scrooge had observed at the baker's), that notwithstanding his gigantic size, he could accommodate himself to any place with ease; and that he stood beneath a low roof quite as gracefully and like a supernatural creature, as it was possible he could have done in any lofty hall.

And perhaps it was the pleasure the good Spirit had in showing off this power of his, or else it was his own kind, generous, hearty nature, and his sympathy with all poor men, that led him straight to Scrooge's clerk's; for there he went, and took Scrooge with him, holding to his robe; and on the threshold of the door the Spirit smiled, and stopped to bless Bob Cratchit's dwelling with the sprinkling of his torch. Think of that! Bob had but fifteen bob a-week himself; he pocketed on Saturdays but fifteen copies of his Christian name; and yet the Ghost of Christmas Present blessed his four-roomed house!

Then up rose Mrs. Cratchit, Cratchit's wife, dressed out but poorly in a twice-turned gown, but brave in ribbons, which are cheap and make a goodly show for sixpence; and she laid the cloth, assisted by Belinda Cratchit, second of her daughters, also brave in ribbons; while Master Peter Cratchit plunged a fork into the saucepan of potatoes, and getting the corners of his monstrous shirt collar (Bob's private property, conferred upon his son and heir in honour of the day) into his mouth, rejoiced to find himself so gallantly attired, and yearned to show his linen in the fashionable Parks. And now two smaller Cratchits, boy and girl, came tearing in, screaming that outside the baker's they had smelt the goose, and known it for their own; and basking in luxurious thoughts of sage and onion, these young Cratchits danced about the table, and exalted Master Peter Cratchit to the skies, while he (not proud, although his collars nearly choked him) blew the fire, until the slow potatoes bubbling up, knocked loudly at the saucepan-lid to be let out and peeled.

'What has ever got your precious father then,' said Mrs. Cratchit. 'And your brother, Tiny Tim! And Martha warn't as late last Christmas Day by half-an-hour!'

'Here's Martha, mother!' said a girl, appearing as she spoke.

'Here's Martha, mother!' cried the two young Cratchits. 'Hurrah! There's such a goose, Martha!'

'Why, bless your heart alive, my dear, how late you are!' said Mrs. Cratchit, kissing her a dozen times, and taking off her shawl and bonnet for her with officious zeal.

'We'd a deal of work to finish up last night,' replied the girl, 'and had to clear away this morning, mother!'

'Well. Never mind so long as you are come,' said Mrs. Cratchit. 'Sit ye down before the fire, my dear, and have a warm, Lord bless ye!'

'No, no! There's father coming,' cried the two young Cratchits, who were everywhere at once. 'Hide, Martha, hide!'

So Martha hid herself, and in came little Bob, the father, with at least three feet of comforter exclusive of the fringe, hanging down before him; and his threadbare clothes darned up and brushed, to look seasonable; and Tiny Tim upon his shoulder. Alas for Tiny Tim, he bore a little crutch, and had his limbs supported by an iron frame.

'Why, where's our Martha?' cried Bob Cratchit, looking round.

'Not coming,' said Mrs. Cratchit.

'Not coming!' said Bob, with a sudden declension in his high spirits; for he had been Tim's blood horse all the way from church, and had come home rampant. 'Not coming upon Christmas Day!'

Martha didn't like to see him disappointed, if it were only in joke; so she came out prematurely from behind the closet door, and ran into his arms, while the two young Cratchits hustled Tiny Tim, and bore him off into the wash-house, that he might hear the pudding singing in the copper.

'And how did little Tim behave?' asked Mrs. Cratchit, when she had rallied Bob on his credulity, and Bob had hugged his daughter to his heart's content.

'As good as gold,' said Bob, 'and better. Somehow he gets thoughtful, sitting by himself so much, and thinks the strangest things you ever heard. He told me, coming home, that he hoped the people saw him in the church, because he was a cripple, and it might be pleasant to them to remember upon Christmas Day, who made lame beggars walk, and blind men see.'

Bob's voice was tremulous when he told them this, and trembled more when he said that Tiny Tim was growing strong and hearty.

His active little crutch was heard upon the floor, and back came Tiny Tim before another word was spoken, escorted by his brother and sister to his stool before the fire; and while Bob, turning up his cuffs—as if, poor fellow, they were capable of being made more shabby—compounded some hot mixture in a jug with gin and lemons, and stirred it round and round and put it on the hob to simmer; Master Peter, and the two ubiquitous young Cratchits went to fetch the goose, with which they soon returned in high procession.

Such a bustle ensued that you might have thought a goose the rarest of all birds; a feathered phenomenon, to which a black swan was a matter of course—and in truth it was something very like it in that house. Mrs. Cratchit made the gravy (ready beforehand in a little saucepan) hissing hot; Master Peter mashed the potatoes with incredible vigour; Miss Belinda sweetened up the apple-sauce; Martha dusted the hot plates; Bob took Tiny Tim beside him in a tiny corner at the table; the two young Cratchits set chairs for everybody, not forgetting themselves, and mounting guard upon their posts, crammed spoons into their mouths, lest they should shriek for goose before their turn came to be helped. At last the dishes were set on, and grace was said. It was succeeded by a breathless pause, as Mrs. Cratchit, looking slowly all along the carving-knife, prepared to plunge it in the breast; but when she did, and when the long expected gush of stuffing issued forth, one murmur of delight arose all round the board, and even Tiny Tim, excited by the two young Cratchits, beat on the table with the handle of his knife, and feebly cried Hurrah!

There never was such a goose. Bob said he didn't believe there ever was such a goose cooked. Its tenderness and flavour, size and cheapness, were the themes of universal admiration. Eked out by apple-sauce and mashed potatoes, it was a sufficient dinner for the whole family; indeed, as Mrs. Cratchit said with great delight (surveying one small atom of a bone upon the dish), they hadn't ate it all at last. Yet every one had had enough, and the youngest Cratchits in particular, were steeped in sage and onion to the eyebrows. But now, the plates being changed by Miss Belinda, Mrs. Cratchit left the room alone—too nervous to bear witnesses—to take the pudding up and bring it in.

Suppose it should not be done enough! Suppose it should break in turning out! Suppose somebody should have got over the wall of the back-yard, and stolen it, while they were merry with the goose—a supposition at which the two young Cratchits became livid. All sorts of horrors were supposed.

Hallo! A great deal of steam! The pudding was out of the copper. A smell like a washing-day! That was the cloth. A smell like an eating-house and a pastrycook's next door to each other, with a laundress's next door to that! That was the pudding. In half a minute Mrs Cratchit entered—flushed, but smiling proudly—with the pudding, like a speck-led cannon-ball, so hard and firm, blazing in half of half-a-quartern of ignited brandy, and bedight with Christmas holly stuck into the top.

Oh, a wonderful pudding! Bob Cratchit said, and calmly too, that he regarded it as the greatest success achieved by Mrs. Cratchit since their marriage. Mrs. Cratchit said that now the weight was off her mind, she would confess she had had her doubts about the quantity of flour. Everybody had something to say about it, but nobody said or thought it was at all a small pudding for a large family. It would have been flat heresy to do so. Any Cratchit would have blushed to hint at such a thing.

At last the dinner was all done, the cloth was cleared, the hearth swept, and the fire made up. The compound in the jug being tasted, and considered perfect, apples and oranges were put upon the table, and a shovel-full of chestnuts on the fire. Then all the Cratchit family drew round the hearth, in what Bob Cratchit called a circle, meaning half a one; and at Bob Cratchit's elbow stood the family display of glass. Two tumblers, and a custard-cup without a handle.

These held the hot stuff from the jug, however, as well as golden goblets would have done; and Bob served it out with beaming looks, while the chestnuts on the fire sput-tered and cracked noisily. Then Bob proposed:

'A Merry Christmas to us all, my dears. God bless us!'

Which all the family re-echoed.

'God bless us every one!' said Tiny Tim, the last of all.

He sat very close to his father's side upon his little stool. Bob held his withered little hand in his, as if he loved the child, and wished to keep him by his side, and dreaded that he might be taken from him.

'Spirit,' said Scrooge, with an interest he had never felt before, 'tell me if Tiny Tim will live.'

'I see a vacant seat,' replied the Ghost, 'in the poor chimney-corner, and a crutch without an owner, carefully preserved. If these shadows remain unaltered by the Future, the child will die.'

'No, no,' said Scrooge. 'Oh, no, kind Spirit! say he will be spared.'

'If these shadows remain unaltered by the Future, none other of my race,' returned the Ghost, 'will find him here. What then? If he be like to die, he had better do it, and decrease the surplus population.'

Scrooge hung his head to hear his own words quoted by the Spirit, and was overcome with penitence and grief. 'Man,' said the Ghost, 'if man you be in heart, not adamant, forbear that wicked cant until you have discovered What the surplus is, and Where it is. Will you decide what men shall live, what men shall die? It may be, that in the sight of Heaven, you are more worthless and less fit to live than millions like this poor man's child. Oh God! to hear the Insect on the leaf pronouncing on the too much life among his hungry brothers in the dust!'

Scrooge bent before the Ghost's rebuke, and trembling cast his eyes upon the ground. But he raised them speedily, on hearing his own name.

'Mr. Scrooge!' said Bob; 'I'll give you Mr. Scrooge, the Founder of the Feast!'

'The Founder of the Feast indeed!' cried Mrs. Cratchit, reddening. 'I wish I had him here. I'd give him a piece of my mind to feast upon, and I hope he'd have a good appetite for it.'

'My dear,' said Bob, 'the children. Christmas Day.'

'It should be Christmas Day, I am sure,' said she, 'on which one drinks the health of such an odious, stingy, hard, unfeeling man as Mr. Scrooge. You know he is, Robert! Nobody knows it better than you do, poor fellow.'

'My dear,' was Bob's mild answer, 'Christmas Day.'

'I'll drink his health for your sake and the Day's,' said Mrs. Cratchit, 'not for his. Long life to him! A merry Christmas and a happy new year! He'll be very merry and very happy, I have no doubt!'

The children drank the toast after her. It was the first of their proceedings which had no heartiness. Tiny Tim drank it last of all, but he didn't care twopence for it. Scrooge was the Ogre of the family. The mention of his name cast a dark shadow on the party, which was not dispelled for full five minutes.

After it had passed away, they were ten times merrier than before, from the mere relief of Scrooge the Baleful being done with. Bob Cratchit told them how he had a situation in his eye for Master Peter, which would bring in, if obtained, full five-and-sixpence weekly. The two young Cratchits laughed tremendously at the idea of Peter's being a man of business; and Peter himself looked thoughtfully at the fire from between his collars, as if he were deliberating what particular investments he should favour when he came into the receipt of that bewildering income. Martha, who was a poor apprentice at a milliner's, then told them what kind of work she had to do, and how many hours she worked at a stretch, and how she meant to lie abed tomorrow morning for a good long rest; to-morrow being a holiday she passed at home. Also how she had seen a countess and a lord some days before, and how the lord was much about as tall as Peter; at which Peter pulled up his collars so high that you couldn't have seen his head if you had been there. All this time the chestnuts and the jug went round and round; and by-and-bye they had a song, about a lost child travelling in the snow, from Tiny Tim, who had a plaintive little voice, and sang it very well indeed.

There was nothing of high mark in this. They were not a handsome family; they were not well dressed; their shoes were far from being waterproof; their clothes were scanty; and Peter might have known, and very likely did, the inside of a pawnbroker's. But, they were happy, grateful, pleased with one another, and contented with the time; and when they faded, and looked happier yet in the bright sprinklings of the Spirit's torch at parting, Scrooge had his eye upon them, and especially on Tiny Tim, until the last.

By this time it was getting dark, and snowing pretty heavily; and as Scrooge and the Spirit went along the streets, the brightness of the roaring fires in kitchens, parlours, and all sorts of rooms, was wonderful. Here, the flickering of the blaze showed preparations for a cosy dinner, with hot plates baking through and through before the fire, and deep red curtains, ready to be drawn to shut out cold and darkness. There all the children of the house were running out into the snow to meet their married sisters, brothers, cousins, uncles, aunts, and be the first to greet them. Here, again, were shadows on the window-blind of guests assembling; and there a group of handsome girls, all hooded and fur-booted, and all chattering at once, tripped lightly off to some near neighbour's house; where, woe upon the single man who saw them enter—artful witches, well they knew it—in a glow!

But, if you had judged from the numbers of people on their way to friendly gatherings, you might have thought that no one was at home to give them welcome when they got there, instead of every house expecting company, and piling up its fires half-chimney high. Blessings on it, how the Ghost exulted! How it bared its breadth of breast, and opened its capacious palm, and floated on, outpouring, with a generous hand, its bright and harmless mirth on everything within its reach! The very lamplighter, who ran on before, dotting the dusky street with specks of light, and who was dressed to spend the evening somewhere, laughed out loudly as the Spirit passed, though little kenned the lamplighter that he had any company but Christmas!

And now, without a word of warning from the Ghost, they stood upon a bleak and desert moor, where monstrous masses of rude stone were cast about, as though it were the burial-place of giants; and water spread itself wheresoever it listed, or would have done so, but for the frost that held it prisoner; and nothing grew but moss and furze, and coarse rank grass. Down in the west the setting sun had left a streak of fiery red, which glared upon the desolation for an instant, like a sullen eye, and frowning lower, lower, lower yet, was lost in the thick gloom of darkest night.

'What place is this?' asked Scrooge.

'A place where Miners live, who labour in the bowels of the earth,' returned the Spirit. 'But they know me. See!'

A light shone from the window of a hut, and swiftly they advanced towards it. Passing through the wall of mud and stone, they found a cheerful company assembled round a glowing fire. An old, old man and woman, with their children and their children's children, and another generation beyond that, all decked out gaily in their holiday attire. The old man, in a voice that seldom rose above the howling of the wind upon the barren waste, was singing them a Christmas song—it had been a very old song when he was a boy—and from time to time they all joined in the chorus. So surely as they raised their voices, the old man got quite blithe and loud; and so surely as they stopped, his vigour sank again.

The Spirit did not tarry here, but bade Scrooge hold his robe, and passing on above the moor, sped—whither? Not to sea? To sea. To Scrooge's horror, looking back, he saw the last of the land, a frightful range of rocks, behind them; and his ears were deafened by the thundering of water, as it rolled and roared, and raged among the dreadful caverns it had worn, and fiercely tried to undermine the earth.

Built upon a dismal reef of sunken rocks, some league or so from shore, on which the waters chafed and dashed, the wild year through, there stood a solitary lighthouse. Great heaps of sea-weed clung to its base, and storm-birds— born of the wind one might suppose, as seaweed of the water—rose and fell about it, like the waves they skimmed.

But even here, two men who watched the light had made a fire, that through the loop-hole in the thick stone wall shed out a ray of brightness on the awful sea. Joining their horny hands over the rough table at which they sat, they wished each other Merry Christmas in their can of grog; and one of them: the elder, too, with his face all damaged and scarred with hard weather, as the figure-head of an old ship might be: struck up a sturdy song that was like a Gale in itself.

Again the Ghost sped on, above the black and heaving sea—on, on—until, being far away, as he told Scrooge, from any shore, they lighted on a ship. They stood beside the helmsman at the wheel, the look-out in the bow, the officers who had the watch; dark, ghostly figures in their several stations; but every man among them hummed a Christmas tune, or had a Christmas thought, or spoke below his breath to his companion of some bygone Christmas Day, with homeward hopes belonging to it. And every man on board, waking or sleeping, good or bad, had had a kinder word for another on that day than on any day in the year; and had shared to some extent in its festivities; and had remembered those he cared for at a distance, and had known that they delighted to remember him.

It was a great surprise to Scrooge, while listening to the moaning of the wind, and thinking what a solemn thing it was to move on through the lonely darkness over an unknown abyss, whose depths were secrets as profound as Death: it was a great surprise to Scrooge, while thus engaged, to hear a hearty laugh. It was a much greater surprise to Scrooge to recognise it as his own nephew's and to find himself in a bright, dry, gleaming room, with the Spirit standing smiling by his side, and looking at that same nephew with approving affability!

'Ha, ha!' laughed Scrooge's nephew. 'Ha, ha, ha!'

If you should happen, by any unlikely chance, to know a man more blest in a laugh than Scrooge's nephew, all I can say is, I should like to know him too. Introduce him to me, and I'll cultivate his acquaintance.

It is a fair, even-handed, noble adjustment of things, that while there is infection in disease and sorrow, there is nothing in the world so irresistibly contagious as laughter and good-humour. When Scrooge's nephew laughed in this way: holding his sides, rolling his head, and twisting his face into the most extravagant contortions: Scrooge's niece, by marriage, laughed as heartily as he. And their assembled friends being not a bit behindhand, roared out lustily.

'Ha, ha! Ha, ha, ha, ha!'

'He said that Christmas was a humbug, as I live!' cried Scrooge's nephew. 'He believed it too!'

'More shame for him, Fred!' said Scrooge's niece, indignantly. Bless those women; they never do anything by halves. They are always in earnest.

She was very pretty: exceedingly pretty. With a dimpled, surprised-looking, capital face; a ripe little mouth, that seemed made to be kissed—as no doubt it was; all kinds of good little dots about her chin, that melted into one another when she laughed; and the sunniest pair of eyes you ever saw in any little creature's head. Altogether she was what you would have called provoking, you know; but satisfactory.

'He's a comical old fellow,' said Scrooge's nephew, 'that's the truth: and not so pleasant as he might be. However, his offences carry their own punishment, and I have nothing to say against him.'

'I'm sure he is very rich, Fred,' hinted Scrooge's niece. 'At least you always tell me so.'

'What of that, my dear!' said Scrooge's nephew. 'His wealth is of no use to him. He don't do any good with it. He don't make himself comfortable with it. He hasn't the satisfaction of thinking—ha, ha, ha!—that he is ever going to benefit us with it.'

'I have no patience with him,' observed Scrooge's niece. Scrooge's niece's sisters, and all the other ladies, expressed the same opinion.

'Oh, I have!' said Scrooge's nephew. 'I am sorry for him; I couldn't be angry with him if I tried. Who suffers by his ill whims? Himself, always. Here, he takes it into his head to dislike us, and he won't come and dine with us. What's the consequence? He don't lose much of a dinner.'

'Indeed, I think he loses a very good dinner,' interrupted Scrooge's niece. Everybody else said the same, and they must be allowed to have been competent judges, because they had just had dinner; and, with the dessert upon the table, were clustered round the fire, by lamplight.

'Well. I'm very glad to hear it,' said Scrooge's nephew, 'because I haven't great faith in these young housekeepers. What do you say, Topper?'

Topper had clearly got his eye upon one of Scrooge's niece's sisters, for he answered that a bachelor was a wretched outcast, who had no right to express an opinion on the subject. Whereat Scrooge's niece's sister—the plump one with the lace tucker: not the one with the roses—blushed.

'Do go on, Fred,' said Scrooge's niece, clapping her hands. 'He never finishes what he begins to say! He is such a ridiculous fellow!'

Scrooge's nephew revelled in another laugh, and as it was impossible to keep the infection off; though the plump sister tried hard to do it with aromatic vinegar; his example was unanimously followed.

'I was only going to say,' said Scrooge's nephew, 'that the consequence of his taking a dislike to us, and not making merry with us, is, as I think, that he loses some pleasant moments, which could do him no harm. I am sure he loses pleasanter companions than he can find in his own thoughts, either in his mouldy old office, or his dusty chambers. I mean to give him the same chance every year, whether he likes it or not, for I pity him. He may rail at Christmas till he dies, but he can't help thinking better of it—I defy him—if he finds me going there, in good temper, year after year, and saying Uncle

Scrooge, how are you? If it only puts him in the vein to leave his poor clerk fifty pounds, that's something; and I think I shook him yesterday.'

It was their turn to laugh now at the notion of his shaking Scrooge. But being thoroughly good-natured, and not much caring what they laughed at, so that they laughed at any rate, he encouraged them in their merriment, and passed the bottle joyously.

After tea, they had some music. For they were a musical family, and knew what they were about, when they sung a Glee or Catch, I can assure you: especially Topper, who could growl away in the bass like a good one, and never swell the large veins in his forehead, or get red in the face over it. Scrooge's niece played well upon the harp; and played among other tunes a simple little air (a mere nothing: you might learn to whistle it in two minutes), which had been familiar to the child who fetched Scrooge from the boarding-school, as he had been reminded by the Ghost of Christmas Past. When this strain of music sounded, all the things that Ghost had shown him, came upon his mind; he softened more and more; and thought that if he could have listened to it often, years ago, he might have cultivated the kindnesses of life for his own happiness with his own hands, without resorting to the sexton's spade that buried Jacob Marley.

But they didn't devote the whole evening to music. After a while they played at forfeits; for it is good to be children sometimes, and never better than at Christmas, when its mighty Founder was a child himself. Stop! There was first a game at blind-man's buff. Of course there was. And I no more believe Topper was really blind than I believe he had eyes in his boots. My opinion is, that it was a done thing between him and Scrooge's nephew; and that the Ghost of Christmas Present knew it. The way he went after that plump sister in the lace tucker, was an outrage on the credulity of human nature. Knocking down the fire-irons, tumbling over the chairs, bumping against the piano, smothering himself among the curtains, wherever she went, there went he. He always knew where the plump sister was. He wouldn't catch anybody else. If you had fallen up against him (as some of them did), on purpose, he would have made a feint of endeavouring to seize you, which would have been an affront to your understanding, and would instantly have sidled off in the direction of the plump sister. She often cried out that it wasn't fair; and it really was not. But when at last, he caught her; when, in spite of all her silken rustlings, and her rapid flutterings past him, he got her into a corner whence there was no escape; then his conduct was the most execrable. For his pretending not to know her; his pretending that it was necessary to touch her head-dress, and further to assure himself of her identity by pressing a certain ring upon her finger, and a certain chain about her neck; was vile, monstrous! No doubt she told him her opinion of it, when, another blind-man being in office, they were so very confidential together, behind the curtains.

Scrooge's niece was not one of the blind-man's buff party, but was made comfortable with a large chair and a footstool, in a snug corner, where the Ghost and Scrooge were close behind her. But she joined in the forfeits, and loved her love to admiration with all the letters of the alphabet. Likewise at the game of How, When, and Where, she was very great, and to the secret joy of Scrooge's nephew, beat her sisters hollow: though they were sharp girls too, as Topper could have told you. There might have been twenty people there, young and old, but they all played, and so did Scrooge, for, wholly forgetting the interest he had in what was going on, that his voice made no sound in their ears, he sometimes came out with his guess quite loud, and very often guessed quite right, too; for the sharpest needle, best Whitechapel, warranted not to cut in the eye, was not sharper than Scrooge; blunt as he took it in his head to be.

The Ghost was greatly pleased to find him in this mood, and looked upon him with such favour, that he begged like a boy to be allowed to stay until the guests departed. But this the Spirit said could not be done.

'Here is a new game,' said Scrooge. 'One half hour, Spirit, only one!'

It was a Game called Yes and No, where Scrooge's nephew had to think of something, and the rest must find out what; he only answering to their questions yes or no, as the case was. The brisk fire of questioning to which he was exposed, elicited from him that he was thinking of an animal, a live animal, rather a disagreeable animal, a savage animal, an animal that growled and grunted sometimes, and talked sometimes, and lived in London, and walked about the streets, and wasn't made a show of, and wasn't led by anybody, and didn't live in a menagerie, and was never killed in a market, and was not a horse, or an ass, or a cow, or a bull, or a tiger, or a dog, or a pig, or a cat, or a bear. At every fresh question that was put to him, this nephew burst into a fresh roar of laughter; and was so inexpressibly tickled, that he was obliged to get up off the sofa and stamp. At last the plump sister, falling into a similar state, cried out:

'I have found it out! I know what it is, Fred! I know what it is!'

'What is it?' cried Fred.

'It's your Uncle Scrooge!'

Which it certainly was. Admiration was the universal sentiment, though some objected that the reply to 'Is it a bear?' ought to have been 'Yes;' inasmuch as an answer in the negative was sufficient to have diverted their thoughts from Mr. Scrooge, supposing they had ever had any tendency that way.

'He has given us plenty of merriment, I am sure,' said Fred, 'and it would be ungrateful not to drink his health. Here is a glass of mulled wine ready to our hand at the moment; and I say, "Uncle Scrooge!"'

'Well! Uncle Scrooge!' they cried.

'A Merry Christmas and a Happy New Year to the old man, whatever he is!' said Scrooge's nephew. 'He wouldn't take it from me, but may he have it, nevertheless. Uncle Scrooge!'

Uncle Scrooge had imperceptibly become so gay and light of heart, that he would have pledged the unconscious company in return, and thanked them in an inaudible speech, if the Ghost had given him time. But the whole scene passed off in the breath of the last word spoken by his nephew; and he and the Spirit were again upon their travels.

Much they saw, and far they went, and many homes they visited, but always with a happy end. The Spirit stood beside sick beds, and they were cheerful; on foreign lands, and they were close at home; by struggling men, and they were patient in their greater hope; by poverty, and it was rich. In almshouse, hospital, and jail, in misery's every refuge, where vain man in his little brief authority had not made fast the door and barred the Spirit out, he left his blessing, and taught Scrooge his precepts.

It was a long night, if it were only a night; but Scrooge had his doubts of this, because the Christmas Holidays appeared to be condensed into the space of time they passed together. It was strange, too, that while Scrooge remained unaltered in his outward form, the Ghost grew older, clearly older. Scrooge had observed this change, but never spoke of it, until they left a children's Twelfth Night party, when, looking at the Spirit as they stood together in an open place, he noticed that its hair was grey.

'Are spirits' lives so short?' asked Scrooge.

'My life upon this globe, is very brief,' replied the Ghost. 'It ends to-night.'

'To-night!' cried Scrooge.

'To-night at midnight. Hark! The time is drawing near.'

The chimes were ringing the three quarters past eleven at that moment.

'Forgive me if I am not justified in what I ask,' said Scrooge, looking intently at the Spirit's robe, 'but I see something strange, and not belonging to yourself, protruding from your skirts. Is it a foot or a claw?'

'It might be a claw, for the flesh there is upon it,' was the Spirit's sorrowful reply. 'Look here.'

From the foldings of its robe, it brought two children; wretched, abject, frightful, hideous, miserable. They knelt down at its feet, and clung upon the outside of its garment.

'Oh, Man! look here. Look, look, down here!' exclaimed the Ghost.

They were a boy and a girl. Yellow, meagre, ragged, scowling, wolfish; but prostrate, too, in their humility. Where graceful youth should have filled their features out, and touched them with its freshest tints, a stale and shrivelled hand, like that of age, had pinched, and twisted them, and pulled them into shreds. Where angels might have sat enthroned, devils lurked, and glared out menacing. No change, no degradation, no perversion of humanity, in any grade, through all the mysteries of wonderful creation, has monsters half so horrible and dread.

Scrooge started back, appalled. Having them shown to him in this way, he tried to say they were fine children, but the words choked themselves, rather than be parties to a lie of such enormous magnitude.

'Spirit! are they yours?' Scrooge could say no more.

'They are Man's,' said the Spirit, looking down upon them. 'And they cling to me, appealing from their fathers. This boy is Ignorance. This girl is Want. Beware them both, and all of their degree, but most of all beware this boy, for on his brow I see that written which is Doom, unless the writing be erased. Deny it!' cried the Spirit, stretching out its hand towards the city. 'Slander those who tell it ye! Admit it for your factious purposes, and make it worse! And abide the end!'

'Have they no refuge or resource?' cried Scrooge.

'Are there no prisons?' said the Spirit, turning on him for the last time with his own words. 'Are there no workhouses?' The bell struck twelve.

Scrooge looked about him for the Ghost, and saw it not. As the last stroke ceased to vibrate, he remembered the prediction of old Jacob Marley, and lifting up his eyes, beheld a solemn Phantom, draped and hooded, coming, like a mist along the ground, towards him.

Stave 4: The Last of the Spirits

The Phantom slowly, gravely, silently approached. When it came, Scrooge bent down upon his knee; for in the very air through which this Spirit moved it seemed to scatter gloom and mystery.

It was shrouded in a deep black garment, which concealed its head, its face, its form, and left nothing of it visible save one outstretched hand. But for this it would have been difficult to detach its figure from the night, and separate it from the darkness by which it was surrounded.

He felt that it was tall and stately when it came beside him, and that its mysterious presence filled him with a solemn dread. He knew no more, for the Spirit neither spoke nor moved.

'I am in the presence of the Ghost of Christmas Yet To Come?' said Scrooge.

The Spirit answered not, but pointed onward with its hand.

'You are about to show me shadows of the things that have not happened, but will happen in the time before us,' Scrooge pursued. 'Is that so, Spirit?'

The upper portion of the garment was contracted for an instant in its folds, as if the Spirit had inclined its head. That was the only answer he received.

Although well used to ghostly company by this time, Scrooge feared the silent shape so much that his legs trembled beneath him, and he found that he could hardly stand when he prepared to follow it. The Spirit pauses a moment, as observing his condition, and giving him time to recover.

But Scrooge was all the worse for this. It thrilled him with a vague uncertain horror, to know that behind the dusky shroud, there were ghostly eyes intently fixed upon him, while he, though he stretched his own to the utmost, could see nothing but a spectral hand and one great heap of black.

'Ghost of the Future!' he exclaimed, 'I fear you more than any spectre I have seen. But as I know your purpose is to do me good, and as I hope to live to be another man from what I was, I am prepared to bear you company, and do it with a thankful heart. Will you not speak to me?'

It gave him no reply. The hand was pointed straight before them.

'Lead on!' said Scrooge. 'Lead on! The night is waning fast, and it is precious time to me, I know. Lead on, Spirit!'

The Phantom moved away as it had come towards him. Scrooge followed in the shadow of its dress, which bore him up, he thought, and carried him along.

They scarcely seemed to enter the city; for the city rather seemed to spring up about them, and encompass them of its own act. But there they were, in the heart of it; on Change, amongst the merchants; who hurried up and down, and chinked the money in their pockets, and conversed in groups, and looked at their watches, and trifled thoughtfully with their great gold seals; and so forth, as Scrooge had seen them often.

The Spirit stopped beside one little knot of business men. Observing that the hand was pointed to them, Scrooge advanced to listen to their talk.

'No,' said a great fat man with a monstrous chin, 'I don't know much about it, either way. I only know he's dead.'

'When did he die?' inquired another.

'Last night, I believe.'

'Why, what was the matter with him?' asked a third, taking a vast quantity of snuff out of a very large snuff-box. 'I thought he'd never die.'

'God knows,' said the first, with a yawn.

'What has he done with his money?' asked a red-faced gentleman with a pendulous excrescence on the end of his nose, that shook like the gills of a turkey-cock.

'I haven't heard,' said the man with the large chin, yawning again. 'Left it to his company, perhaps. He hasn't left it to me. That's all I know.'

This pleasantry was received with a general laugh.

'It's likely to be a very cheap funeral,' said the same speaker; 'for upon my life I don't know of anybody to go to it. Suppose we make up a party and volunteer?'

'I don't mind going if a lunch is provided,' observed the gentleman with the excrescence on his nose. 'But I must be fed, if I make one.'

Another laugh.

'Well, I am the most disinterested among you, after all,' said the first speaker, 'for I never wear black gloves, and I never eat lunch. But I'll offer to go, if anybody else will. When I come to think of it, I'm not at all sure that I wasn't his most particular friend; for we used to stop and speak whenever we met. Bye, bye!'

Speakers and listeners strolled away, and mixed with other groups. Scrooge knew the men, and looked towards the Spirit for an explanation.

The Phantom glided on into a street. Its finger pointed to two persons meeting. Scrooge listened again, thinking that the explanation might lie here.

He knew these men, also, perfectly. They were men of business: very wealthy, and of great importance. He had made a point always of standing well in their esteem: in a business point of view, that is; strictly in a business point of view.

'How are you?' said one.

'How are you?' returned the other.

'Well!' said the first. 'Old Scratch has got his own at last, hey?'

'So I am told,' returned the second. 'Cold, isn't it?'

'Seasonable for Christmas time. You're not a skater, I suppose?'

'No. No. Something else to think of. Good morning!'

Not another word. That was their meeting, their conversation, and their parting.

Scrooge was at first inclined to be surprised that the Spirit should attach importance to conversations apparently so trivial; but feeling assured that they must have some hidden purpose, he set himself to consider what it was likely to be. They could scarcely be supposed to have any bearing on the death of Jacob, his old partner, for that was Past, and this Ghost's province was the Future. Nor could he think of any one immediately connected with himself, to whom he could apply them. But nothing doubting that to whomsoever they applied they had some latent moral for his own improvement, he resolved to treasure up every word he heard, and everything he saw; and especially to observe the shadow of himself when it appeared. For he had an expectation that the conduct of his future self would give him the clue he missed, and would render the solution of these riddles easy.

He looked about in that very place for his own image; but another man stood in his accustomed corner, and though the clock pointed to his usual time of day for being there, he saw no likeness of himself among the multitudes that poured in through the Porch. It gave him little surprise, however; for he had been revolving in his mind a change of life, and thought and hoped he saw his new-born resolutions carried out in this.

Quiet and dark, beside him stood the Phantom, with its outstretched hand. When he roused himself from his thoughtful quest, he fancied from the turn of the hand, and its situation in reference to himself, that the Unseen Eyes were looking at him keenly. It made him shudder, and feel very cold.

They left the busy scene, and went into an obscure part of the town, where Scrooge had never penetrated before, although he recognised its situation, and its bad repute. The ways were foul and narrow; the shops and houses wretched; the people half-naked, drunken, slipshod, ugly. Alleys and archways, like so many cesspools, disgorged their offences of smell, and dirt, and life, upon the straggling streets; and the whole quarter reeked with crime, with filth, and misery.

Far in this den of infamous resort, there was a low-browed, beetling shop, below a penthouse roof, where iron, old rags, bottles, bones, and greasy offal, were bought. Upon the floor within, were piled up heaps of rusty keys, nails, chains, hinges, files, scales, weights, and refuse iron of all kinds. Secrets that few would like to scrutinise were bred and hidden in mountains of unseemly rags, masses of corrupted fat, and sepulchres of bones. Sitting in among the wares he dealt in, by a charcoal stove, made of old bricks, was a grey-haired rascal, nearly seventy years of age; who had screened himself from the cold air without, by a frousy curtaining of miscellaneous tatters, hung upon a line; and smoked his pipe in all the luxury of calm retirement.

Scrooge and the Phantom came into the presence of this man, just as a woman with a heavy bundle slunk into the shop. But she had scarcely entered, when another woman, similarly laden, came in too; and she was closely followed by a man in faded black, who was no less startled by the sight of them, than they had been upon the recognition of each other. After a short period of blank astonishment, in which the old man with the pipe had joined them, they all three burst into a laugh.

'Let the charwoman alone to be the first!' cried she who had entered first. 'Let the laundress alone to be the second; and let the undertaker's man alone to be the third. Look here, old Joe, here's a chance. If we haven't all three met here without meaning it!'

'You couldn't have met in a better place,' said old Joe, removing his pipe from his mouth. 'Come into the parlour. You were made free of it long ago, you know; and the other two an't strangers. Stop till I shut the door of the shop. Ah! How it skreeks! There an't such a rusty bit of metal in the place as its own hinges, I believe; and I'm sure there's no such old bones here, as mine. Ha, ha! We're all suitable to our calling, we're well matched. Come into the parlour. Come into the parlour.'

The parlour was the space behind the screen of rags. The old man raked the fire together with an old stair-rod, and having trimmed his smoky lamp (for it was night), with the stem of his pipe, put it in his mouth again.

While he did this, the woman who had already spoken threw her bundle on the floor, and sat down in a flaunting manner on a stool; crossing her elbows on her knees, and looking with a bold defiance at the other two.

'What odds then! What odds, Mrs. Dilber?' said the woman. 'Every person has a right to take care of themselves. *He* always did!'

'That's true, indeed!' said the laundress. 'No man more so.'

'Why then, don't stand staring as if you was afraid, woman; who's the wiser? We're not going to pick holes in each other's coats, I suppose.'

'No, indeed!' said Mrs. Dilber and the man together. 'We should hope not.'

'Very well, then!' cried the woman. 'That's enough. Who's the worse for the loss of a few things like these? Not a dead man, I suppose.'

'No, indeed!' said Mrs. Dilber, laughing.

'If he wanted to keep them after he was dead, a wicked old screw,' pursued the woman, 'why wasn't he natural in his lifetime? If he had been, he'd have had somebody to look after him when he was struck with Death, instead of lying gasping out his last there, alone by himself.'

'It's the truest word that ever was spoke,' said Mrs. Dilber. 'It's a judgment on him.'

'I wish it was a little heavier judgment,' replied the woman; 'and it should have been, you may depend upon it, if I could have laid my hands on anything else. Open that bundle, old Joe, and let me know the value of it. Speak out plain. I'm not afraid to be the first, nor afraid for them to see it. We know pretty well that we were helping ourselves, before we met here, I believe. It's no sin. Open the bundle, Joe.'

But the gallantry of her friends would not allow of this; and the man in faded black, mounting the breach first, produced his plunder. It was not extensive. A seal or two, a pencil-case, a pair of sleeve-buttons, and a brooch of no great value, were all. They were severally examined and appraised by old Joe, who chalked the sums he was disposed to give for each, upon the wall, and added them up into a total when he found there was nothing more to come.

'That's your account,' said Joe,' and I wouldn't give another sixpence, if I was to be boiled for not doing it. Who's next?'

Mrs. Dilber was next. Sheets and towels, a little wearing apparel, two old-fashioned silver teaspoons, a pair of sugar-tongs, and a few boots. Her account was stated on the wall in the same manner.

'I always give too much to ladies. It's a weakness of mine, and that's the way I ruin myself,' said old Joe. 'That's your account. If you asked me for another penny, and made it an open question, I'd repent of being so liberal and knock off half-a-crown.'

'And now undo my bundle, Joe,' said the first woman.

Joe went down on his knees for the greater convenience of opening it, and having unfastened a great many knots, dragged out a large and heavy roll of some dark stuff.

'What do you call this?' said Joe. 'Bed-curtains!'

'Ah!' returned the woman, laughing and leaning forward on her crossed arms. 'Bed-curtains!'

'You don't mean to say you took them down, rings and all, with him lying there?' said Joe.

'Yes I do,' replied the woman. 'Why not?'

'You were born to make your fortune,' said Joe, 'and you'll certainly do it.'

'I certainly shan't hold my hand, when I can get anything in it by reaching it out, for the sake of such a man as he was, I promise you, Joe,' returned the woman coolly. 'Don't drop that oil upon the blankets, now.'

'His blankets?' asked Joe.

'Whose else's do you think?' replied the woman. 'He isn't likely to take cold without them, I dare say.'

'I hope he didn't die of any thing catching? Eh?' said old Joe, stopping in his work, and looking up.

'Don't you be afraid of that,' returned the woman. 'I an't so fond of his company that I'd loiter about him for such things, if he did. Ah! you may look through that shirt till your eyes ache; but you won't find a hole in it, nor a threadbare place. It's the best he had, and a fine one too. They'd have wasted it, if it hadn't been for me.'

'What do you call wasting of it?' asked old Joe.

'Putting it on him to be buried in, to be sure,' replied the woman with a laugh. 'Somebody was fool enough to do it, but I took it off again. If calico an't good enough for such a purpose, it isn't good enough for anything. It's quite as becoming to the body. He can't look uglier than he did in that one.'

Scrooge listened to this dialogue in horror. As they sat grouped about their spoil, in the scanty light afforded by the old man's lamp, he viewed them with a detestation and disgust, which could hardly have been greater, though they had been obscene demons, marketing the corpse itself.

'Ha, ha!' laughed the same woman, when old Joe, producing a flannel bag with money in it, told out their several gains upon the ground. 'This is the end of it, you see! He frightened every one away from him when he was alive, to profit us when he was dead! Ha, ha, ha!'

'Spirit!' said Scrooge, shuddering from head to foot. 'I see, I see. The case of this unhappy man might be my own. My life tends that way, now. Merciful Heaven, what is this!'

He recoiled in terror, for the scene had changed, and now he almost touched a bed: a bare, uncurtained bed: on which, beneath a ragged sheet, there lay a something covered up, which, though it was dumb, announced itself in awful language.

The room was very dark, too dark to be observed with any accuracy, though Scrooge glanced round it in obedience to a secret impulse, anxious to know what kind of room it was. A pale light, rising in the outer air, fell straight upon the bed; and on it, plundered and bereft, unwatched, unwept, uncared for, was the body of this man.

Scrooge glanced towards the Phantom. Its steady hand was pointed to the head. The cover was so carelessly adjusted that the slightest raising of it, the motion of a finger upon Scrooge's part, would have disclosed the face. He thought of it, felt how easy it would be to do, and longed to do it; but had no more power to withdraw the veil than to dismiss the spectre at his side.

Oh cold, cold, rigid, dreadful Death, set up thine altar here, and dress it with such terrors as thou hast at thy command: for this is thy dominion! But of the loved, revered, and honoured head, thou canst not turn one hair to thy dread purposes, or make one feature odious. It is not that the hand is heavy and will fall down when released; it is not that the heart and pulse are still; but that the hand was open, generous, and true; the heart brave, warm, and tender; and the pulse a man's. Strike, Shadow, strike! And see his good deeds springing from the wound, to sow the world with life immortal!

No voice pronounced these words in Scrooge's ears, and yet he heard them when he looked upon the bed. He thought, if this man could be raised up now, what would be his foremost thoughts? Avarice, hard-dealing, griping cares? They have brought him to a rich end, truly!

He lay, in the dark empty house, with not a man, a woman, or a child, to say that he was kind to me in this or that, and for the memory of one kind word I will be kind to him. A cat was tearing at the door, and there was a sound of gnawing rats beneath the hearth-stone. What they wanted in the room of death, and why they were so restless and disturbed, Scrooge did not dare to think.

'Spirit!' he said, 'this is a fearful place. In leaving it, I shall not leave its lesson, trust me. Let us go!'

Still the Ghost pointed with an unmoved finger to the head.

'I understand you,' Scrooge returned, 'and I would do it, if I could. But I have not the power, Spirit. I have not the power.'

Again it seemed to look upon him.

'If there is any person in the town, who feels emotion caused by this man's death,' said Scrooge quite agonised, 'show that person to me, Spirit, I beseech you!'

The Phantom spread its dark robe before him for a moment, like a wing; and withdrawing it, revealed a room by daylight, where a mother and her children were.

She was expecting some one, and with anxious eagerness; for she walked up and down the room; started at every sound; looked out from the window; glanced at the clock; tried, but in vain, to work with her needle; and could hardly bear the voices of the children in their play.

At length the long-expected knock was heard. She hurried to the door, and met her husband; a man whose face was careworn and depressed, though he was young. There was a remarkable expression in it now; a kind of serious delight of which he felt ashamed, and which he struggled to repress.

He sat down to the dinner that had been boarding for him by the fire; and when she asked him faintly what news (which was not until after a long silence), he appeared embarrassed how to answer.

'Is it good.' she said, 'or bad?'—to help him.

'Bad,' he answered.

'We are quite ruined?'

'No. There is hope yet, Caroline.'

'If he relents,' she said, amazed, 'there is! Nothing is past hope, if such a miracle has happened.'

'He is past relenting,' said her husband. 'He is dead.'

She was a mild and patient creature if her face spoke truth; but she was thankful in her soul to hear it, and she said so, with clasped hands. She prayed forgiveness the next moment, and was sorry; but the first was the emotion of her heart.

'What the half-drunken woman whom I told you of last night, said to me, when I tried to see him and obtain a week's delay; and what I thought was a mere excuse to avoid me; turns out to have been quite true. He was not only very ill, but dying, then.'

'To whom will our debt be transferred?'

'I don't know. But before that time we shall be ready with the money; and even though we were not, it would be a bad fortune indeed to find so merciless a creditor in his successor. We may sleep to-night with light hearts, Caroline!'

Yes. Soften it as they would, their hearts were lighter. The children's faces, hushed and clustered round to hear what they so little understood, were brighter; and it was a happier house for this man's death. The only emotion that the Ghost could show him, caused by the event, was one of pleasure.

'Let me see some tenderness connected with a death,' said Scrooge; 'or that dark chamber, Spirit, which we left just now, will be for ever present to me.'

The Ghost conducted him through several streets familiar to his feet; and as they went along, Scrooge looked here and there to find himself, but nowhere was he to be seen. They entered poor Bob Cratchit's house; the dwelling he had visited before; and found the mother and the children seated round the fire.

Quiet. Very quiet. The noisy little Cratchits were as still as statues in one corner, and sat looking up at Peter, who had a book before him. The mother and her daughters were engaged in sewing. But surely they were very quiet.

'And he took a child, and set him in the midst of them.'

Where had Scrooge heard those words? He had not dreamed them. The boy must have read them out, as he and the Spirit crossed the threshold. Why did he not go on?

The mother laid her work upon the table, and put her hand up to her face.

'The colour hurts my eyes,' she said.

The colour? Ah, poor Tiny Tim!

'They're better now again,' said Cratchit's wife. 'It makes them weak by candle-light; and I wouldn't show weak eyes to your father when he comes home, for the world. It must be near his time.'

'Past it rather,' Peter answered, shutting up his book. 'But I think he has walked a little slower than he used, these few last evenings, mother.'

They were very quiet again. At last she said, and in a steady, cheerful voice, that only faltered once:

'I have known him walk with—I have known him walk with Tiny Tim upon his shoulder, very fast indeed.'

'And so have I,' cried Peter. 'Often.'

'And so have I!' exclaimed another. So had all.

'But he was very light to carry,' she resumed, intent upon her work, 'and his father loved him so, that it was no trouble: no trouble. And there is your father at the door!'

She hurried out to meet him; and little Bob in his comforter—he had need of it, poor fellow—came in. His tea was ready for him on the hob, and they all tried who should help him to it most. Then the two young Cratchits got upon his knees and laid, each child a little cheek, against his face, as if they said, 'Don't mind it, father. Don't be grieved!'

Bob was very cheerful with them, and spoke pleasantly to all the family. He looked at the work upon the table, and praised the industry and speed of Mrs. Cratchit and the girls. They would be done long before Sunday, he said.

'Sunday! You went to-day, then, Robert?' said his wife.

'Yes, my dear,' returned Bob. 'I wish you could have gone. It would have done you good to see how green a place it is. But you'll see it often. I promised him that I would walk there on a Sunday. My little, little child!' cried Bob. 'My little child!'

He broke down all at once. He couldn't help it. If he could have helped it, he and his child would have been farther apart perhaps than they were.

He left the room, and went up-stairs into the room above, which was lighted cheerfully, and hung with Christmas. There was a chair set close beside the child, and there were signs of some one having been there, lately. Poor Bob sat down in it, and when he had thought a little and composed himself, he kissed the little face. He was reconciled to what had happened, and went down again quite happy.

They drew about the fire, and talked; the girls and mother working still. Bob told them of the extraordinary kindness of Mr. Scrooge's nephew, whom he had scarcely seen but

once, and who, meeting him in the street that day, and seeing that he looked a little—
'just a little down you know,' said Bob, inquired what had happened to distress him. 'On which,' said Bob, 'for he is the pleasantest-spoken gentleman you ever heard, I told him. 'I am heartily sorry for it, Mr. Cratchit,' he said, 'and heartily sorry for your good wife.' By the bye, how he ever knew that, I don't know.'

'Knew what, my dear?'

'Why, that you were a good wife,' replied Bob.

'Everybody knows that!' said Peter.

'Very well observed, my boy!' cried Bob. 'I hope they do. 'Heartily sorry,' he said, 'for your good wife. If I can be of service to you in any way,' he said, giving me his card, 'that's where I live. Pray come to me.' Now, it wasn't,' cried Bob, 'for the sake of anything he might be able to do for us, so much as for his kind way, that this was quite delightful. It really seemed as if he had known our Tiny Tim, and felt with us.'

'I'm sure he's a good soul!' said Mrs. Cratchit.

'You would be surer of it, my dear,' returned Bob, 'if you saw and spoke to him. I shouldn't be at all surprised—mark what I say!—if he got Peter a better situation.'

'Only hear that, Peter,' said Mrs. Cratchit.

'And then,' cried one of the girls, 'Peter will be keeping company with some one, and setting up for himself.'

'Get along with you!' retorted Peter, grinning.

'It's just as likely as not,' said Bob, 'one of these days; though there's plenty of time for that, my dear. But however and when ever we part from one another, I am sure we shall none of us forget poor Tiny Tim—shall we—or this first parting that there was among us?'

'Never, father!' cried they all.

'And I know,' said Bob, 'I know, my dears, that when we recollect how patient and how mild he was; although he was a little, little child; we shall not quarrel easily among ourselves, and forget poor Tiny Tim in doing it.'

'No, never, father!' they all cried again.

'I am very happy,' said little Bob, 'I am very happy!'

Mrs. Cratchit kissed him, his daughters kissed him, the two young Cratchits kissed him, and Peter and himself shook hands. Spirit of Tiny Tim, thy childish essence was from God!

'Spectre,' said Scrooge, 'something informs me that our parting moment is at hand. I know it, but I know not how. Tell me what man that was whom we saw lying dead.'

The Ghost of Christmas Yet To Come conveyed him, as before—though at a different time, he thought: indeed, there seemed no order in these latter visions, save that they were in the Future—into the resorts of business men, but showed him not himself. Indeed, the Spirit did not stay for anything, but went straight on, as to the end just now desired, until besought by Scrooge to tarry for a moment.

'This court,' said Scrooge,' through which we hurry now, is where my place of occupation is, and has been for a length of time. I see the house. Let me behold what I shall be, in days to come.'

The Spirit stopped; the hand was pointed elsewhere.

'The house is yonder,' Scrooge exclaimed. 'Why do you point away.'

The inexorable finger underwent no change.

Scrooge hastened to the window of his office, and looked in. It was an office still, but not his. The furniture was not the same, and the figure in the chair was not himself. The Phantom pointed as before.

He joined it once again, and wondering why and whither he had gone, accompanied it until they reached an iron gate. He paused to look round before entering.

A churchyard. Here, then, the wretched man whose name he had now to learn, lay underneath the ground. It was a worthy place. Walled in by houses; overrun by grass and weeds, the growth of vegetation's death, not life; choked up with too much burying; fat with repleted appetite. A worthy place!

The Spirit stood among the graves, and pointed down to One. He advanced towards it trembling. The Phantom was exactly as it had been, but he dreaded that he saw new meaning in its solemn shape.

'Before I draw nearer to that stone to which you point,' said Scrooge, 'answer me one question. Are these the shadows of the things that Will be, or are they shadows of things that May be, only?'

Still the Ghost pointed downward to the grave by which it stood.

'Men's courses will foreshadow certain ends, to which, if persevered in, they must lead,' said Scrooge. 'But if the courses be departed from, the ends will change. Say it is thus with what you show me!'

The Spirit was immovable as ever.

Scrooge crept towards it, trembling as he went; and following the finger, read upon the stone of the neglected grave his own name, EBENEZER SCROOGE.

'Am I that man who lay upon the bed?' he cried, upon his knees.

The finger pointed from the grave to him, and back again.

'No, Spirit! Oh no, no!'

The finger still was there.

'Spirit!' he cried, tight clutching at its robe, 'hear me! I am not the man I was. I will not be the man I must have been but for this intercourse. Why show me this, if I am past all hope!'

For the first time the hand appeared to shake.

'Good Spirit,' he pursued, as down upon the ground he fell before it:' Your nature intercedes for me, and pities me. Assure me that I yet may change these shadows you have shown me, by an altered life!'

The kind hand trembled.

'I will honour Christmas in my heart, and try to keep it all the year. I will live in the Past, the Present, and the Future. The Spirits of all Three shall strive within me. I will not shut out the lessons that they teach. Oh, tell me I may sponge away the writing on this stone!'

In his agony, he caught the spectral hand. It sought to free itself, but he was strong in his entreaty, and detained it. The Spirit, stronger yet, repulsed him.

Holding up his hands in a last prayer to have his fate reversed, he saw an alteration in the Phantom's hood and dress. It shrunk, collapsed, and dwindled down into a bedpost.

Stave 5: The End of It

Yes! and the bedpost was his own. The bed was his own, the room was his own. Best and happiest of all, the Time before him was his own, to make amends in!

'I will live in the Past, the Present, and the Future!' Scrooge repeated, as he scrambled out of bed. 'The Spirits of all Three shall strive within me. Oh Jacob Marley! Heaven, and the Christmas Time be praised for this! I say it on my knees, old Jacob, on my knees!'

He was so fluttered and so glowing with his good intentions, that his broken voice would scarcely answer to his call. He had been sobbing violently in his conflict with the Spirit, and his face was wet with tears.

'They are not torn down,' cried Scrooge, folding one of his bed-curtains in his arms, 'they are not torn down, rings and all. They are here—I am here—the shadows of the things that would have been, may be dispelled. They will be. I know they will!'

His hands were busy with his garments all this time; turning them inside out, putting them on upside down, tearing them, mislaying them, making them parties to every kind of extravagance.

'I don't know what to do,' cried Scrooge, laughing and crying in the same breath; and making a perfect Laocoön of himself with his stockings. 'I am as light as a feather, I am as happy as an angel, I am as merry as a schoolboy. I am as giddy as a drunken man. A merry Christmas to everybody! A happy New Year to all the world. Hallo here! Whoop! Hallo!'

He had frisked into the sitting-room, and was now standing there: perfectly winded.

'There's the saucepan that the gruel was in!' cried Scrooge, starting off again, and going round the fireplace. 'There's the door, by which the Ghost of Jacob Marley entered! There's the corner where the Ghost of Christmas Present, sat! There's the window where I saw the wandering Spirits! It's all right, it's all true, it all happened. Ha ha ha!'

Really, for a man who had been out of practice for so many years, it was a splendid laugh, a most illustrious laugh. The father of a long, long line of brilliant laughs!

'I don't know what day of the month it is!' said Scrooge, 'I don't know how long I've been among the Spirits. I don't know anything. I'm quite a baby. Never mind. I don't care. I'd rather be a baby. Hallo! Whoop! Hallo here!'

He was checked in his transports by the churches ringing out the lustiest peals he had ever heard. Clash, clang, hammer; ding, dong, bell. Bell, dong, ding; hammer, clang, clash! Oh, glorious, glorious!

Running to the window, he opened it, and put out his head. No fog, no mist; clear, bright, jovial, stirring, cold; cold, piping for the blood to dance to; Golden sunlight; Heavenly sky; sweet fresh air; merry bells. Oh, glorious. Glorious!

'What's to-day?' cried Scrooge, calling downward to a boy in Sunday clothes, who perhaps had loitered in to look about him.

'Eh?' returned the boy, with all his might of wonder.

'What's to-day, my fine fellow?' said Scrooge.

'To-day!' replied the boy. 'Why, Christmas Day.'

'It's Christmas Day!' said Scrooge to himself. 'I haven't missed it. The Spirits have done it all in one night. They can do anything they like. Of course they can. Of course they can. Hallo, my fine fellow!'

'Hallo!' returned the boy.

'Do you know the Poulterer's, in the next street but one, at the corner?' Scrooge inquired.

'I should hope I did,' replied the lad.

'An intelligent boy!' said Scrooge. 'A remarkable boy! Do you know whether they've sold the prize Turkey that was hanging up there—Not the little prize Turkey: the big one?'

'What, the one as big as me?' returned the boy.

'What a delightful boy!' said Scrooge. 'It's a pleasure to talk to him. Yes, my buck!'

'It's hanging there now,' replied the boy.

'Is it?' said Scrooge. 'Go and buy it.'

'Walk-er!' exclaimed the boy.

'No, no,' said Scrooge, 'I am in earnest. Go and buy it, and tell them to bring it here, that I may give them the direction where to take it. Come back with the man, and I'll give you a shilling. Come back with him in less than five minutes and I'll give you half-a-crown!'

The boy was off like a shot. He must have had a steady hand at a trigger who could have got a shot off half so fast.

'I'll send it to Bob Cratchit's!' whispered Scrooge, rubbing his hands, and splitting with a laugh. 'He shan't know who sends it. It's twice the size of Tiny Tim. Joe Miller never made such a joke as sending it to Bob's will be!'

The hand in which he wrote the address was not a steady one, but write it he did, somehow, and went down-stairs to open the street door, ready for the coming of the poulterer's man. As he stood there, waiting his arrival, the knocker caught his eye.

'I shall love it, as long as I live!' cried Scrooge, patting it with his hand. 'I scarcely ever looked at it before. What an honest expression it has in its face! It's a wonderful knocker!—Here's the Turkey. Hallo! Whoop! How are you! Merry Christmas!'

It *was* a Turkey. He never could have stood upon his legs, that bird. He would have snapped them short off in a minute, like sticks of sealing-wax.

'Why, it's impossible to carry that to Camden Town,' said Scrooge. 'You must have a cab.'

The chuckle with which he said this, and the chuckle with which he paid for the Turkey, and the chuckle with which he paid for the cab, and the chuckle with which he recompensed the boy, were only to be exceeded by the chuckle with which he sat down breathless in his chair again, and chuckled till he cried.

Shaving was not an easy task, for his hand continued to shake very much; and shaving requires attention, even when you don't dance while you are at it. But if he had cut the end of his nose off, he would have put a piece of sticking-plaster over it, and been quite satisfied.

He dressed himself all in his best, and at last got out into the streets. The people were by this time pouring forth, as he had seen them with the Ghost of Christmas Present; and walking with his hands behind him, Scrooge regarded every one with a delighted smile. He looked so irresistibly pleasant, in a word, that three or four good-humoured fellows said, 'Good morning, sir! A merry Christmas to you!' And Scrooge said often afterwards, that of all the blithe sounds he had ever heard, those were the blithest in his ears.

He had not gone far, when coming on towards him he beheld the portly gentleman, who had walked into his counting-house the day before, and said, 'Scrooge and Marley's, I believe?' It sent a pang across his heart to think how this old gentleman would look upon him when they met; but he knew what path lay straight before him, and he took it.

'My dear sir,' said Scrooge, quickening his pace, and taking the old gentleman by both his hands. 'How do you do? I hope you succeeded yesterday. It was very kind of you. A merry Christmas to you, sir!'

'Mr. Scrooge?'

'Yes,' said Scrooge. 'That is my name, and I fear it may not be pleasant to you. Allow me to ask your pardon. And will you have the goodness'—here Scrooge whispered in his ear.

'Lord bless me!' cried the gentleman, as if his breath were taken away. 'My dear Mr. Scrooge, are you serious?'

'If you please,' said Scrooge. 'Not a farthing less. A great many back-payments are included in it, I assure you. Will you do me that favour?'

'My dear sir,' said the other, shaking hands with him. 'I don't know what to say to such munificence.'

'Don't say anything please,' retorted Scrooge. 'Come and see me. Will you come and see me?'

'I will!' cried the old gentleman. And it was clear he meant to do it.

'Thank you,' said Scrooge. 'I am much obliged to you. I thank you fifty times. Bless you!'

He went to church, and walked about the streets, and watched the people hurrying to and fro, and patted children on the head, and questioned beggars, and looked down into the kitchens of houses, and up to the windows, and found that everything could yield him pleasure. He had never dreamed that any walk—that anything—could give him so much happiness. In the afternoon he turned his steps towards his nephew's house.

He passed the door a dozen times, before he had the courage to go up and knock. But he made a dash, and did it:

'Is your master at home, my dear?' said Scrooge to the girl. Nice girl! Very.

'Yes, sir.'

'Where is he, my love?' said Scrooge.

'He's in the dining-room, sir, along with mistress. I'll show you up-stairs, if you please.'

'Thank you. He knows me,' said Scrooge, with his hand already on the dining-room lock. 'I'll go in here, my dear.'

He turned it gently, and sidled his face in, round the door. They were looking at the table (which was spread out in great array); for these young housekeepers are always nervous on such points, and like to see that everything is right.

'Fred!' said Scrooge.

Dear heart alive, how his niece by marriage started! Scrooge had forgotten, for the moment, about her sitting in the corner with the footstool, or he wouldn't have done it, on any account.

'Why bless my soul!' cried Fred, 'who's that?'

'It's I. Your uncle Scrooge. I have come to dinner. Will you let me in, Fred?'

Let him in! It is a mercy he didn't shake his arm off. He was at home in five minutes. Nothing could be heartier. His niece looked just the same. So did Topper when he came. So did the plump sister when she came. So did every one when they came. Wonderful party, wonderful games, wonderful unanimity, wonderful happiness!

But he was early at the office next morning. Oh, he was early there. If he could only be there first, and catch Bob Cratchit coming late. That was the thing he had set his heart upon.

And he did it; yes, he did! The clock struck nine. No Bob. A quarter past. No Bob. He was full eighteen minutes and a half behind his time. Scrooge sat with his door wide open, that he might see him come into the Tank.

His hat was off, before he opened the door; his comforter too. He was on his stool in a jiffy; driving away with his pen, as if he were trying to overtake nine o'clock.

'Hallo!' growled Scrooge, in his accustomed voice, as near as he could feign it. 'What do you mean by coming here at this time of day?'

'I am very sorry, sir,' said Bob. 'I am behind my time.'

'You are!' repeated Scrooge. 'Yes. I think you are. Step this way, sir, if you please.'

'It's only once a year, sir,' pleaded Bob, appearing from the Tank. 'It shall not be repeated. I was making rather merry yesterday, sir.'

'Now, I'll tell you what, my friend,' said Scrooge, 'I am not going to stand this sort of thing any longer. And therefore,' he continued, leaping from his stool, and giving Bob such a dig in the waistcoat that he staggered back into the Tank again; 'and therefore I am about to raise your salary!'

Bob trembled, and got a little nearer to the ruler. He had a momentary idea of knocking Scrooge down with it, holding him, and calling to the people in the court for help and a strait-waistcoat.

'A merry Christmas, Bob!' said Scrooge, with an earnestness that could not be mistaken, as he clapped him on the back. 'A merrier Christmas, Bob, my good fellow, than I have given you for many a year! I'll raise your salary, and endeavour to assist your struggling family, and we will discuss your affairs this very afternoon, over a Christmas bowl of smoking bishop, Bob! Make up the fires, and buy another coal-scuttle before you dot another i, Bob Cratchit!'

Scrooge was better than his word. He did it all, and infinitely more; and to Tiny Tim, who did not die, he was a second father. He became as good a friend, as good a master, and as good a man, as the good old city knew, or any other good old city, town, or borough, in the good old world. Some people laughed to see the alteration in him, but he let them laugh, and little heeded them; for he was wise enough to know that nothing ever happened on this globe, for good, at which some people did not have their fill of laughter in the outset; and knowing that such as these would be blind anyway, he thought it quite as well that they should wrinkle up their eyes in grins, as have the malady in less attractive forms. His own heart laughed: and that was quite enough for him.

He had no further intercourse with Spirits, but lived upon the Total Abstinence Principle, ever afterwards; and it was always said of him, that he knew how to keep Christmas well, if any man alive possessed the knowledge. May that be truly said of us, and all of us! And so, as Tiny Tim observed, God Bless Us, Every One!

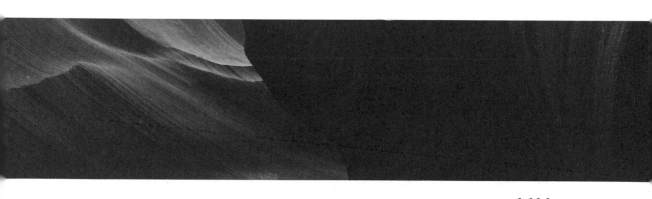

VII

Leo Tolstoy

Editors' Introduction

"Ivan Ilych's life had been most simple and most ordinary and therefore most terrible." This somber judgment expresses the central focus of Tolstoy's short novel. To understand the reason for this judgment is to gain an insight into some of Tolstoy's deepest convictions concerning the best way to live.

For most of his life (1828–1910) Lev Tolstoy was engaged in an unrelenting process of self-examination. In both his fiction and non-fiction he returns over and over again to questions about how we should live. Like many of the great novelists, his work reflects the struggles involved in his own ongoing conversion. Even when not explicitly so (as in St. Augustine's *Confessions*), Tolstoy's writings are fundamentally autobiographical.

Tolstoy came from an old, aristocratic, and wealthy Russian family (he was, in fact, referred to as Count Tolstoy). His parents died before he was ten years old, and he and his siblings were raised by a succession of female relatives. He attended Kazan University, but left without ever attaining his degree. He and his brother Nikolai also spent time in the army, serving in the Caucasus for several years (1851–56). In 1852 he published his first significant work, the novel *Childhood*, which brought him acclaim and instant recognition as one of Russia's most talented new writers. Tolstoy's diaries from this period in his life reveal a self-centered young man who is obsessed with schemes for self-improvement while simultaneously preoccupied with gambling, sex, and a desire for fame. But they also reveal someone who reflects frequently on spiritual and religious questions.

When Tolstoy turned twenty years of age he inherited his family's estate at Yasnaya Polyana ("Clear Glade" in English). For the rest of his life this would be his permanent home. Tolstoy was a person of many enthusiasms, and after returning to Yasnaya Polyana after his stint in the army he threw himself into the project of providing education for the children of the peasants on his estate. His interest in education led him to tour Europe for ten months in 1860–61. In 1862 he entered into the most important relationship of his life—his marriage to Sofia Andreevna Behrs. Entire books could be (and have been) written on the Tolstoys' marriage. Suffice it to say that theirs was an intense, close, complicated, and often tumultuous relationship, one that produced thirteen children.

After writing his two greatest novels, *War and Peace* (1869) and *Anna Karenina* (1877), Tolstoy entered into a period in which he began to question the meaning and purpose of life. His marriage had brought him stability and happiness well into the 1870s, but his restless search concerning the best way to live led him to become increasingly dissatisfied with the kind of life he was leading. He was already being acclaimed as Russia's greatest writer, his family life was generally good, and by the standards of his time (as well as ours) he had achieved great success. But the question "So what?" would give him no rest, and the crisis of meaning in which he was embroiled led him to even contemplate suicide. Tolstoy chronicled his struggle during these years in his *Confession* (1879). At first he tried to find meaning by throwing himself fully into the practices and beliefs of the Russian Orthodox faith in which he had been raised. However, he found himself increasingly questioning the doctrines of the Church, and he devoted several years to the study of Orthodox theology and the gospels. The result of these studies was that Tolstoy found it difficult to believe much of what he had been taught concerning religious doctrine. However, he also concluded that Christianity, pruned of the accretions that had been added to it by church authorities, did contain the answers he was seeking about the meaning of life. It can certainly be argued that for the rest of his life he devoted himself to working out the implications of his newly reformulated understanding of the Christian message, both in writing and in practice. He became convinced that the gospel teaching on love implied an uncompromising attitude of non-violence and pacifism. Consequently, he came to denounce war, capital punishment, and all other forms of coercion. He came to see all government as a form of violence, leading him to become an outspoken critic of the Russian authorities and their policies. Tolstoy's espousal of religious views contrary to Orthodox teaching and his public criticism of the Orthodox Church eventually led to him being excommunicated by the Holy Synod in 1901.

Tolstoy's attempts to put his newly found views into practice also led to increasing friction within his family. In particular, he experienced a good deal of resistance from his wife and from many of his children when he attempted to divest himself of his property and to renounce the copyright to many of his literary works. His friend and devoted disciple Vladimir Chertkov, encouraged (some would say manipulated) Tolstoy to take these dramatic actions, further exacerbating Tolstoy's increasingly strained relationship with his wife. Eventually his domestic situation reached a point that Tolstoy found intolerable, and in November 1910, without telling his wife, he left home (along with his youngest daughter Alexandra and his physician/friend Dushan Makovitsky), hoping to spend the rest of his days in quiet and contemplation. Shortly after leaving home he caught pneumonia and died at the train station in the village of Astapovo. In accordance with his wishes, he was buried on his estate without any religious ceremony. The Russian government tried to prevent people from attending the burial, but despite these attempts, thousands made their way to Yasnaya Polyana and lined the road as the funeral procession made its way.

The Death of Ivan Ilych was written in 1886. It is Tolstoy's first "post-conversion" work of fiction and is generally considered one of his best works. On one level the novel offers a scathing satire of the life of the professional classes in the Russia of the time. On a deeper level the story raises profound and disturbing questions about the purpose of life and the meaning of success. Unlike such novelists as Dickens and Dostoevsky, who excel at exaggerating certain features of their characters in order to convey their message, Tolstoy had a knack for disclosing just how spiritually empty and alienating are the lives that we take to be "normal" and successful. Nowhere is this ability displayed with greater power than in *The Death of Ivan Ilych*.

During the time in which the story was being written, Tolstoy was becoming increasingly dissatisfied with the life he and his family were leading. He was becoming more and more convinced that he and others of his class were parasites, living off the work of others. His attempts to convince his family to adopt his new view toward life met with incomprehension. A diary entry from 1884 reflects this situation:

> "It's very depressing in the family. Depressing, because I can't sympathize with them. All their joys, the examination, social successes, music furniture, shopping—I consider them all a misfortune and an evil for them, and I can't tell them so. I can and do speak, but my words don't get through to anyone. . . I've been assigned the role of a querulous old man, and in their eyes I can't escape from it: if I take part in their life I renounce the truth, and they would be the first to cast this renunciation in my teeth. If I look sadly, as now, at their madness—I'm a querulous old man, like all old men."

A year later he writes in a similar vein:

> "Thought about my unhappy family: my wife, sons and daughters who live side by side with me and deliberately put barriers between me and themselves in order not to see the truth and the good, which would expose the falseness of their lives, but would also save them from suffering. . . I thought further: to do the will of Him who sent me—that is my food. What simple and profound significance. You can only be at peace and always content when you take as your purpose not something external, but doing the will of Him who sent you."

These glimpses into Tolstoy's state of mind at the time of the writing of the novel offer important clues as to why he considered the life of Ivan Ilych to be most simple, most ordinary, and most terrible.

THE DEATH OF IVAN ILYCH

I

During an interval in the Melvinski trial in the large building of the Law Courts the members and public prosecutor met in Ivan Egorovich Shebek's private room, where the conversation turned on the celebrated Krasovski case. Fedor Vasilievich warmly maintained that it was not subject to their jurisdiction, Ivan Egorovich maintained the contrary, while Peter Ivanovich, not having entered into the discussion at the start, took no part in it but looked through the *Gazette* which had just been handed in.

"Gentlemen," he said, "Ivan Ilych has died!"

"You don't say so!"

"Here, read it yourself," replied Peter Ivanovich, handing Fedor Vasilievich the paper still damp from the press. Surrounded by a black border were the words: "Praskovya Fedorovna Golovina, with profound sorrow, informs relatives and friends of the demise of her beloved husband Ivan Ilych Golovin, Member of the Court of Justice, which occurred on February the 4th of this year 1882. The funeral will take place on Friday at one o'clock in the afternoon."

Ivan Ilych had been a colleague of the gentlemen present and was liked by them all. He had been ill for some weeks with an illness said to be incurable. His post had been kept open for him, but there had been conjectures that in case of his death Alexeev might receive his appointment, and that either Vinnikov or Shtabel would succeed Alexeev. So on receiving the news of Ivan Ilych's death the first thought of each of the gentlemen in that private room was of the changes and promotions it might occasion among themselves or their acquaintances.

"I shall be sure to get Shtabel's place or Vinnikov's," thought Fedor Vasilievich. "I was promised that long ago, and the promotion means an extra eight hundred rubles a year for me besides the allowance."

"Now I must apply for my brother-in-law's transfer from Kaluga," thought Peter Ivanovich. "My wife will be very glad, and then she won't be able to say that I never do anything for her relations."

"I thought he would never leave his bed again," said Peter Ivanovich aloud. "It's very sad."

"But what really was the matter with him?"

"The doctors couldn't say—at least they could, but each of them said something different. When last I saw him I thought he was getting better."

"And I haven't been to see him since the holidays. I always meant to go."

"Had he any property?"

"I think his wife had a little—but something quite trifling."

"We shall have to go to see her, but they live so terribly far away."

"Far away from you, you mean. Everything's far away from your place."

"You see, he never can forgive my living on the other side of the river," said Peter Ivanovich, smiling at Shebek. Then, still talking of the distances between different parts of the city, they returned to the Court.

Besides considerations as to the possible transfers and promotions likely to result from Ivan Ilych's death, the mere fact of the death of a near acquaintance aroused, as usual, in all who heard of it the complacent feeling that, "it is he who is dead and not I."

Each one thought or felt, "Well, he's dead but I'm alive!" But the more intimate of Ivan Ilych's acquaintances, his so-called friends, could not help thinking also that they would now have to fulfil the very tiresome demands of propriety by attending the funeral service and paying a visit of condolence to the widow.

Fedor Vasilievich and Peter Ivanovich had been his nearest acquaintances. Peter Ivanovich had studied law with Ivan Ilych and had considered himself to be under obligations to him.

Having told his wife at dinner-time of Ivan Ilych's death, and of his conjecture that it might be possible to get her brother transferred to their circuit, Peter Ivanovich sacrificed his usual nap, put on his evening clothes and drove to Ivan Ilych's house.

At the entrance stood a carriage and two cabs. Leaning against the wall in the hall downstairs near the cloakstand was a coffin-lid covered with cloth of gold, ornamented with gold cord and tassels, that had been polished up with metal powder. Two ladies in black were taking off their fur cloaks. Peter Ivanovich recognized one of them as Ivan Ilych's sister, but the other was a stranger to him. His colleague Schwartz was just coming downstairs, but on seeing Peter Ivanovich enter he stopped and winked at him, as if to say: "Ivan Ilych has made a mess of things—not like you and me."

Schwartz's face with his Piccadilly whiskers, and his slim figure in evening dress, had as usual an air of elegant solemnity which contrasted with the playfulness of his character and had a special piquancy here, or so it seemed to Peter Ivanovich.

Peter Ivanovich allowed the ladies to precede him and slowly followed them upstairs. Schwartz did not come down but remained where he was, and Peter Ivanovich understood that he wanted to arrange where they should play bridge that evening. The ladies went upstairs to the widow's room, and Schwartz with seriously compressed lips but a playful looking his eyes, indicated by a twist of his eyebrows the room to the right where the body lay.

Peter Ivanovich, like everyone else on such occasions, entered feeling uncertain what he would have to do. All he knew was that at such times it is always safe to cross oneself. But he was not quite sure whether one should make obseisances while doing so. He therefore adopted a middle course. On entering the room he began crossing himself and made a slight movement resembling a bow. At the same time, as far as the motion of his head and arm allowed, he surveyed the room. Two young men—apparently nephews, one of whom was a high-school pupil—were leaving the room, crossing themselves as they did so. An old woman was standing motionless, and a lady with strangely arched eyebrows was saying something to her in a whisper. A vigorous, resolute Church Reader, in a frock-coat, was reading something in a loud voice with an expression that precluded any contradiction. The butler's assistant, Gerasim, stepping lightly in front of Peter Ivanovich, was strewing something on the floor. Noticing this, Peter Ivanovich was immediately aware of a faint odour of a decomposing body.

The last time he had called on Ivan Ilych, Peter Ivanovich had seen Gerasim in the study. Ivan Ilych had been particularly fond of him and he was performing the duty of a sick nurse.

Peter Ivanovich continued to make the sign of the cross slightly inclining his head in an intermediate direction between the coffin, the Reader, and the icons on the table in a corner of the room. Afterwards, when it seemed to him that this movement of his arm in crossing himself had gone on too long, he stopped and began to look at the corpse.

The dead man lay, as dead men always lie, in a specially heavy way, his rigid limbs sunk in the soft cushions of the coffin, with the head forever bowed on the pillow. His yellow waxen brow with bald patches over his sunken temples was thrust up in the way peculiar to the dead, the protruding nose seeming to press on the upper lip. He was much changed and grown even thinner since Peter Ivanovich had last seen him, but, as is always the case with the dead, his face was handsomer and above all more dignified than when he was alive, the expression on the face said that what was necessary had been accomplished, and accomplished rightly. Besides this there was in that expression a reproach and a warning to the living. This warning seemed to Peter Ivanovich out of place, or at least not applicable to him. He felt a certain discomfort and so he hurriedly crossed himself once more and turned and went out of the door—too hurriedly and too regardless of propriety, as he himself was aware.

Schwartz was waiting for him in the adjoining room with legs spread wide apart and both hands toying with his top-hat behind his back. The mere sight of that playful, well-groomed, and elegant figure refreshed Peter Ivanovich. He felt that Schwartz was above all these happenings and would not surrender to any depressing influences. His very look said that this incident of a church service for Ivan Ilych could not be a sufficient reason for infringing the order of the session—in other words, that it would certainly not prevent his unwrapping a new pack of cards and shuffling them that evening while a footman placed fresh candles on the table: in fact, that there was no reason for supposing that this incident would hinder their spending the evening agreeably. Indeed he said this in a whisper as Peter Ivanovich passed him, proposing that they should meet for a game at Fedor Vasilievich's. But apparently Peter Ivanovich was not destined to play bridge that evening. Praskovya Fedorovna (a short, fat woman who despite all efforts to the contrary had continued to broaden steadily from her shoulders downwards and who had the same extraordinarily arched eyebrows as the lady who had been standing by the coffin), dressed all in black, her head covered with lace, came out of her own room with some other ladies, conducted them to the room where the dead body lay, and said: "The service will begin immediately. Please go in."

Schwartz, making an indefinite bow, stood still, evidently neither accepting nor declining this invitation. Praskovya Fedorovna recognizing Peter Ivanovich, sighed, went close up to him, took his hand, and said: "I know you were a true friend to Ivan Ilych ..." and looked at him awaiting some suitable response. And Peter Ivanovich knew that, just as it had been the right thing to cross himself in that room, so what he had to do here was to press her hand, sigh, and say, "Believe me ..." So he did all this and as he did it felt that the desired result had been achieved: that both he and she were touched.

"Come with me. I want to speak to you before it begins," said the widow. "Give me your arm."

Peter Ivanovich gave her his arm and they went to the inner rooms, passing Schwartz who winked at Peter Ivanovich compassionately.

"That does for our bridge! Don't object if we find another player. Perhaps you can cut in when you do escape," said his playful look.

Peter Ivanovich sighed still more deeply and despondently, and Praskovya Fedorovna pressed his arm gratefully. When they reached the drawing-room, upholstered in pink cretonne and lighted by a dim lamp, they sat down at the table—she on a sofa and Peter Ivanovich on a low pouffe, the springs of which yielded spasmodically under his weight. Praskovya Fedorovna had been on the point of warning him to take another seat, but felt that such a warning was out of keeping with her present condition and so changed her mind. As he sat down on the pouffe Peter Ivanovich recalled how Ivan Ilych had arranged this room and had consulted him regarding this pink cretonne with green leaves. The whole room was full of furniture and knick-knacks, and on her way to the sofa the lace of the widow's black shawl caught on the edge of the table. Peter Ivanovich rose to detach it, and the springs of the pouffe, relieved of his weight, rose also and gave him a push. The widow began detaching her shawl herself, and Peter Ivanovich again sat down, suppressing the rebellious springs of the pouffe under him. But the widow had not quite freed herself and Peter Ivanovich got up again, and again the pouffe rebelled and even creaked. When this was all over she took out a clean cambric handkerchief and began to weep. The episode with the shawl and the struggle with the pouffe had cooled Peter Ivanovich's emotions and he sat there with a sullen look on his face. This awkward situation was interrupted by Sokolov, Ivan Ilych's butler, who came to report that the plot in the cemetery that Praskovya Fedorovna had chosen would cost two hundred rubles. She stopped weeping and, looking at Peter Ivanovich with the air of a victim, remarked in French that it was very hard for her. Peter Ivanovich made a silent gesture signifying his full conviction that it must indeed be so.

"Please smoke," she said in a magnanimous yet crushed voice, and turned to discuss with Sokolov the price of the plot for the grave.

Peter Ivanovich while lighting his cigarette heard her inquiring very circumstantially into the prices of different plots in the cemetery and finally decide which she would take, when that was done she gave instructions about engaging the choir. Sokolov then left the room.

"I look after everything myself," she told Peter Ivanovich, shifting the albums that lay on the table; and noticing that the table was endangered by his cigarette-ash, she immediately passed him an ash-tray, saying as she did so: "I consider it an affectation to say that my grief prevents my attending to practical affairs. On the contrary, if anything can—I won't say console me, but— distract me, it is seeing to everything concerning him." She again took out her handkerchief as if preparing to cry, but suddenly, as if mastering her feeling, she shook herself and began to speak calmly. "But there is something I want to talk to you about."

Peter Ivanovich bowed, keeping control of the springs of the pouffe, which immediately began quivering under him.

"He suffered terribly the last few days."

"Did he?" said Peter Ivanovich.

"Oh, terribly! He screamed unceasingly, not for minutes but for hours, for the last three days he screamed incessantly. It was unendurable. I cannot understand how I bore it; you could hear him three rooms off. Oh, what I have suffered!"

"Is it possible that he was conscious all that time?" asked Peter Ivanovich.

"Yes," she whispered. "To the last moment. He took leave of us a quarter of an hour before he died, and asked us to take Volodya away."

The thought of the suffering of this man he had known so intimately, first as a merry little boy, then as a schoolmate, and later as a grownup colleague, suddenly struck Peter Ivanovich with horror, despite an unpleasant consciousness of his own and this woman's dissimulation. He again saw that brow, and that nose pressing down on the lip, and felt afraid for himself.

"Three days of frightful suffering and the death! Why, that might suddenly, at any time, happen to me," he thought, and for a moment felt terrified. But—he did not himself know how—the customary reflection at once occurred to him that this had happened to Ivan Ilych and not to him, and that it should not and could not happen to him, and that to think that it could would be yielding to depression which he ought not to do, as Schwartz's expression plainly showed. After which reflection Peter Ivanovich felt reassured, and began to ask with interest about the details of Ivan Ilych's death, as though death was an accident natural to Ivan Ilych but certainly not to himself.

After many details of the really dreadful physical sufferings Ivan Ilych had endured (which details he learnt only from the effect those sufferings had produced on Praskovya Fedorovna's nerves) the widow apparently found it necessary to get to business.

"Oh, Peter Ivanovich, how hard it is! How terribly, terribly hard!" and she again began to weep.

Peter Ivanovich sighed and waited for her to finish blowing her nose. When she had done so he said, "Believe me . . ." and she again began talking and brought out what was evidently her chief concern with him—namely, to question him as to how she could obtain a grant of money from the government on the occasion of her husband's death. She made it appear that she was asking Peter Ivanovich's advice about her pension, but he soon saw that she already knew about that to the minutest detail, more even than he did himself. She knew how much could be got out of the government in consequence of her husband's death, but wanted to find out whether she could not possibly extract something more. Peter Ivanovich tried to think of some means of doing so, but after reflecting for a while and, out of propriety, condemning the government for its niggardliness, he said he thought that nothing more could be got. Then she sighed and evidently began to devise means of getting rid of her visitor. Noticing this, he put out his cigarette, rose, pressed her hand, and went out into the anteroom.

In the dining-room where the clock stood that Ivan Ilych had liked so much and had bought at an antique shop, Peter Ivanovich met a priest and a few acquaintances who had come to attend the service, and he recognized Ivan Ilych's daughter, a handsome young woman. She was in black and her slim figure appeared slimmer than ever. She had a gloomy, determined, almost angry expression, and bowed to Peter Ivanovich as though he were in some way to blame. Behind her, with the same offended look, stood a wealthy young man, an examining magistrate, whom Peter Ivanovich also knew and who was her fiancé, as he had heard. He bowed mournfully to them and was about to pass into the death-chamber, when from under the stairs appeared the figure of Ivan Ilych's schoolboy son, who was extremely like his father. He seemed a little Ivan Ilych, such as Peter Ivanovich remembered when they studied law together. His tear-stained eyes had in them the look that is seen in the eyes of boys of thirteen or fourteen who are not pure-minded. When he saw Peter Ivanovich he scowled morosely and shamefacedly. Peter Ivanovich nodded to him and entered the death-chamber. The service began: candles, groans, incense, tears, and sobs. Peter Ivanovich stood looking gloomily down at his feet. He did not look once at the dead man, did not yield to any depressing influence, and was one of the first to leave the room. There was no one in the anteroom, but Gerasim darted out of the dead man's room, rummaged with his strong hands among the fur coats to find Peter Ivanovich's and helped him on with it.

"Well, friend Gerasim," said Peter Ivanovich, so as to say something. "It's a sad affair, isn't it?"

"It's God will. We shall all come to it some day," said Gerasim, displaying his teeth—the even white teeth of a healthy peasant—and, like a man in the thick of urgent work, he briskly opened the front door, called the coachman, helped Peter Ivanovich into the sledge, and sprang back to the porch as if in readiness for what he had to do next.

Peter Ivanovich found the fresh air particularly pleasant after the smell of incense, the dead body, and carbolic acid.

"Where to sir?" asked the coachman.

"It's not too late even now. . . . I'll call round on Fedor Vasilievich."

He accordingly drove there and found them just finishing the first rubber, so that it was quite convenient for him to cut in.

II

Ivan Ilych's life had been most simple and most ordinary and therefore most terrible.

He had been a member of the Court of Justice, and died at the age of forty-five. His father had been an official who after serving in various ministries and departments in Petersburg had made the sort of career which brings men to positions from which by reason of their long service they cannot be dismissed, though they are obviously unfit to hold any responsible position, and for whom therefore posts are specially created, which though fictitious carry salaries of from six to ten thousand rubles that are not fictitious, and in receipt of which they live on to a great age.

Such was the Privy Councillor and superfluous member of various superfluous institutions, Ilya Epimovich Golovin.

He had three sons, of whom Ivan Ilych was the second. The eldest son was following in his father's footsteps only in another department, and was already approaching that stage in the service at which a similar sinecure would be reached. The third son was a failure. He had ruined his prospects in a number of positions and was now serving in the railway department. His father and brothers, and still more their wives, not merely disliked meeting him, but avoided remembering his existence unless compelled to do so. His sister had married Baron Greff, a Petersburg official of her father's type. Ivan Ilych was *le phenix de la famille* as people said. He was neither as cold and formal as his elder brother nor as wild as the younger, but was a happy mean between them—an intelligent polished, lively and agreeable man. He had studied with his younger brother at the School of Law, but the latter had failed to complete the course and was expelled when he was in the fifth class. Ivan Ilych finished the course well. Even when he was at the School of Law he was just what he remained for the rest of his life: a capable, cheerful, good-natured, and sociable man, though strict in the fulfillment of what he considered to be his duty: and he considered his duty to be what was so considered by those in authority. Neither as a boy nor as a man was he a toady, but from early youth was by nature attracted to people of high station as a fly is drawn to the light, assimilating their ways and views of life and establishing friendly relations with them. All the enthusiasms of childhood and youth passed without leaving much trace on him; he succumbed to sensuality, to vanity, and latterly among the highest classes to liberalism, but always within limits which his instinct unfailingly indicated to him as correct.

At school he had done things which had formerly seemed to him very horrid and made him feel disgusted with himself when he did them; but when later on he saw that such actions were done by people of good position and that they did not regard them as wrong, he was able not exactly to regard them as right, but to forget about them entirely or not be at all troubled at remembering them.

Having graduated from the School of Law and qualified for the tenth rank of the civil service, and having received money from his father for his equipment, Ivan Ilych ordered himself clothes at Scharmer's, the fashionable tailor, hung a medallion inscribed *respice finem* on his watch-chain, took leave of his professor and the prince who was patron of the school, had a farewell dinner with his comrades at Donon's first-class restaurant, and with his new and fashionable portmanteau, linen, clothes, shaving and other toilet appliances, and a travelling rug, all purchased at the best shops, he set off for one of the provinces where through his father's influence, he had been attached to the governor as an official for special service.

In the province Ivan Ilych soon arranged as easy and agreeable a position for himself as he had had at the School of Law. He performed his official task, made his career, and at the same time amused himself pleasantly and decorously. Occasionally he paid official visits to country districts where he behaved with dignity both to his superiors and inferiors, and performed the duties entrusted to him, which related chiefly to the sectarians, with an exactness and incorruptible honesty of which he could not but feel proud.

In official matters, despite his youth and taste for frivolous gaiety, he was exceedingly reserved, punctilious, and even severe; but in society he was often amusing and witty, and always good-natured, correct in his manner, and *bon enfant*, as the governor and his wife—with whom he was like one of the family—used to say of him.

In the province he had an affair with a lady who made advances to the elegant young lawyer, and there was also a milliner; and there were carousals with aides-de-camp who visited the district, and after-supper visits to a certain outlying street of doubtful reputation; and there was too some obsequiousness to his chief and even to his chief's wife, but all this was done with such a tone of good breeding that no hard names could be applied to it. It all came under the heading of the French saying: "*Il faut que jeunesse se passe.*" It was all done with clean hands, in clean linen, with French phrases, and above all among people of the best society and consequently with the approval of people of rank.

So Ivan Ilych served for five years and then came a change in his official life. The new and reformed judicial institutions were introduced, and new men were needed. Ivan Ilych became such a new man. He was offered the post of examining magistrate, and he accepted it though the post was in another province and obliged him to give up the connexions he had formed and to make new ones. His friends met to give him a send-off; they had a group photograph taken and presented him with a silver cigarette-case, and he set off to his new post.

As examining magistrate Ivan Ilych was just as *comme il faut* and decorous a man, inspiring general respect and capable of separating his official duties from his private life, as he had been when acting as an official on special service. His duties now as examining magistrate were far more interesting and attractive than before. In his former position it had been pleasant to wear an undress uniform made by Scharmer, and to pass through the crowd of petitioners and officials who were timorously awaiting an audience with the governor, and who envied him as with free and easy gait he went straight into his chief's private room to have a cup of tea and a cigarette with him. But not many people had then been directly dependent on him—only police officials and the sectarians when he went on special missions—and he liked to treat them politely, almost as comrades, as if he were letting them feel that he who had the power to crush them was treating them in this simple, friendly way. There were then but few such people. But now, as an examining magistrate, Ivan Ilych felt that everyone without exception, even the most important and self-satisfied, was in his power, and that he need only write a few words on a sheet of paper with a certain heading, and this or that important, self-satisfied person would be brought before him in the role of an accused person or a witness, and if he did not choose to allow him to sit down, would have to stand before him and answer his questions. Ivan Ilych never abused his power; he tried on the contrary to soften its expression, but the consciousness of it and the possibility of softening its effect, supplied the chief interest and attraction of his office. In his work itself, especially in his examinations, he very soon acquired a method of eliminating all considerations irrelevant to the legal aspect of the case, and reducing even the most complicated case to a form in which it would be presented on paper only in its externals, completely excluding his personal opinion of the matter, while above all observing every prescribed formality. The work was new and Ivan Ilych was one of the first men to apply the new Code of 1864.

On taking up the post of examining magistrate in a new town, he made new acquaintances and connexions, placed himself on a new footing and assumed a somewhat different tone. He took up an attitude of rather dignified aloofness towards the provincial authorities, but picked out the best circle of legal gentlemen and wealthy gentry living in the town and assumed a tone of slight dissatisfaction with the government, of moderate liberalism, and of enlightened citizenship. At the same time, without at all altering the elegance of his toilet, he ceased shaving his chin and allowed his beard to grow as it pleased.

Ivan Ilych settled down very pleasantly in this new town. The society there, which inclined towards opposition to the governor was friendly, his salary was larger, and he began to play *vint* [a form of bridge], which he found added not a little to the pleasure of life, for he had a capacity for cards, played good-humouredly, and calculated rapidly and astutely, so that he usually won.

After living there for two years he met his future wife, Praskovya Fedorovna Mikhel, who was the most attractive, clever, and brilliant girl of the set in which he moved, and among other amusements and relaxations from his labours as examining magistrate, Ivan Ilych established light and playful relations with her.

While he had been an official on special service he had been accustomed to dance, but now as an examining magistrate it was exceptional for him to do so. If he danced now, he did it as if to show that though he served under the reformed order of things, and had reached the fifth official rank, yet when it came to dancing he could do it better than most people. So at the end of an evening he sometimes danced with Praskovya Fedorovna, and it was chiefly during these dances that he captivated her. She fell in love with him. Ivan Ilych had at first no definite intention of marrying, but when the girl fell in love with him he said to himself: "Really, why shouldn't I marry?"

Praskovya Fedorovna came of a good family, was not bad looking, and had some little property. Ivan Ilych might have aspired to a more brilliant match, but even this was good. He had his salary, and she, he hoped, would have an equal income. She was well connected, and was a sweet, pretty, and thoroughly correct young woman. To say that Ivan Ilych married because he fell in love with Praskovya Fedorovna and found that she sympathized with his views of life would be as incorrect as to say that he married because his social circle approved of the match. He was swayed by both these considerations: the marriage gave him personal satisfaction, and at the same time it was considered the right thing by the most highly placed of his associates.

So Ivan Ilych got married.

The preparations for marriage and the beginning of married life, with its conjugal caresses, the new furniture, new crockery, and new linen, were very pleasant until his wife became pregnant—so that Ivan Ilych had begun to think that marriage would not impair the easy, agreeable, gay and always decorous character of his life, approved of by society and regarded by himself as natural, but would even improve it. But from the first months of his wife's pregnancy, something new, unpleasant, depressing, and unseemly, and from which there was no way of escape, unexpectedly showed itself.

His wife, without any reason—*de gaiete de coeur* as Ivan Ilych expressed it to himself—began to disturb the pleasure and propriety of their life. She began to be jealous without any cause, expected him to devote his whole attention to her, found fault with everything, and made coarse and ill-mannered scenes.

At first Ivan Ilych hoped to escape from the unpleasantness of this state of affairs by the same easy and decorous relation to life that had served him heretofore: he tried to ignore his wife's disagreeable moods, continued to live in his usual easy and pleasant way, invited friends to his house for a game of cards, and also tried going out to his club or spending his evenings with friends. But one day his wife began upbraiding him so vigorously, using such coarse words, and continued to abuse him every time he did not fulfil her demands, so resolutely and with such evident determination not to give way till he submitted—that is, till he stayed at home and was bored just as she was—that he became alarmed. He now realized that matrimony—at any rate with Praskovya Fedorovna—was not always conducive to the pleasures and amenities of life, but on the contrary often infringed both comfort and propriety, and that he must therefore entrench himself against such infringement. And Ivan Ilych began to seek for means of doing so. His official duties were the one thing that imposed upon Praskovya Fedorovna, and by means of his official work and the duties attached to it he began struggling with his wife to secure his own independence.

With the birth of their child, the attempts to feed it and the various failures in doing so, and with the real and imaginary illnesses of mother and child, in which Ivan Ilych's sympathy was demanded but about which he understood nothing, the need of securing for himself an existence outside his family life became still more imperative.

As his wife grew more irritable and exacting and Ivan Ilych transferred the center of gravity of his life more and more to his official work, so did he grow to like his work better and became more ambitious than before.

Very soon, within a year of his wedding, Ivan Ilych had realized that marriage, though it may add some comforts to life, is in fact a very intricate and difficult affair towards which in order to perform one's duty, that is, to lead a decorous life approved of by society, one must adopt a definite attitude just as towards one's official duties.

And Ivan Ilych evolved such an attitude towards married life. He only required of it those conveniences—dinner at home, housewife, and bed—which it could give him, and above all that propriety of external forms required by public opinion. For the rest he looked for lighthearted pleasure and propriety, and was very thankful when he found them, but if he met with antagonism and querulousness he at once retired into his separate fenced-off world of official duties, where he found satisfaction.

Ivan Ilych was esteemed a good official, and after three years was made Assistant Public Prosecutor. His new duties, their importance, the possibility of indicting and imprisoning anyone he chose, the publicity his speeches received, and the success he had in all these things, made his work still more attractive.

More children came. His wife became more and more querulous and ill-tempered, but the attitude Ivan Ilych had adopted towards his home life rendered him almost impervious to her grumbling.

After seven years' service in that town he was transferred to another province as Public Prosecutor. They moved, but were short of money and his wife did not like the place they moved to. Though the salary was higher the cost of living was greater, besides which two of their children died and family life became still more unpleasant for him.

Praskovya Fedorovna blamed her husband for every inconvenience they encountered in their new home. Most of the conversations between husband and wife, especially as to the children's education, led to topics which recalled former disputes, and these disputes were apt to flare up again at any moment. There remained only those rare periods of amorousness which still came to them at times but did not last long. These were islets at which they anchored for a while and then again set out upon that ocean of veiled hostility which showed itself in their aloofness from one another. This aloofness might have grieved Ivan Ilych had he considered that it ought not to exist, but he now regarded the position as normal, and even made it the goal at which he aimed in family life. His aim was to free himself more and more from those unpleasantness and to give them a semblance of harmlessness and propriety. He attained this by spending less and less time with his family, and when obliged to be at home he tried to safeguard his position by the presence of outsiders. The chief thing however was that he had his official duties. The whole interest of his life now centered in the official world and that interest absorbed him. The consciousness of his power, being able to ruin anybody he wished to ruin, the importance, even the external dignity of his entry into court, or meetings with his subordinates, his success with superiors and inferiors, and above all his masterly handling of cases, of which he was conscious—all this gave him pleasure and filled his life, together with chats with his colleagues, dinners, and bridge. So that on the whole Ivan Ilych's life continued to flow as he considered it should do—pleasantly and properly.

So things continued for another seven years. His eldest daughter was already sixteen, another child had died, and only one son was left, a schoolboy and a subject of dissension. Ivan Ilych wanted to put him in the School of Law, but to spite him Praskovya Fedorovna entered him at the High School. The daughter had been educated at home and had turned out well: the boy did not learn badly either.

III

So Ivan Ilych lived for seventeen years after his marriage. He was already a Public Prosecutor of long standing, and had declined several proposed transfers while awaiting a more desirable post, when an unanticipated and unpleasant occurrence quite upset the peaceful course of his life. He was expecting to be offered the post of presiding judge in a University town, but Happe somehow came to the front and obtained the appointment instead. Ivan Ilych became irritable, reproached Happe, and quarrelled both with him and with his immediate superiors—who became colder to him and again passed him over when other appointments were made.

This was in 1880, the hardest year of Ivan Ilych's life. It was then that it became evident on the one hand that his salary was insufficient for them to live on, and on the other that he had been forgotten, and not only this, but that what was for him the greatest and most cruel injustice appeared to others a quite ordinary occurrence. Even his father did not consider it his duty to help him. Ivan Ilych felt himself abandoned by everyone, and that they regarded his position with a salary of 3,500 rubles as quite normal and even fortunate. He alone knew that with the consciousness of the injustices done him, with his wife's incessant nagging, and with the debts he had contracted by living beyond his means, his position was far from normal.

In order to save money that summer he obtained leave of absence and went with his wife to live in the country at her brother's place.

In the country, without his work, he experienced *ennui* for the first time in his life, and not only *ennui* but intolerable depression, and he decided that it was impossible to go on living like that, and that it was necessary to take energetic measures.

Having passed a sleepless night pacing up and down the veranda, he decided to go to Petersburg and bestir himself, in order to punish those who had failed to appreciate him and to get transferred to another ministry.

Next day, despite many protests from his wife and her brother, he started for Petersburg with the sole object of obtaining a post with a salary of five thousand rubles a year. He was no longer bent on any particular department, or tendency, or kind of activity. All he now wanted was an appointment to another post with a salary of five thousand rubles, either in the administration, in the banks, with the railways in one of the Empress Marya's Institutions, or even in the customs—but it had to carry with it a salary of five thousand rubles and be in a ministry other than that in which they had failed to appreciate him.

And this quest of Ivan Ilych's was crowned with remarkable and unexpected success. At Kursk an acquaintance of his, F. I. Ilyin, got into the first-class carriage, sat down beside Ivan Ilych, and told him of a telegram just received by the governor of Kursk announcing that a change was about to take place in the ministry: Peter Ivanovich was to be superseded by Ivan Semonovich.

The proposed change, apart from its significance for Russia, had a special significance for Ivan Ilych, because by bringing forward a new man, Peter Petrovich, and consequently his friend Zachar Ivanovich, it was highly favourable for Ivan Ilych, since Sachar Ivanovich was a friend and colleague of his.

In Moscow this news was confirmed, and on reaching Petersburg Ivan Ilych found Zachar Ivanovich and received a definite promise of an appointment in his former Department of Justice.

A week later he telegraphed to his wife: "Zachar in Miller's place. I shall receive appointment on presentation of report."

Thanks to this change of personnel, Ivan Ilych had unexpectedly obtained an appointment in his former ministry which placed him two states above his former colleagues besides giving him five thousand rubles salary and three thousand five hundred rubles for expenses connected with his removal. All his ill humour towards his former enemies and the whole department vanished, and Ivan Ilych was completely happy.

He returned to the country more cheerful and contented than he had been for a long time. Praskovya Fedorovna also cheered up and a truce was arranged between them. Ivan Ilych told of how he had been feted by everybody in Petersburg, how all those who had been his enemies were put to shame and now fawned on him, how envious they were of his appointment, and how much everybody in Petersburg had liked him.

Praskovya Fedorovna listened to all this and appeared to believe it. She did not contradict anything, but only made plans for their life in the town to which they were going. Ivan Ilych saw with delight that these plans were his plans, that he and his wife agreed, and that, after a stumble, his life was regaining its due and natural character of pleasant lightheartedness and decorum.

Ivan Ilych had come back for a short time only, for he had to take up his new duties on the 10th of September. Moreover, he needed time to settle into the new place, to move all his belongings from the province, and to buy and order many additional things: in a word, to make such arrangements as he had resolved on, which were almost exactly what Praskovya Fedorovna too had decided on.

Now that everything had happened so fortunately, and that he and his wife were at one in their aims and moreover saw so little of one another, they got on together better than they had done since the first years of marriage. Ivan Ilych had thought of taking his family away with him at once, but the insistence of his wife's brother and her sister-in-law, who had suddenly become particularly amiable and friendly to him and his family, induced him to depart alone.

So he departed, and the cheerful state of mind induced by his success and by the harmony between his wife and himself, the one intensifying the other, did not leave him. He found a delightful house, just the thing both he and his wife had dreamt of. Spacious, lofty reception rooms in the old style, a convenient and dignified study, rooms for his wife and daughter, a study for his son—it might have been specially built for them. Ivan Ilych himself superintended the arrangements, chose the wallpapers, supplemented the furniture (preferably with antiques which he considered particularly *comme il faut*), and supervised the upholstering. Everything progressed and progressed and approached the ideal he had set himself: even when things were only half completed they exceeded his expectations. He saw what a refined and elegant character, free from vulgarity, it would all have when it was ready. On falling asleep he pictured to himself how the reception room would look. Looking at the yet unfinished drawing room he could see the fireplace, the screen, the what-not, the little chairs dotted here and there, the dishes and plates on the walls, and the bronzes, as they would be when everything was in place. He was pleased by the thought of how his wife and daughter, who shared his taste in this matter, would be impressed by it. They were certainly not expecting as much. He had been particularly successful in finding, and buying cheaply, antiques which gave a particularly aristocratic character to the whole place. But in his letters he intentionally understated everything in order to be able to surprise them. All this so absorbed him that his new duties—though he liked his official work—interested him less than he had expected. Sometimes he even had moments of absent-mindedness during the court sessions and would consider whether he should have straight or curved cornices for his curtains. He was so interested in it all that he often did things himself, rearranging the furniture, or re-hanging the curtains. Once when mounting a step-ladder to show the upholsterer, who did not understand, how he wanted the hangings draped, he made a false step and slipped, but being a strong and agile man he clung on and only knocked his side against the knob of the window frame. The bruised place was painful but the pain soon passed, and he felt particularly bright and well just then. He wrote: "I feel fifteen years younger." He thought he would have everything ready by September, but it dragged on till mid-October. But the result was charming not only in his eyes but to everyone who saw it.

In reality it was just what is usually seen in the houses of people of moderate means who want to appear rich, and therefore succeed only in resembling others like themselves: there are damasks, dark wood, plants, rugs, and dull and polished bronzes—all the things people of a certain class have in order to resemble other people of that class. His house was so like the others that it would never have been noticed, but to him it all seemed to be quite exceptional. He was very happy when he met his family at the station and brought them to the newly furnished house all lit up, where a footman in a white tie opened the door into the hall decorated with plants, and when they went on into the drawing-room and the study uttering exclamations of delight. He conducted them everywhere, drank in their praises eagerly, and beamed with pleasure. At tea that evening, when Praskovya Fedorovna among others things asked him about his fall, he laughed, and showed them how he had gone flying and had frightened the upholsterer.

"It's a good thing I'm a bit of an athlete. Another man might have been killed, but I merely knocked myself, just here; it hurts when it's touched, but it's passing off already—it's only a bruise."

So they began living in their new home—in which, as always happens, when they got thoroughly settled in they found they were just one room short—and with the increased income, which as always was just a little (some five hundred rubles) too little, but it was all very nice.

Things went particularly well at first, before everything was finally arranged and while something had still to be done: this thing bought, that thing ordered, another thing moved, and something else adjusted. Though there were some disputes between husband and wife, they were both so well satisfied and had so much to do that it all passed off without any serious quarrels. When nothing was left to arrange it became rather dull and something seemed to be lacking, but they were then making acquaintances, forming habits, and life was growing fuller.

Ivan Ilych spent his mornings at the law court and came home to dinner, and at first he was generally in a good humour, though he occasionally became irritable just on account of his house. (Every spot on the tablecloth or the upholstery, and every broken window-blind string, irritated him. He had devoted so much trouble to arranging it all that every disturbance of it distressed him.) But on the whole his life ran its course as he believed life should do: easily, pleasantly, and decorously.

He got up at nine, drank his coffee, read the paper, and then put on his undress uniform and went to the law courts. There the harness in which he worked had already been stretched to fit him and he donned it without a hitch: petitioners, inquiries at the chancery, the chancery itself, and the sittings public and administrative. In all this the thing was to exclude everything fresh and vital, which always disturbs the regular course of official business, and to admit only official relations with people, and then only on official grounds. A man would come, for instance, wanting some information. Ivan Ilych, as one in whose sphere the matter did not lie, would have nothing to do with him: but if the man had some business with him in his official capacity, something that could be expressed on officially stamped paper, he would do everything, positively everything he could within the limits of such relations, and in doing so would maintain the semblance of friendly human relations, that is, would observe the courtesies of life. As soon as the official relations ended, so did everything else. Ivan Ilych possessed this capacity to separate his real life from the official side of affairs and not mix the two, in the highest degree, and by long practice and natural aptitude had brought it to such a pitch that sometimes, in the manner of a virtuoso, he would even allow himself to let the human and official relations mingle. He let himself do this just because he felt that he could at any time he chose resume the strictly official attitude again and drop the human relation, and he did it all easily, pleasantly, correctly, and even artistically. In the intervals between the sessions he smoked, drank tea, chatted a little about politics, a little about general topics, a little about cards, but most of all about official appointments. Tired, but with the feelings of a virtuoso—one of the first violins who has played his part in an orchestra with precision—he would return home to find that his wife and daughter had been out paying calls, or had a visitor, and that his son had been to school, had done his homework with his tutor, and was surely learning what is taught at High Schools. Everything was as it should be. After dinner, if they had no visitors, Ivan Ilych sometimes read a book that was being much discussed at the time, and in the evening settled down to work, that is, read official papers, compared the depositions of witnesses, and noted paragraphs of the Code applying to them. This was neither dull nor amusing. It was dull when he might have been playing bridge, but if no bridge was available it was at any rate better than doing nothing or sitting with his wife. Ivan Ilych's chief pleasure was giving little dinners to which he invited men and women of good social position, and just as his drawing-room resembled all other drawing-rooms so did his enjoyable little parties resemble all other such parties.

Once they even gave a dance. Ivan Ilych enjoyed it and everything went off well, except that it led to a violent quarrel with his wife about the cakes and sweets. Praskovya Fedorovna had made her own plans, but Ivan Ilych insisted on getting everything from an expensive confectioner and ordered too many cakes, and the quarrel occurred because some of those cakes were left over and the confectioner's bill came to forty-five rubles. It was a great and disagreeable quarrel. Praskovya Fedorovna called him "a fool and an imbecile," and he clutched at his head and made angry allusions to divorce.

But the dance itself had been enjoyable. The best people were there, and Ivan Ilych had danced with Princess Trufonova, a sister of the distinguished founder of the Society "Bear My Burden."

The pleasures connected with his work were pleasures of ambition; his social pleasures were those of vanity; but Ivan Ilych's greatest pleasure was playing bridge. He acknowledged that whatever disagreeable incident happened in his life, the pleasure that beamed like a ray of light above everything else was to sit down to bridge with good players, not noisy partners, and of course to four-handed bridge (with five players it was annoying to have to stand out, though one pretended not to mind), to play a clever and serious game (when the cards allowed it) and then to have supper and drink a glass of wine. After a game of bridge, especially if he had won a little (to win a large sum was unpleasant), Ivan Ilych went to bed in a specially good humour.

So they lived. They formed a circle of acquaintances among the best people and were visited by people of importance and by young folk. In their views as to their acquaintances, husband, wife and daughter were entirely agreed, and tacitly and unanimously kept at arm's length and shook off the various shabby friends and relations who, with much show of affection, gushed into the drawing-room with its Japanese plates on the walls. Soon these shabby friends ceased to obtrude themselves and only the best people remained in the Golovins' set.

Young men made up to Lisa, and Petrishchev, an examining magistrate and Dmitri Ivanovich Petrishchev's son and sole heir, began to be so attentive to her that Ivan Ilych had already spoken to Praskovya Fedorovna about it, and considered whether they should not arrange a party for them, or get up some private theatricals.

So they lived, and all went well, without change, and life flowed pleasantly.

IV

They were all in good health. It could not be called ill health if Ivan Ilych sometimes said that he had a queer taste in his mouth and felt some discomfort in his left side.

But this discomfort increased and, though not exactly painful, grew into a sense of pressure in his side accompanied by ill humour. And his irritability became worse and worse and began to mar the agreeable, easy, and correct life that had established itself in the Golovin family. Quarrels between husband and wife became more and more frequent, and soon the ease and amenity disappeared and even the decorum was barely maintained. Scenes again became frequent, and very few of those islets remained on which husband and wife could meet without an explosion. Praskovya Fedorovna now had good reason to say that her husband's temper was trying. With characteristic exaggeration she said he had always had a dreadful temper, and that it had needed all her good nature to put up with it for twenty years. It was true that now the quarrels were started by him. His bursts of temper always came just before dinner, often just as he began to eat his soup. Sometimes he noticed that a plate or dish was chipped, or the food was not right, or his son put his elbow on the table, or his daughter's hair was not done as he liked it, and for all this he blamed Praskovya Fedorovna. At first she retorted and said disagreeable things to him, but once or twice he fell into such a rage at the beginning of dinner that she realized it was due to some physical derangement brought on by taking food, and so she restrained herself and did not answer, but only hurried to get the dinner over. She regarded this self-restraint as highly praiseworthy. Having come to the conclusion that her husband had a dreadful temper and made her life miserable, she began to feel sorry for herself, and the more she pitied herself the more she hated her husband. She began to wish he would die; yet she did not want him to die because then his salary would cease. And this irritated her against him still more. She considered herself dreadfully unhappy just because not even his death could save her, and though she concealed her exasperation, that hidden exasperation of hers increased his irritation also.

After one scene in which Ivan Ilych had been particularly unfair and after which he had said in explanation that he certainly was irritable but that it was due to his not being well, she said that he was ill it should be attended to, and insisted on his going to see a celebrated doctor.

He went. Everything took place as he had expected and as it always does. There was the usual waiting and the important air assumed by the doctor, with which he was so familiar (resembling that which he himself assumed in court), and the sounding and listening, and the questions which called for answers that were foregone conclusions and were evidently unnecessary, and the look of importance which implied that "if only you put yourself in our hands we will arrange everything—we know indubitably how it has to be done, always in the same way for everybody alike." It was all just as it was in the law courts. The doctor put on just the same air towards him as he himself put on towards an accused person.

The doctor said that so-and-so indicated that there was so-and-so inside the patient, but if the investigation of so-and-so did not confirm this, then he must assume that and that. If he assumed that and that, then . . . and so on. To Ivan Ilych only one question was important: was his case serious or not? But the doctor ignored that inappropriate question. From his point of view it was not the one under consideration, the real question was to decide between a floating kidney, chronic catarrh, or appendicitis. It was not a question the doctor solved brilliantly, as it seemed to Ivan Ilych, in favour of the appendix, with the reservation that should an examination of the urine give fresh indications the matter would be reconsidered. All this was just what Ivan Ilych had himself brilliantly accomplished a thousand times in dealing with men on trial. The doctor summed up just as brilliantly, looking over his spectacles triumphantly and even gaily at the accused. From the doctor's summing up Ivan Ilych concluded that things were bad, but that for the doctor, and perhaps for everybody else, it was a matter of indifference, though for him it was bad. And this conclusion struck him painfully, arousing in him a great feeling of pity for himself and of bitterness towards the doctor's indifference to a matter of such importance.

He said nothing of this, but rose, placed the doctor's fee on the table, and remarked with a sigh: "We sick people probably often put inappropriate questions. But tell me, in general, is this complaint dangerous, or not? . . ."

The doctor looked at him sternly over his spectacles with one eye, as if to say: "Prisoner, if you will not keep to the questions put to you, I shall be obliged to have you removed from the court."

"I have already told you what I consider necessary and proper. The analysis may show something more." And the doctor bowed.

Ivan Ilych went out slowly, seated himself disconsolately in his sledge, and drove home. All the way home he was going over what the doctor had said, trying to translate those complicated, obscure, scientific phrases into plain language and find in them an answer to the question: "Is my condition bad? Is it very bad? Or is there as yet nothing much wrong?" And it seemed to him that the meaning of what the doctor had said was that it was very bad. Everything in the streets seemed depressing. The cabmen, the houses, the passers-by, and the shops, were dismal. His ache, this dull gnawing ache that never ceased for a moment, seemed to have acquired a new and more serious significance from the doctor's dubious remarks. Ivan Ilych now watched it with a new and oppressive feeling.

He reached home and began to tell his wife about it. She listened, but in the middle of his account his daughter came in with her hat on, ready to go out with her mother. She sat down reluctantly to listen to this tedious story, but could not stand it long, and her mother too did not hear him to the end.

"Well, I am very glad," she said. "Mind now to take your medicine regularly. Give me the prescription and I'll send Gerasim to the chemist's." And she went to get ready to go out.

While she was in the room Ivan Ilych had hardly taken time to breathe, but he sighed deeply when she left it.

"Well," he thought, "perhaps it isn't so bad after all."

He began taking his medicine and following the doctor's directions, which had been altered after the examination of the urine, but then it happened that there was a contradiction between the indications drawn from the examination of the urine and the symptoms that showed themselves. It turned out that what was happening differed from what the doctor had told him, and that he had either forgotten or blundered, or hidden something from him. He could not, however, be blamed for that, and Ivan Ilych still obeyed his orders implicitly and at first derived some comfort from doing so.

From the time of his visit to the doctor, Ivan Ilych's chief occupation was the exact fulfillment of the doctor's instructions regarding hygiene and the taking of medicine, and the observation of his pain and his excretions. His chief interest came to be people's ailments and people's health. When sickness, deaths, or recoveries were mentioned in his presence, especially when the illness resembled his own, he listened with agitation which he tried to hide, asked questions, and applied what he heard to his own case.

The pain did not grow less, but Ivan Ilych made efforts to force himself to think that he was better. And he could do this so long as nothing agitated him. But as soon as he had any unpleasantness with his wife, any lack of success in his official work, or held bad cards at bridge, he was at once acutely sensible of his disease. He had formerly borne such mischances, hoping soon to adjust what was wrong, to master it and attain success, or make a grand slam. But now every mischance upset him and plunged him into despair. He would say to himself: "there now, just as I was beginning to get better and the medicine had begun to take effect, comes this accursed misfortune, or unpleasantness . . ." And he was furious with the mishap, or with the people who were causing the unpleasantness and killing him, for he felt that this fury was killing him but he could not restrain it. One would have thought that it should have been clear to him that this exasperation with circumstances and people aggravated his illness, and that he ought therefore to ignore unpleasant occurrences. But he drew the very opposite conclusion: he said that he needed peace, and he watched for everything that might disturb it and became irritable at the slightest infringement of it. His condition was rendered worse by the fact that he read medical books and consulted doctors. The progress of his disease was so gradual that he could deceive himself when comparing one day with another— the difference was so slight. But when he consulted the doctors it seemed to him that he was getting worse, and even very rapidly. Yet despite this he was continually consulting them.

That month he went to see another celebrity, who told him almost the same as the first had done but put his questions rather differently, and the interview with this celebrity only increased Ivan Ilych's doubts and fears. A friend of a friend of his, a very good doctor, diagnosed his illness again quite differently from the others, and though he predicted recovery, his questions and suppositions bewildered Ivan Ilych still more and increased his doubts. A homeopathist diagnosed the disease in yet another way, and prescribed medicine which Ivan Ilych took secretly for a week. But after a week, not feeling any improvement and having lost confidence both in the former doctor's treatment and in this one's, he became still more despondent. One day a lady acquaintance mentioned a cure effected by a wonder-working icon. Ivan Ilych caught himself listening attentively and beginning to believe that it had occurred. This incident alarmed him. "Has my mind really weakened to such an extent?" he asked himself. "Nonsense! It's all rubbish. I mustn't give way to nervous fears but having chosen a doctor must keep strictly to his treatment. That is what I will do. Now it's all settled. I won't think about it, but will follow the treatment seriously till summer, and then we shall see. From now there must be no more of this wavering!" This was easy to say but impossible to carry out. The pain in his side oppressed him and seemed to grow worse and more incessant, while the taste in his mouth grew stranger and stranger. It seemed to him that his breath had a disgusting smell, and he was conscious of a loss of appetite and strength. There was no deceiving himself: something terrible, new, and more important than anything before in his life, was taking place within him of which he alone was aware. Those about him did not understand or would not understand it, but thought everything in the world was going on as usual. That tormented Ivan Ilych more than anything. He saw that his household, especially his wife and daughter who were in a perfect whirl of visiting, did not understand anything of it and were annoyed that he was so depressed and so exacting, as if he were to blame for it. Though they tried to disguise it he saw that he was an obstacle in their path, and that his wife had adopted a definite line in regard to his illness and kept to it regardless of anything he said or did. Her attitude was this: "You know," she would say to her friends, "Ivan Ilych can't do as other people do, and keep to the treatment prescribed for him. One day he'll take his drops and keep strictly to his diet and go to bed in good time, but the next day unless I watch him he'll suddenly forget his medicine, eat sturgeon—which is forbidden—and sit up playing cards till one o'clock in the morning."

"Oh, come, when was that?" Ivan Ilych would ask in vexation. "Only once at Peter Ivanovich's."

"And yesterday with Shebek."

"Well, even if I hadn't stayed up, this pain would have kept me awake."

"Be that as it may you'll never get well like that, but will always make us wretched."

Praskovya Fedorovna's attitude to Ivan Ilych's illness, as she expressed it both to others and to him, was that it was his own fault and was another of the annoyances he caused her. Ivan Ilych felt that this opinion escaped her involuntarily—but that did not make it easier for him.

At the law courts too, Ivan Ilych noticed, or thought he noticed, a strange attitude towards himself. It sometimes seemed to him that people were watching him inquisitively as a man whose place might soon be vacant. Then again, his friends would suddenly begin to chaff him in a friendly way about his low spirits, as if the awful, horrible, and unheard-of thing that was going on within him, incessantly gnawing at him and irresistibly drawing him away, was a very agreeable subject for jests. Schwartz in particular irritated him by his jocularity, vivacity, and *savoir-faire*, which reminded him of what he himself had been ten years ago.

Friends came to make up a set and they sat down to cards. They dealt, bending the new cards to soften them, and he sorted the diamonds in his hand and found he had seven. His partner said "No trumps" and supported him with two diamonds. What more could be wished for? It ought to be jolly and lively. They would make a grand slam. But suddenly Ivan Ilych was conscious of that gnawing pain, that taste in his mouth, and it seemed ridiculous that in such circumstances he should be pleased to make a grand slam.

He looked at his partner Mikhail Mikhaylovich, who rapped the table with his strong hand and instead of snatching up the tricks pushed the cards courteously and indulgently towards Ivan Ilych that he might have the pleasure of gathering them up without the trouble of stretching out his hand for them. "Does he think I am too weak to stretch out my arm?" thought Ivan Ilych, and forgetting what he was doing he over-trumped his partner, missing the grand slam by three tricks. And what was most awful of all was that he saw how upset Mikhail Mikhaylovich was about it but did not himself care. And it was dreadful to realize why he did not care.

They all saw that he was suffering, and said: "We can stop if you are tired. Take a rest." Lie down? No, he was not at all tired, and he finished the rubber. All were gloomy and silent. Ivan Ilych felt that he had diffused this gloom over them and could not dispel it. They had supper and went away, and Ivan Ilych was left alone with the consciousness that his life was poisoned and was poisoning the lives of others, and that this poison did not weaken but penetrated more and more deeply into his whole being.

With this consciousness, and with physical pain besides the terror, he must go to bed, often to lie awake the greater part of the night. Next morning he had to get up again, dress, go to the law courts, speak, and write; or if he did not go out, spend at home those twenty-four hours a day each of which was a torture. And he had to live thus all alone on the brink of an abyss, with no one who understood or pitied him.

V

So one month passed and then another. Just before the New Year his brother-in-law came to town and stayed at their house. Ivan Ilych was at the law courts and Praskovya Fedorovna had gone shopping. When Ivan Ilych came home and entered his study he found his brother-in-law there—a healthy, florid man—unpacking his portmanteau himself. He raised his head on hearing Ivan Ilych's footsteps and looked up at him for a moment without a word. That stare told Ivan Ilych everything. His brother-in-law opened his mouth to utter an exclamation of surprise but checked himself, and that action confirmed it all.

"I have changed, eh?"

"Yes, there is a change."

And after that, try as he would to get his brother-in-law to return to the subject of his looks, the latter would say nothing about it. Praskovya Fedorovna came home and her brother went out to her. Ivan Ilych locked the door and began to examine himself in the glass, first full face, then in profile. He took up a portrait of himself taken with his wife, and compared it with what he saw in the glass. The change in him was immense. Then he bared his arms to the elbow, looked at them, drew the sleeves down again, sat down on an ottoman, and grew blacker than night.

"No, no, this won't do!" he said to himself, and jumped up, went to the table, took up some law papers and began to read them, but could not continue. He unlocked the door and went into the reception-room. The door leading to the drawing-room was shut. He approached it on tiptoe and listened.

"No, you are exaggerating!" Praskovya Fedorovna was saying.

"Exaggerating! Don't you see it? Why, he's a dead man! Look at his eyes—there's no life in them. But what is it that is wrong with him?"

"No one knows. Nikolaevich [that was another doctor] said something, but I don't know what. And Seshchetitsky [this was the celebrated specialist] said quite the contrary . . ."

Ivan Ilych walked away, went to his own room, lay down, and began musing; "The kidney, a floating kidney." He recalled all the doctors had told him of how it detached itself and swayed about. And by an effort of imagination he tried to catch that kidney and arrest it and support it. So little was needed for this, it seemed to him. "No, I'll go to see Peter Ivanovich again." [That was the friend whose friend was a doctor.] He rang, ordered the carriage, and got ready to go.

"Where are you going, Jean?" asked his wife with a specially sad and exceptionally kind look.

This exceptionally kind look irritated him. He looked morosely at her.

"I must go to see Peter Ivanovich."

He went to see Peter Ivanovich, and together they went to see his friend, the doctor. He was in, and Ivan Ilych had a long talk with him.

Reviewing the anatomical and physiological details of what in the doctor's opinion was going on inside him, he understood it all.

There was something, a small thing, in the vermiform appendix. It might all come right. Only stimulate the energy of one organ and check the activity of another, then absorption would take place and everything would come right. He got home rather late for dinner, ate his dinner, and conversed cheerfully, but could not for a long time bring himself to go back to work in his room. At last, however, he went to his study and did what was necessary, but the consciousness that he had put something aside—an important, intimate matter which he would revert to when his work was done—never left him. When he had finished his work he remembered that this intimate matter was the thought of his vermiform appendix. But he did not give himself up to it, and went to the drawing-room for tea. There were callers there, including the examining magistrate who was a desirable match for his daughter, and they were conversing, playing the piano, and singing. Ivan Ilych, as Praskovya Fedorovna remarked, spent that evening more cheerfully than usual, but he never for a moment forgot that he had postponed the important mater of the appendix. At eleven o'clock he said goodnight and went to his bedroom. Since his illness he had slept alone in a small room next to his study. He undressed and took up a novel by Zola, but instead of reading it he fell into thought, and in his imagination that desired improvement in the vermiform appendix occurred. There was the absorption and evacuation and the re-establishment of normal activity. "Yes, that's it!" he said to himself. "One need only assist nature, that's all." He remembered his medicine, rose, took it, and lay down on his back watching for the beneficent action of the medicine and for it to lessen the pain. "I need only take it regularly and avoid all injurious influences. I am already feeling better, much better." He began touching his side: it was not painful to the touch. "There, I really don't feel it. It's much better already." He put out the light and turned on his side. . . "The appendix is getting better, absorption is occurring." Suddenly he felt the old, familiar, dull, gnawing pain, stubborn and serious. There was the same familiar loathsome taste in his mouth. His heart sank and he felt dazed. "My God! My God!" he muttered. "Again, again! And it will never cease." And suddenly the matter presented itself in a quite different aspect. "Vermiform appendix! Kidney!" he said to himself. "It's not a question of appendix or kidney, but of life and . . . death. Yes, life was there and now it is going, going and I cannot stop it. Yes. Why deceive myself? Isn't it obvious to everyone but me that I'm dying, and that it's only a question of weeks, days . . . it may happen this moment. There was light and now there is darkness. I was here and now I'm going there! Where?" A chill came over him, his breathing ceased, and he felt only the throbbing of his heart.

"When I am not, what will there be? There will be nothing. Then where shall I be when I am no more? Can this be dying? No, I don't want to!" He jumped up and tried to light the candle, felt for it with trembling hands, dropped candle and candlestick on the floor, and fell back on his pillow.

"What's the use? It makes no difference," he said to himself, staring with wide-open eyes into the darkness. "Death. Yes, death. And none of them knows or wishes to know it, and they have no pity for me. Now they are playing." (He heard through the door the distant sound of a song and its accompaniment.) "It's all the same to them, but they will die too! Fools! I first, and they later, but it will be the same for them. And now they are merry . . . the beasts!"

Anger choked him and he was agonizingly, unbearably miserable. "It is impossible that all men have been doomed to suffer this awful horror!" He raised himself.

"Something must be wrong. I must calm myself—must think it all over from the beginning." And he again began thinking. "Yes, the beginning of my illness: I knocked my side, but I was still quite well that day and the next. It hurt a little, then rather more.

I saw the doctors, then followed despondency and anguish, more doctors, and I drew nearer to the abyss. My strength grew less and I kept coming nearer and nearer, and now I have wasted away and there is no light in my eyes. I think of the appendix—but this is death! I think of mending the appendix, and all the while here is death! Can it really be death?" Again terror seized him and he gasped for breath. He leant down and began feeling for the matches, pressing with his elbow on the stand beside the bed. It was in his way and hurt him, he grew furious with it, pressed on it still harder, and upset it. Breathless and in despair he fell on his back, expecting death to come immediately.

Meanwhile the visitors were leaving. Praskovya Fedorovna was seeing them off. She heard something fall and came in.

"What has happened?"

"Nothing. I knocked it over accidentally."

She went out and returned with a candle. He lay there panting heavily, like a man who has run a thousand yards, and stared upwards at her with a fixed look.

"What is it, Jean?"

"No . . . o . . . thing. I upset it." ("Why speak of it? She won't understand," he thought.)

And in truth she did not understand. She picked up the stand, lit his candle, and hurried away to see another visitor off. When she came back he still lay on his back, looking upwards.

"What is it? Do you feel worse?"

"Yes."

She shook her head and sat down.

"Do you know, Jean, I think we must ask Leshchetitsky to come and see you here."

This meant calling in the famous specialist, regardless of expense. He smiled malignantly and said "No." She remained a little longer and then went up to him and kissed his forehead.

While she was kissing him he hated her from the bottom of his soul and with difficulty refrained from pushing her away.

"Good night. Please God you'll sleep."

"Yes."

VI

Ivan Ilych saw that he was dying, and he was in continual despair.

In the depth of his heart he knew he was dying, but not only was he not accustomed to the thought, he simply did not and could not grasp it.

The syllogism he had learnt from Kiesewetter's Logic: "Caius is a man, men are mortal, therefore Caius is mortal," had always seemed to him correct as applied to Caius, but certainly not as applied to himself. That Caius—man in the abstract—was mortal, was perfectly correct, but he was not Caius, not an abstract man, but a creature quite, quite separate from all others. He had been little Vanya, with a mamma and a papa, with Mitya and Volodya, with the toys, a coachman and a nurse, afterwards with Katenka and with all the joys, griefs, and delights of childhood, boyhood, and youth. What did Caius know of the smell of that striped leather ball Vanya had been so fond of? Had Caius kissed his mother's hand like that, and did the silk of her dress rustle so for Caius? Had he rioted like that at school when the pastry was bad? Had Caius been in love like that? Could Caius preside at a session as he did? "Caius really was mortal, and it was right for him to die; but for me, little Vanya, Ivan Ilych, with all my thoughts and emotions, it's altogether a different matter. It cannot be that I ought to die. That would be too terrible."

Such was his feeling.

"If I had to die like Caius I would have known it was so. An inner voice would have told me so, but there was nothing of the sort in me and I and all my friends felt that our case was quite different from that of Caius. and now here it is!" he said to himself. "It can't be. It's impossible! But here it is. How is this? How is one to understand it?"

He could not understand it, and tried to drive this false, incorrect, morbid thought away and to replace it by other proper and healthy thoughts. But that thought, and not the thought only but the reality itself, seemed to come and confront him.

And to replace that thought he called up a succession of others, hoping to find in them some support. He tried to get back into the former current of thoughts that had once screened the thought of death from him. But strange to say, all that had formerly shut off, hidden, and destroyed his consciousness of death, no longer had that effect. Ivan Ilych now spent most of his time in attempting to re-establish that old current. He would say to himself: "I will take up my duties again—after all I used to live by them." And banishing all doubts he would go to the law courts, enter into conversation with his colleagues, and sit carelessly as was his wont, scanning the crowd with a thoughtful look and leaning both his emaciated arms on the arms of his oak chair; bending over as usual to a colleague and drawing his papers nearer he would interchange whispers with him, and then suddenly raising his eyes and sitting erect would pronounce certain words and open the proceedings. But suddenly in the midst of those proceedings the pain in his side, regardless of the stage the proceedings had reached, would begin its own gnawing work. Ivan Ilych would turn his attention to it and try to drive the thought of it away, but without success. *It* would come and stand before him and look at him, and he would be petrified and the light would die out of his eyes, and he would again begin asking himself whether *It* alone was true. And his colleagues and subordinates would see with surprise and distress that he, the brilliant and subtle judge, was becoming confused and making mistakes. He would shake himself, try to pull himself together, manage somehow to bring the sitting to a close, and return home with the sorrowful consciousness that his judicial labours could not as formerly hide from him what he wanted them to hide, and could not deliver him from *It*. And what was worst of all was that *It* drew his attention to itself not in order to make him take some action but only that he should look at *It*, look it straight in the face: look at it and without doing anything, suffer inexpressibly.

And to save himself from this condition Ivan Ilych looked for consolations—new screens—and new screens were found and for a while seemed to save him, but then they immediately fell to pieces or rather became transparent, as if *It* penetrated them and nothing could veil *It*.

In these latter days he would go into the drawing-room he had arranged—that drawing-room where he had fallen and for the sake of which (how bitterly ridiculous it seemed) he had sacrificed his life—for he knew that his illness originated with that knock. He would enter and see that something had scratched the polished table. He would look for the cause of this and find that it was the bronze ornamentation of an album, that had got bent. He would take up the expensive album which he had lovingly arranged, and feel vexed with his daughter and her friends for their untidiness—for the album was torn here and there and some of the photographs turned upside down. He would put it carefully in order and bend the ornamentation back into position. Then it would occur to him to place all those things in another corner of the room, near the plants. He would call the footman, but his daughter or wife would come to help him. They would not agree, and his wife would contradict him, and he would dispute and grow angry. But that was all right, for then he did not think about *It*. *It* was invisible.

But then, when he was moving something himself, his wife would say: "Let the servants do it. You will hurt yourself again." And suddenly *It* would flash through the screen and he would see it. It was just a flash, and he hoped it would disappear, but he would involuntarily pay attention to his side. "It sits there as before, gnawing just the same!" And he could no longer forget *It*, but could distinctly see it looking at him from behind the flowers. "What is it all for?"

"It really is so! I lost my life over that curtain as I might have done when storming a fort. Is that possible? How terrible and how stupid. It can't be true! It can't, but it is."

He would go to his study, lie down, and again be alone with *It*: face to face with *It*. And nothing could be done with *It* except to look at it and shudder.

VII

How it happened it is impossible to say because it came about step by step, unnoticed, but in the third month of Ivan Ilych's illness, his wife, his daughter, his son, his acquaintances, the doctors, the servants, and above all he himself, were aware that the whole interest he had for other people was whether he would soon vacate his place, and at last release the living from the discomfort caused by his presence and be himself released from his sufferings.

He slept less and less. He was given opium and hypodermic injections of morphine, but this did not relieve him. The dull depression he experienced in a somnolent condition at first gave him a little relief, but only as something new; afterwards it became as distressing as the pain itself or even more so.

Special foods were prepared for him by the doctors' orders, but all those foods became increasingly distasteful and disgusting to him.

For his excretions also special arrangements had to be made, and this was a torment to him every time—a torment from the uncleanliness, the unseemliness, and the smell, and from knowing that another person had to take part in it.

But just through this most unpleasant matter, Ivan Ilych obtained comfort. Gerasim, the butler's young assistant, always came in to carry the things out. Gerasim was a clean, fresh peasant lad, grown stout on town food and always cheerful and bright. At first the sight of him, in his clean Russian peasant costume, engaged on that disgusting task embarrassed Ivan Ilych.

Once when he got up from the commode too weak to draw up his trousers, he dropped into a soft armchair and looked with horror at his bare, enfeebled thighs with the muscles so sharply marked on them.

Gerasim with a firm light tread, his heavy boots emitting a pleasant smell of tar and fresh winter air, came in wearing a clean Hessian apron, the sleeves of his print shirt tucked up over his strong bare young arms; and refraining from looking at his sick master out of consideration for his feelings, and restraining the joy of life that beamed from his face, he went up to the commode.

"Gerasim!" said Ivan Ilych in a weak voice.

Gerasim started, evidently afraid he might have committed some blunder, and with a rapid movement turned his fresh, kind, simple young face which just showed the first downy signs of a beard.

"Yes, sir?"

"That must be very unpleasant for you. You must forgive me. I am helpless."

"Oh, why, sir," and Gerasim's eyes beamed and he showed his glistening white teeth, "what's a little trouble? It's a case of illness with you, sir."

And his deft strong hands did their accustomed task, and he went out of the room stepping lightly. Five minutes later he as lightly returned.

Ivan Ilych was still sitting in the same position in the armchair.

"Gerasim," he said when the latter had replaced the freshly-washed utensil. "Please come here and help me." Gerasim went up to him. "Lift me up. It is hard for me to get up, and I have sent Dmitri away."

Gerasim went up to him, grasped his master with his strong arms deftly but gently, in the same way that he stepped—lifted him, supported him with one hand, and with the other drew up his trousers and would have set him down again, but Ivan Ilych asked to be led to the sofa. Gerasim, without an effort and without apparent pressure, led him, almost lifting him, to the sofa and placed him on it.

"Thank you. How easily and well you do it all!"

Gerasim smiled again and turned to leave the room. But Ivan Ilych felt his presence such a comfort that he did not want to let him go.

"One thing more, please move up that chair. No, the other one—under my feet. It is easier for me when my feet are raised."

Gerasim brought the chair, set it down gently in place, and raised Ivan Ilych's legs on it. It seemed to Ivan Ilych that he felt better while Gerasim was holding up his legs.

"It's better when my legs are higher," he said. "Place that cushion under them."

Gerasim did so. He again lifted the legs and placed them, and again Ivan Ilych felt better while Gerasim held his legs. When he set them down Ivan Ilych fancied he felt worse.

"Gerasim," he said. "Are you busy now?"

"Not at all, sir," said Gerasim, who had learnt from the townsfolk how to speak to gentlefolk.

"What have you still to do?"

"What have I to do? I've done everything except chopping the logs for tomorrow."

"Then hold my legs up a bit higher, can you?"

"Of course I can. Why not?" and Gerasim raised his master's legs higher and Ivan Ilych thought that in that position he did not feel any pain at all.

"And how about the logs?"

"Don't trouble about that, sir. There's plenty of time."

Ivan Ilych told Gerasim to sit down and hold his legs, and began to talk to him. And strange to say it seemed to him that he felt better while Gerasim held his legs up.

After that Ivan Ilych would sometimes call Gerasim and get him to hold his legs on his shoulders, and he liked talking to him. Gerasim did it all easily, willingly, simply, and with a good nature that touched Ivan Ilych. Health, strength, and vitality in other people were offensive to him, but Gerasim's strength and vitality did not mortify but soothed him.

What tormented Ivan Ilych most was the deception, the lie, which for some reason they all accepted, that he was not dying but was simply ill, and he only need keep quiet and undergo a treatment and then something very good would result. He however knew that do what they would nothing would come of it, only still more agonizing suffering and death. This deception tortured him—their not wishing to admit what they all knew and what he knew, but wanting to lie to him concerning his terrible condition, and wishing and forcing him to participate in that lie. Those lies—lies enacted over him on the eve of his death and destined to degrade this awful, solemn act to the level of their visitings, their curtains, their sturgeon for dinner—were a terrible agony for Ivan Ilych. And strangely enough, many times when they were going through their antics over him he had been within a hairbreadth of calling out to them: "Stop lying! You know and I know that I am dying. Then at least stop lying about it!" But he had never had the spirit to do it. The awful, terrible act of his dying was, he could see, reduced by those about him to the level of a casual, unpleasant, and almost indecorous incident (as if someone entered a drawing room defusing an unpleasant odour) and this was done by that very decorum which he had served all his life long. He saw that no one felt for him, because no one even wished to grasp his position. Only Gerasim recognized it and pitied him. And so Ivan Ilych felt at ease only with him. He felt comforted when Gerasim supported his legs (sometimes all night long) and refused to go to bed, saying: "Don't you worry, Ivan Ilych. I'll get sleep enough later on," or when he suddenly became familiar and exclaimed: "If you weren't sick it would be another matter, but as it is, why should I grudge a little trouble?" Gerasim alone did not lie; everything showed that he alone understood the facts of the case and did not consider it necessary to disguise them, but simply felt sorry for his emaciated and enfeebled master. Once when Ivan Ilych was sending him away he even said straight out: "We shall all of us die, so why should I grudge a little trouble?"—expressing the fact that he did not think his work burdensome, because he was doing it for a dying man and hoped someone would do the same for him when his time came.

Apart from this lying, or because of it, what most tormented Ivan Ilych was that no one pitied him as he wished to be pitied. At certain moments after prolonged suffering he wished most of all (though he would have been ashamed to confess it) for someone to pity him as a sick child is pitied. He longed to be petted and comforted. He knew he was an important functionary, that he had a beard turning grey, and that therefore what he longed for was impossible, but still he longed for it. And in Gerasim's attitude towards him there was something akin to what he wished for, and so that attitude comforted him. Ivan Ilych wanted to weep, wanted to be petted and cried over, and then his colleague Shebek would come, and instead of weeping and being petted, Ivan Ilych would assume a serious, severe, and profound air, and by force of habit would express his opinion on a decision of the Court of Cassation and would stubbornly insist on that view. This falsity around him and within him did more than anything else to poison his last days.

VIII

It was morning. He knew it was morning because Gerasim had gone, and Peter the footman had come and put out the candles, drawn back one of the curtains, and begun quietly to tidy up. Whether it was morning or evening, Friday or Sunday, made no difference, it was all just the same: the gnawing, unmitigated, agonizing pain, never ceasing for an instant, the consciousness of life inexorably waning but not yet extinguished, the approach of that ever dreaded and hateful Death which was the only reality, and always the same falsity. What were days, weeks, hours, in such a case?

"Will you have some tea, sir?"

"He wants things to be regular, and wishes the gentlefolk to drink tea in the morning," thought Ivan Ilych, and only said "No."

"Wouldn't you like to move onto the sofa, sir?"

"He wants to tidy up the room, and I'm in the way. I am uncleanliness and disorder," he thought, and said only:

"No, leave me alone."

The man went on bustling about. Ivan Ilych stretched out his hand. Peter came up, ready to help.

"What is it, sir?"

"My watch."

Peter took the watch which was close at hand and gave it to his master.

"Half-past eight. Are they up?"

"No sir, except Vladimir Ivanovich" (the son) "who has gone to school. Praskovya Fedorovna ordered me to wake her if you asked for her. Shall I do so?"

"No, there's no need to." "Perhaps I'd better have some tea," he thought, and added aloud: "Yes, bring me some tea."

Peter went to the door, but Ivan Ilych dreaded being left alone. "How can I keep him here? Oh yes, my medicine." "Peter, give me my medicine." "Why not? Perhaps it may still do some good." He took a spoonful and swallowed it. "No, it won't help. It's all tomfoolery, all deception," he decided as soon as he became aware of the familiar, sickly, hopeless taste. "No, I can't believe in it any longer. But the pain, why this pain? If it would only cease just for a moment!" And he moaned. Peter turned towards him. "It's all right. Go and fetch me some tea."

Peter went out. Left alone Ivan Ilych groaned not so much with pain, terrible though that was, as from mental anguish. Always and for ever the same, always these endless days and nights. If only it would come quicker! If only *what* would come quicker? Death, darkness? . . . No, no! anything rather than death!

When Peter returned with the tea on a tray, Ivan Ilych stared at him for a time in perplexity, not realizing who and what he was. Peter was disconcerted by that look and his embarrassment brought Ivan Ilych to himself.

"Oh, tea! All right, put it down. Only help me to wash and put on a clean shirt."

And Ivan Ilych began to wash. With pauses for rest, he washed his hands and then his face, cleaned his teeth, brushed his hair, looked in the glass. He was terrified by what he saw, especially by the limp way in which his hair clung to his pallid forehead.

While his shirt was being changed he knew that he would be still more frightened at the sight of his body, so he avoided looking at it. Finally he was ready. He drew on a dressing-gown, wrapped himself in a plaid, and sat down in the armchair to take his tea. For a moment he felt refreshed, but as soon as he began to drink the tea he was again aware of the same taste, and the pain also returned. He finished it with an effort, and then lay down stretching out his legs, and dismissed Peter.

Always the same. Now a spark of hope flashes up, then a sea of despair rages, and always pain; always pain, always despair, and always the same. When alone he had a dreadful and distressing desire to call someone, but he knew beforehand that with others present it would be still worse. "Another dose of morphine—to lose consciousness. I will tell him, the doctor, that he must think of something else. It's impossible, impossible, to go on like this."

An hour and another pass like that. But now there is a ring at the door bell. Perhaps it's the doctor? It is. He comes in fresh, hearty, plump, and cheerful, with that look on his face that seems to say: "There now, you're in a panic about something, but we'll arrange it all for you directly!" The doctor knows this expression is out of place here, but he has put it on once for all and can't take it off—like a man who has put on a frock-coat in the morning to pay a round of calls.

The doctor rubs his hands vigorously and reassuringly.

"Brr! How cold it is! There's such a sharp frost; just let me warm myself!" he says, as if it were only a matter of waiting till he was warm, and then he would put everything right.

"Well now, how are you?"

Ivan Ilych feels that the doctor would like to say: "Well, how are our affairs?" but that even he feels that this would not do, and says instead: "What sort of a night have you had?"

Ivan Ilych looks at him as much as to say: "Are you really never ashamed of lying?" But the doctor does not wish to understand this question, and Ivan Ilych says: "Just as terrible as ever. The pain never leaves me and never subsides. If only something . . ."

"Yes, you sick people are always like that . . . There, now I think I am warm enough. Even Praskovya Fedorovna, who is so particular, could find no fault with my temperature. Well, now I can say good-morning," and the doctor presses his patient's hand.

Then dropping his former playfulness, he begins with a most serious face to examine the patient, feeling his pulse and taking his temperature, and then begins the sounding and auscultation.

Ivan Ilych knows quite well and definitely that all this is nonsense and pure deception, but when the doctor, getting down on his knee, leans over him, putting his ear first higher then lower, and performs various gymnastic movements over him with a significant expression on his face, Ivan Ilych submits to it all as he used to submit to the speeches of the lawyers, though he knew very well that they were all lying and why they were lying.

The doctor, kneeling on the sofa, is still sounding him when Praskovya Fedorovna's silk dress rustles at the door and she is heard scolding Peter for not having let her know of the doctor's arrival.

She comes in, kisses her husband, and at once proceeds to prove that she has been up a long time already, and only owing to a misunderstanding failed to be there when the doctor arrived.

Ivan Ilych looks at her, scans her all over, sets against her the whiteness and plumpness and cleanness of her hands and neck, the gloss of her hair, and the sparkle of her vivacious eyes. He hates her with his whole soul. And the thrill of hatred he feels for her makes him suffer from her touch.

Her attitude towards him and his disease is still the same. Just as the doctor had adopted a certain relation to his patient which he could not abandon, so had she formed one towards him—that he was not doing something he ought to do and was himself to blame, and that she reproached him lovingly for this—and she could not now change that attitude.

"You see he doesn't listen to me and doesn't take his medicine at the proper time. And above all he lies in a position that is no doubt bad for him—with his legs up."

She described how he made Gerasim hold his legs up.

The doctor smiled with a contemptuous affability that said: "What's to be done? These sick people do have foolish fancies of that kind, but we must forgive them."

When the examination was over the doctor looked at his watch, and then Praskovya Fedorovna announced to Ivan Ilych that it was of course as he pleased, but she had sent today for a celebrated specialist who would examine him and have a consultation with Michael Danilovich (their regular doctor).

"Please don't raise any objections. I am doing this for my own sake," she said ironically, letting it be felt that she was doing it all for his sake and only said this to leave him no right to refuse. He remained silent, knitting his brows. He felt that he was surrounded and involved in a mesh of falsity that it was hard to unravel anything.

Everything she did for him was entirely for her own sake, and she told him she was doing for herself what she actually was doing for herself, as if that was so incredible that he must understand the opposite.

At half-past eleven the celebrated specialist arrived. Again the sounding began and the significant conversations in his presence and in another room, about the kidneys and the appendix, and the questions and answers, with such an air of importance that again, instead of the real question of life and death which now alone confronted him, the question arose of the kidney and appendix which were not behaving as they ought to and would now be attached by Michael Danilovich and the specialist and forced to amend their ways.

The celebrated specialist took leave of him with a serious though not hopeless look, and in reply to the timid question Ivan Ilych, with eyes glistening with fear and hope, put to him as to whether there was a chance of recovery, said that he could not vouch for it but there was a possibility. The look of hope with which Ivan Ilych watched the doctor out was so pathetic that Praskovya Fedorovna, seeing it, even wept as she left the room to hand the doctor his fee.

The gleam of hope kindled by the doctor's encouragement did not last long. The same room, the same pictures, curtains, wall-paper, medicine bottles, were all there, and the same aching suffering body, and Ivan Ilych began to moan. They gave him a subcutaneous injection and he sank into oblivion.

It was twilight when he came to. They brought him his dinner and he swallowed some beef tea with difficulty, and then everything was the same again and night was coming on.

After dinner, at seven o'clock, Praskovya Fedorovna came into the room in evening dress, her full bosom pushed up by her corset, and with traces of powder on her face. She had reminded him in the morning that they were going to the theatre. Sarah Bernhardt was visiting the town and they had a box, which he had insisted on their taking. Now he had forgotten about it and her toilet offended him, but he concealed his vexation when he remembered that he had himself insisted on their securing a box and going because it would be an instructive and aesthetic pleasure for the children.

Praskovya Fedorovna came in, self-satisfied but yet with a rather guilty air. She sat down and asked how he was, but, as he saw, only for the sake of asking and not in order to learn about it, knowing that there was nothing to learn—and then went on to what she really wanted to say: that she would not on any account have gone but that the box had been taken and Helen and their daughter were going, as well as Petrishchev (the examining magistrate, their daughter's fiancé) and that it was out of the question to let them go alone; but that she would have much preferred to sit with him for a while; and he must be sure to follow the doctor's orders while she was away.

"Oh, and Fedor Petrovich" (the fiancé) "would like to come in. May he? And Lisa?"

"All right."

Their daughter came in in full evening dress, her fresh young flesh exposed (making a show of that very flesh which in his own case caused so much suffering), strong, healthy, evidently in love, and impatient with illness, suffering, and death, because they interfered with her happiness.

Fedor Petrovich came in too, in evening dress, his hair curled *a la Capoul*, a tight stiff collar round his long sinewy neck, an enormous white shirt-front and narrow black trousers tightly stretched over his strong thighs. He had one white glove tightly drawn on, and was holding his opera hat in his hand.

Following him the schoolboy crept in unnoticed, in a new uniform, poor little fellow, and wearing gloves. Terribly dark shadows showed under his eyes, the meaning of which Ivan Ilych knew well.

His son had always seemed pathetic to him, and now it was dreadful to see the boy's frightened look of pity. It seemed to Ivan Ilych that Vasya was the only one besides Gerasim who understood and pitied him.

They all sat down and again asked how he was. A silence followed. Lisa asked her mother about the opera glasses, and there was an altercation between mother and daughter as to who had taken them and where they had been put. This occasioned some unpleasantness.

Fedor Petrovich inquired of Ivan Ilych whether he had ever seen Sarah Bernhardt. Ivan Ilych did not at first catch the question, but then replied: "No, have you seen her before?"

"Yes, in *Adrienne Lecouvreur*."

Praskovya Fedorovna mentioned some roles in which Sarah Bernhardt was particularly good. Her daughter disagreed. Conversation sprang up as to the elegance and realism of her acting—the sort of conversation that is always repeated and is always the same.

In the midst of the conversation Fedor Petrovich glanced at Ivan Ilych and became silent. The others also looked at him and grew silent. Ivan Ilych was staring with glittering eyes straight before him, evidently indignant with them. This had to be rectified, but it was impossible to do so. The silence had to be broken, but for a time no one dared to break it and they all became afraid that the conventional deception would suddenly become obvious and the truth become plain to all. Lisa was the first to pluck up courage and break that silence, but by trying to hide what everybody was feeling, she betrayed it.

"Well, if we are going it's time to start," she said, looking at her watch, a present from her father, and with a faint and significant smile at Fedor Petrovich relating to something known only to them. She got up with a rustle of her dress.

They all rose, said good-night, and went away.

When they had gone it seemed to Ivan Ilych that he felt better; the falsity had gone with them. But the pain remained—that same pain and that same fear that made everything monotonously alike, nothing harder and nothing easier. Everything was worse.

Again minute followed minute and hour followed hour. Everything remained the same and there was no cessation. And the inevitable end of it all became more and more terrible.

"Yes, send Gerasim here," he replied to a question Peter asked.

IX

His wife returned late at night. She came in on tiptoe, but he heard her, opened his eyes, and made haste to close them again. She wished to send Gerasim away and to sit with him herself, but he opened his eyes and said: "No, go away."

"Are you in great pain?"

"Always the same."

"Take some opium."

He agreed and took some. She went away.

Till about three in the morning he was in a state of stupefied misery. It seemed to him that he and his pain were being thrust into a narrow, deep black sack, but though they were pushed further and further in they could not be pushed to the bottom. And this, terrible enough in itself, was accompanied by suffering. He was frightened yet wanted to fall through the sack, he struggled but yet co-operated. And suddenly he broke through, fell, and regained consciousness. Gerasim was sitting at the foot of the bed dozing quietly and patiently, while he himself lay with his emaciated stockinged legs resting on Gerasim's shoulders; the same shaded candle was there and the same unceasing pain.

"Go away, Gerasim," he whispered.

"It's all right, sir. I'll stay a while."

"No. Go away."

He removed his legs from Gerasim's shoulders, turned sideways onto his arm, and felt sorry for himself. He only waited till Gerasim had gone into the next room and then restrained himself no longer but wept like a child. He wept on account of his helplessness, his terrible loneliness, the cruelty of man, the cruelty of God, and the absence of God.

"Why hast Thou done all this? Why hast Thou brought me here? Why, why dost Thou torment me so terribly?"

He did not expect an answer and yet wept because there was no answer and could be none. The pain again grew more acute, but he did not stir and did not call. He said to himself: "Go on! Strike me! But what is it for? What have I done to Thee? What is it for?"

Then he grew quiet and not only ceased weeping but even held his breath and became all attention. It was as though he were listening not to an audible voice but to the voice of his soul, to the current of thoughts arising within him.

"What is it you want?" was the first clear conception capable of expression in words, that he heard.

"What do you want? What do you want?" he repeated to himself.

"What do I want? To live and not to suffer," he answered.

And again he listened with such concentrated attention that even his pain did not distract him.

"To live? How?" asked his inner voice.

"Why, to live as I used to—well and pleasantly."

"As you lived before, well and pleasantly?" the voice repeated.

And in imagination he began to recall the best moments of his pleasant life. But strange to say none of those best moments of his pleasant life now seemed at all what they had then seemed—none of them except the first recollections of childhood. There, in child-hood, there had been something really pleasant with which it would be possible to live if it could return. But the child who had experienced that happiness existed no longer, it was like a reminiscence of somebody else.

As soon as the period began which had produced the present Ivan Ilych, all that had then seemed joys now melted before his sight and turned into something trivial and often nasty.

And the further he departed from childhood and the nearer he came to the present the more worthless and doubtful were the joys. This began with the School of Law. A little that was really good was still found there—there was light-heart-edness, friendship, and hope. But in the upper classes there had already been fewer of such good moments. Then during the first years of his official career, when he was in the service of the governor, some pleasant moments again occurred: they were the memories of love for a woman. Then all became confused and there was still less of what was good; later on again there was still less that was good, and the further he went the less there was. His marriage, a mere accident, then the disenchantment that followed it, his wife's bad breath and the sensuality and hypocrisy: then that deadly official life and those preoccupations about money, a year of it, and two, and ten, and twenty, and always the same thing. And the longer it lasted the more deadly it became. "It is as if I had been going downhill while I imagined I was going up. And that is really what it was. I was going up in public opin-ion, but to the same extent life was ebbing away from me. And now it is all done and there is only death.

"Then what does it mean? Why? It can't be that life is so senseless and horrible. But if it really has been so horrible and senseless, why must I die and die in agony? There is something wrong!

"Maybe I did not live as I ought to have done," it suddenly occurred to him. "But how could that be, when I did everything properly?" he replied, and immediately dismissed from his mind this, the sole solution of all the riddles of life and death, as something quite impossible.

"Then what do you want now? To live? Live how? Live as you lived in the law courts when the usher proclaimed 'The judge is coming!' The judge is coming, the judge!" he repeated to himself. "Here he is, the judge. But I am not guilty!" he exclaimed angrily. "What is it for?" And he ceased crying, but turning his face to the wall continued to ponder on the same question: Why, and for what purpose, is there all this horror? But however much he pondered he found no answer. And whenever the thought occurred to him, as it often did, that it all resulted from his not having lived as he ought to have done, he at once recalled the correctness of his whole life and dismissed so strange an idea.

X

Another fortnight passed. Ivan Ilych now no longer left his sofa. He would not lie in bed but lay on the sofa, facing the wall nearly all the time. He suffered ever the same unceasing agonies and in his loneliness pondered always on the same insoluble question: "What is this? Can it be that it is Death?" And the inner voice answered: "Yes, it is Death."

"Why these sufferings?" And the voice answered, "For no reason—they just are so." Beyond and besides this there was nothing.

From the very beginning of his illness, ever since he had first been to see the doctor, Ivan Ilych's life had been divided between two contrary and alternating moods: now it was despair and the expectation of this uncomprehended and terrible death, and now hope and an intently interested observation of the functioning of his organs. Now before his eyes there was only a kidney or an intestine that temporarily evaded its duty, and now only that incomprehensible and dreadful death from which it was impossible to escape.

These two states of mind had alternated from the very beginning of his illness, but the further it progressed the more doubtful and fantastic became the conception of the kidney, and the more real the sense of impending death.

He had but to call to mind what he had been three months before and what he was now, to call to mind with what regularity he had been going downhill, for every possibility of hope to be shattered.

Latterly during the loneliness in which he found himself as he lay facing the back of the sofa, a loneliness in the midst of a populous town and surrounded by numerous acquaintances and relations but that yet could not have been more complete anywhere—either at the bottom of the sea or under the earth—during that terrible loneliness Ivan Ilych had lived only in memories of the past. Pictures of his past rose before him one after another. They always began with what was nearest in time and then went back to what was most remote—to his childhood—and rested there. If he thought of the stewed prunes that had been offered him that day, his mind went back to the raw shrivelled French plums of his childhood, their peculiar flavour and the flow of saliva when he sucked their stones, and along with the memory of that taste came a whole series of memories of those days: his nurse, his brother, and their toys. "No, I mustn't think of that . . . It is too painful," Ivan Ilych said to himself, and brought himself back to the present—to the button on the back of the sofa and the creases in its morocco. "Morocco is expensive, but it does not wear well: there had been a quarrel about it. It was a different kind of quarrel and a different kind of morocco that time when we tore father's portfolio and were punished, and mamma brought us some tarts . . . ." And again his thoughts dwelt on his childhood, and again it was painful and he tried to banish them and fix his mind on something else.

Then again together with that chain of memories another series passed through his mind—of how his illness had progressed and grown worse. There also the further back he looked the more life there had been. There had been more of what was good in life and more of life itself. The two merged together. "Just as the pain went on getting worse and worse, so my life grew worse and worse," he thought. "There is one bright spot there at the back, at the beginning of life, and afterwards all becomes blacker and blacker and proceeds more and more rapidly—in inverse ratio to the square of the distance from death," thought Ivan Ilych. And the example of a stone falling downwards with increasing velocity entered his mind. Life, a series of increasing sufferings, flies further and further towards its end—the most terrible suffering. "I am flying. . . " He shuddered, shifted himself, and tried to resist, but was already aware that resistance was impossible, and again with eyes weary of gazing but unable to cease seeing what was before them, he stared at the back of the sofa and waited—awaiting that dreadful fall and shock and destruction.

"Resistance is impossible!" he said to himself. "If I could only understand what it is all for! But that too is impossible. An explanation would be possible if it could be said that I have not lived as I ought to. But it is impossible to say that," and he remembered all the legality, correctitude, and propriety of his life. "That at any rate can certainly not be admitted," he thought, and his lips smiled ironically as if someone could see that smile and be taken in by it. "There is no explanation! Agony, death. . . What for?"

XI

Another two weeks went by in this way and during that fortnight an event occurred that Ivan Ilych and his wife had desired. Petrishchev formally proposed. It happened in the evening. The next day Praskovya Fedorovna came into her husband's room considering how best to inform him of it, but that very night there had been a fresh change for the worse in his condition. She found him still lying on the sofa but in a different position. He lay on his back, groaning and staring fixedly straight in front of him.

She began to remind him of his medicines, but he turned his eyes towards her with such a look that she did not finish what she was saying; so great an animosity, to her in particular, did that look express.

"For Christ's sake let me die in peace!" he said.

She would have gone away, but just then their daughter came in and went up to say good morning. He looked at her as he had done at his wife, and in reply to her inquiry about his health said dryly that he would soon free them all of himself. They were both silent and after sitting with him for a while went away.

"Is it our fault?" Lisa said to her mother. "It's as if we were to blame! I am sorry for papa, but why should we be tortured?"

The doctor came at his usual time. Ivan Ilych answered "Yes" and "No," never taking his angry eyes from him, and at last said: "You know you can do nothing for me, so leave me alone."

"We can ease your sufferings."

"You can't even do that. Let me be."

The doctor went into the drawing room and told Praskovya Fedorovna that the case was very serious and that the only resource left was opium to allay her husband's sufferings, which must be terrible.

It was true, as the doctor said, that Ivan Ilych's physical sufferings were terrible, but worse than the physical sufferings were his mental sufferings which were his chief torture.

His mental sufferings were due to the fact that that night, as he looked at Gerasim's sleepy, good-natured face with its prominent cheek-bones, the question suddenly occurred to him: "What if my whole life has been wrong?"

It occurred to him that what had appeared perfectly impossible before, namely that he had not spent his life as he should have done, might after all be true. It occurred to him that his scarcely perceptible attempts to struggle against what was considered good by the most highly placed people, those scarcely noticeable impulses which he had immediately suppressed, might have been the real thing, and all the rest false. And his professional duties and the whole arrangement of his life and of his family, and all his social and official interests, might all have been false. He tried to defend all those things to himself and suddenly felt the weakness of what he was defending. There was nothing to defend.

"But if that is so," he said to himself, "and I am leaving this life with the consciousness that I have lost all that was given me and it is impossible to rectify it—what then?"

He lay on his back and began to pass his life in review in quite a new way. In the morning when he saw first his footman, then his wife, then his daughter, and then the doctor, their every word and movement confirmed to him the awful truth that had been revealed to him during the night. In them he saw himself—all that for which he had lived—and saw clearly that it was not real at all, but a terrible and huge deception which had hidden both life and death. This consciousness intensified his physical suffering tenfold. He groaned and tossed about, and pulled at his clothing which choked and stifled him. And he hated them on that account.

He was given a large dose of opium and became unconscious, but at noon his sufferings began again. He drove everybody away and tossed from side to side.

His wife came to him and said:

"Jean, my dear, do this for me. It can't do any harm and often helps. Healthy people often do it."

He opened his eyes wide.

"What? Take communion? Why? It's unnecessary! However. . . "

She began to cry.

"Yes, do, my dear. I'll send for our priest. He is such a nice man."

"All right. Very well," he muttered.

When the priest came and heard his confession, Ivan Ilych was softened and seemed to feel a relief from his doubts and consequently from his sufferings, and for a moment there came a ray of hope. He again began to think of the vermiform appendix and the possibility of correcting it. He received the sacrament with tears in his eyes.

When they laid him down again afterwards he felt a moment's ease, and the hope that he might live awoke in him again. He began to think of the operation that had been suggested to him. "To live! I want to live!" he said to himself.

His wife came in to congratulate him after his communion, and when uttering the usual conventional words she added:

"You feel better, don't you?"

Without looking at her he said "Yes."

Her dress, her figure, the expression of her face, the tone of her voice, all revealed the same thing. "This is wrong, it is not as it should be. All you have lived for and still live for is falsehood and deception, hiding life and death from you." And as soon as he admitted that thought, his hatred and his agonizing physical suffering again sprang up, and with that suffering a consciousness of the unavoidable, approaching end. And to this was added a new sensation of grinding shooting pain and a feeling of suffocation.

The expression of his face when he uttered that "Yes" was dreadful. Having uttered it, he looked her straight in the eyes, turned on his face with a rapidity extraordinary in his weak state and shouted:

"Go away! Go away and leave me alone!"

XII

From that moment the screaming began that continued for three days, and was so terrible that one could not hear it through two closed doors without horror. At the moment he answered his wife realized that he was lost, that there was no return, that the end had come, the very end, and his doubts were still unsolved and remained doubts.

"Oh! Oh! Oh!" he cried in various intonations. He had begun by screaming "I won't!" and continued screaming on the letter "O".

For three whole days, during which time did not exist for him, he struggled in that black sack into which he was being thrust by an invisible, resistless force. He struggled as a man condemned to death struggles in the hands of the executioner, knowing that he cannot save himself. And every moment he felt that despite all his efforts he was drawing nearer and nearer to what terrified him. He felt that his agony was due to his being thrust into that black hole and still more to his not being able to get right into it. He was hindered from getting into it by his conviction that his life had been a good one. That very justification of his life held him fast and prevented his moving forward, and it caused him most torment of all.

Suddenly some force struck him in the chest and side, making it still harder to breathe, and he fell through the hole and there at the bottom was a light. What had happened to him was like the sensation one sometimes experiences in a railway carriage when one thinks one is going backwards while one is really going forwards and suddenly becomes aware of the real direction.

"Yes, it was not the right thing," he said to himself, "but that's no matter. It can be done. But what *is* the right thing?" he asked himself, and suddenly grew quiet.

This occurred at the end of the third day, two hours before his death. Just then his schoolboy son had crept softly in and gone up to the bedside. The dying man was still screaming desperately and waving his arms. His hand fell on the boy's head, and the boy caught it, pressed it to his lips, and began to cry.

At that very moment Ivan Ilych fell through and caught sight of the light, and it was revealed to him that though his life had not been what it should have been, this could still be rectified. He asked himself, "What *is* the right thing?" and grew still, listening. Then he felt that someone was kissing his hand. He opened his eyes, looked at his son, and felt sorry for him. His wife came up to him and he glanced at her. She was gazing at him open-mouthed, with undried tears on her nose and cheek and a despairing look on her face. He felt sorry for her too.

"Yes, I am making them wretched," he thought. "They are sorry, but it will be better for them when I die." He wished to say this but had not the strength to utter it. "Besides, why speak? I must act," he thought. With a look at his wife he indicated his son and said: "Take him away . . . sorry for him . . . sorry for you too . . ." He tried to add, "Forgive me," but said "Forego" and waved his hand, knowing that He whose understanding mattered would understand.

And suddenly it grew clear to him that what had been oppressing him and would not leave him was all dropping away at once from two sides, from ten sides, and from all sides. He was sorry for them, he must act so as not to hurt them: release them and free himself from these sufferings. "How good and how simple!" he thought. "And the pain?" he asked himself. "What has become of it? Where are you, pain?"

He turned his attention to it.

"Yes, here it is. Well, what of it? Let the pain be."

"And death . . . where is it?"

He sought his former accustomed fear of death and did not find it. "Where is it? What death?" There was no fear because there was no death.

In place of death there was light.

"So that's what it is!" he suddenly exclaimed aloud. "What joy!"

To him all this happened in a single instant, and the meaning of that instant did not change.

For those present his agony continued for another two hours. Something rattled in his throat, his emaciated body twitched, then the gasping and rattle became less and less frequent.

"It is finished!" said someone near him.

He heard these words and repeated them in his soul.

"Death is finished," he said to himself. "It is no more!"

He drew in a breath, stopped in the midst of a sigh, stretched out, and died.

VIII

Pope Benedict XVI

Editors' Introduction

Cardinal Joseph Ratzinger was elected pope on April 19, 2005, taking the name Benedict. Born in the southern German state of Bavaria in 1927, Ratzinger came to the papacy having served in the Vatican since 1981 as prefect (director) of the Vatican Congregation for the Doctrine of the Faith. As is evident from the title of the Congregation, this is the body within the Vatican that oversees Catholic doctrine. Cardinal Ratzinger came to this position as a well-known and respected theologian. During the Second Vatican Council (see the introduction to *Nostra Aetate*), Ratzinger had a reputation as one of the leading reformers among the theologians involved in the Council's deliberations. Some commentators have come to the conclusion that over the years Ratzinger's thought has taken a more conservative turn. He, however, has always maintained that his theological views, while they developed over time, have remained consistent, and that there has been no break with his earlier writings. The question as to just what constitutes "liberal/reformer" and "conservative/traditional," and whether these terms are at all useful in describing the work of a nuanced thinker like Joseph Ratzinger, needs to be understood within the wider context of the ongoing debate concerning the meaning and proper interpretation of the Second Vatican Council.

God Is Love is the first encyclical of Benedict XVI. An encyclical was originally understood as a letter from a bishop that was circulated within a particular territory. In Roman Catholicism the term has come to mean a letter from the pope (who is the bishop of Rome). Usually, the title of the encyclical is taken from its first few words. Sometimes an encyclical is addressed to the pope's fellow bishops, but it can also be directed to the entire church (as is the case with *God Is Love*). Encyclicals vary in terms of content; some might deal with particular issues involving social justice, sexual morality, liturgical matters, etc., while others take up and explore theological themes. In some cases (such as *God Is Love*), an encyclical will combine both themes. In the Roman Catholic tradition, a papal encyclical is taken very seriously, since it is an expression of the pope's thinking on a particular theme or issue.

If, as some believe, the first encyclical of a pope gives some indication of the themes or concerns that will animate his papacy, then it is noteworthy that Benedict's first offering in this genre focuses on love. The title of the encyclical is inspired by the affirmation that God is love found in the New Testament in the First Letter of John (1 John 4:16). Beginning with this text, Benedict offers an extended reflection on the nature of love as understood within the Christian tradition. True to his philosophical and theological background, he interweaves these reflections with other views of love taken largely from the traditions of classical Greek culture. In particular, Benedict explores the relationship between the notion of love (*agape* in Greek) emphasized in the New Testament and the Greek idea of love as *eros*. This theological exploration of the nature of love constitutes the first part of the encyclical. In the second part, Benedict moves from a primarily theoretical perspective to an application of the Christian understanding of love to the life of the Church and society.

GOD IS LOVE (DEUS CARITAS EST) **(SELECTIONS)**

Introduction

1. "God is love, and he who abides in love abides in God, and God abides in him" (*1 Jn* 4:16). These words from the *First Letter of John* express with remarkable clarity the heart of the Christian faith: the Christian image of God and the resulting image of mankind and its destiny. In the same verse, Saint John also offers a kind of summary of the Christian life: "We have come to know and to believe in the love God has for us."

    We have come to believe in God's love: in these words the Christian can express the fundamental decision of his life. Being Christian is not the result of an ethical choice or a lofty idea, but the encounter with an event, a person, which gives life a new horizon and a decisive direction. Saint John's Gospel describes that event in these words: "God so loved the world that he gave his only Son, that whoever believes in him should . . . have eternal life" (3:16). In acknowledging the centrality of love, Christian faith has retained the core of Israel's faith, while at the same time giving it new depth and breadth. The pious Jew prayed daily the words of the *Book of Deuteronomy* which expressed the heart of his existence: "Hear, O Israel: the Lord our God is one Lord, and you shall love the Lord your God with all your heart, and with all your soul and with all your might" (6:4–5). Jesus united into a single precept this commandment of love for God and the commandment of love for neighbour found in the *Book of Leviticus*: "You shall love your neighbour as yourself" (19:18; cf. *Mk* 12:29–31). Since God has first loved us (cf. *1 Jn* 4:10), love is now no longer a mere "command"; it is the response to the gift of love with which God draws near to us.

    In a world where the name of God is sometimes associated with vengeance or even a duty of hatred and violence, this message is both timely and significant. For this reason, I wish in my first Encyclical to speak of the love which God lavishes upon us and which we in turn must share with others. That, in essence, is what the two main parts of this Letter are about, and they are profoundly interconnected. The first part is more speculative, since I wanted here—at the beginning of my Pontificate— to clarify some essential facts concerning the love which God mysteriously and gratuitously offers to man, together with the intrinsic link between that Love and the reality of human love. The second part is more concrete, since it treats the ecclesial exercise of the commandment of love of neighbour. The argument has vast implications, but a lengthy treatment would go beyond the scope of the present Encyclical. I wish to emphasize some basic elements, so as to call forth in the world renewed energy and commitment in the human response to God's love.

Part I

The Unity of Love in Creation and in Salvation History

A Problem of Language

2. God's love for us is fundamental for our lives, and it raises important questions about who God is and who we are. In considering this, we immediately find ourselves hampered by a problem of language. Today, the term "love" has become one of the most frequently used and misused of words, a word to which we attach quite different meanings. Even though this Encyclical will deal primarily with the understanding and practice of love in sacred Scripture and in the Church's Tradition, we cannot simply prescind from the meaning of the word in the different cultures and in present-day usage.

    Let us first of all bring to mind the vast semantic range of the word "love": we speak of love of country, love of one's profession, love between friends, love of work, love between parents and children, love between family members, love of neighbour and love of God. Amid this multiplicity of meanings, however, one in particular stands out: love between man and woman, where body and soul are inseparably joined and human beings glimpse an apparently irresistible promise of happiness. This would seem to be the very epitome of love; all other kinds of love immediately seem to fade in comparison. So we need to ask: are all these forms of love basically one, so that love, in its many and varied manifestations, is ultimately a single reality, or are we merely using the same word to designate totally different realities?

"Eros" and "Agape"—Difference and Unity

3. That love between man and woman which is neither planned nor willed, but somehow imposes itself upon human beings, was called *eros* by the ancient Greeks. Let us note straight away that the Greek Old Testament uses the word *eros* only twice, while the New Testament does not use it at all: of the three Greek words for love, *eros*, *philia* (the love of friendship) and *agape*, New Testament writers prefer the last, which occurs rather infrequently in Greek usage. As for the term *philia*, the love of friendship, it is used with added depth of meaning in Saint John's Gospel in order to express the relationship between Jesus and his disciples. The tendency to avoid the word *eros*, together with the new vision of love expressed through the word *agape*, clearly point to something new and distinct about the Christian understanding of love. In the critique of Christianity which began with the Enlightenment and grew progressively more radical, this new element was seen as something thoroughly negative. According to Friedrich Nietzsche, Christianity had poisoned *eros*, which for its part, while not completely succumbing, gradually degenerated into vice. Here the German philosopher was expressing a widely-held

perception: doesn't the Church, with all her commandments and prohibitions, turn to bitterness the most precious thing in life? Doesn't she blow the whistle just when the joy which is the Creator's gift offers us a happiness which is itself a certain foretaste of the Divine?

4. But is this the case? Did Christianity really destroy *eros*? Let us take a look at the pre-Christian world. The Greeks—not unlike other cultures—considered *eros* principally as a kind of intoxication, the overpowering of reason by a "divine madness" which tears man away from his finite existence and enables him, in the very process of being overwhelmed by divine power, to experience supreme happiness. All other powers in heaven and on earth thus appear secondary: "*Omnia vincit amor*" says Virgil in the *Bucolics*—love conquers all—and he adds: "*et nos cedamus amori*"—let us, too, yield to love. In the religions, this attitude found expression in fertility cults, part of which was the "sacred" prostitution which flourished in many temples. *Eros* was thus celebrated as divine power, as fellowship with the Divine.

The Old Testament firmly opposed this form of religion, which represents a powerful temptation against monotheistic faith, combating it as a perversion of religiosity. But it in no way rejected *eros* as such; rather, it declared war on a warped and destructive form of it, because this counterfeit divinization of eros actually strips it of its dignity and dehumanizes it. Indeed, the prostitutes in the temple, who had to bestow this divine intoxication, were not treated as human beings and persons, but simply used as a means of arousing "divine madness": far from being goddesses, they were human persons being exploited. An intoxicated and undisciplined *eros*, then, is not an ascent in "ecstasy" towards the Divine, but a fall, a degradation of man. Evidently, *eros* needs to be disciplined and purified if it is to provide not just fleeting pleasure, but a certain foretaste of the pinnacle of our existence, of that beatitude for which our whole being yearns.

5. Two things emerge clearly from this rapid overview of the concept of *eros* past and present. First, there is a certain relationship between love and the Divine: love promises infinity, eternity—a reality far greater and totally other than our everyday existence. Yet we have also seen that the way to attain this goal is not simply by submitting to instinct. Purification and growth in maturity are called for; and these also pass through the path of renunciation. Far from rejecting or "poisoning" *eros*, they heal it and restore its true grandeur.

This is due first and foremost to the fact that man is a being made up of body and soul. Man is truly himself when his body and soul are intimately united; the challenge of *eros* can be said to be truly overcome when this unification is achieved. Should he aspire to be pure spirit and to reject the flesh as pertaining to his animal nature alone, then spirit and body would both lose their dignity. On the other hand, should he deny the spirit and consider matter, the body, as the only reality, he would likewise lose his greatness. The epicure Gassendi used to offer Descartes the humorous greeting: "O Soul!" And Descartes would reply: "O Flesh!" Yet it is neither the spirit alone nor the body alone that loves: it is man, the person, a unified creature composed of body and soul, who loves. Only when both dimensions are truly united, does man attain his full stature. Only thus is love —eros—able to mature and attain its authentic grandeur.

Nowadays Christianity of the past is often criticized as having been opposed to the body; and it is quite true that tendencies of this sort have always existed. Yet the contemporary way of exalting the body is deceptive. *Eros*, reduced to pure "sex," has become a commodity, a mere "thing" to be bought and sold, or rather, man himself becomes a commodity. This is hardly man's great "yes" to the body. On the contrary, he now considers his body and his sexuality as the purely material part of himself, to be used and exploited at will. Nor does he see it as an arena for the exercise of his freedom, but as a mere object that he attempts, as he pleases, to make both enjoyable and harmless. Here we are actually dealing with a debasement of the human body: no longer is it integrated into our overall existential freedom; no longer is it a vital expression of our whole being, but it is more or less relegated to the purely biological sphere. The apparent exaltation of the body can quickly turn into a hatred of bodiliness. Christian faith, on the other hand, has always considered man a unity in duality, a reality in which spirit and matter compenetrate, and in which each is brought to a new nobility. True, *eros* tends to rise "in ecstasy" towards the Divine, to lead us beyond ourselves; yet for this very reason it calls for a path of ascent, renunciation, purification and healing.

6. Concretely, what does this path of ascent and purification entail? How might love be experienced so that it can fully realize its human and divine promise? Here we can find a first, important indication in the *Song of Songs*, an Old Testament book well known to the mystics. According to the interpretation generally held today, the poems contained in this book were originally love-songs, perhaps intended for a Jewish wedding feast and meant to exalt conjugal love. In this context it is highly instructive to note that in the course of the book two different Hebrew words are used to indicate "love." First there is the word *doctim*, a plural form suggesting a love that is still insecure, indeterminate and searching. This comes to be replaced by the word *ahaba*, which the Greek version of the Old Testament translates with the similar-sounding *agape*, which, as we have seen, becomes the typical expression for the biblical notion of love. By contrast with an indeterminate, "searching" love, this word expresses the experience of a love which involves a real discovery of the other, moving beyond the selfish character that prevailed earlier. Love now becomes concern and care for the other. No longer is it self-seeking, a sinking in

the intoxication of happiness; instead it seeks the good of the beloved: it becomes renunciation and it is ready, and even willing, for sacrifice.

It is part of love's growth towards higher levels and inward purification that it now seeks to become definitive, and it does so in a twofold sense: both in the sense of exclusivity (this particular person alone) and in the sense of being "for ever." Love embraces the whole of existence in each of its dimensions, including the dimension of time. It could hardly be otherwise, since its promise looks towards its definitive goal: love looks to the eternal. Love is indeed "ecstasy," not in the sense of a moment of intoxication, but rather as a journey, an ongoing exodus out of the closed inward-looking self towards its liberation through self-giving, and thus towards authentic self-discovery and indeed the discovery of God: "Whoever seeks to gain his life will lose it, but whoever loses his life will preserve it" (*Lk* 17:33), as Jesus says throughout the Gospels (cf. *Mt* 10:39; 16:25; *Mk* 8:35; *Lk* 9:24; *Jn* 12:25). In these words, Jesus portrays his own path, which leads through the Cross to the Resurrection: the path of the grain of wheat that falls to the ground and dies, and in this way bears much fruit. Starting from the depths of his own sacrifice and of the love that reaches fulfilment therein, he also portrays in these words the essence of love and indeed of human life itself.

7. By their own inner logic, these initial, somewhat philosophical reflections on the essence of love have now brought us to the threshold of biblical faith. We began by asking whether the different, or even opposed, meanings of the word "love" point to some profound underlying unity, or whether on the contrary they must remain unconnected, one alongside the other. More significantly, though, we questioned whether the message of love proclaimed to us by the Bible and the Church's Tradition has some points of contact with the common human experience of love, or whether it is opposed to that experience. This in turn led us to consider two fundamental words: *eros*, as a term to indicate "worldly" love and *agape*, referring to love grounded in and shaped by faith. The two notions are often contrasted as "ascending" love and "descending" love. There are other, similar classifications, such as the distinction between possessive love and oblative love (*amor concupiscentiae—amor benevolentiae*), to which is sometimes also added love that seeks its own advantage.

In philosophical and theological debate, these distinctions have often been radicalized to the point of establishing a clear antithesis between them: descending, oblative love—*agape*—would be typically Christian, while on the other hand ascending, possessive or covetous love—*eros*—would be typical of non-Christian, and particularly Greek culture. Were this antithesis to be taken to extremes, the essence of Christianity would be detached from the vital relations fundamental to human existence, and would become a world apart, admirable perhaps, but decisively cut off from the complex fabric of human life. Yet *eros* and *agape*—ascending love and descending love—can never be completely separated. The more the two, in their different aspects, find a proper unity in the one reality of love, the more the true nature of love in general is realized. Even if *eros* is at first mainly covetous and ascending, a fascination for the great promise of happiness, in drawing near to the other, it is less and less concerned with itself, increasingly seeks the happiness of the other, is concerned more and more with the beloved, bestows itself and wants to "be there for" the other. The element of *agape* thus enters into this love, for otherwise *eros* is impoverished and even loses its own nature. On the other hand, man cannot live by oblative, descending love alone. He cannot always give, he must also receive. Anyone who wishes to give love must also receive love as a gift. Certainly, as the Lord tells us, one can become a source from which rivers of living water flow (cf. *Jn* 7:37–38). Yet to become such a source, one must constantly drink anew from the original source, which is Jesus Christ, from whose pierced heart flows the love of God (cf. *Jn* 19:34).

In the account of Jacob's ladder, the Fathers of the Church saw this inseparable connection between ascending and descending love, between *eros* which seeks God and *agape* which passes on the gift received, symbolized in various ways. In that biblical passage we read how the Patriarch Jacob saw in a dream, above the stone which was his pillow, a ladder reaching up to heaven, on which the angels of God were ascending and descending (cf. *Gen* 28:12; *Jn* 1:51). A particularly striking interpretation of this vision is presented by Pope Gregory the Great in his *Pastoral Rule*. He tells us that the good pastor must be rooted in contemplation. Only in this way will he be able to take upon himself the needs of others and make them his own: "*per pietatis viscera in se infirmitatem caeterornm transferat.*" Saint Gregory speaks in this context of Saint Paul, who was borne aloft to the most exalted mysteries of God, and hence, having descended once more, he was able to become all things to all men (cf. *2 Cor* 12:2–4; *1 Cor* 9:22). He also points to the example of Moses, who entered the tabernacle time and again, remaining in dialogue with God, so that when he emerged he could be at the service of his people. "Within [the tent] he is borne aloft through contemplation, while without he is completely engaged in helping those who suffer: *intus in contemplationem rapitur, foris infirmantium negotiis urgetur.*"

8. We have thus come to an initial, albeit still somewhat generic response to the two questions raised earlier. Fundamentally, "love" is a single reality, but with different dimensions; at different times, one or other dimension may emerge more clearly. Yet when the two dimensions are totally cut off from one another, the result is a caricature or at least an impoverished form of love. And we have also seen, synthetically, that biblical faith does not set up a parallel universe, or one opposed to that

primordial human phenomenon which is love, but rather accepts the whole man; it intervenes in his search for love in order to purify it and to reveal new dimensions of it. This newness of biblical faith is shown chiefly in two elements which deserve to be highlighted: the image of God and the image of man.

The Newness of Biblical Faith

9. First, the world of the Bible presents us with a new image of God. In surrounding cultures, the image of God and of the gods ultimately remained unclear and contradictory. In the development of biblical faith, however, the content of the prayer fundamental to Israel, the *Shema*, became increasingly clear and unequivocal: "Hear, O Israel, the Lord our God is one Lord" (*Dt* 6:4). There is only one God, the Creator of heaven and earth, who is thus the God of all. Two facts are significant about this statement: all other gods are not God, and the universe in which we live has its source in God and was created by him. Certainly, the notion of creation is found elsewhere, yet only here does it become absolutely clear that it is not one god among many, but the one true God himself who is the source of all that exists; the whole world comes into existence by the power of his creative Word. Consequently, his creation is dear to him, for it was willed by him and "made" by him. The second important element now emerges: this God loves man. The divine power that Aristotle at the height of Greek philosophy sought to grasp through reflection, is indeed for every being an object of desire and of love—and as the object of love this divinity moves the world—but in itself it lacks nothing and does not love: it is solely the object of love. The one God in whom Israel believes, on the other hand, loves with a personal love. His love, moreover, is an elective love: among all the nations he chooses Israel and loves her—but he does so precisely with a view to healing the whole human race. God loves, and his love may certainly be called *eros*, yet it is also totally *agape*. The Prophets, particularly Hosea and Ezekiel, described God's passion for his people using boldly erotic images. God's relationship with Israel is described using the metaphors of betrothal and marriage; idolatry is thus adultery and prostitution. Here we find a specific reference—as we have seen—to the fertility cults and their abuse of *eros*, but also a description of the relationship of fidelity between Israel and her God. The history of the love-relationship between God and Israel consists, at the deepest level, in the fact that he gives her the *Torah*, thereby opening Israel's eyes to man's true nature and showing her the path leading to true humanism. It consists in the fact that man, through a life of fidelity to the one God, comes to experience himself as loved by God, and discovers joy in truth and in righteousness—a joy in God which becomes his essential happiness: "Whom do I have in heaven but you? And there is nothing upon earth that I desire besides you . . . for me it is good to be near God" (*Ps* 73 [72]:25, 28).

10. We have seen that God's *eros* for man is also totally *agape*. This is not only because it is bestowed in a completely gratuitous manner, without any previous merit, but also because it is love which forgives. Hosea above all shows us that this *agape* dimension of God's love for man goes far beyond the aspect of gratuity. Israel has committed "adultery" and has broken the covenant; God should judge and repudiate her. It is precisely at this point that God is revealed to be God and not man: "How can I give you up, O Ephraim! How can I hand you over, O Israel! . . . My heart recoils within me, my compassion grows warm and tender. I will not execute my fierce anger, I will not again destroy Ephraim; for I am God and not man, the Holy One in your midst" (*Hos* 11:8–9). God's passionate love for his people—for humanity—is at the same time a forgiving love. It is so great that it turns God against himself, his love against his justice. Here Christians can see a dim prefigurement of the mystery of the Cross: so great is God's love for man that by becoming man he follows him even into death, and so reconciles justice and love.

The philosophical dimension to be noted in this biblical vision, and its importance from the standpoint of the history of religions, lies in the fact that on the one hand we find ourselves before a strictly metaphysical image of God: God is the absolute and ultimate source of all being; but this universal principle of creation—the *Logos*, primordial reason—is at the same time a lover with all the passion of a true love. *Eros* is thus supremely ennobled, yet at the same time it is so purified as to become one with *agape*. We can thus see how the reception of the *Song of Songs* in the canon of sacred Scripture was soon explained by the idea that these love songs ultimately describe God's relation to man and man's relation to God. Thus the *Song of Songs* became, both in Christian and Jewish literature, a source of mystical knowledge and experience, an expression of the essence of biblical faith: that man can indeed enter into union with God—his primordial aspiration. But this union is no mere fusion, a sinking in the nameless ocean of the Divine; it is a unity which creates love, a unity in which both God and man remain themselves and yet become fully one. As Saint Paul says: "He who is united to the Lord becomes one spirit with him" (*1 Cor* 6:17).

11. The first novelty of biblical faith consists, as we have seen, in its image of God. The second, essentially connected to this, is found in the image of man. The biblical account of creation speaks of the solitude of Adam, the first man, and God's decision to give him a helper. Of all other creatures, not one is capable of being the helper that man needs, even though he has assigned a name to all the wild beasts and birds and thus made them fully a part of his life. So God forms woman from the rib of man. Now Adam finds the helper that he needed: "This at last is bone of my bones and flesh of my flesh" (*Gen* 2:23). Here one might detect hints of ideas that are also found, for example, in the myth mentioned by Plato, according to which man was

originally spherical, because he was complete in himself and self-sufficient. But as a punishment for pride, he was split in two by Zeus, so that now he longs for his other half, striving with all his being to possess it and thus regain his integrity. While the biblical narrative does not speak of punishment, the idea is certainly present that man is somehow incomplete, driven by nature to seek in another the part that can make him whole, the idea that only in communion with the opposite sex can he become "complete." The biblical account thus concludes with a prophecy about Adam: "Therefore a man leaves his father and his mother and cleaves to his wife and they become one flesh" (*Gen* 2:24).

Two aspects of this are important. First, *eros* is somehow rooted in man's very nature; Adam is a seeker, who "abandons his mother and father" in order to find woman; only together do the two represent complete humanity and become "one flesh." The second aspect is equally important. From the standpoint of creation, *eros* directs man towards marriage, to a bond which is unique and definitive; thus, and only thus, does it fulfil its deepest purpose. Corresponding to the image of a monotheistic God is monogamous marriage. Marriage based on exclusive and definitive love becomes the icon of the relationship between God and his people and vice versa. God's way of loving becomes the measure of human love. This close connection between *eros* and marriage in the Bible has practically no equivalent in extra-biblical literature.

Jesus Christ—The Incarnate Love of God

12. Though up to now we have been speaking mainly of the Old Testament, nevertheless the profound compenetration of the two Testaments as the one Scripture of the Christian faith has already become evident. The real novelty of the New Testament lies not so much in new ideas as in the figure of Christ himself, who gives flesh and blood to those concepts—an unprecedented realism. In the Old Testament, the novelty of the Bible did not consist merely in abstract notions but in God's unpredictable and in some sense unprecedented activity. This divine activity now takes on dramatic form when, in Jesus Christ, it is God himself who goes in search of the "stray sheep," a suffering and lost humanity. When Jesus speaks in his parables of the shepherd who goes after the lost sheep, of the woman who looks for the lost coin, of the father who goes to meet and embrace his prodigal son, these are no mere words: they constitute an explanation of his very being and activity. His death on the Cross is the culmination of that turning of God against himself in which he gives himself in order to raise man up and save him. This is love in its most radical form. By contemplating the pierced side of Christ (cf. 19:37), we can understand the starting-point of this Encyclical Letter: "God is love" (*1 Jn* 4:8). It is there that this truth can be contemplated. It is from there that our definition of love must

begin. In this contemplation the Christian discovers the path along which his life and love must move.

13. Jesus gave this act of oblation an enduring presence through his institution of the Eucharist at the Last Supper. He anticipated his death and resurrection by giving his disciples, in the bread and wine, his very self, his body and blood as the new manna (cf. *Jn* 6:31–33). The ancient world had dimly perceived that man's real food—what truly nourishes him as man—is ultimately the *Logos*, eternal wisdom: this same *Logos* now truly becomes food for us—as love. The Eucharist draws us into Jesus' act of self-oblation. More than just statically receiving the incarnate *Logos*, we enter into the very dynamic of his self-giving. The imagery of marriage between God and Israel is now realized in a way previously inconceivable: it had meant standing in God's presence, but now it becomes union with God through sharing in Jesus' self-gift, sharing in his body and blood. The sacramental "mysticism," grounded in God's condescension towards us, operates at a radically different level and lifts us to far greater heights than anything that any human mystical elevation could ever accomplish.

14. Here we need to consider yet another aspect: this sacramental "mysticism" is social in character, for in sacramental communion I become one with the Lord, like all the other communicants. As Saint Paul says, "Because there is one bread, we who are many are one body, for we all partake of the one bread" (*1 Cor* 10:17). Union with Christ is also union with all those to whom he gives himself. I cannot possess Christ just for myself; I can belong to him only in union with all those who have become, or who will become, his own. Communion draws me out of myself towards him, and thus also towards unity with all Christians. We become "one body", completely joined in a single existence. Love of God and love of neighbour are now truly united: God incarnate draws us all to himself. We can thus understand how *agape* also became a term for the Eucharist: there God's own *agape* comes to us bodily, in order to continue his work in us and through us. Only by keeping in mind this Christological and sacramental basis can we correctly understand Jesus' teaching on love. The transition which he makes from the Law and the Prophets to the twofold commandment of love of God and of neighbour, and his grounding the whole life of faith on this central precept, is not simply a matter of morality—something that could exist apart from and alongside faith in Christ and its sacramental re-actualization. Faith, worship and *ethos* are interwoven as a single reality which takes shape in our encounter with God's *agape*. Here the usual contraposition between worship and ethics simply falls apart. "Worship" itself, Eucharistic communion, includes the reality both of being loved and of loving others in turn. A Eucharist which does not pass over into the concrete practice of love is intrinsically fragmented. Conversely, as we shall have to consider in greater

detail below, the "commandment" of love is only possible because it is more than a requirement. Love can be "commanded" because it has first been given.

15. This principle is the starting-point for understanding the great parables of Jesus. The rich man (cf. *Lk* 16:19–31) begs from his place of torment that his brothers be informed about what happens to those who simply ignore the poor man in need. Jesus takes up this cry for help as a warning to help us return to the right path. The parable of the Good Samaritan (cf. *Lk* 10:25–37) offers two particularly important clarifications. Until that time, the concept of "neighbour" was understood as referring essentially to one's countrymen and to foreigners who had settled in the land of Israel; in other words, to the closely-knit community of a single country or people. This limit is now abolished. Anyone who needs me, and whom I can help, is my neighbour. The concept of "neighbour" is now universalized, yet it remains concrete. Despite being extended to all mankind, it is not reduced to a generic, abstract and undemanding expression of love, but calls for my own practical commitment here and now. The Church has the duty to interpret ever anew this relationship between near and far with regard to the actual daily life of her members. Lastly, we should especially mention the great parable of the Last Judgement (cf. *Mt* 25:31–46), in which love becomes the criterion for the definitive decision about a human life's worth or lack thereof. Jesus identifies himself with those in need, with the hungry, the thirsty, the stranger, the naked, the sick and those in prison. "As you did it to one of the least of these my brethren, you did it to me" (*Mt* 25:40). Love of God and love of neighbour have become one: in the least of the brethren we find Jesus himself, and in Jesus we find God.

Love of God and Love of Neighbour

16. Having reflected on the nature of love and its meaning in biblical faith, we are left with two questions concerning our own attitude: can we love God without seeing him? And can love be commanded? Against the double commandment of love these questions raise a double objection. No one has ever seen God, so how could we love him? Moreover, love cannot be commanded; it is ultimately a feeling that is either there or not, nor can it be produced by the will. Scripture seems to reinforce the first objection when it states: "If anyone says, 'I love God,' and hates his brother, he is a liar; for he who does not love his brother whom he has seen, cannot love God whom he has not seen" (*1 Jn* 4:20). But this text hardly excludes the love of God as something impossible. On the contrary, the whole context of the passage quoted from the *First Letter of John* shows that such love is explicitly demanded. The unbreakable bond between love of God and love of neighbour is emphasized. One is so closely connected to the other that to say that we love God becomes a lie if we are closed to our neighbour or hate him altogether. Saint John's words should rather

be interpreted to mean that love of neighbour is a path that leads to the encounter with God, and that closing our eyes to our neighbour also blinds us to God.

17. True, no one has ever seen God as he is. And yet God is not totally invisible to us; he does not remain completely inaccessible. God loved us first, says the *Letter of John* quoted above (cf. 4:10), and this love of God has appeared in our midst. He has become visible in as much as he "has sent his only Son into the world, so that we might live through him" (1 *Jn* 4:9). God has made himself visible: in Jesus we are able to see the Father (cf. *Jn* 14:9). Indeed, God is visible in a number of ways. In the love-story recounted by the Bible, he comes towards us, he seeks to win our hearts, all the way to the Last Supper, to the piercing of his heart on the Cross, to his appearances after the Resurrection and to the great deeds by which, through the activity of the Apostles, he guided the nascent Church along its path. Nor has the Lord been absent from subsequent Church history: he encounters us ever anew, in the men and women who reflect his presence, in his word, in the sacraments, and especially in the Eucharist. In the Church's Liturgy, in her prayer, in the living community of believers, we experience the love of God, we perceive his presence and we thus learn to recognize that presence in our daily lives. He has loved us first and he continues to do so; we too, then, can respond with love. God does not demand of us a feeling which we ourselves are incapable of producing. He loves us, he makes us see and experience his love, and since he has "loved us first," love can also blossom as a response within us.

In the gradual unfolding of this encounter, it is clearly revealed that love is not merely a sentiment. Sentiments come and go. A sentiment can be a marvellous first spark, but it is not the fullness of love. Earlier we spoke of the process of purification and maturation by which *eros* comes fully into its own, becomes love in the full meaning of the word. It is characteristic of mature love that it calls into play all man's potentialities; it engages the whole man, so to speak. Contact with the visible manifestations of God's love can awaken within us a feeling of joy born of the experience of being loved. But this encounter also engages our will and our intellect. Acknowledgment of the living God is one path towards love, and the "yes" of our will to his will unites our intellect, will and sentiments in the all-embracing act of love. But this process is always open-ended; love is never "finished" and complete; throughout life, it changes and matures, and thus remains faithful to itself. *Idem velle atque idem nolle*—to want the same thing, and to reject the same thing—was recognized by antiquity as the authentic content of love: the one becomes similar to the other, and this leads to a community of will and thought. The love-story between God and man consists in the very fact that this communion of will increases in a communion of thought and sentiment, and thus our will and God's will increasingly coincide: God's will is no longer for me an alien will, something imposed on me from without by the commandments, but it is now my own will, based on the realization that God is in fact more deeply present to me than I am to myself. Then self-abandonment to God increases and God becomes our joy (cf. *Ps* 73 [72]:23–28).

18. Love of neighbour is thus shown to be possible in the way proclaimed by the Bible, by Jesus. It consists in the very fact that, in God and with God, I love even the person whom I do not like or even know. This can only take place on the basis of an intimate encounter with God, an encounter which has become a communion of will, even affecting my feelings. Then I learn to look on this other person not simply with my eyes and my feelings, but from the perspective of Jesus Christ. His friend is my friend. Going beyond exterior appearances, I perceive in others an interior desire for a sign of love, of concern. This I can offer them not only through the organizations intended for such purposes, accepting it perhaps as a political necessity. Seeing with the eyes of Christ, I can give to others much more than their outward necessities; I can give them the look of love which they crave. Here we see the necessary interplay between love of God and love of neighbour which the *First Letter of John* speaks of with such insistence. If I have no contact whatsoever with God in my life, then I cannot see in the other anything more than the other, and I am incapable of seeing in him the image of God. But if in my life I fail completely to heed others, solely out of a desire to be "devout" and to perform my "religious duties," then my relationship with God will also grow arid. It becomes merely "proper," but loveless. Only my readiness to encounter my neighbour and to show him love makes me sensitive to God as well. Only if I serve my neighbour can my eyes be opened to what God does for me and how much he loves me. The saints—consider the example of Blessed Teresa of Calcutta—constantly renewed their capacity for love of neighbour from their encounter with the Eucharistic Lord, and conversely this encounter acquired its realism and depth in their service to others. Love of God and love of neighbour are thus inseparable, they form a single commandment. But both live from the love of God who has loved us first. No longer is it a question, then, of a "commandment" imposed from without and calling for the impossible, but rather of a freely-bestowed experience of love from within, a love which by its very nature must then be shared with others. Love grows through love. Love is "divine" because it comes from God and unites us to God; through this unifying process it makes us a "we" which transcends our divisions and makes us one, until in the end God is "all in all" (*1 Cor* 15:28).

Part II: Caritas

The Practice of Love by the Church as a "Community of Love"

The Church's Charitable Activity as a Manifestation of Trinitarian Love

19. "If you see charity, you see the Trinity," wrote Saint Augustine. In the foregoing reflections, we have been able to focus our attention on the Pierced one (cf. *Jn* 19:37, *Zech* 12:10), recognizing the plan of the Father who, moved by love (cf. *Jn* 3:16), sent his only-begotten Son into the world to redeem man. By dying on the Cross—as Saint John tells us—Jesus "gave up his Spirit" (*Jn* 19:30), anticipating the gift of the Holy Spirit that he would make after his Resurrection (cf. *Jn* 20:22). This was to fulfil the promise of "rivers of living water" that would flow out of the hearts of believers, through the outpouring of the Spirit (cf. *Jn* 7:38–39). The Spirit, in fact, is that interior power which harmonizes their hearts with Christ's heart and moves them to love their brethren as Christ loved them, when he bent down to wash the feet of the disciples (cf. *Jn* 13:1–13) and above all when he gave his life for us (cf. *Jn* 13:1, 15:13).

The Spirit is also the energy which transforms the heart of the ecclesial community, so that it becomes a witness before the world to the love of the Father, who wishes to make humanity a single family in his Son. The entire activity of the Church is an expression of a love that seeks the integral good of man: it seeks his evangelization through Word and Sacrament, an undertaking that is often heroic in the way it is acted out in history; and it seeks to promote man in the various arenas of life and human activity. Love is therefore the service that the Church carries out in order to attend constantly to man's sufferings and his needs, including material needs. And this is the aspect, this *service of charity*, on which I want to focus in the second part of the Encyclical.

Charity as a Responsibility of the Church

20. Love of neighbour, grounded in the love of God, is first and foremost a responsibility for each individual member of the faithful, but it is also a responsibility for the entire ecclesial community at every level: from the local community to the particular Church and to the Church universal in its entirety. As a community, the Church must practise love. Love thus needs to be organized if it is to be an ordered service to the community. The awareness of this responsibility has had a constitutive relevance in the Church from the beginning: "All who believed were together and had all things in common; and they sold their possessions and goods and distributed them to all, as any had need" (*Acts* 2:44–5). In these words, Saint Luke provides a kind of definition of the Church, whose constitutive elements include

fidelity to the "teaching of the Apostles," "communion" (*koinonia*), "the breaking of the bread" and "prayer" (cf. *Acts* 2:42). The element of "communion" (*koinonia*) is not initially defined, but appears concretely in the verses quoted above: it consists in the fact that believers hold all things in common and that among them, there is no longer any distinction between rich and poor (cf. also *Acts* 4:32–37). As the Church grew, this radical form of material communion could not in fact be preserved. But its essential core remained: within the community of believers there can never be room for a poverty that denies anyone what is needed for a dignified life.

21. A decisive step in the difficult search for ways of putting this fundamental ecclesial principle into practice is illustrated in the choice of the seven, which marked the origin of the diaconal office (cf. *Acts* 6:5–6). In the early Church, in fact, with regard to the daily distribution to widows, a disparity had arisen between Hebrew speakers and Greek speakers. The Apostles, who had been entrusted primarily with "prayer" (the Eucharist and the liturgy) and the "ministry of the word," felt overburdened by "serving tables," so they decided to reserve to themselves the principal duty and to designate for the other task, also necessary in the Church, a group of seven persons. Nor was this group to carry out a purely mechanical work of distribution: they were to be men "full of the Spirit and of wisdom" (cf. *Acts* 6:1–6). In other words, the social service which they were meant to provide was absolutely concrete, yet at the same time it was also a spiritual service; theirs was a truly spiritual office which carried out an essential responsibility of the Church, namely a well-ordered love of neighbour. With the formation of this group of seven, "*diaconia*"—the ministry of charity exercised in a communitarian, orderly way—became part of the fundamental structure of the Church.

22. As the years went by and the Church spread further afield, the exercise of charity became established as one of her essential activities, along with the administration of the sacraments and the proclamation of the word: love for widows and orphans, prisoners, and the sick and needy of every kind, is as essential to her as the ministry of the sacraments and preaching of the Gospel. The Church cannot neglect the service of charity any more than she can neglect the Sacraments and the Word. A few references will suffice to demonstrate this. Justin Martyr († *c.* 155) in speaking of the Christians' celebration of Sunday, also mentions their charitable activity, linked with the Eucharist as such. Those who are able make offerings in accordance with their means, each as he or she wishes; the Bishop in turn makes use of these to support orphans, widows, the sick and those who for other reasons find themselves in need, such as prisoners and foreigners. The great Christian writer Tertullian († after 220) relates how the pagans were struck by the Christians' concern for the needy of every sort. And when Ignatius of Antioch († *c.* 117) described the Church of Rome as

"presiding in charity (*agape*)," we may assume that with this definition he also intended in some sense to express her concrete charitable activity.

23. Here it might be helpful to allude to the earliest legal structures associated with the service of charity in the Church. Towards the middle of the fourth century we see the development in Egypt of the "*diaconia*": the institution within each monastery responsible for all works of relief, that is to say, for the service of charity. By the sixth century this institution had evolved into a corporation with full juridical standing, which the civil authorities themselves entrusted with part of the grain for public distribution. In Egypt not only each monastery, but each individual Diocese eventually had its own *diaconia*; this institution then developed in both East and West. Pope Gregory the Great († 604) mentions the *diaconia* of Naples, while in Rome the *diaconiae* are documented from the seventh and eighth centuries. But charitable activity on behalf of the poor and suffering was naturally an essential part of the Church of Rome from the very beginning, based on the principles of Christian life given in the *Acts of the Apostles*. It found a vivid expression in the case of the deacon Lawrence († 258). The dramatic description of Lawrence's martyrdom was known to Saint Ambrose († 397) and it provides a fundamentally authentic picture of the saint. As the one responsible for the care of the poor in Rome, Lawrence had been given a period of time, after the capture of the Pope and of Lawrence's fellow deacons, to collect the treasures of the Church and hand them over to the civil authorities. He distributed to the poor whatever funds were available and then presented to the authorities the poor themselves as the real treasure of the Church. Whatever historical reliability one attributes to these details, Lawrence has always remained present in the Church's memory as a great exponent of ecclesial charity.

24. A mention of the emperor Julian the Apostate († 363) can also show how essential the early Church considered the organized practice of charity. As a child of six years, Julian witnessed the assassination of his father, brother and other family members by the guards of the imperial palace; rightly or wrongly, he blamed this brutal act on the Emperor Constantius, who passed himself off as an outstanding Christian. The Christian faith was thus definitively discredited in his eyes. Upon becoming emperor, Julian decided to restore paganism, the ancient Roman religion, while reforming it in the hope of making it the driving force behind the empire. In this project he was amply inspired by Christianity. He established a hierarchy of metropolitans and priests who were to foster love of God and neighbour. In one of his letters, he wrote that the sole aspect of Christianity which had impressed him was the Church's charitable activity. He thus considered it essential for his new pagan religion that, alongside the system of the Church's charity, an equivalent activity of its own be established. According to him, this was the reason for the popularity of the "Galileans." They needed now to be imitated and outdone. In this way, then,

the Emperor confirmed that charity was a decisive feature of the Christian community, the Church.

25. Thus far, two essential facts have emerged from our reflections:

a. The Church's deepest nature is expressed in her three-fold responsibility: of proclaiming the word of God (*kerygma-martyria*), celebrating the sacraments (*leitourgia*), and exercising the ministry of charity (*diakonia*). These duties presuppose each other and are inseparable. For the Church, charity is not a kind of welfare activity which could equally well be left to others, but is a part of her nature, an indispensable expression of her very being.

b. The Church is God's family in the world. In this family no one ought to go without the necessities of life. Yet at the same time *caritas-agape* extends beyond the frontiers of the Church. The parable of the Good Samaritan remains as a standard which imposes universal love towards the needy whom we encounter "by chance" (cf. *Lk* 10:31), whoever they may be. Without in any way detracting from this commandment of universal love, the Church also has a specific responsibility: within the ecclesial family no member should suffer through being in need. The teaching of the *Letter to the Galatians* is emphatic: "So then, as we have opportunity, let us do good to all, and especially to those who are of the household of faith" (6:10).

Justice and Charity

26. Since the nineteenth century, an objection has been raised to the Church's charitable activity, subsequently developed with particular insistence by Marxism: the poor, it is claimed, do not need charity but justice. Works of charity—almsgiving—are in effect a way for the rich to shirk their obligation to work for justice and a means of soothing their consciences, while preserving their own status and robbing the poor of their rights. Instead of contributing through individual works of charity to maintaining the *status quo*, we need to build a just social order in which all receive their share of the world's goods and no longer have to depend on charity. There is admittedly some truth to this argument, but also much that is mistaken. It is true that the pursuit of justice must be a fundamental norm of the State and that the aim of a just social order is to guarantee to each person, according to the principle of subsidiarity, his share of the community's goods. This has always been emphasized by Christian teaching on the State and by the Church's social doctrine. Historically, the issue of the just ordering of the collectivity had taken a new dimension with the industrialization of society in the nineteenth century. The rise of modern industry caused the old social structures to collapse, while the growth of a class of salaried workers provoked radical changes in the fabric of society. The relationship between capital and labour now became the decisive issue—an issue

which in that form was previously unknown. Capital and the means of production were now the new source of power which, concentrated in the hands of a few, led to the suppression of the rights of the working classes, against which they had to rebel.

27. It must be admitted that the Church's leadership was slow to realize that the issue of the just structuring of society needed to be approached in a new way. There were some pioneers, such as Bishop Ketteler of Mainz († 1877), and concrete needs were met by a growing number of groups, associations, leagues, federations and, in particular, by the new religious orders founded in the nineteenth century to combat poverty, disease and the need for better education. In 1891, the papal magisterium intervened with the Encyclical *Rerum Novarum* of Leo XIII. This was followed in 1931 by Pius XI's Encyclical *Quadragesimo Anno*. In 1961 Blessed John XXIII published the Encyclical *Mater et Magistra*, while Paul VI, in the Encyclical *Populorum Progressio* (1967) and in the Apostolic Letter *Octogesima Adveniens* (1971), insistently addressed the social problem, which had meanwhile become especially acute in Latin America. My great predecessor John Paul II left us a trilogy of social Encyclicals: *Laborem Exercens* (1981), *Sollicitudo Rei Socialis* (1987) and finally *Centesimus Annus* (1991). Faced with new situations and issues, Catholic social teaching thus gradually developed, and has now found a comprehensive presentation in the *Compendium of the Social Doctrine of the Church* published in 2004 by the Pontifical Council *Iustitia et Pax*. Marxism had seen world revolution and its preliminaries as the panacea for the social problem: revolution and the subsequent collectivization of the means of production, so it was claimed, would immediately change things for the better. This illusion has vanished. In today's complex situation, not least because of the growth of a globalized economy, the Church's social doctrine has become a set of fundamental guidelines offering approaches that are valid even beyond the confines of the Church: in the face of ongoing development these guidelines need to be addressed in the context of dialogue with all those seriously concerned for humanity and for the world in which we live.

28. In order to define more accurately the relationship between the necessary commitment to justice and the ministry of charity, two fundamental situations need to be considered:

   a. The just ordering of society and the State is a central responsibility of politics. As Augustine once said, a State which is not governed according to justice would be just a bunch of thieves: "*Remota itaque iustitia quid sunt regna nisi magna latrocinia?*" Fundamental to Christianity is the distinction between what belongs to Caesar and what belongs to God (cf. *Mt* 22:21), in other words, the distinction between Church and State, or, as the Second Vatican Council puts it, the autonomy of the temporal sphere. The State may not impose religion, yet it must guarantee religious freedom and harmony between the followers of different religions. For her part, the Church, as the social expression of Christian faith, has a proper independence and is structured on the basis of her faith as a community which the State must recognize. The two spheres are distinct, yet always interrelated.

Justice is both the aim and the intrinsic criterion of all politics. Politics is more than a mere mechanism for defining the rules of public life: its origin and its goal are found in justice, which by its very nature has to do with ethics. The State must inevitably face the question of how justice can be achieved here and now. But this presupposes an even more radical question: what is justice? The problem is one of practical reason; but if reason is to be exercised properly, it must undergo constant purification, since it can never be completely free of the danger of a certain ethical blindness caused by the dazzling effect of power and special interests.

Here politics and faith meet. Faith by its specific nature is an encounter with the living God—an encounter opening up new horizons extending beyond the sphere of reason. But it is also a purifying force for reason itself. From God's standpoint, faith liberates reason from its blind spots and therefore helps it to be ever more fully itself. Faith enables reason to do its work more effectively and to see its proper object more clearly. This is where Catholic social doctrine has its place: it has no intention of giving the Church power over the State. Even less is it an attempt to impose on those who do not share the faith ways of thinking and modes of conduct proper to faith. Its aim is simply to help purify reason and to contribute, here and now, to the acknowledgment and attainment of what is just.

The Church's social teaching argues on the basis of reason and natural law, namely, on the basis of what is in accord with the nature of every human being. It recognizes that it is not the Church's responsibility to make this teaching prevail in political life. Rather, the Church wishes to help form consciences in political life and to stimulate greater insight into the authentic requirements of justice as well as greater readiness to act accordingly, even when this might involve conflict with situations of personal interest. Building a just social and civil order, wherein each person receives what is his or her due, is an essential task which every generation must take up anew. As a political task, this cannot be the Church's immediate responsibility. Yet, since it is also a most important human responsibility, the Church is duty-bound to offer, through the purification of reason and through ethical formation, her own specific contribution towards understanding the requirements of justice and achieving them politically.

The Church cannot and must not take upon herself the political battle to bring about the most just society possible. She cannot and must not replace the State. Yet at the same time she cannot and must not remain on the sidelines in the fight for justice. She has to play her part through rational argument and she has to reawaken the spiritual energy without which justice, which always demands sacrifice, cannot prevail and prosper. A just society must be the achievement of politics, not of the Church. Yet the promotion of justice through efforts to bring about openness of mind and will to the demands of the common good is something which concerns the Church deeply.

b.   Love—*caritas*—will always prove necessary, even in the most just society. There is no ordering of the State so just that it can eliminate the need for a service of love. Whoever wants to eliminate love is preparing to eliminate man as such. There will always be suffering which cries out for consolation and help. There will always be loneliness. There will always be situations of material need where help in the form of concrete love of neighbour is indispensable. The State which would provide everything, absorbing everything into itself, would ultimately become a mere bureaucracy incapable of guaranteeing the very thing which the suffering person—every person—needs: namely, loving personal concern. We do not need a State which regulates and controls everything, but a State which, in accordance with the principle of subsidiarity, generously acknowledges and supports initiatives arising from the different social forces and combines spontaneity with closeness to those in need. The Church is one of those living forces: she is alive with the love enkindled by the Spirit of Christ. This love does not simply offer people material help, but refreshment and care for their souls, something which often is even more necessary than material support. In the end, the claim that just social structures would make works of charity superfluous masks a materialist conception of man: the mistaken notion that man can live "by bread alone" (*Mt* 4:4; cf. *Dt* 8:3)—a conviction that demeans man and ultimately disregards all that is specifically human.

29.   We can now determine more precisely, in the life of the Church, the relationship between commitment to the just ordering of the State and society on the one hand, and organized charitable activity on the other. We have seen that the formation of just structures is not directly the duty of the Church, but belongs to the world of politics, the sphere of the autonomous use of reason. The Church has an indirect duty here, in that she is called to contribute to the purification of reason and to the reawakening of those moral forces without which just structures are neither established nor prove effective in the long run.

The direct duty to work for a just ordering of society, on the other hand, is proper to the lay faithful. As citizens of the State, they are called to take part in public life in a personal capacity. So they cannot relinquish their participation "in the many different economic, social, legislative, administrative and cultural areas, which are intended to promote organically and institutionally the *common good*." The mission of the lay faithful is therefore to configure social life correctly, respecting its legitimate autonomy and cooperating with other citizens according to their respective competences and fulfilling their own responsibility. Even if the specific expressions of ecclesial charity can never be confused with the activity of the State, it still remains true that charity must animate the entire lives of the lay faithful and therefore also their political activity, lived as "social charity."

The Church's charitable organizations, on the other hand, constitute an *opus proprium*, a task agreeable to her, in which she does not cooperate collaterally, but acts as a subject with direct responsibility, doing what corresponds to her nature. The Church can never be exempted from practising charity as an organized activity of believers, and on the other hand, there will never be a situation where the charity of each individual Christian is unnecessary, because in addition to justice man needs, and will always need, love.

IX

Thomas Merton

Editors' Introduction

In an age where higher learning and the university system have come more to resemble a technical school preparing worker drones to occupy cubicles in multinational corporations than a place of profound thought and deep intellectual and spiritual reflection upon the meaning of life and the formation of the soul, Thomas Merton's essay "Learning to Live" may come as both a shock and a challenge to how you approach your education here at Seton Hall. In one of the oft quoted lines from this incredible essay, Merton exhorts his readers, "If I had a message to my contemporaries, I said, it is surely this: Be anything you like, be madmen, drunks and bastards of every shape and form, but at all costs avoid one thing: success."

Merton spent most of his adult life as a Roman Catholic Cistercian monk (more commonly called Trappists) and a priest. He found great similarity between his education at Columbia University, where he was trained to think and reflect through a core of courses not unlike the "Journey of Transformation" and its sequel, "Christianity and Culture in Dialogue," and his life as a cloistered contemplative monk. Eventually, toward the end of his life (he died suddenly in 1968 while on a trip to Asia), Merton lived as a hermit, separated from the rest of his fellow monks. Merton spent most of his day in prayer, study, and labor (the three pillars of all Christian monks) in a small cabin deep in the woods on the land owned by the monastery to which he was attached, The Abbey of Our Lady Gethsemane, in Trappist, Kentucky. It is about an hour's drive from nearby Louisville.

If there was ever a poster child for the journey of transformation, Merton is it. In many ways, his life story parallels the Confessions of St. Augustine. Merton's most famous book, The Seven Storey Mountain (an autobiography), is his personal version of Augustine's *Confessions*. In *The Seven Storey Mountain* Merton details how he went from living the life of a Bohemian, hedonistic, non-conformist, journalist, poet and novelist to the Christian hermit who practiced Zen Buddhist meditation. Merton studied the religions of the world with as much depth and determination as he did the Roman Catholic faith into which he was baptized (as a convert in his adult life) in November 1938. As a result of a life of prayer, study, and work, eventually Merton became one of the most powerful voices of conscience of the twentieth century, widely read by Catholics, Protestants, Jews, Buddhists, and atheists. Particularly through his social writings, Merton challenged the Catholic Church and modern society in general in relation to issues such as war (Merton was a pacifist), the use of technology (of which Merton was highly suspicious and worried about the negative and the numbing effects technology would have on the human spirit), on civil rights for African Americans and, ultimately, for the liberation of oppressed persons the world over. Merton was also one of the pioneers of what is now referred to as "inter-religiosity." While there are some in the Catholic Church who would disagree with this claim, Merton did indeed figure out how to be Christian (and thus Roman Catholic) "interreligiously." In his numerous correspondence, Merton refers to himself as a Catholic, a Quaker, a Buddhist, and a Sufi. In the essay you are about to read, Merton sees the university as a place that provides many opportunities to plumb the depths of our being through the subject matter of the courses taught as part of the university curriculum. Merton writes that, in taking various courses, students can create for themselves the soul that will be their guiding light for the rest of their lives. Monks, Merton claims, are engaged in a similar process. He wrote, "A university, like a monastery, (and here I have medievalists to back me up, but presume that footnotes are not needed), is at once a microcosm and a paradise. Both monastery and university came into being in a civilization open to the sacred, that is to say in a civilization which paid a great deal of attention to what it considered to be its own primordial roots in a mythical and archetypal holy ground, a spiritual creation." In fact, monasteries have often been referred to as universities of the soul in the manuals that serve as the rule for living by which Christian monks of the Western and the Eastern Church guide and pattern their lives either in community or as solitary seekers after Truth and in pursuit of union with the Divine Presence.

Merton fully understood that when it comes to the journey of transformation that is the life of the intellect as much as it is the life of the soul, one simply does not know where the journey will or could end. Merton's journey of transformation ended tragically (but also joyfully in a strange sort of way), when on December 10, 1968, suddenly and somewhat providentially (for Merton had many premonitions that his death was near), he was accidentally electrocuted by the faulty wiring in a fan he touched as he was getting out of the shower while attending a conference for Asian, American, and European monks and nuns in Bangkok, Thailand. As you read through this, one of the best and most challenging of Merton's essays, please keep in mind what Merton writes within its pages: "The whole of life is learning to ignite without dependence on any specific external means, whether cloistered, Zenist, Tantric, psychedelic or what have you." The essay provides a good opportunity for you to ponder more deeply why you enrolled in a university, why Seton Hall in particular, and for what purpose you might use your education: To become a "successful" corporate drone in a cubical or in order to create the soul Merton references above and provide you with the deep values that will be your guide through the course of your life with all its joys and sufferings.

"LEARNING TO LIVE"

Life consists in learning to live on one's own, spontaneous, freewheeling: to do this one must recognize what is one's own—be familiar and at home with oneself. This means basically learning who one is, and learning what one has to offer to the contemporary world, and then learning how to make that offering valid.

The purpose of education is to show a person how to define himself authentically and spontaneously in relation to his world—not to impose a prefabricated definition of the world, still less an arbitrary definition of the individual himself. The world is made up of the people who are fully alive in it: that is, of the people who can be themselves in it and can enter into a living and fruitful relationship with each other in it. The world is, therefore, more real in proportion as the people in it are able to be more fully and more humanly alive: that is to say, better able to make a lucid and conscious use of their free-dom. Basically, this freedom must consist first of all in the capacity to choose their own lives, to find themselves on the deepest possible level. A superficial freedom to wander aimlessly here or there, to taste this or that, to make a choice of distractions (in Pascal's sense) is simply a sham. It claims to be a freedom of "choice" when it has evaded the basic task of discovering who it is that chooses. It is not free because it is unwilling to face the risk of self-discovery.

The function of a university is, then, first of all to help the student to discover himself: to recognize himself, and to identify who it is that chooses.

This description will be recognized at once as unconventional and, in fact, monastic. To put it in even more outrageous terms, the function of the university is to help men and women save their souls and, in so doing, to save their society: from what? From the hell of meaninglessness, of obsession, of complex artifice, of systematic lying, of criminal evasions and neglects, of self-destructive futilities.

It will be evident from my context that the business of saving one's soul means more than taking an imaginary object, "a soul," and entrusting it to some institutional bank for deposit until it is recovered with interest in heaven.

Speaking as a Christian existentialist, I mean by "soul" not simply the Aristotelian es-sential form but the mature personal identity, the creative fruit of an authentic and lucid search, the "self" that is found after other partial and exterior selves have been discarded as masks.

This metaphor must not mislead: this inner identity is not "found" as an object, but is the very self that finds. It is lost when it forgets to find, when it does not know how to seek, or when it seeks itself as an object. (Such a search is futile and self-contradictory.)

Hence the paradox that it finds best when it stops seeking: and the graduate level of learning is when one learns to sit still and be what one has become, which is what one does not know and does not need to know. In the language of Sufism, the end of the ascetic life is *Rida*, satisfaction. Debts are paid (and they were largely imaginary). One no longer seeks something else. One no longer seeks to be told by another who one is. One no longer demands reassurance. But there is the whole infinite depth of *what is* remaining to be revealed. And it is not revealed to those who seek it from others.

Education in this sense means more than learning; and for such education, one is awarded no degree. One graduates by rising from the dead. Learning to be oneself means, therefore, learning to die in order to live. It means discovering in the ground of one's being a "self" which is ultimate and indestructible, which not only survives the destruction of all other more superficial selves but finds its identity affirmed and clarified by their destruction.

The inmost self is naked. Nakedness is not socially acceptable except in certain crude forms which can be commercialized without any effort of imagination (topless waitresses). Curiously, this cult of bodily nakedness is a veil and a distraction, a communion in futility, where all identities get lost in their nerve endings. Everybody claims to like it. Yet no one is really happy with it. It makes money.

Spiritual nakedness, on the other hand, is far too stark to be useful. It strips life down to the root where life and death are equal, and this is what nobody likes to look at. But it is where freedom really begins: the freedom that cannot be guaranteed by the death of somebody else. The point where you become free not to kill, not to exploit, not to destroy, not to compete, because you are no longer afraid of death or the devil or poverty or failure. If you discover this nakedness, you'd better keep it private. People don't like it. But can you keep it private? Once you are exposed . . . Society continues to do you the service of keeping you in disguises, not for your comfort, but for its own. It is quite willing to strip you of this or that outer skin (a stripping which is a normal ritual and which everybody enjoys). The final metaphysical stripping goes too far, unless you happen to be in Auschwitz.

If I say this description is "monastic," I do not necessarily mean "theological." The terms in which it has been stated here are open to interpretation on several levels: theologically, ascetically, liturgically, psychologically. Let's assume that this last is the more acceptable level for most readers. And let's assume that I am simply speaking from experience as one who, from a French lycée and an English public school, has traveled through various places of "learning" and has, in these, learned one thing above all: to keep on going. I have described the itinerary elsewhere, but perhaps a few new ideas may be added here. The journey went from Europe to America, from Cambridge to Columbia. At

Columbia, having got the necessary degrees, I crossed the boundary that separates those who learn as students from those who learn as teachers. Then I went to teach English at a Catholic college (St. Bonaventure).* After which I went to be a novice in a Trappist monastery, where I also "learned" just enough theology to renounce all desire to be a theologian. Here also (for I am still in Kentucky) I learned by teaching: not theology as such, but the more hazardous and less charted business of monastic education, which deals with the whole person in a situation of considerable ambiguity and hazard: the novice, the young monk who wants to become a contemplative and who is (you sooner or later discover) trapped both by the institution and by his own character in a situation where what he desperately wants beyond all else on earth will probably turn out to be impossible. Perhaps I would have been safer back at Columbia teaching elementary English composition. Fortunately, I am no longer teaching anybody anything.

On the basis of this experience, I can, anyhow, take up an ancient position that views monastery and university as having the same kind of function. After all, that is natural enough to one who could walk about Cambridge saying to himself, "Here were the Franciscans at one time, here the Dominicans, here—at my own college—Chaucer was perhaps a clerk."

A university, like a monastery (and here I have medievalists to back me up, but presume that footnotes are not needed), is at once a microcosm and a paradise. Both monastery and university came into being in a civilization open to the sacred, that is to say, in a civilization which paid a great deal of attention to what it considered to be its own primordial roots in a mythical and archetypal holy ground, a spiritual creation. Thus the *Logos or Ratio*** of both monastery and university is pretty much the same. Both are "schools," and they teach not so much by imparting information as by bringing the clerk (in the university) or the monk (in the monastery) to direct contact with "the beginning," the archetypal paradise world. This was often stated symbolically by treating the various disciplines of university and monastic life, respectively, as the "four rivers of paradise." At the same time, university and monastery tended sometimes to be in very heated conflict, for though they both aimed at "participation" in and "experience" of the hidden and sacred values implanted in the "ground" and the "beginning," they arrived there by different means: the university by *scientia*, intellectual knowledge, and the monastery by *sapientia*, or mystical contemplation. (Of course, the monastery itself easily tended to concentrate on *scientia*—the science of the Scriptures—and in the university there could be mystics like Aquinas, Scotus, and Eckhart. So that in the end, in spite of all the fulminations of the Cistercian St. Bernard, a deeper *sapientia* came sometimes from schools than from monasteries.)

---

* Now St. Bonaventure University

** [Purpose.]

The point I am making here is this: far from suggesting that Columbia ought to return to the ideal of Chartres and concentrate on the trivium and quadrivium, I am insinuating that this archetypal approach, this "microcosm-paradise" type of sacred humanism, is basically personalistic.

I admit that all through the Middle Ages men were actively curious about the exact location of the earthly paradise. This curiosity was not absent from the mind of Columbus. The Pilgrim Fathers purified it a little, spiritualized it a little, but New England to them was a kind of paradise: and to make sure of a paradisic institution they created, of all things, Harvard. But the monks of the Middle Ages, and the clerks too, believed that the inner paradise was the ultimate ground of freedom in man's heart. To find it one had to travel, as Augustine had said, not with steps, but with yearnings. The journey was from man's "fallen" condition, in which he was not free not to be untrue to himself, to that original freedom in which, made in the image and likeness of God, he was no longer able to be untrue to himself. Hence, he recovered that nakedness of Adam which needed no fig leaves of law, of explanation, of justification, and no social garments of skins (Gregory of Nyssa). Paradise is simply the person, the self, but the radical self in its uninhibited freedom. The self no longer clothed with an ego.

One must not forget the dimension of relatedness to others. True freedom is openness, availability, the capacity for gift. But we must also remember that the difficult dialectic of fidelity to others in fidelity to oneself requires one to break through the veils of infidelity which, as individual egoists or as a selfish community, we set up to prevent ourselves from living in the truth.

This sacred humanism was, of course, abused and perverted by the sacred institution, and in the end monasticism, by a curious reversal that is so usual in the evolution of societies, identified the fig leaf with the paradise condition and insisted on the monk having at least enough of a self to serve the organization itself pressed into the service of more mundane interests. Freedom, then, consisted in blind obedience, and contemplation consisted in renouncing nakedness in favor of elaborate and ritual vestments. The "person" was only what he was in the eyes of the institution because the institution was, for all intents and purposes, Paradise, the domain of God, and indeed God himself. To be in Paradise, then, consisted in being defined by the paradisic community—or by Academe. Hence, the dogmatic absolutism for which the late Middle Ages are all too well known—and for which they are by no means uniquely responsible.

The original and authentic "paradise" idea, both in the monastery (*paradisus claustralis*)*** and in the university, implied not simply a celestial store of theoretic ideas to which the Magistri and Doctores held the key, but the inner self of the student who,

---

*** [Cloistered paradise.]

in discovering the ground of his own personality as it opened out into the center of all created being, found in himself the light and the wisdom of his Creator, a light and wisdom in which everything comprehensible could be comprehended and what was not comprehensible could nevertheless be grasped in the darkness of contemplation by a direct and existential contact.

Thus, the fruit of education, whether in the university (as for Eckhart) or in the monastery (as for Ruysbroeck) was the activation of that inmost center, that *scintilla animae*, that "apex" or "spark" which is a freedom beyond freedom, an identity beyond essence, a self beyond all ego, a being beyond the created realm, and a consciousness that transcends all division, all separation. To activate this spark is not to be, like Plotinus, "alone with the Alone," but to recognize the Alone which is by itself in everything because there is nothing that can be apart from It and yet nothing that can be with It, and nothing that can realize It. It can only realize itself. The "spark" which is my true self is the flash of the Absolute recognizing itself in me.

This realization at the apex is a coincidence of all opposites (as Nicholas of Cusa might say), a fusion of freedom and unfreedom, being and unbeing, life and death, self and nonself, man and God. The "spark" is not so much a stable entity which one finds but an event, an explosion which happens as all opposites clash within oneself. Then it is seen that the ego is not. It vanishes in its non-seeing when the flash of the spark alone is. When all things are reduced to the spark, who sees it? Who knows it? If you say "God," you are destroyed; and if you say no one, you will plunge into hell; and if you say I, you prove you are not even in the ballgame.

The purpose of all learning is to dispose man for this kind of event.

The purpose of various disciplines is to provide ways or paths which lead to this capacity for ignition.

Obviously it would be a grave mistake to do, as some have done and still do, and declare that the only way is to be found in a cloister and the only discipline is asceticism or Zen sitting or, for that matter, turning on with a new drug. The whole of life is learning to ignite without dependence on any specific external means, whether cloistered, Zenist Tantric, psychedelic, or what have you. It is learning that the spark, being a flash at the apex and explosion of all freedoms, can never be subject to control or to enlightenment, can never be got by pressing buttons. A spark that goes off when you swallow something or stick yourself with something may be a fairly passable imitation of the real thing, but it is not the real thing. (I will not argue that it cannot teach you a great deal about the real thing.) In the same way a cloistered complacency—a "peace" that is guaranteed only by getting out of the traffic, turning off the radio, and forgetting the world—is not by itself the real thing either.

The danger of education, I have found, is that it so easily confuses means with ends. Worse than that, it quite easily forgets both and devotes itself merely to the mass production of uneducated graduates—people literally unfit for anything except to take part in an elaborate and completely artificial charade which they and their contemporaries have conspired to call "life."

A few years ago a man who was compiling a book entitled *Success* wrote and asked me to contribute a statement on how I got to be a success. I replied indignantly that I was not able to consider myself a success in any terms that had a meaning to me. I swore I had spent my life strenuously avoiding success. If it so happened that I had once written a best seller, this was a pure accident, due to inattention and naïveté, and I would take very good care never to do the same again. If I had a message to my contemporaries, I said, it was surely this: Be anything you like, be madmen, drunks, and bastards of every shape and form, but at all costs avoid one thing: success. I heard no more from him and I am not aware that my reply was published with the other testimonials.

Thus, I have undercut all hope of claiming that Columbia made me a success. On the contrary, I believe I can thank Columbia, among so many other things, for having helped me learn the value of unsuccess. Columbia was for me a microcosm, a little world, where I exhausted myself in time. Had I waited until after graduation, it would have been too late. During the few years in which I was there, I managed to do so many wrong things that I was ready to blow my mind. But fortunately I learned, in so doing, that this was good. I might have ended up on Madison Avenue if I hadn't. Instead of preparing me for one of those splendid jobs, Columbia cured me forever of wanting one. Instead of adapting me to the world downtown, Columbia did me the favor of lobbing me half conscious into the Village, where I occasionally came to my senses and where I continued to learn. I think I have sufficiently explained, elsewhere, how much I owed, in this regard, to people like Mark Van Doren (who lived around the corner from me in the Village) and Joseph Wood Krutch (who became, as I have become, a hermit). Such people taught me to imitate not Rockefeller but Thoreau. Of course, I am not trying to say that one has to be Thoreau rather than Rockefeller, nor am I slyly intimating that I have discovered a superior form of resentment, an off-beat way of scoring on everybody by refusing to keep score.

What I am saying is this: the score is not what matters. Life does not have to be regarded as a game in which scores are kept and somebody wins. If you are too intent on winning, you will never enjoy playing. If you are too obsessed with success, you will forget to live. If you have learned only how to be a success, your life has probably been wasted. If a university concentrates on producing successful people, it is lamentably failing in its obligation to society and to the students themselves.

Now I know that even in the thirties, at Columbia, the business of wanting to be a success was very much in the air. There was, in fact, a scandal about the yearbook senior poll. The man who was voted "most likely to succeed" was accused of having doctored the results in his own favor after a surreptitious deal with a yearbook staff member who was voted "best dressed." Incidentally, I was voted best writer. I was not accused of trickery, but everyone understood that the vote, which had been between me and Hank Liebermann, had been decided by my fraternity brothers. (Incidentally, whatever became of the man "most likely to succeed"?)

In any case, no one really cared. Since that time many of my classmates have attained to eminence with all its joys and all its sorrows, and the ones I have seen since then are marked by the signature of anguish. So am I. I do not claim exemption. Yet I never had the feeling that our alma mater just wanted us to become well-paid operators, or to break our necks to keep on the front pages of the *Times*. On the contrary—maybe this is a delusion, but if it is a delusion it is a salutary one—I always felt at Columbia that people around me, half amused and perhaps at times half incredulous, were happy to let me be myself. (I add that I seldom felt this way at Cambridge.) The thing I always liked best about Columbia was the sense that the university was on the whole glad to turn me loose in its library, its classrooms, and among its distinguished faculty, and let me make what I liked out of it all. I did. And I ended up by being turned on like a pinball machine by Blake, Thomas Aquinas, Augustine, Eckhart, Coomaraswamy, Traherne, Hopkins, Maritain, and the sacraments of the Catholic Church. After which I came to the monastery in which (this is public knowledge) I have continued to be the same kind of maverick and have, in fact, ended as a hermit who is also fully identified with the peace movement, with Zen, with a group of Latin American hippie poets, etc., etc.

The least of the work of learning is done in classrooms. I can remember scores of incidents, remarks, happenings, encounters that took place all over the campus and sometimes far from the campus: small bursts of light that pointed out my way in the dark of my own identity. For instance, Mark Van Doren saying to me as we crossed Amsterdam Avenue: "Well, if you have a vocation to the monastic life, it will not be possible for you to decide not to enter" (or words to that effect). I grasped at once the existential truth of this statement.

One other scene, much later on. A room in Butler Hall, over-looking some campus buildings. Daisetz Suzuki, with his great bushy eyebrows and the hearing aid that aids nothing. Mihoko, his beautiful secretary, has to repeat everything. She is making tea. Tea ceremony, but a most unconventional one, for there are no rites and no rules. I drink my tea as reverently and attentively as I can. She goes into the other room. Suzuki, as if waiting for her to go, hastily picks up his cup and drains it.

It was at once as if nothing at all had happened and as if the roof had flown off the building. But in reality nothing had happened. A very very old deaf Zen man with bushy eyebrows had drunk a cup of tea, as though with the complete wakefulness of a child and as though at the same time declaring with utter finality: "This is not important!"

The function of a university is to teach a man how to drink tea, not because anything is important, but because it is usual to drink tea, or, for that matter, anything else under the sun. And whatever you do, every act, however small, can teach you everything—provided you see who it is that is acting.